*Brownfield Application
Development in .NET*

D1249343

# *Brownfield Application Development in .NET*

KYLE BALEY
DONALD BELCHAM

MANNING

Greenwich
(74° w. long.)

For online information and ordering of this and other Manning books, please visit
www.manning.com. The publisher offers discounts on this book when ordered in quantity.
For more information, please contact

    Special Sales Department
    Manning Publications Co.
    Sound View Court 3B
    Greenwich, CT 06830
    Email: orders@manning.com

Manning Publications Co.
Sound View Court 3B
Greenwich, CT 06830

Development editor:  Cynthia Kane
Copyeditor:  Liz Welch
Proofreader:  Katie Tennant
Typesetter:  Gordan Salinovic

ISBN 978-1-933988-71-9
Printed in the United States of America
1 2 3 4 5 6 7 8 9 10 – MAL – 14 13 12 11 10

*To brownfield developers everywhere.*
*We feel for you, we really do.*

# brief contents

# contents

# *foreword*

I believe it takes a certain kind of psychology, a brand of will, to succeed in tackling technical debt and wrangling out-of-control code. I also believe that values should drive the selection of tools and practices and techniques. Through direct conversations over the course of a couple of years, I know that Kyle Baley and Donald Belcham share these values. They're the kind of developers who embody and evangelize this way of thinking, and it's apparent in the words you're about to absorb.

A few values help guide you through working with legacy or unmanageable codebases, times that are often frustrating or even dark: passion, patience, and collaboration. I'm certain there are more, but in the interest of keeping this foreword short and letting the content speak for itself, we'll start here.

Passion is what drives the best developers to find and master new tools that work and inspire those around them to do the same. Developers who have a passion for crafting elegant, maintainable solutions and a drive for learning new techniques to do so are the best of the best. You might be one of these folks—after all, you're reading this book.

Working with brownfield codebases requires a particular kind of passion; they tend to be chock-full of brain-teasing problems. It helps if you're a developer who doesn't mind getting her hands dirty. It helps if you're the kind of developer who throws himself headlong into a mess, thriving on creating simple solutions to complicated problems. It helps if you can lead by example, motivating your fellow team members to bring new ideas and moves to the table. These examples are all expressions of passion.

Technical debt is a drag not only on your customer's bottom line but on your will to live in a project community. Does anyone enjoy showing up at work and treading water for days, weeks, or months on end? Sometimes a codebase can seem so daunting and so hopeless, yet a rewrite is impossible due to political reasons, budgetary constraints, or a more insidious lack of long-term investment thinking. Chances are your customers won't give you a blank check to do it right a second time, and you'll be thrown into the fray of a brownfield project that's supporting a successful revenue stream with a backlog of features with no end in sight. I hear this kind of story on the road all the time.

If this is your scenario, it helps to have patience, methodically finding areas where you can make improvements small and large. You might have to be patient with your project sponsors, building up trust that turns into influence that you can trade for permission to make more ambitious and systemic changes. You'll have to exhibit patience when dealing with the more frustrating corners of the codebase; good leaders tend to have good attitudes, keeping morale steady, especially when the going gets tough.

Getting people aboard the improvement train is key. Collaborate with your customers and fellow developers, testers, and analysts to succeed and sustain a turnaround of unmaintainable code.

Business folks need to understand the long-term benefits of deep refactoring, restructuring, or rewriting; they'll ultimately have to approve such efforts. Work with them to achieve consensus. Make the case with supporting data in terms they understand. Formulate a plan and communicate that plan early and often. People don't enjoy being kept in the dark. Secrecy and unilateralism are not ways to build trust.

When you discover how to apply one of the techniques from this book (or any source) to a real-world problem, share it with your teammates. Build a doctrine over time that you can apply to similar debt items you find in the code. In my experience, true collaboration builds in a snowball effect: it only takes one leader on the team to get it rolling, and that might as well be you.

A couple of years ago, Donald and Kyle pulled me aside at a software development conference in Vancouver and asked me to review an outline for a book they were shopping around called *Brownfield Application Development in .NET*. Here we are in the present, and I'm wrapping up the foreword for that very book: this book!

So what can I say about the project and its authors almost two years later?

I'll take this opportunity to congratulate my friends on their achievement: job well done, Donald and Kyle. I remember remarking on the promise of the outline and giving mostly picky, take-it-or-leave-it notes. My reaction was simple: "This book needs writing." And, having read it, I'm not disappointed. I see it as a significant contribution to our craft.

Donald and Kyle have managed to assemble and describe an extremely useful and comprehensive bag of tricks that you can apply to your brownfield applications. Now when you get to it, remember to apply your new toolbox in the context of your value system: passion will inspire your teammates and supply you energy; patience will get you through the long stretches; collaboration will grow trust and accelerate improvement over time.

DAVID LARIBEE, AGILE COACH

# *preface*

It's not easy inheriting another team's project. If you haven't been in a situation like this already, clearly you're new to the industry and we welcome you into our midst. Whether you join a project as a replacement or as an additional developer, it's rare for someone to go through their entire career working solely on so-called "greenfield" applications (ones with no prior history). Even if you do start a greenfield project, it doesn't take long before the application starts to show signs of contamination.

We've been on many projects in different stages of progress, and it's the exception, rather than the rule, that you find strong coding practices or frictionless processes throughout the codebase. Instead there always seem to be glaring issues causing the team, and ultimately the project, massive amounts of pain. Usually the team has either become numb to the pain or everyone has become resigned to the fact that it "just has to be this way." Having seen it so often and with so many of the same problems repeated, we decided that something needed to be said about it. Hence, the book before you.

When we first started to talk about the contents of the book, we were looking to define the types of applications that drove us to write. We knew that they definitely weren't greenfield, but were they legacy? Both of us had read Michael Feathers' *Working Effectively with Legacy Code* (Prentice Hall PTR, 2004) and decided that the style of project we'd encountered wasn't fully described by his definition of legacy. After some time searching on Google and reading Wikipedia (http://en.wikipedia.org/wiki/Brownfield_land), we both decided the definition of brownfield as it pertained to land management was much closer than anything else we'd come up with:

*[B]rownfield land (or simply a brownfield) is land previously used for industrial purposes or certain commercial uses. The land may be contaminated by low concentrations of hazardous waste or pollution, and has the potential to be reused once it is cleaned up.*

So we absconded with the term and set about trying to make the land management definition work for software development.

You should note two things about this book. First, although we decided to write within the confines of our brownfield terminology, all the practices, techniques, and tools mentioned in the book apply equally well to any project. Greenfield, brownfield, or legacy, we've used these techniques to help our teams succeed. Don't be scared to use them on other types of projects. Without them, we'd probably have many more failed projects under our belts than we do now.

The second thing to note is that this book isn't meant to be a definitive guide on tools or practices. We continually evolve both to fit the projects we're on as well as to improve the skills we currently have. Just because you've read this book, don't stop your quest to gain knowledge and challenge both your techniques and those that are believed to be conventional.

With those two caveats in mind, we present to you our thoughts on brownfield application development.

# acknowledgments

First off, kudos to the Manning team for letting us miss deadline after deadline without breaking from their professionalism, guidance, and nudging. We felt it was only appropriate that we try to mimic the current failures of our industry when writing this book, and missing as many deadlines as we did certainly proved that we can. Without the Manning team, we'd probably still be sitting in a hotel lobby in some city discussing what the topic of the book should be.

So special thanks to publisher Marjan Bace, our technical editor Andrew Siemer, our copyeditor Liz Welch, our development editor Cynthia Kane, our proofreader Katie Tennant, and everyone else at Manning who worked with us on the manuscript during its development and production. A big thank-you to our editor Mike Stephens who showed incredible patience, tact, and negotiation skills throughout the journey.

Many of the ideas in this book are offshoots of others from people we respect in the industry. Specifically, thanks to Robert C. "Uncle Bob" Martin, whose principles formed the basis for part 2 of the book, and Michael Feathers, whose book *Working Effectively With Legacy Code* essentially inspired this book. Thank you to James Kovacs for allowing us to use his title for chapter 9 and to Josh Schwartzberg who provided us with the anecdote to open chapter 2.

We'd also like to thank the many reviewers who read the manuscript at different stages and provided invaluable input: Ayende Rahien, Mike Tian-Jiang Jiang, Berndt Hamboeck, Dave Corun, Derik Whittaker, Josh Schwartzberg, Nikander Bruggeman, Margriet Bruggeman, Liam McLennan, Mark Needham, Peter Ritchie, Philippe Vialatte, Alan Ruth, Rick Wagner, Wendy Friedlander, Horaci Macias, Gary Pronych,

Philipp K. Janert, Stuart Caborn, Eric Swanson, Jason Drews, Adam Willie, Rob Windsor, Barabbas Jiang, Ted Neward, and Timothy Binkley-Jones.

Finally, thanks to David Laribee for his encouragement and for having graciously agreed to write the foreword to our book.

## Kyle Baley

I'll start with an apology to my late grandfather. When I was young, I used to watch the Academy Awards with him. When an acceptance speech started to run too long, he'd throw his hands in the air and say, "Oh, for heaven's sake, thank God and your mother and get the &*%$ off the stage!" Sorry, Grandpa, I may never be here again.

A big thank-you to my parents, brothers, grandparents, aunts, uncle, and extended family who taught me the importance of a sense of humility and humor, not necessarily in that order. A special shout-out to my cousin Jocelyn, whose emails and notes of encouragement always seemed to come at the right time.

Finally, although I always thought it was a cliché for an author to thank his spouse and children, now I know where they're coming from. A huge thank-you to my beautiful wife Liza and my charming daughter Sydney, both of whom showed infinitely more patience than I did throughout the process. They are Sunshine and Starshine, respectively, to my Moonshine. I also want to throw some thanks to my son Jake, who was born during the writing process. Although he wasn't quite as patient as the ladies were, he was a consistent source of inspiration nonetheless.

## Donald Belcham

I'd like to thank many of my non-IT friends for what they've done both for my career path and this book. These are the people who implored me to attend school, set me up with a strong foundational knowledge of how to work as a professional when I first entered the industry, and have continued to support me during the good and the bad that I've been through. Without any of you I'd probably still be farming in the hinterlands of northern Canada.

A big apology goes to all the people who, for the last two years, have had to deal with hearing about "the book." Thank you for understanding that I couldn't make many social engagements and that, when I did, I'd have a laptop in tow to write down any fleeting ideas that I may have had.

I'd also like to thank the greater software development community for providing so many thought-provoking ideas and chances to learn, and doing so in an open way. Whether it was coding practices, professional advice, or general business knowledge, I'm thankful to have had the chance to absorb what you've had to offer. Without the interaction and learning that you allowed me to participate in, I'd still be writing code in darkness and frustration.

Finally, to *The Sixteen Men of Tain*, thank you for helping me through the writing process so nicely.

# *about this book*

This book is intended for developers who work on both greenfield and brownfield projects. We've tried to cover content that will be thought-provoking for developers of many different skill levels. As a result, the discussions range from being very high-level all the way down to raw code.

We've split the book into two parts: "The ecosystem" and "The code." In our experience they're the two major areas where we encounter issues on a brownfield project. It made the most sense to us to discuss the ecosystem in part 1 because it sets the foundation for being able to do many different things with any project.

In part 1, we decided to cover everything from the most obvious (we hope), version control, through continuous integration (CI), automated testing, metrics, and defect tracking in the order that we generally approach them on a brownfield project.

Some would, and did, argue that automated testing should come before continuous integration. We disagree. There's no prerequisite to have automated tests before implementing CI. Having a CI environment that compiles the codebase on each code check-in will add an enormous benefit to any project, brownfield or not. In the end we do want to strive for CI that executes automated tests, but waiting to implement CI until your project has a functioning test may be putting off a process that could solve some problems you may be encountering.

That said, feel free to wait until you have functioning automated tests before you implement CI. This book reflects the order that has worked for us in the past. Every project is different. CI before automated test, or vice versa, could vary depending on what you encounter when joining a brownfield project.

Part 2 is dedicated to code techniques and practices that we feel can benefit all the "-abilities" (maintainability, readability, extensibility, reversibility…). Again, there's no magic formula for which order they should appear. In the name of flow and simplicity we decided to start with fundamentals (OO concepts, layering) and then address the main areas of the application working from the user interface to the data access layer.

Again, you can address any one before the other, but with regard to the application tiers, we've found the most benefit and easiest refactorings to occur when working from the UI layer toward the data store. Our experience has shown that working with "consumer" code (code that calls other code) allows us to better see how the code being called needs to be organized and formulated. If you write the UI tier to call the service layer in the way that makes most sense for the UI, then the service layer's exposed API/interface will be as efficient and meaningful as possible. That alone will help you to improve the "-abilities" of your codebase.

## Roadmap

A brief summary of what you will find in each chapter follows:

Chapter 1 explores the foundation of what brownfield projects are and some of the issues that are commonly found when working on them.

Chapter 2 starts our discussion on the development ecosystem with version control systems and how they can be used to benefit both brownfield and greenfield projects.

Chapter 3 tackles the idea of continuous integration and adding automated build scripts to an existing project.

Chapter 4 looks at automated testing fundamentals, managing existing tests on a brownfield project and how to approach adding automated testing to an existing project.

Chapter 5 delves into metrics and code analysis to explore how the ideas and tools can help you get a better handle on an existing code base.

Chapter 6 covers the oft-forgotten defect tracking component of any project. The chapter takes a long look at how to manage existing defect backlogs and how to use past defects to direct your development efforts.

Chapter 7 introduces the code-specific portion of the book by discussing object-oriented fundamentals. This chapter lays the foundation for coding practices that will be suggested and discussed through the remainder of the book.

Chapter 8 explores layering of code in an application both at a conceptual level as well as what efforts and approaches will be beneficial when working in a brownfield code base.

Chapter 9 covers decoupling a code base through the use of interfaces, dependency inversion, and inversion of control containers, both in general and specifically for existing code bases.

Chapter 10 is dedicated to discussing user interface patterns and how they pertain to a brownfield project.

Chapter 11 tackles the sticky subject of data access from both theoretical and practical brownfield standpoints.

Chapter 12 explores the problems introduced by third-party dependencies and how to manage them within a code base.

Chapter 13 wraps up the book with a discussion about how to keep the momentum built through the book to continue to flow in your projects.

## Sidebars

Interspersed through the book you'll find a couple of different types of sidebars. One is titled "Tales from the trenches." These are real-life situations we've encountered or instigated. Hopefully you can learn from some of our mistakes and successes.

Another common sidebar is "Challenge your assumptions." When we started working on the book, we wanted to present some ideas that stretched readers out of their traditional comfort zones. Although there are a number of these sidebars in the book, don't stop when you've finished reading them. Constantly look at the situations you're in and consider options and thoughts that push boundaries. There's a lot of great content on the internet that presents ideas that would fall into this category. Make the time to search out the sources of this content. Consider their ideas and see if they apply to your situations. You'll use some and you'll discard more. The thing is, you'll be putting yourself into a mind-set to do what is best for the project, not just what is "normal."

## Code conventions and downloads

All source code in listings or in the text is in a `fixed-width font like this` to separate it from ordinary text. Code annotations accompany some of the listings, highlighting important concepts. In most cases, numbered bullets link to explanations that follow in the text.

You can download the source code for this book from the publisher's website at www.manning.com/BrownfieldApplicationDevelopmentin.NET. The code available for download requires Visual Studio 2008 or higher.

## Author Online

Purchase of *Brownfield Application Development in .NET* includes free access to a private web forum run by Manning where you can make comments about the book, ask technical questions, and receive help from the authors and from other users. To access the forum and subscribe to it, point your web browser to www.manning.com/Brownfield ApplicationDevelopmentin.Net. This page provides information on how to get on the forum once you're registered, what kind of help is available, and the rules of conduct on the forum.

Manning's commitment to our readers is to provide a venue where a meaningful dialogue between individual readers and between readers and the authors can take place. It's not a commitment to any specific amount of participation on the part of the authors, whose contribution to the book's forum remains voluntary (and unpaid). We suggest you try asking the authors some challenging questions, lest their interest stray!

The Author Online forum and the archives of previous discussions will be accessible from the publisher's website as long as the book is in print.

### Sample project and living ideas

In addition to the Author Online forum, this book is supported by a website (www.brownfieldappdev.com) that contains living records of our experiences and tools. It also hosts a sample brownfield refactoring project that outlines and demonstrates many of the techniques espoused in this book.

### About the authors

Kyle Baley is uncomfortable talking about himself in the third person so he'd just like to say he's a guy who writes code for a living.

Donald Belcham is just another developer trying to be as productive, professional, and client-focused as possible.

### About the cover illustration

The figure on the cover of *Brownfield Application Development in .NET* is "The Merchant," taken from a late 18th century edition of Sylvain Maréchal's four-volume compendium of regional dress customs published in France. Each illustration is finely drawn and colored by hand. The rich variety of Maréchal's collection reminds us vividly of how culturally apart the world's towns and regions were just 200 years ago. Isolated from each other, people spoke different dialects and languages. In the streets or in the countryside, it was easy to identify where they lived and what their trade or station in life was just by what they were wearing.

Dress codes have changed since then and the diversity by region, so rich at the time, has faded away. It is now hard to tell apart the inhabitants of different continents, let alone different towns or regions. Perhaps we have traded cultural diversity for a more varied personal life-certainly for a more varied and fast-paced technological life.

At a time when it is hard to tell one computer book from another, Manning celebrates the inventiveness and initiative of the computer business with book covers based on the rich diversity of regional life of two centuries ago, brought back to life by Maréchal's pictures.

# Understanding brownfield applications

1

**This chapter covers**

- Defining brownfield applications
- Inheriting an application
- Facing challenges in brownfield applications

An industrial *brownfield* is a commercial site contaminated by hazardous waste that has the potential to be reused once it's cleaned up. To a software developer, a *brownfield application* is an existing project, or codebase, that may be contaminated by poor practices, structure, and design, but that has the potential to be revived through comprehensive and directed refactoring.

Many of the established applications you'll encounter fit this description. By the time you start working on them, the core technology and architectural decisions have already been made, but architectures and technologies are still more easily repaired than replaced. In this chapter, we'll explore the various components of a brownfield application. We'll talk about the challenges inherent in taking on brownfield applications, particularly the social and political aspects surrounding your work. We'll include in our discussion ways you can convince your boss that the

1

effort is worthwhile and that it will result in lower costs and higher productivity in the long run. We'll also look at the unique benefits working on brownfield apps offers to you as a developer.

As you move through this book, you'll learn (or relearn) numerous techniques for dealing with brownfield applications. Many are the same techniques you should be applying to new development projects to prevent the "contamination" characteristic of brownfields. But they can present some interesting challenges when you apply them to established code.

To set the stage, we'll open with an anecdote—contrived, to be sure, but very much based on personal experience and observations.

## 1.1   *Welcome to Twilight Stars!*

"Welcome to Twilight Stars! Where fading stars can shine again!"

So claims the welcome package you receive on your first day. You've just started as a consultant for Twilight Stars, a company that provides bookings for bands of fading popularity. The website that manages these bookings has had a storied past, and you've been told that your job is to turn that site around. This is your first gig as an independent consultant, so your optimism runs high!

### 1.1.1   *Reality check*

Then Michael walks in. He props himself up against the door and watches you unpack for a while. You exchange introductions and discover he's one of the senior programmers on the team. As you explain some of your ideas, Michael's smirk becomes increasingly prominent.

"How much do you really know?" he says. Without waiting for an answer, he launches into a diatribe that he has clearly recounted many times before…

"Did they tell you our delivery date is in 6 weeks? Didn't think so. That's a hard deadline, too; they'll miss their window of opportunity if we don't deliver by then. The big shots still cling to the hope that we'll meet it but the rest of us know better. If we hold to that date, this app is going to have more bugs than an entomology convention. As it is, the client has zero confidence in us. He stopped coming to the status meetings months ago.

"Anyway, you'll be hard pressed just to keep up since Huey and Lewis both left last week. They're only the latest to go, too. Despite what he may have told you about refactoring, the PM, Jackson, had to bring you in just to get this sucker out the door on time. Yeah, we know it's a mess and we need to clean it up and all, but I've seen guys like you come through here on a regular basis. It'll be all you can do just to keep up with the defects. Which, by the way, we're mandated to resolve before delivery. Each and every one of them."

With that, Michael excuses himself after suggesting (somewhat ominously) that you review the defect list. You locate the Excel file on the server that stores them and are taken aback. There are some 700 open defects, some more than 2 years old! Some are one-liners like "Can't log in" and many were reported by people who no longer work on the project.

Without knowing what else to do, you scan the list for a seemingly simple bug to fix: display an appropriate page title in the title bar of the window. "That should be an easy one to pick off," you think.

Luckily, your welcome package contains instructions on getting the latest version of the code. Unluckily, the instructions are out of date and it's a good 45 minutes before you realize you're looking at the wrong code.

After retrieving the latest version, you open the solution and do what comes naturally: compile. Errors abound. References to third-party controls that you haven't installed and code files that don't exist. As you investigate, you also discover references to local web services and databases that you have yet to install. In one case, it even appears unit tests are running against a production database. (Upon further investigation, you realize the tests are being ignored. Phew!)

You spend the rest of the day tracking down the external dependencies and missing code from various team members' machines. As you drive home, you realize that the entire day was spent simply getting the application to compile. "No matter," you say to yourself, "now I'm in a position to be productive."

### 1.1.2 Day two

You arrive early on day two ready to do some coding. As you settle in to find that elusive line of code that sets the window title, you realize the code itself is going to be a significant obstacle to cramming the work required into the remaining time before release.

Eventually, you find the code to change a window title. It's buried deep in what appears to be a half-finished generic windowing framework. Tentatively, you "fix" the bug and test it the only way you can at the moment: by pressing F5. *Crash!*

Fast-forward to two o'clock. In the intervening hours, you've touched every major layer of the application after you discovered that the window title was being stored in the database (explained one team member, "At one point, we were going to offer the app in Spanish."). Near as you can tell, the new title you were trying to set is too big for the corresponding database column.

Stop us if any of this starts to sound familiar.

In the meantime, you still aren't able to even fix the bug because key files have been checked out by others (including the recently departed Huey) and the version control system doesn't allow files to be modified by more than one person. Also, though some areas appear to be protected by automated tests, these tests are ignored, not testing what they claim, or outright failing. Clearly the team doesn't run them often. One class containing over 10,000 lines of code is "covered" by a single test. Disturbingly, it passes.

### 1.1.3 Settling in

Over the ensuing weeks, the longer you spend working with the code, the more questions you have. The architecture looks as though it's in the process of moving to a new

UI pattern. The architect behind it steadfastly refuses requests for meetings to explain it, claiming it should be self-explanatory. The designers of the original code are long gone, so you're left to cobble together solutions that make use of both the original and the new patterns. You know it's not the best you can do, but you're scared to even suggest to the PM that it needs to be revamped.

Eventually, you're told that you'll be taking over the test-fix-test cycle for one area of the application (or as some developers call it, fix-release-pray-fix). Changes to the code have indeterminate impacts. Verifying any change requires a full release and testing cycle that involves the end users. The result is uncontrollable code, sliding morale, and no confidence among the parties involved.

In the end your team makes the deadline, but at a cost. More developers have left for greener fields and lower stress. Management begins a process of imposing crippling accountability practices on the team. As you sit down to start on phase 2, you pause to reflect on your initial optimism in the project. An email notification interrupts your reverie:

*Issue #3,787 Created: Window title incorrect.*

### 1.1.4   *Taking stock*

Twilight Stars may be a fictional company, but the issues facing it are real. We've touched on only a scant few of the problems here that often face a brownfield application. We'll come back to our intrepid hero again in chapter 13 after he's had a chance to peruse the book and implement some of the solutions he encounters. In the meantime, let's see what makes up a brownfield application.

## 1.2   *The components of a brownfield application*

Like the industrial definition, the salient components of a brownfield application are

- Existing codebase
- Contamination by poor practices
- Potential for reuse or improvement

Figure 1.1 shows the three components and as you can see, they're interrelated.

It's easy to distinguish brownfield applications from greenfield ones. Greenfield applications have no previous project or technical history, whereas brownfield applications are typically burdened with it. Similarly, we make a distinction between brownfield and legacy applications as well. We'll come back to legacy codebases shortly, but for now consider them to be applications that are long forgotten and that are worked on only when absolutely necessary.

**Figure 1.1   Brownfield applications have three components that distinguish them from greenfield and legacy applications.**

Brownfield applications generally fall between greenfield and legacy. Table 1.1 compares the three types of projects.

**Table 1.1   A comparison of the major project concerns and how they relate to greenfield, brownfield, and legacy applications**

| Concern | Greenfield | Brownfield | Legacy |
|---|---|---|---|
| Project state | Early in the development lifecycle; focuses on new features | New feature development and testing and/or production environment maintenance | Primarily maintenance mode |
| Code maturity | All code actively being worked on | Some code being worked on for new development; all code actively maintained for defect resolution | Very little code actively developed, except for defect resolution |
| Architectural review | Reviewed and modified at all levels and times as the codebase grows | Only when significant changes (business or technical) are requested | Rarely, if ever, reviewed or modified |
| Practices and processes | Developed as work progresses | Mostly in place, though not necessarily working for the team/project | Focused on maintaining the application and resolving critical defects |
| Project team | Newly formed group that is looking to identify the direction of its processes and practices | Mix of new and old, bringing together fresh ideas and historical biases | Very small team that maintains the status quo |

In short, brownfield applications fall into that gray area between when an application is shiny and new and when it's strictly in maintenance mode. Now that we've provided the criteria for a brownfield application, let's examine the components from figure 1.1 in more detail.

### 1.2.1   Existing codebase

One of the defining characteristics of a greenfield application is that there's little or no prior work. There's no previous architecture or structure to deal with. By contrast, brownfield projects are ones that have a significant codebase already in place.

We don't mean that when you leave work after the first day, your greenfield application magically turns into a brownfield one overnight. Typically, it has been in development for some period of time (or has been left unattended) and now has some concrete and measurable work that needs to be done on it. Often, this work takes the form of a phase of a project or even a full-fledged project.

There are a couple of points worth mentioning with respect to existing codebases, even if they're a little obvious:

- You must have access to the code.
- The code should be in active development.

**Your brownfield application may already be in production**

Because you're dealing with an existing codebase, there's a chance it has already been released into production. If so, this will have some bearing on your project's direction but not necessarily on the techniques we'll talk about in this book. Whether you're responding to user requests for new features, addressing bugs in the existing version, or simply trying to complete an existing project, the methods in this book still apply.

These two points disqualify certain types of applications from being brownfield ones—for example, an application that requires occasional maintenance to fix bugs or add the odd feature. Perhaps the company doesn't make enough money on it to warrant more than a few developer hours a week, or maybe it's not a critical application for your organization. This application isn't being actively developed. It's being maintained and falls more into the category of a legacy application.

Instead, a brownfield codebase is an active one. It has a team assigned to it and a substantial budget behind it. New features are considered and bugs tracked.

The next component of a brownfield application is the degree to which it's contaminated. Let's see why this is an important aspect of the definition.

### 1.2.2   *Contaminated by poor programming practices*

Besides being an existing, actively developed codebase, brownfield applications are defined by their level of contamination, or *smell*—that is, how bad the code is. This determination is subjective in the best of cases, but in many instances, everyone agrees that *something* is wrong, even if the team can't quite put their finger on it or agree on how to fix it.

Different levels of contamination exist in any codebase. It's a rare application indeed that's completely free of bad code and/or infrastructure. Even if you follow good coding practices and have comprehensive testing and continuous integration, chances are you've accrued technical debt to some degree.

**Technical debt**

*Technical debt* is a term used to describe the quainter areas of your code. They're pieces that you know need some work but that you don't have the time, experience, or staff to address at the moment. Perhaps you've got a data access class with hand-coded SQL that you know is ripe for a SQL injection attack. Or each of your forms has the same boilerplate code cut and pasted into it to check the current user. Your team recognizes that it's bad code but isn't able to fix it at the moment.

It's akin to the to-do list on your refrigerator taunting you with tasks like "clean out the garage" and "find out what that smell is in the attic." They're easily put off but need to be done eventually.

*(continued)*

The nasty side effect of technical debt is the bad design and code decisions. They're like the weekend you had that one time in college. It seemed like a good idea at the time, but now you constantly have to deal with it. In code, at some point you've made decisions about design and architectures that may have made sense at the time but now come back to haunt you regularly. It may now take an inordinate amount of time to add a new screen to the application, or it might be that you have to change something in several different places instead of just one. Like that weekend in college, these are painful, and regular, reminders of your past transgression. But unlike your college past, you can change code.

Along the same lines, contamination means different things to different people. You'll need to fight the urge to call code contaminated simply because it doesn't match your coding style.

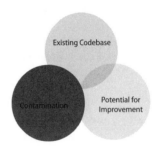

The point is that you need to evaluate the degree to which the code is contaminated. If it already follows good coding practices and has a relatively comprehensive set of tests but you don't like the way it's accessing the database, you could argue that it isn't a full-fledged brownfield application—merely one that needs a new data access strategy.

Although it may be hard to pinpoint the exact degree of contamination, you can watch for warning signs that might give you a gut feeling:

- How quickly are you able to fix bugs?
- How confident do you feel when bugs are fixed?
- How easy is it to extend the application and add new features?
- How easy would it be to change how you log error messages in the application?

If your answer to any or all of these questions is a chagrined "Not very," chances are you have a lot of contamination.

Bear in mind that every application can be improved upon. Often, all it takes is a new perspective. And like any homeowner will tell you, you're never truly finished renovating until you leave (or the money runs out).

So far we've discussed the nature of the application and talked about its negative aspects. With the final core component of a brownfield application, we'll look at the positive side of things and see what can be done to make our app better.

### 1.2.3 *Potential for reuse or improvement*

The final criterion, potential for reuse or improvement, is important. It means that despite the problems you've identified, you're confident that the application can be improved. Your application isn't only salvageable but you'll be making an active effort to improve it. Often, it's an application that you're still actively developing (perhaps even still working toward version 1). Other times, it's one that has been put on hold for some time and that you're resurrecting.

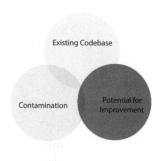

Compare this with a traditional legacy application. Projects that have aged significantly, or that have been moved into maintenance mode, fall into the legacy category. Such applications aren't so much *maintained* as they are *dealt with*. These applications are left alone and resurrected only when a critical bug needs to be fixed. No attempts are made to improve the code's design or to refactor existing functionality.

**NOTE**   In his book *Working Effectively with Legacy Code* (Prentice Hall PTR, 2004), Michael Feathers defines legacy code as any code that doesn't have tests. This definition works for the purpose of his book, but we're using a more traditional definition: really, really old code.

As you can see, it isn't hard to come up with an example of a brownfield application. Any time you work on an application greater than version 1.0, you're two-thirds of the way to the core definition of a brownfield application. Often, even applications working toward version 1.0 fall into this category.

Our next step is to crystallize some of the vague notions we feel when dealing with brownfield applications.

## 1.3   *Inheriting an application*

The idea of working in a codebase that has been thrown together haphazardly, patched up on the fly, and allowed to incur ongoing technical debt doesn't always inspire one to great heights. So consider this section of the book your rallying cry. Dealing with someone else's code (or even your own code, months or years later) is rarely easy, even if it does follow good design practices. And in many cases, you'll be making changes that end users, and even your own managers, don't notice. The person who will truly benefit from your work is either you or the developer who comes after you.

> **Reasons to be excited about brownfield applications**
> - Business logic already exists in some form.
> - You can be productive from day one.
> - Fixing code is easier than writing it.
> - The project may already be in use and generating revenue.

It's the *contaminated* nature of the code that makes your task exciting. Software developers, as a group, love to solve problems, and brownfield applications are fantastic problems to solve. The answers are already there in the existing code; you just need to filter out the noise and reorganize.

The nice thing about brownfield applications is that you see progress almost from day one. They're great for getting quick wins—expending a little effort for a big gain. This is especially true at the beginning of the project where a small, obvious refactoring can have a huge positive effect on the overall maintainability of the application. And right from the start, we'll be making things easier by encouraging good version control practices (chapter 2) and implementing a continuous integration process (chapter 3), two tasks that are easier to accomplish than you might think.

In addition, most developers find it much easier to "fix" code than to write it from scratch. How many times have you looked at code you've done even 6 months ago and thought, "I could write this so much better now"? It's human nature. Things are easier to modify and improve than they are to create, because all the boring stuff (project setup, form layout) has already been done.

Compare this with greenfield applications, where the initial stages are spent setting up the infrastructure for code not yet written. Or compare it with writing tests at a relatively granular level and agonizing over whether you should create a separate Services project to house that new class you're testing.

Finally, the application may already be in production and may even be generating revenue for your company! That alone should be reason enough to make a concerted effort to improve it.

In short, brownfield applications shouldn't be viewed as daunting. Quite the contrary. Throughout this book, you'll find that once you start improving an application and its ecosystem, the process becomes addictive.

But before we go any further, this is a good point to lay some groundwork for the brownfield revitalization task that lies ahead of you. To do that, we'll talk about some concepts that will be recurring themes throughout the remainder of the book, starting with the concept of *pain points*. Although pain points are only a sampling of problems that you may encounter on your brownfield project, they'll show you how to identify and act on issues.

### 1.3.1  Pain points

A *pain point* is a process that's causing you grief—one that causes you to search for a solution or alternative. For example, if every test in a certain area requires the same code to prime it, it may signal that the common code needs to be either moved to the test's setup or, at the very least, into a separate method.

Pain points come in all sizes. The easy ones are those that can be codified or for which solutions can be purchased. These include refactorings like Extract to Method or Introduce Variable (which can be done with a couple of keystrokes within Visual Studio).

The harder ones take more thought and might require drastic changes to the code. Don't shy away from these—they've been identified as pain points. But always keep in mind the cost-benefit ratio before undertaking major changes.

One of the things that differentiate a brownfield application from a greenfield application is that pain points are more prevalent at the start. Pain points in greenfield applications don't stick around long because you remove them as soon as you discover them—which is easier because there isn't as much code. In brownfield applications, pain points have been allowed to linger and fester and grow.

Pain points are especially relevant to brownfield applications because they define areas in need of improvement. Without pain points, there's no need to make changes. It's only when you're typing the same boilerplate code repeatedly, or having to cut and paste more than once, or are unable to quickly respond to feature requests, and so on and so forth, that you need to take a look at finding a better way.

> **Be on the lookout for pain**
>
> Very often, we aren't even aware of pain points, or we accept them as a normal part of the development process. For example, we might have a web application that restricts access to certain pages to administrators. In these pages, you've peppered your code with calls to `IsAdmin()` to ensure regular users can't access them. But after you've made this call for the third time, your "hack alert" should trigger you to find out if this problem can be solved some other way (like, say, with a `<location>` tag in your web.config).

We'll talk about pain points throughout this book. Almost every piece of advice is predicated on solving some common pain point. Each remaining chapter will begin with a scenario describing at least one pain point (and usually several) that we'll address in that chapter.

Identifying pain points is normally the result of some kind of productivity friction, which we'll discuss next.

## 1.3.2  *Identifying friction*

Another thing you'll encounter when inheriting a brownfield application is friction. Anything that gets in the way of a developer's normal process causes friction. Things that cause friction aren't necessarily painful but they're a noticeable burden, and you should take steps to reduce friction.

An example of friction is if the build process is excessively long. Perhaps this is due to automated tests dropping and re-creating a database (we'll cover automated builds and integration tests in chapters 3 and 4, respectively). Perhaps it's calling out to an unreliable web service. Whatever the reason, building the application is a regular event in a developer's day-to-day process, and if left unchecked, this friction could add up to quite a bit of money over the length of the project.

Like pain points, friction may go unnoticed. You should constantly be on the alert when anything distracts you from your core task: developing software. If anything gets in your way, it must be evaluated to see if the process can be improved upon. Very often, we can get so wrapped up in our work that we forget computers can automate all but the most complex of tasks.

Noticing and acting on friction and pain points takes a clarity of thought that often subsides as your involvement in a project lengthens. As a result you have to explicitly expend effort thinking outside your current box, or as we like to say, challenging your assumptions.

### 1.3.3   *Challenging your assumptions*

When you inherit a brownfield application, you're at a unique point in its development in that you're actively trying to improve it. It behooves you to challenge the way you have thought about certain techniques and practices in the past in order to deliver on that promise.

> **Challenge your assumptions**
>
> Throughout the book, we'll call attention to ideas that may be unintuitive or that may not be commonly known. These won't be traditional pieces of advice that you should follow heedlessly. Rather, they should be taken as a new perspective—an idea worth considering that might fit in with your style or that might solve a particular problem you're having.

Examples of challenging your assumptions can range from the mundane to the far-reaching. It could be as simple as raising your monitor to eye level to reduce strain. Or it could be reexamining your data access layer to see if it can be refactored to an object-relational mapper (see chapter 11). Do you find yourself typing the same code over and over again? Maybe you can create a code snippet for it. Or maybe it's the symptom of some design flaw in your application. Whatever the case, developers, more than anyone, should recognize that doing the same thing over and over again is a sign that something can be improved.

Challenging assumptions is a good practice in any project but more so in brownfield applications. There's a good chance that some questionable assumptions led to the code being contaminated in the first place. Usually, bad assumptions are the root cause of pain points and friction.

But by the same token, there's a fine line between critical thinking and outright irreverence. You should be practical with your challenges. At all times, you should weigh the costs and benefits of any major changes you make. Although we developers would rather not consider it most of the time, the expectations of clients and management need to play into our decision-making process.

### 1.3.4   *Balancing the client's expectations*

There's a common metaphor in the software industry: the Iron Triangle. It's depicted in figure 1.2.

Here's one way the triangle has been summed up: the project can be done on time, on budget, and feature complete. Which two do you want? The idea is that in order to increase the quality (the area of the triangle), one or more of the other aspects will need to give. Conversely, if we reduce the resources, for example, without changing anything else, quality will suffer.

Figure 1.2   The Iron Triangle. Changes in any of the three vertices will affect the project's overall quality.

The Iron Triangle metaphor is somewhat flawed. One example is that if you reduce the scope of an application without reducing anything else, it implies the quality will go down.

Instead, we feel the relationship is more akin to a scale, as shown in figure 1.3. On the left, we have (estimated) time and resources, representing things we want to keep low. On the right are quality and features, which we want to be high. The important thing to remember is that the scale must remain balanced at all times. If you want to add a new feature, you must add an appropriate amount of time and resources to keep the balance. If you lose some funding, you have a decision to make: sacrifice quality or features in order to rebalance.

Figure 1.3   Generally speaking, your job will be to balance time and resources against code quality and features.

The development team has influence in all aspects of this equation except cost. We have the ability to work in ways that will ensure that we provide the functionality that the client wants. We can also use different tools, techniques, and practices that will enhance the quality of the application. Although more limited, the development team does have the ability to meet or miss deadlines. More effective, though, is our ability to influence deadlines and set realistic and attainable expectations.

The relationship between time/resources and quality/scope is of particular interest in a brownfield application. This is because the scale needs constant adjustment as time goes on. As you progress, you may discover that your estimates were off and need adjustment. You may not be physically able to deliver the application at the current scope and quality within the existing timeframe and budget. In effect, external factors have shifted the balance so that the left side of the scale is too light. You need to either increase the schedule or resources, or lower the quality or scope, in order to balance it out.

As developers, we're often focused on one aspect of the scale: quality. By contrast, project managers and clients typically need to balance all four. Brownfield applications, in particular, may require some radical decisions. Almost by definition, you'll be affecting the quality of the code. As you outline the changes that have to be made, be sure you consider their impact on the scale, especially from the standpoint of your client.

In itself, balancing the scale is a complex task. Management courses and development methodologies exist by the dozens simply to try to address it. With a brownfield application, subtle complexities come into play. One of those subtleties is the decision to refactor or to do a big rewrite.

### 1.3.5 *The big rewrite*

When you inherit a brownfield project, at some point someone will ask the question: "Should we just rewrite this thing from scratch?" Often, the obvious answer is no. The codebase might be too large, the current problems with it too small, and/or the benefit of the work too minor.

But on rare occasions, you'll encounter a project where the answer should be yes. In our experience, this is dictated by a few factors. For example, the current brownfield codebase may not address the client's desired goals. Perhaps it's a completely synchronous system and the need is for an asynchronous one. In this case, trying to shoehorn asynchronous, or messaging-based, practices and patterns into the existing codebase would probably lead to maintainability issues, and possibly even a failure to achieve the stated architecture. As a result, the disconnect between the current architectures and the desired one will probably dictate that we perform a major rewrite of the application.

Be cautious when evaluating whether a brownfield codebase should be rewritten. As a rule, developers often prematurely jump to the conclusion that an application is unmaintainable simply because we don't want to deal with "someone else's" problems. We feel like the guy in the parade who has to follow behind the horses with a shovel.

But in many cases, issues such as poor coding practices, lack of a good ecosystem, and defect-ridden code can be overcome through strong and focused refactoring, not from a ground-up rewrite. We refer to Joel Spolsky's still-relevant article from 2000 titled "Things You Should Never Do"[1] on the dangers of rewriting from scratch.

That said, if you perform your due diligence and decide that rewriting the application is more cost-effective than refactoring and tweaking the existing one, you'll face some unique challenges. In some ways, it's easier than a straight greenfield project because you're starting from scratch, yet you still have a reference application that defines the functionality. At the same time, you're essentially rebooting an application that, from the users' perspective, may work. Maybe it has some quirks but few users will trade the devil they know for the devil they don't.

In the end, the refactor/rewrite decision should come down to business value. Will it cost less over the long term to maintain the current application versus creating a whole new one? It may be hard for us to put aside emotion and not inflate the cost of maintenance for the current application, but it's even more detrimental to ignore the economics of any project.

Now that we've looked at some aspects of inheriting an application, let's explore some of the challenges you'll face as you start your brownfield project.

---

[1] http://www.joelonsoftware.com/articles/fog0000000069.html

## 1.4   *The challenges of a brownfield application*

Your task won't be an easy one. There will be technical and not-so-technical challenges ahead.

Unlike with a greenfield project, there's a good chance your application comes with some baggage. Perhaps the current version has been released to production and has been met with a less-than-enthusiastic response from the customers. Maybe there are developers who worked on the original codebase and they aren't too keen on their work being dissected. Or maybe management is pressuring you to finally get the application out the door so it doesn't look like such a blemish on the IT department.

These are but a few of the scenarios that will affect the outcome of your project (see figure 1.4). Unfortunately, they can't be ignored. Sometimes they can be managed, but at the very least, you must be cognizant of the political and social aspects of the project so that you can try to stay focused on the task at hand.

**Figure 1.4   There are many challenges to a brownfield application. As developers, we often focus only on the technical ones.**

We'll start the discussion with the easy ones: technical factors.

### 1.4.1   *Technical factors*

Almost by definition, brownfield applications are rife with technical problems. The deployment process might be cumbersome. The web application may not work in all browsers. Perhaps it doesn't print properly on the obscure printer on the third floor. You likely have a list of many of the problems in some form already. And if you're new to the project, you'll certainly find more. Rare is the project that holds up well under scrutiny by a new pair of eyes.

In many ways, the technical challenges will be easiest to manage. This is, after all, what you were trained to do. And the good thing is that help is everywhere. Other developers, user groups, newsgroups, blogs—virtually any problem has already been solved in some format, save those in bleeding-edge technology. Usually, the issue isn't finding a solution exists—the issue is finding one that works in your environment.

One of the keys to successfully overcoming the technical factors that you inherit is to focus on one at a time and to prioritize them based on pain. Trying to solve all the technical issues on a project is impossible. Even trying to solve many of them at one time is overwhelming. Instead of trying to take on two, three, or more technical refactorings at one time, focus on one and be sure to complete that task as best as you possibly can.

> **Stay focused!**
>
> When you start looking for problems in a brownfield application, you'll find them. Chances are they'll be everywhere. You may face a tendency to start down one path, then get distracted by another problem. Call it the "I'll-just-refactor-this-one-piece-of-code-first" syndrome.
>
> Fight this impulse if you can. Nothing adds technical debt to a project like several half-finished refactorings. Leaving a problem partially solved is more a hindrance than a solution. Not only does the problem remain, but you have introduced inconsistency. This makes it that much harder for the next developer to figure out what's going on.

Working on some technical factors will be daunting. Looking to introduce something like inversion of control and dependency injection (see chapter 9) into a tightly coupled application can be an overwhelming experience. This is why it's important to bite off pieces that you can chew completely. Occasionally, those pieces will be large and require a significant amount of mastication. That's when it's crucial to have the motivation and drive to see the task through to completion. For a developer, nothing is more rewarding than completing a task, knowing that it was worthwhile and, subsequently, seeing that the effort is paying off.

Unfortunately, technical problems aren't the only ones you'll face. Unless you work for yourself, you'll at least need to be aware of political issues. We'll discuss political factors next.

## 1.4.2 *Political factors*

Whether or not you like it, politics plays a factor in all but the smallest companies. Brownfield applications, by their very nature, are sure to come with their own brand of political history. By the time an application has become brownfield, the politics can become entrenched.

Political factors can take many forms, depending on the nature of the application, its visibility within the organization, and the personality of the stakeholders. And it doesn't take much to create a politically charged situation. The application could be high profile and several months late. It could be in production already but so unstable that the customers refuse to use it. The company may be going through a merger with another company that makes similar software. All of these situations will have an effect on you.

Political factors exist mostly at a macro level. Rarely do politics dip into the daily domain of the individual programmer. But programmers will usually feel the ramifications of politics indirectly.

One of the most direct manifestations is in the morale of the team, especially the ones who have been on the project longer. Perhaps you have a highly skilled senior programmer on the team who has long stopped voicing her opinions out of resignation or frustration. Alternatively, there's the not-so-skilled developer who has enough political clout to convince the project manager that the entire application's data storage mechanism should be XML files to make it easier to read them into typed datasets. Sure, you could make the case against this particular issue, and possibly win, but the root cause (the misinformed developer) is still running rampant through the project.

Another common example is when management, project sponsors, or some component of the organization has soured to your project and they've decided, rightly or wrongly, to point the blame at the technology being used. As the implementers of the technology, the developers are often dragged into the fray. In such cases, we're almost always on the defensive, having to explain every single decision we make, from the choice of programming language to the number of assemblies we deploy.

Regardless of the forces causing them to influence a project, politics are the single most difficult thing to change when on the project. They're usually based on longstanding corporate or business relationships that have a strong emotional backing to them, and this is difficult to strip away. It's nearly impossible to meet these situations head on and make changes.

Dealing with political situations is never an easy undertaking. Our natural tendency is to hide in the code and let others worry about the political landscape. Indeed, if you're able to safely ignore these problems, we highly recommend doing so. But we have yet to encounter a situation in a brownfield application where we've been able to disregard them completely. And in our experience, burying your head in the sand tends to make things worse (or at the very least, it certainly doesn't make things better).

Instead, subtlety and patience are often the best ways to address politically charged situations. Tread lightly at first. As when working in code, learning the pain points is the key to success. In the case of negative politics, learning what triggers and fuels the situation sets the foundation for solving the problem. Once you know the reasoning for individual or group resistance, you can begin appealing to those points.

### Tales from the trenches: "Get it done with fewer defects"

One of the projects we worked on had a poor track record of releasing new features that were littered with defects and/or missed functionality. This had continued to the point where management and clients intervened with the mandate that the team must "...get it done with fewer defects." And they were right—we had to.

At the time, one of our first suggestions was to implement a policy of test-driven design (TDD) to force the development team to spend more time defining the requirements, designing their code around those requirements, and generating a set of lasting artifacts that could be used to verify the expectations of the requirements. As is often the case when proposing TDD to management, the added coding effort was perceived as a drain on resources and a problem for meeting schedules or deadlines. The idea of doing more work up-front to ensure successful implementation—rather than doing more after-the-fact work to fix defects—didn't compute well with them.

**(continued)**

As we backed away from the (heated) conversations, it became quite apparent to us that there was a historically based set of prejudices surrounding TDD. Past experience and the ensuing politics surrounding a visible failure were creating a great deal of resistance to our ideas.

Instead of selling a technique known as test-driven design, we proposed a combination of practices that would allow us to specifically address the quality problems the project was seeing, without boring the client about what they were. With the implementation of these practices, delivered quality improved and management's confidence in our abilities increased.

To this day we're not sure if that management team understood that we were doing TDD on their project, but that didn't matter. The political charge around the term was so high that it was never going to succeed when packaged in that manner. Research into the reasoning behind that level of negativity pointed to a past implementation and execution experience. By rebundling the practices, we were able to circumvent the resistance and still deliver what was requested of us by management.

In the end, your goal in a project that has some political charge isn't to meet the politics directly. Instead, you should be looking to quell the emotion and stay focused on the business problems being solved by your application. Strike a happy balance between groups who have interests they want addressed. You'll never make everyone fully happy all the time, but if you can get the involved parties to rationally discuss the project, or specific parts of the project, you're starting to succeed.

That was kind of a superficial, Dr. Phil analysis of politics, but this is a technical book, after all. And we don't want to give the impression that we have all the answers with regard to office politics ourselves. For now, we can only point out the importance of recognizing and anticipating problems. In the meantime, we'll continue our talk on challenges with a discussion on morale.

### 1.4.3 Team morale

When you first start on a brownfield project, you'll usually be bright eyed and bushy tailed. But the existing members of that team may not share your enthusiasm. Because this is a brownfield application, they'll have some history with the project. They've probably been through some battles and lost on occasion. In the worst situations, there may be feelings of pessimism, cynicism, and possibly even anger among the team members. This type of morale problem brings with it project stresses such as degradation in quality, missed deadlines, and poor or caustic communication.

It's also a self-perpetuating problem. When quality is suffering, the testing team may suffer from bad morale. It's frustrating to feel that no matter how many defects you catch and send back for fixing, the returned code always has a new problem caused by fixing the original problem. The testing team's frustration reflects on the developers and the quality degrades even more.

Because every team reacts differently to project stresses, resolving the issues will vary. One thing is certain, though: for team morale to improve, a better sense of "team" has to be built.

One of the most interesting problems that we've encountered is Hero Programmer Syndrome (HPS). On some teams, or in some organizations, there are a few developers who will work incredible numbers of hours to meet what seem like impossible deadlines. Management loves what these people do. They become the go-to guys when times are tough, crunches are needed, or deadlines are looming.

It may seem counterintuitive (and a little anticapitalist), but HPS should be discouraged. Instead of rewarding individual acts of heroism, look for ways to reward the team as a whole. Although rewarding individuals is nice, having the whole team on board will usually provide better results both in the short and long terms.

**NOTE**  The project will run much smoother if the team feels a sense of collective ownership. The team succeeds and faces challenges together. When a bug is encountered, it's the team's fault, not the fault of any one developer. When the project succeeds, it's due to the efforts of everyone, not any one person.

One of the benefits you get from treating the team as a single unit is a sense of collective code ownership. No one person feels personally responsible for any one piece of the application. Rather, each team member is committed to the success of the application as a whole. Bugs are caused by the team, not a team member. Features are added by the team—not Paul, who specializes in data access, or Anne, who's a whiz at UI.

When everyone feels as if they have a stake in the application as a whole, there's no "Well, I'm pulling my weight but I feel like the rest of the team is dragging me down." You can get a quick sense of how the project is going by talking to individual members of the team. If they use the words *we* and *our* a lot, their attitude is likely reflected by the rest of the team. If they say, *I* and *my*, you have to talk to other members to get their side of the story.

HPS is of particular importance in brownfield applications. A pervasive individualistic attitude may be one of the factors contributing to the project's existing political history. If you get the impression that it exists on your team, you have that much more work ahead of you moving toward collective code ownership.

It isn't always an easy feat to achieve. Team dynamics are a topic unto themselves. At best, we can only recognize that they're important here and relate them to brownfield applications in general.

Unfortunately, the development team members aren't the only people you have to worry about when it comes to morale. If your team members are disenchanted, imagine how your client feels.

### 1.4.4  *Client morale*

It's easy to think of morale only in terms of the team doing the construction of the software. As developers, we're most in touch with this group. But we're also heavily influenced by the morale of our clients. Their feeling toward the project and working on it will ebb and flow just as it does for a developer and the team in general.

Because the client is usually outside our sphere of direct influence, there's little that we can do to affect their overall morale. The good news is that the biggest way we can affect their mood is simply by doing what we were trained to do: build and deliver software.

Clients have fairly simple concerns when it comes to software development projects. They want to get software that works the way they need it to (without fail), when they need it, and for a reasonable cost. This doesn't change between projects or between clients.

The great thing for developers is that many of the things that will make working in the code easier will also address the concerns of the client. Introducing automated testing (see chapter 4) will help to increase quality. Applying good object-oriented (OO) principles to the codebase (chapter 7) will increase the speed with which changes and new features can be implemented with confidence. Applying agile principles, such as increased stakeholder/end user involvement, will show clients firsthand that the development team has their interests at heart.

Any combination of these things will increase the morale of the client at the same time as, and possibly correlated to, increasing their confidence in the development team. The increased confidence that they have will significantly reduce friction and increase communication within the team. Those are two things that will positively influence the project's success.

To relate this again back to brownfield applications, remember that the client likely is coming into the project with some preconceived notions of the team and the project based on direct experience. If some bad blood exists between the client and the development team, you have your work cut out for you. In our experience, constant and open communication with the client can go a long way to rebuilding any broken relationships.

Whatever bad blood has existed in the past, you should make every attempt to repair damaged relationships. Don't be afraid to humble yourself. It's helpful to remember that you're there for your client's benefit, not the other way around.

### Tales from the trenches: Involving the client

For one of our clients, quality assurance (QA) testing had historically been a bottleneck on projects. Without a dedicated QA team, the business analyst was taking on these duties...whenever she could fit it in with her regular duties. Development charged ahead at full steam but nothing could be taken off our "completed features" list until the QA had been completed.

Unfortunately, the business analyst wasn't receptive when we suggested she work an 80-hour week. So our alternate solution was to engage the end users directly for the QA testing. Three people who were going to use the application dedicated a certain number of hours each week to QA testing.

> **(continued)**
> The advantages were so quick and so numerous, we felt foolish for not thinking of it sooner. Not only did our QA bottleneck all but disappear, but also the users provided invaluable feedback on the direction of the features, they got "on-the-job" training on how the application worked, and each team gained a greater appreciation for the needs of the other. The business users became much more interested in the development process because their feedback was being heard and they got responses quickly. Because of this, the relationship between the developers and the client flourished, setting the stage for a much smoother experience in the next project.
>
> We cannot overstate this: involving the client is A Good Thing.

So far, we've psychoanalyzed our team and our client. That just leaves the management team in the middle. Let's talk about how they feel.

### 1.4.5    Management morale

We've discussed the morale of the team and the client. In between those two usually sits a layer of management. These are the people tasked with herding the cats. Like everyone else, they can fall victim to poor morale. From the perspective of the developer, management morale problems manifest themselves in the same way that client morale problems do.

It's helpful to think of management as another client for the development team, albeit one with slightly different goals. They have deliverables that they expect from the development team, but they're happiest when the client is happiest. As such, you can influence their morale the same way you influence the client's: by building quality software on time and on budget.

A good method we've found for improving management morale is to keep open communication lines. This is true for your client as well, but nothing saps a project manager's energy like a problem that has been allowed to fester unchecked until it bubbles over. Even if there is nothing actionable, most managers like to know what's going on, both good and bad. At the beginning of the project there may be more bad than good, but as long as you stay focused on the goal of improving the application, managers can help navigate to where the effort should be focused.

That covers everybody. In the next section, we'll focus on change.

### 1.4.6    Being an agent for change

As a software developer, you likely don't have a problem embracing change at a personal level. After all, change is one of the defining characteristics of our industry. The challenge will be effecting change on a broader level in your project.

This being a brownfield application, change *must be* inevitable. Clearly, the path that led to the codebase being a brownfield application didn't work too well, and the fact that you're reading this book probably indicates that the project is in need of some fresh ideas.

Not everyone has the stomach for change. Clients dread it and have grown accustomed to thinking that technical people are only concerned with the cool new stuff. Management fears it because it introduces risk around areas of the application that they've become comfortable with assuming are now risk free. Testers loath it as it will add extra burden to their short-term workload. Finally, some developers reject it because they're comfortable having "always done it this way." (See section 1.2.3 earlier in this chapter.)

## Tales from the trenches: Dealing with skepticism

Over the course of our careers, we've heard countless excuses from people who, for one reason or another, simply don't want to learn anything new. Examples include "I don't have time to learn, I'm too busy getting work done" and "How is a college summer student going to support this?" and "This is too different from the way we're used to" and "We've never had a problem with the old way of doing things."

On one project where we met considerable skepticism, the response required some planning and more than a little good fortune. We sought out others on the team who were more receptive to our goals. We worked directly with them to train them on different techniques and help instill a sense of continuous improvement.

The good fortune came in the form of a manager with a long-term goal that the team would be trained within the next 3 to 5 years. Whenever we met with particularly strong resistance, he'd act as the arbitrator to decide the direction the team should go. Sometimes he would decide in our favor; sometimes he wouldn't. But whatever the final decision, it was always explained clearly that it was in support of the long-term goal.

If this sounds a little too "mom-and-apple-pie," that's because we're sugarcoating it. Success wasn't total and the team didn't look the same way at the end of the project as it did at the beginning. But over time, we were able to introduce some useful tools into their arsenal and get most of them into the mind-set of continuous improvement.

In the end, it was a measured response and more than a little support from above that helped.

Even with all these barriers to change, people in each of those roles will be thankful after the fact that change has taken place. We do assume that the change was successful and, just as important, that the team members can see the effects of the change. If change happens and there is nothing that can be used for comparison, or nothing that can be trotted out in a meeting that indicates the effect of the change, it will be hard for team members to agree that the effort required was worth the gain received. It might be as simple as creating a report, such as the one shown in figure 1.5, which visually describes the progress being made in different areas of the project's work effort.

As a person who thinks of development effort in terms of quality, maintainability, timeliness, and completeness, you have all the information and tools to present the case for change, both before and after it has occurred. Remember, you'll have to convince

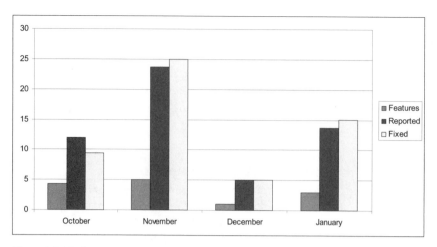

**Figure 1.5    Before starting any change, be sure you can measure how successful it will be when you're done.**

people to allow you to implement the change (whether in its entirety or in isolation) and to get the ball rolling. You'll also be involved in providing the proof that the effect(s) of the change were worth the effort. You have to be the agent for change.

This ability will come with experience, but in the meantime here are a couple of tactics you can try. The first is "It's better to beg forgiveness than to ask permission." Now, we're not espousing anarchy as a way of getting things done, but if you can defend your actions and you feel the consequences are reasonable, going ahead and, say, adding a unit-test project to your application can get things rolling. If your decision is easily reversible, that's all the better.

Also, be efficient. Talk only to the people you need to talk to and tell them only pertinent details. Users don't care if you want to implement an object-relational mapper (see chapter 11). If you aren't talking about cash dollars, leave them and your VPs out of the conversation.

## Challenge your assumptions: Making change

When talking about working on poorly performing projects, a developer we both highly respect said to us, "Change your environment, or change your environment." That is, if you can't change the way things are done in your organization, consider moving on to a new environment.

Sometimes you'll find environments where, no matter how well you prepare, present, and follow through on a proposed change, you won't be able to implement it. If you can't make changes in your environment, you're not going to make it any better, and that's frustrating. No matter how change resistant your current organization may be, you can always make a change in your personal situation. That could be moving to a different team, department, or company. Regardless of what the change ends up being, make sure that you're in the situation that you can be most comfortable in.

Acting as an agent is similar to how a business analyst or client works for the business needs. You have to represent the needs of your project to your team. But change doesn't just happen; someone has to advocate it, to put their neck on the line (sometimes a little, sometimes a lot). Someone has to get the ball rolling. It takes a special kind of personality to achieve this. You have to be confident in the arguments you make. You need to inspire others on the project team where change needs to occur. You don't necessarily have to orate at the same level as Martin Luther King Jr., JFK, or Mahatma Gandhi, but you need to inspire some passion from people. If you can, you should be that person.

If you're joining a brownfield project, you're in the perfect situation to advocate change. You're looking at the code, the process, and the team with fresh eyes. You're seeing what others with more time on the project may have already become numb to. You may have fresh ideas about tools and practices that you bring from other projects. You, above all else, can bring enthusiasm and energy to a project that's simply moving forward in the monotony of the day to day.

As we've mentioned before, you'll want to tread lightly at the start. First, get the lay of the land and find (or create) allies within the project. More than anything, you'll want to proceed with making change.

During our time talking about change with different groups and implementing it in our own work, we have come up with one clear thought: the process of change is about hearts and minds, not shock and awe. Running into a new project with your technical and process guns blazing will alienate and offend some of the existing team. They'll balk at the concepts simply because you're the new person. Negativity will be attached to your ideas because the concerned parties will, without thought, think that they're nothing more than fads or the ideas of a rogue or cowboy developer. Once you've entered a project in this fashion, it's extremely difficult to have the team think of you in any other way.

Hearts and minds is all about winning people over. Take one developer at a time. Try something new with a person who's fighting a pain point and, if you're successful at solving the problem area, you'll have a second advocate spreading ideas of change. People with historical relevance on the project usually carry more weight than a new person when proposing change. Don't be afraid to find and use these people.

---

**Tales from the trenches: Don't get emotionally involved**

In one project we were on, tensions started to run high as the team fragmented into a consultants-versus-employees mentality. On the one side were the consultants who wanted to "throw in a bunch of advanced code that the others couldn't understand or support." On the other were the employees who were "so far behind in their skills, they may as well be coding in COBOL." The frustration culminated in an email from one employee to one of us copied to not only the current team but everyone in the entire group as well as a couple of managers. Some of the complaints in the email were valid; some less so. Among the rational ones: we removed code that we had thought wasn't being called, not counting on direct calls made to it from an Active Server Pages Framework (ASPX) page.

*(continued)*

The first off-the-cuff email response we made sat in our draft box for a couple of hours before we deleted it. We took a deep breath and wrote a second one. The cc list was reduced only to the direct team. We included a sincere apology for removing the code and a request that we keep our focus on delivering value to the client. This was followed up with a telephone call reiterating the apology.

In this case, there are many reasons we could've given to defend ourselves: Why are we calling code directly from an ASPX page? Why does the app still compile and pass all its tests? And why does something like this warrant such a melodramatic response?

All of these are subjective and would have prolonged, and likely escalated, the situation. By admitting wrongdoing, we were able to diffuse the situation and get back on track quickly.

Emotionally charged situations will arise in your brownfield projects. As tough as it will be at the time, it's imperative that you keep your wits about you and stay focused on the goal: delivering an application the client is happy with.

Being an agent of change is about playing politics, suggesting ideas, formulating reasoning for adoption, and following through with the proposals. In some environments, none of these things will be simple. The problem is, if someone doesn't promote ideas for change, they'll never happen. That's where you (and, we hope, this book) come in. One of the common places that you'll have to sell these changes is to management. Let's take a look at what can happen there.

## 1.5   *Selling it to your boss*

There may be some reluctance and possibly outright resistance to making large-scale changes to an application's architecture and design. This is especially true when the application already "works" in some fashion. After all, users don't typically see any noticeable difference when you refactor. It's only when you're able to deliver features and fix defects much quicker that the efforts get noticed.

Often, managers even recognize that an application isn't particularly well written but are still hesitant. They will ease developers' concerns by claiming that "We'll refactor it in the next release but for the time being, let's just get it done."

### The technical debt phase

As mentioned in section 1.1.2, technical debt is the laundry list of items that eventually should get done but that are easy to put off. Every project incurs technical debt, and many projects deal with it through a big push phase (if they deal with it at all). This is some major undertaking where all work on the application stops until you've worked through at least a good chunk of your technical debt.

> **(continued)**
>
> This isn't the way to go. Instead, we promote the idea of a time-boxed task every, or every other, coding cycle (whether that be development iterations or releases to testing). The sole purpose of this task is to pay down some technical debt.
>
> This doesn't have to be a team-wide task. It may take only one person working half a day a week. And it's limited by time, not by tasks. The person working on technical debt works on it for the allotted time, then stops, regardless of how much is left on the technical debt list. (The person should finish what she's started and plan accordingly.)

This sentiment is understandable and may even be justified. Just as there are managers who ignore the realities of technical debt, many developers ignore the realities of basic cost-benefit equations. As a group, we have a tendency to suggest changes for some shaky reasons:

- We want to learn a new technology or technique.
- We read a white paper/blog post suggesting this is the thing to do.
- We don't want to take the time to understand the current codebase.
- We believe that doing it another way will make all our problems go away and not introduce a different set of issues.
- We're bored with the tasks that have been assigned to us.

So before we talk about how to convince your boss to undertake a massive rework in the next phase of the project, it's worth taking stock of the reasons why we're suggesting it. Are we doing it for the client's benefit? Or is it for ours?

The reason we ask is that there are many valid business reasons why you shouldn't undertake this kind of work. Understanding them will help put your desires to try something new in perspective:

- The project's shelf life is short.
- The application does follow good design patterns—just not ones you agree with.
- The risk associated with the change is too large to mitigate before the next release.
- The current team or the maintenance team won't be able to technically understand the changed code and need training first.
- Significant UI changes may risk alienating the client or end user.

**WARNING**   Be cautious when someone suggests a project's shelf life will be short. Applications have a tendency to outlive their predicted retirement date. Like shelf life, people often minimize the perceived technical complexity of a project. Don't let this fool you. We've seen many "simple" applications turn into monstrous beasts that have required advanced technical implementations to achieve the goals and needs of the business. Never buy this line of rhetoric. Instead, prepare yourself and your codebase for the likely eventuality of increasing technical complexity.

NOTE    Lack of time and money are two common reasons given for choosing not to perform a large-scale refactoring. Neither one is valid unless the person making the decision outright admits they're hoping for a short-term gain in exchange for long-term pain.

You won't have an easy time trying to justify the expense of large-scale changes. It's hard to find good solid information on this that's written in a way meant to convince management to adopt. Even if you do find a good piece of writing, it's common for management to dismiss the article on the grounds that the writer doesn't have a name known to them, or that the situation doesn't apply.

By far, the best way to alter management's opinion is to show concrete results with clear business value. Attempt to convince them to let you try a prototype in a small and controlled situation. This will give them the comfort that if the trial goes sour, they'll have protected the rest of the project and not spent a lot of money. And if it goes well, they now have the data to support their decision to go ahead.

For these same reasons, you shouldn't be looking at the proof of concept solely as a way to convince your management that you are right. You should always consider that your suggestion may not be the best thing for the project and approach the trial objectively. This allows you to detach yourself from any one technology and focus on the success of the project itself. If the experiment succeeds, you now have a way of helping the project succeed. If it fails, at least you didn't go too far down the wrong road.

In figure 1.6, we show something akin to a mockup but with notes on how it can work within our existing infrastructure.

Another advantage of proofs of concept is that because you're constrained to a small area, you can be protected from external factors. You can then focus on the task at hand and increase your chances to succeed—which is your ideal goal.

When you're discussing change with decision makers, it's a good idea to discuss benefits and costs in terms of cash dollars whenever possible. Doing so may not be as difficult as it first sounds.

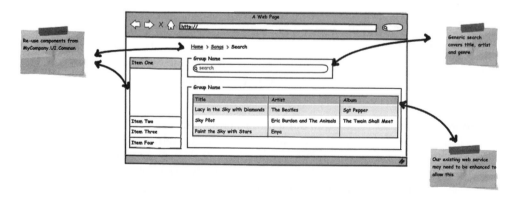

**Figure 1.6  Proofs of concept and mockups can help convince your boss of the value of a concept and can help you work out kinks before implementing it large-scale.**

Previously, we discussed the concept of pain points and friction. This is the first step in quantifying the money involved: isolate the pain point down to specific steps that can be measured. The steps that are causing pain for the development team can then be translated into business terms.

There are two kinds of cost savings you can focus on. The first is direct savings from being able to work faster. If you spend 2 hours implementing a change and that change saves half a day for each of four developers on the project, the task can be justified.

Another way to look at this method of cost savings is as an opportunity cost. How much money is the company forgoing by not completing a particular cost-saving task?

The second method of cost savings is what keeps insurance companies in business: How much money will it cost if we don't implement a certain task and things go wrong? Can we spend a little money up front to reduce our risk exposure in the event something goes horribly wrong?

In the end, the discussion points for selling management or clients on the idea of reworking the codebase are going to include the concepts of cost and risk. By using prototypes and proofs of concept, along with examples of inefficiency and risk, you'll be more likely to address significant points of concern held by your audience.

Once we've addressed the concerns of management and clients, it's time to start doing some work. That's a great point for us to get you into the technology. Chapter 2 starts at a seemingly innocuous part of the process: version control.

## 1.6 Summary

Like so many in software development, you'll spend more time on projects that are incomplete or in ongoing development than you will on projects that aren't. It's much more common for projects to need our services once they've been started and resource shortages or inadequacies have bubbled to the surface.

With these projects, we inherit all the problems that come with them. Problems will include technical, social, and managerial concerns, and in some way you'll be interacting with all of these. The degree of influence that you have over changing them will vary depending on both the project environment and the position that you have in it.

Remember that you probably won't solve all the problems all the time. Don't get wrapped up in the magnitude of everything that's problematic. Instead, focus on little pieces where the negative impact on the project, at whatever level, is high and where you're in a position to make or direct the change. These pain points are the ones that will provide the biggest gain.

Positive change works wonders on the project, no matter what the change is. Remember to look at pain points that have cross-discipline benefits. Implementing a solution for a problem that's felt by developers, management, testers, and the clients will have a positive influence on each of those disciplines. More importantly, positive cross-discipline improvements will increase the communication and rapport between the groups that may exist within the project team.

No matter the effect that you have said that a change will have on a project team, there will still be people who resist. Convincing these people will become a large part of the work that you do when trying to implement a new technique or process. One of the most effective ways is to sell the change using terms and conditions that will appeal to the resister. If part of their role, as in management, is to be concerned with money and timeline, then sell to those points. For technical people, appeal to the sense of learning new techniques and bettering their craft.

Even with the tactical use of this technique, you'll often run into people and topics that take more selling. If you feel as if you're at a dead end, ask for a time-boxed task where you can prove the technique or practice on a small scale and in an isolated environment. Often, results from these trial or temporary implementations will speak volumes to the person who's blocking their use.

The changes that you, as a developer, make to a project, whether permanently or on a trial basis, will fall into two different concerns: ecosystem and code. No matter how well schooled a project is in one of those two areas, deficiencies in the other can still drag it down. Don't concentrate on one over the other. Instead, focus on the areas in the project where the most significant pain points are occurring. Address those first and then move on to the next largest pain point.

As we step through this book, you'll see a number of categories that pain points will occur in. Although we have tried to address them in a specific order, and each builds on the previous, your project may need an order of its own. This is fine. Adapt what you see in the book and the sample project that provides the best results for you.

With that, let's move on to addressing some common pain points.

# *Part 1*

## *The ecosystem*

There's more to your application than code, but many tend to ignore the ecosystem when reviewing a brownfield project. Instead, they focus on the code, and that focus ignores the surrounding components that are a part of running a successful software development project. When used correctly, these components can create an environment in which any project has a better chance of succeeding.

As in any ecosystem, the health, growth, and potential success (or demise) of a brownfield project are determined by a number of variables working together. The code is only one of those variables.

Think of a tree growing in the desert. That tree has little water and a poor nutrient base from which to sustain itself. When any of us look at that tree, we realize that its prospects seem bleak. But if we provide it with nutrient-rich soil and a steady supply of water, the tree will have a much better chance of living a long life and providing shade to nomads. Although we can't guarantee that it will live, we've taken significant steps toward its ongoing success by controlling those variables.

Now think about your brownfield project. There are a number of controllable variables in its ecosystem: source control, compilation, release management, and defect tracking, among others. The project interacts with these variables on a regular basis. The question is, are you working with those variables in such a way that encourages the project to flourish within its ecosystem?

Part 1 of this book is going to help answer that question. You'll see examples and read discussions of several major variables in a software development ecosystem. We'll show how poor management of these variables can lead to a brownfield project. You'll also explore ways to encourage both yourself and your team to greater productivity. All of these things will be covered before we dive into the code.

As every project's ecosystem is different, our discussion will center on fundamentals. We'll eschew specific prescriptive advice for tool A in favor of a focus on the underlying issues that have traditionally caused pain in your brownfield project. Take the ideas here and think about them as they pertain to your current ecosystem. Apply them in such a way that they'll provide richness to your project by creating the appropriate garden for it to flourish in.

The more that we can control these variables, the more easily our projects can succeed.

# Version control in
# brownfield applications

*2*

**This chapter covers**

- Preparing your app for version control
- Learning the check-in dance
- Working effectively with version control

In chapter 1, we defined a brownfield application and discussed the various challenges you'll face. Now it's time to review your project's ecosystem for pain points and see what you can do to address them. To that end, we're starting with a seemingly basic topic: version control.

Let's begin with a quick look at the worst source control system you're likely to encounter when you tackle a brownfield project.

> You: I'm excited to be furthering the development of your tremendously popular website. How may I gain access to the source control repository?
> Your client: Give me a second.
> <ding! – You've got mail! – sourcecode.zip>

Amusing as this anecdote is, a zipped copy of the code is *technically* a viable method of version control, though it's far more common than it ought to be.

Chances are you already have a version control system (a source control system) of some form in place and are using it daily. Indeed, most developers have a good handle on how version control systems work. Our intent isn't to walk you through the details of checking in and checking out code. Rather, we're using this chapter as a launching pad for one of our underlying goals: to encourage you to take a critical look at your process and see where it can be improved.

In this chapter, we'll consider a brownfield project that either doesn't use version control or has outgrown its existing mechanism and is now looking at switching to a new one. Even if you've already got one, this is a good time to take stock of your system. Is it easy to get code out and put it back in? Does it regularly lose code or history? Are you taking full advantage of it? Later in this chapter, we'll discuss some ways you can use your version control system more effectively.

To get started, let's see where it hurts.

## 2.1   Pain points

As you recall from the previous chapter, we defined a pain point as any aspect of your project that causes you or your client problems. In brownfield apps, pain points often define your initial agenda as you work on the code. Pain deriving from inadequate use of version control can take many forms. We'll start with an anecdote derived from experience.

### 2.1.1   Missing references and assemblies

Lewis scanned the readme file for the application he was about to start working on. In it were instructions for downloading the latest version of the code from the version control system. He located the application's solution file, opened it, and tried to compile. Almost immediately, he was met with a dozen errors, all along the same line (see figure 2.1): the type or namespace name couldn't be found (with messages like "are you missing a `using` directive or an assembly reference?").

| | Description | File | Line | Column |
|---|---|---|---|---|
| 13 | The type or namespace name 'ClassMap' could not be found (are you missing a using directive or an assembly reference?) | CountryMap.cs | 6 | 31 |
| 14 | The type or namespace name 'ClassMap' could not be found (are you missing a using directive or an assembly reference?) | LanguageMap.cs | 6 | 32 |
| 15 | The type or namespace name 'ClassMap' could not be found (are you missing a using directive or an assembly reference?) | LegalDocumentMap.cs | 6 | 37 |
| 16 | The type or namespace name 'Lucene' could not be found (are you missing a using directive or an assembly reference?) | createIndex.aspx.cs | 7 | 7 |
| 17 | The type or namespace name 'Lucene' could not be found (are you missing a using directive or an assembly reference?) | search.aspx.cs | 7 | 7 |
| 18 | The type or namespace name 'ApplicationBlocks' does not exist in the namespace 'Microsoft' (are you missing an assembly reference?) | PetrocashDB.cs | 7 | 17 |
| 19 | The type or namespace name 'Lucene' could not be found (are you missing a using directive or an assembly reference?) | createIndex.aspx.cs | 8 | 7 |
| 20 | The type or namespace name 'FluentNHibernate' could not be found (are you missing a using directive or an assembly reference?) | Global.asax.cs | 8 | 7 |
| 21 | The type or namespace name 'Lucene' could not be found (are you missing a using directive or an assembly reference?) | search.aspx.cs | 8 | 7 |
| 22 | The type or namespace name 'FluentNHibernate' could not be found (are you missing a using directive or an assembly reference?) | Global.asax.cs | 9 | 7 |
| 23 | The type or namespace name 'Lucene' could not be found (are you missing a using directive or an assembly reference?) | search.aspx.cs | 9 | 7 |
| 24 | The type or namespace name 'NHibernate' could not be found (are you missing a using directive or an assembly reference?) | Global.asax.cs | 10 | 7 |
| 25 | The type or namespace name 'Lucene' could not be found (are you missing a using directive or an assembly reference?) | search.aspx.cs | 10 | 7 |
| 26 | The type or namespace name 'ISession' could not be found (are you missing a using directive or an assembly reference?) | RepositoryBase.cs | 10 | 17 |
| 27 | The type or namespace name 'NHibernate' could not be found (are you missing a using directive or an assembly reference?) | Global.asax.cs | 11 | 7 |
| 28 | The type or namespace name 'ISession' could not be found (are you missing a using directive or an assembly reference?) | SessionBuilder.cs | 12 | 24 |

**Figure 2.1   Many brownfield applications will give reference errors when first downloading them from version control.**

Lewis reviewed a couple of the errors and discovered several projects had missing references to certain assemblies (see figure 2.2).

They all appeared to be third-party assemblies that Lewis clearly didn't have on his computer. Sighing to himself, he set about asking his coworkers where to find them. Some he gathered from other machines; others required him to download and run an installation package from the internet. One even required Lewis to map a network drive to a specific location on the network. It was early afternoon before he was able to compile the application.

### 2.1.2 Files locked for checkout

To familiarize himself with the code, Lewis found a simple bug from the defect-tracking system and set about trying to fix it. Quickly, he found the file he needed to change. "Ah!" he said to himself. "It's only my first day and I'm already picking off bugs." Feeling rather smug, he started editing the file. Or at least he tried to edit it…

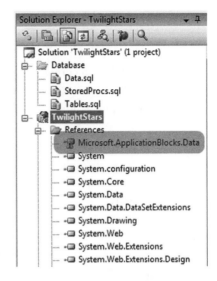

**Figure 2.2   Often, reference errors are due to missing assemblies. The developer must hunt down all the dependencies for the project.**

As soon as Lewis started typing, he was greeted by a message: "TwilightStarsDB.cs is checked out by user (martind) and cannot be edited." Lewis looked at the message dejectedly until Huey walked into his office. He took one look at the dialog and said, "Oh, I get that all the time. Martin went on vacation last week and I'm not sure what he's been working on. I've just been putting my changes up in the user interface project for now and hitting the database straight from there. We can go back and change it when he gets back on Friday and checks in his code… Why are you shuddering? Do you need me to turn the heat up in here?"

### 2.1.3 Maintaining production code

Later that week, Lewis got an email about a bug in the production version of the application. Unfortunately, the team had already made considerable changes to the app since then for the next release. He tracked down Huey again to find out what to do about the bug. Once again, Huey had a quick answer. "Oh, we get those all the time. Every time we deploy the application, we store a copy of it on Martin's machine. Schedule some time with him to fix it and we can do another deploy from there when it's done."

Lewis thought for a moment. "What about the current version of the app?" he asked. Huey looked at him, confused. "What about it?" "Well…" started Lewis slowly, "don't we need to fix the bug in the current version, too?" Huey considered this for a second. "That's a good idea. Be sure you make the same changes to the current app.

That will be a bit of a pain having to do the same thing in both places, but I guess we don't want the same bug biting us again in the future."

Version control is ubiquitous in the industry. You'd be hard-pressed to find a project without it. Most developers are familiar with its obvious advantages:

- Acts as a central location for the current version of the application
- Protects against accidental deletions
- Allows you to roll back changes

But version control isn't always as cut and dried as it first seems, and we don't always take full advantage of its capabilities. Or it's configured in a way that hinders your team's productivity. In our first example, even after getting the latest version of the code from the version control system, Lewis still had a lot of work to do before he was productive. When he was able to start working, the software threw up roadblocks by not allowing him to edit the file he wanted to, leading him to find a workaround. Very often, brownfield applications are rife with these workarounds.

In addition, the scenario where a bug needs to be fixed in two different places is all too common in brownfield projects. Not only that, often they aren't even viewed as pain points. Many people simply accept them as a fact of the industry without ever wondering if there's a better way.

These types of pain points can be fixed by pausing and taking stock of your version control system to make sure it's working for you. For the remainder of the chapter, we'll take a hard look at version control systems and how you can remove related roadblocks from your brownfield application.

But before we do that, we'd like to go back to the basics. Version control is one of those topics that everyone seems to take for granted, but there's value in examining the characteristics of a good version control system before we continue.

## 2.2   *What's in a version control system?*

Ultimately, the mechanics of a version control system (VCS) are the same for brownfield and greenfield applications. But when an app has been developed without a VCS, or the system in place has been used improperly, unnecessary problems due to disorganization can be a source of code contamination. If you're working in an environment that doesn't have a VCS in place, or if you're looking at replacing an existing system, knowing what products are currently on the market will help you choose the right one for your situation. Each product brings its own list of features to the table. In this section, we'll look at which features should be required in any system, as well as some that, although not mandatory, may reduce friction in your team.

### 2.2.1   *Required features*

First we'll discuss the three features that you should always demand in a VCS. But don't expect the discussion to trim down your options when shopping for one. Most, if not all, VCS products include the following in their list of features. That said, it's handy to review it as we'll talk about some of these features later in the chapter.

**RETAIN FILE HISTORY**

A VCS must be able to store old versions of files. This feature relates back to our poor developer who toiled away for several hours on code that eventually needed to be thrown away and reverted to an earlier version.

Also implied is that the previous versions must be easily accessible. Having different versions of a file is of no use if you can't retrieve them. On top of that, you must be able to retrieve the history of files that were deleted. Just because you think you don't need the file now doesn't meant that you won't need to reference it at some point in the future.

And although it's not a strict requirement, most VCS products offer the ability to label different versions of files so that you can more easily locate the one you want (provided you're using labels). You should be able to effectively stamp the existing state of the application with a label so that the current version of the files is associated with that label. The reciprocal is that you should be able to later retrieve the application associated with a particular label. We'll discuss labeling (also known as tagging) later in section 2.5.2.

**CONNECTIVITY**

All your developers must have to connect to the VCS to access the code. Your VCS is going to be the single point of access for your code. If someone asks for the latest version of the code, your VCS is it. It's important that developers be able to use it as such.

**ATOMIC TRANSACTIONS**

If you want to make changes to a group of individual files as a single unit, the files should all be updated entirely or none of them should be updated. If there's a failure when updating one file in the group, the entire transaction should be aborted. Without this criterion there's potential for your code to be left in an unstable state after files are checked in.

**NOTE** You'll often run into the concept of a *changeset*: the list of files and associated meta-information that form a single commit or check-in. Some VCS products will store the file history as a list of changesets rather than entire copies of the application. Others will store *reverse diffs* (they store the current versions of files entirely and then keep track of the differences going backward). Reverse diffs have the advantage of keeping the source code repository small. But the file history is usually stored in a proprietary format that's accessible only by the VCS. Our opinion: this concern is not a deal-breaker when shopping for a VCS.

**EXAMINING THE CRITERIA**

When evaluating a VCS, assume the three features we just discussed are mandatory. Immediately remove from consideration any products that don't offer them. You'll find that almost all products do offer these features at a bare minimum. Any other features you require will vary from project to project and from team to team.

In the opening anecdote, you got your source code via an email attachment. Based on the criteria outlined here, this *could* be a valid version control system. Using file system timestamps or a folder naming convention that segregates each past check-in, you can determine the sequencing of the archived code. And because your code is stored on a centralized file system share, it's easily accessible to the developers. Furthermore, using a compression utility would almost certainly ensure that all files were included in each of the archived versions, thereby ensuring atomicity when you check in.

But this method of version control imposes a lot of friction on the developers. It doesn't solve one of our pain points described in section 2.1: how could two people work on the code at the same time? Someone still needs to manually merge changes into another codebase (in the case where two people update the "latest version" in the same timeframe). In addition, each developer must create the archive file manually and store it on the central file share in the appropriate location—again, manually.

The common theme in this theory is that it's manual. Any time something has to be done manually it's usually much slower and it's almost certainly much more error prone. Neither are features that any software development process wants to add to its list of selling points. So let's see what we can do to make the process smoother.

### 2.2.2  *Greasing the wheels*

What our manual example illustrates is that you need something that not only provides the basic requirements of a version control system but also reduces the friction of the development process.

**NOTE**    Recall from chapter 1 that friction is any process that impedes the forward motion of a developer and keeps her from working on code. If you find yourself working in a way that causes friction, the process should be rethought, reworked, replaced, or simply eliminated. Friction will be a recurring theme throughout this book.

A robust VCS will remove impediments and should answer basic questions each time you check in code to the repository:

- Who made the change?
- What files changed?
- Why were the files changed?

Beyond these, the VCS should provide a few other capabilities to help reduce friction. We'll explore these capabilities next.

#### COMPARE FILE VERSIONS

Although retaining the history of a file is key, being able to compare two versions, as well as compare with a local version on your file system, is of particular interest in brownfield applications. Such a comparison may be the only way you can trace how a file has deteriorated over time. This knowledge can be invaluable when you're working on defects (see chapter 6).

Whether or not your VCS includes this feature natively, text comparison tools are available that do an excellent job of visually displaying differences. Two tools we currently like are Scooter Software's Beyond Compare and the open source WinMerge.

**EASE OF USE**

Many developers may not consider ease of use when using a VCS. Most of the time, that's because they're used to interacting with it from within Visual Studio. Two Microsoft products, SourceSafe and Team Foundation Server, offer Visual Studio integration, and many developers have started with one of these products and never looked into alternatives.

But there are two other common ways of interacting with your VCS:

- Through Windows Explorer
- Via command-line and/or stand-alone applications

> **Challenge your assumptions: Life outside the IDE**
>
> Many developers are hesitant when you suggest they perform some development-related action outside of Visual Studio, especially when there are perfectly viable alternatives inside it. We aren't suggesting you abandon the IDE altogether in favor of Notepad (mostly because there are better text editors than Notepad). But don't automatically discount the idea of, say, checking in code from Windows Explorer or building the application from the command line in a build script (more on this in chapter 3). Often, it can be useful to edit a file and check it in without having to open Visual Studio.

In many cases, more than one of these options will apply, and with some VCS products, third-party utilities or applications that bridge the gap may be available. For example, one popular VCS is Subversion, a command-line application. But third-party applications exist that allow Subversion to integrate with Windows Explorer (such as TortoiseSVN) as well as integrate with Visual Studio (such as AnkhSVN and VisualSVN).

How users work with the VCS is generally a personal preference. Some development teams will be more comfortable, and more productive, if the VCS fully integrates into the IDE. Others may be accustomed to command-line utilities and the flexibility afforded them, especially when used in conjunction with PowerShell.

These features of a VCS aren't strictly required and you can get by without them. But when you join a brownfield project, it's imperative that you look for as many ways as possible to keep your developers focused on code and not process.

Another key topic when discussing VCSs is how they manage files that are checked out. We'll look at the two models of doing this next.

### 2.2.3 *File management*

Another point that factors into how a developer makes use of a VCS is the file management model. There are two models: file locking and version merging.

**FILE LOCKING**

The premise of the file-locking model (also known as the lock-edit-commit model) is that when a developer is editing a file, it's locked and the VCS prevents anyone else from modifying that file. Figure 2.3 shows an example.

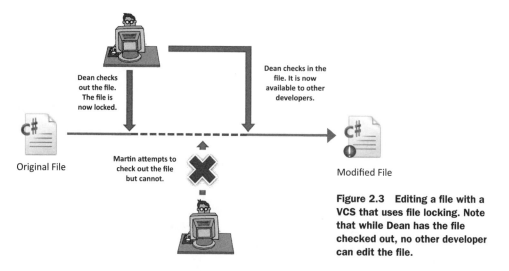

Figure 2.3   Editing a file with a VCS that uses file locking. Note that while Dean has the file checked out, no other developer can edit the file.

The advantage to this model is that it's intuitive and easy to understand. Checking code into the VCS is simple and code conflicts are rare.

The downside is that developers are often fighting over file resources. This conflict is more detrimental than it may seem. Imagine working on a fairly complex piece of code. You edit a `Customer` class to handle some new feature, and then update an application service that retrieves it from the data layer. Next, you move on to the data layer itself and find out that someone else has checked out the file you need to complete your task.

All of a sudden, your momentum grinds to a halt. You have two avenues available to you:

- Stop working and wait for the file to become available
- Find some other location to put your code

### Tales from the trenches: Dispensing with friction

Early in the life of one project, we encountered development friction due to our chosen VCS. At first, adhering to the corporate standard, we had three developers working on the software. As we got started, it took less than a week for the locking-based VCS to block each other's work process. A developer would start a development task and add a new software artifact. In Visual Studio, this means the project file was exclusively checked out to that developer. At the same time, other developers needed to add their own classes but couldn't.

Four days into the development effort, we had one or two developers idle at various times due to constraints imposed by the style of VCS. Rather than allow that friction to impede our development velocity, we took the time to implement and train developers on a different VCS, one that followed the edit-merge-commit method. Although there were some up-front costs due to training and teething issues, the couple of dozen hours it took to address such issues were far cheaper than to use a system that blocked developers from working.

Neither of these options is palatable, to say the least. Project managers and clients don't like portions of their development team sitting idle, and putting code in whatever file is available is a perfect recipe for creating technical debt—something that probably led your application into the mess you're trying to get out of.

The end result is that file locking is often a source of friction to many developers. Luckily, there is another model.

**VERSION MERGING**

In the version merging model (also known as the edit-merge-commit model), any developer can edit any file at any time. In fact, with many VCS products that use this method, you don't even need to explicitly check out a file; you simply start editing it and the file is checked out to you automatically.

This approach can seem like the road to chaos at first because it inevitably leads to instances where a file has been modified by another person while you were making changes to the same file. The VCS gets around this problem by adding another step to the process of checking in: if the file you're checking in has changed since you last retrieved it, you must merge your changes with the current version of the file. Figure 2.4 illustrates this.

At first glance, many people might dismiss such a notion outright, thinking that the seemingly manual merge step will be too cumbersome. In practice, it's not an onerous task. Most VCS products that follow this model provide tools that make it easy to compare your version of the file with the current version. Often, the changes you make are in entirely different areas of the file than the ones that have been modified since you retrieved the latest version, making the merge process easy. Many VCS products automate the merge in simple cases.

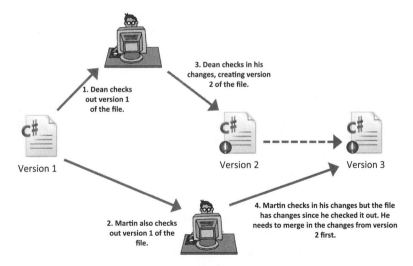

**Figure 2.4   Editing a file with a VCS that uses version merging. Both Dean and Martin are able to make changes to version 1 of the file. But because Dean checks in his changes first, Martin must merge those changes into his version before checking in.**

**Tales from the trenches: The fear of merging**

Any time a project team suggests moving to an edit-merge-commit version control system, it's almost certain that someone will raise concerns about the merging portion of the process. We had this happen to us on a project recently. The developers who had never worked in this manner were terrified of the potential effort that merging required when they committed their code.

Our only remedy was to sit down with the team and train them on the use of common scenarios they'd encounter. This training took about 4 hours, and as each scenario was simulated and discussed, the team became more comfortable with the process. In the end, the combination of the training, strong adherence to the single responsibility principle (see chapter 7), and a culture of checking in fast and often (multiple times per day in our case) meant that a manual merge situation arose only a couple of times per month. By the end of the project, all of the early detractors of the edit-merge-commit style of the version control system had been converted into advocates.

Another way to reduce the pain of merges is to follow a couple of simple guidelines. One is to check in more often (which we talk about later in section 2.5.1). Another is to use the single responsibility principle more often. We'll discuss this principle in detail in chapter 7 (and subsequent chapters), but the general idea is that you ensure each class does one thing and one thing only. That way, when you need to change functionality you typically don't work on the same classes as someone else. By sticking to these guidelines, you'll find that merge conflicts are rare and easily solved by a quick scan.

**WHICH ONE IS RIGHT?**

Both models have advantages and disadvantages, and each team is different. You'll have to decide if your team is capable of handling merge scenarios, if you want to avoid them altogether, or if you want to ease away from locking toward merging.

**NOTE**   We are always in favor of solutions that reduce friction, which makes our personal preference the version merging model. We find that version merging doesn't get in the way of your team's momentum as often as file locking. And in our experience, the potential issues caused by manually resolving occasional merge conflicts is less painful and intrusive than having developers locking files and preventing others from working.

You may need to analyze your codebase to decide if it's written in a way that will cause merge conflicts often. If you have a lot of coupling between your classes and they're generally large, it may be more beneficial to start with a file-locking mechanism and ease into a merging system as you break out dependencies.

But we're getting ahead of ourselves. It's still far too early to start looking at code. We haven't finished evaluating features for our VCS. Next on our list is branching.

### 2.2.4 Branching

Branching, in version control terminology, is when you fork the code
down two or more paths. Starting from
a common codebase, you "branch" the
code essentially into two projects. It's
similar to copying a file and having two
people work on it in tandem, though
most VCSs will use some more-efficient

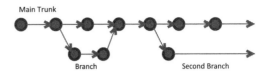

Main Trunk

Branch          Second Branch

**Figure 2.5   The branching process. Each node represents a check-in.**

storage mechanisms to handle branching. The process is shown in figure 2.5.

The idea behind branching is that, on occasion, you need to take your codebase in
a different direction. We've already discussed one scenario in section 2.1 where a
major bug was discovered in the production version of the code but the team has
already started on a new version. We want to release a fix for this bug but we don't
want to include any other changes we've made to the code since it was released to production. So we'd like to branch the production code in another direction while work
continues along its original path.

Another common scenario is the spike. You want to experiment on the current
codebase without affecting other developers. Perhaps you're testing a new UI component, or you want to switch the unit-testing framework used by your application and
want to test the effects of such a change without committing to it fully.

---

**Code spikes**

The term *spike* comes from the agile software development community and is defined
as a means of describing work that can't be estimated without first exploring the solution. It's not uncommon to hear this term used on a regular basis in the development community for this purpose.

Often, a developer will be working on a task in which he doesn't fully understand the
technical implementation requirements. In an effort to better understand the work
that lies ahead, he will put in a limited amount of time attempting to learn as much
about it as possible. Usually this effort is conducted in a throwaway side project or
an isolated branch in the VCS.

There are two key points to a spike. First, the work must be time boxed. Time boxing
is the process of setting a maximum amount of time that you'll spend on the task. If
enough information or understanding hasn't been gathered at the end of that time
box, another spike should be requested. Time boxing is done to limit the effort outlay
in the event that the spike proves the task unachievable.

The second key point is that the spike effort should be considered throwaway. When
working in spike code, it's common and acceptable not to use best practices and
project standards. As a result, any code that's generated can be difficult or impossible to reintegrate with the main development effort.

Remember, we want to learn from the spike, not create something deployable.

Both of these situations illustrate the need to branch the code. In the first case, we want to start from a previous version of the code (the version released to production) and branch it. We want to start working on the previous version as if it were a separate project altogether. In the second case, we branch off from the current version of the code. In both cases, development continues off the main codebase (often called the *trunk*) as if the branch doesn't exist. In effect, you're working on two different versions of the application.

Figure 2.5 (earlier) shows two common scenarios related to branching. Notice that the first branch continues for a short time, and then merges back into the trunk. For example, take the case where you've branched the code to fix a bug. Say you've built a patch to fix the bug and have tested it thoroughly. Naturally, you'll want to apply this patch to the main codebase so you don't reintroduce the bug. Or in the case of our spike, maybe it was a successful test and now you want to incorporate it into the trunk.

But there are also cases when a branch will never be merged back into the trunk. This case is depicted by the second branch in figure 2.5. One example is common in open source projects. When a new version of the .NET Framework is available, the project may upgrade to the new version to take advantage of new language features. A branch is still maintained on the old framework for backward compatibility for a period of time. Eventually, development on the branch stops without ever merging the changes back into the trunk.

### Challenge your assumptions: Frequent branching

Usually teams that are employing branching are doing so based on large piece of work. These may be major refactorings, new versions of the application, or areas to test theories. Although these are valid and commendable reasons to branch your code, there can be benefits to creating branches more frequently.

One option is to branch per feature. Instead of all developers working off one branch, or the trunk, each feature being developed has its own isolated work area. This approach is the ultimate in isolation because each branch has but a single developer working in it. On the downside, it puts more pressure on the team when it comes time to integrate multiple branches into the trunk. This strategy also requires that the team have strong and open communication about the efforts occurring in the branches. Neither of these issues is insurmountable, as successful teams that are trying branch-per-feature development can attest.

Another development model that involves frequent branching is branch per defect. Instead of working on all defects in one location (a defects branch or—*shudder*—the trunk), each defect being resolved is allocated its own branch. Once the defect has been completed and tested, it's integrated back into the appropriate development or maintenance branch. As with branch per feature, you get the benefit of working in isolation. But this approach also gives you more latitude when fixing defects, a process that can often take a relatively long time. With a branch per defect, you can have that work stall (for whatever process, technical, personnel, or other reasons) without affecting the efforts being invested in other defects.

> **(continued)**
> Consider both options as techniques for solving problems of code changes imped-
> ing development or release progress. Branching isn't something to be feared. Use
> it as a tool that can solve problems by providing change isolation.

It's up to the team to decide whether branching and merging is a feature you'll use in
your VCS. But consider that branches aren't usually planned for; they come about
from unforeseen circumstances (as in our two scenarios earlier).

That wraps up our discussion on VCSs. Some of it may have been old hat to you,
but it helps to examine things from the beginning with a brownfield application.
Before we can start effecting real change in a brownfield project, we need to ensure
our VCS is working effectively. Now that we've evaluated the characteristics of a good
one, we'll provide tips on how to get the most from your VCS.

## 2.3 Organizing your project for version control

Now that we've looked at some obvious and not-so-obvious features of a VCS, we'll get
down to the important part: adding your brownfield project to the system.

Typically, this process involves more than simply adding your solution folder to the
VCS—that's the easy part. Here are some things you'll need to consider before you can
start adding files to the repository:

- Does your solution reference any third-party assemblies?
- Is your solution folder structure stable?
- Are there any files/folders in the solution that do *not* need to be versioned?

These are some of the questions you'll need to ask before making the first check-in to
the VCS.

**NOTE** We talk in this section about what to do before your first check-in. But
the concepts also apply if your solution is already in a VCS. For example,
the previous questions apply just as well to an existing code repository as
they do to one that isn't yet versioned.

In this section, we'll look at alternative methods for reorganizing your project's folder
structure. The first step, and a low-hanging fruit in this process, is to address one of
the pain points from the beginning of this chapter. Specifically, how do we deal with
third-party dependencies?

### 2.3.1 Dealing with third-party dependencies

The underlying goal of this section is simple: a developer should be able to retrieve
the latest version of the code at any time and it should work out of the box. The steps
required for a new developer to get up and running on a base development machine
should be as follows:

1   Retrieve the latest version of the code from the VCS.

2   Open the solution (.sln file) in Visual Studio.

3   Compile and run the application.

These steps are outlined in figure 2.6.

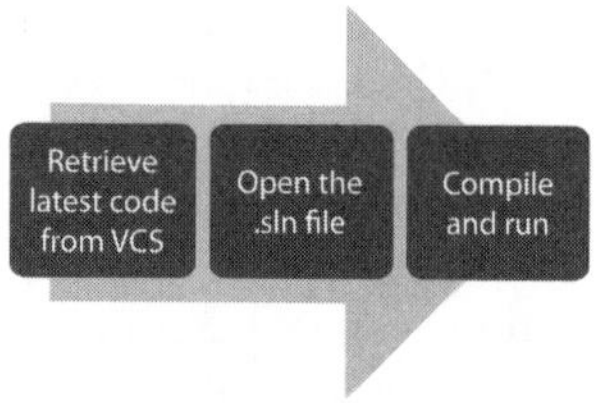

Where many projects fail in this process is the last step. Like Lewis from our opening discussion of pain points, a new developer is often met with a sea of broken references to external libraries or third-party components because

**Figure 2.6   New developers should be able to follow these simple steps to start being productive on a brownfield application. Anything else will result in friction and lost productivity.**

- The required components or libraries haven't been installed on the developer's machine yet.

- The required components or libraries have been installed in a location other than one that was expected.

- Someone has installed an incorrect version.

The solution to this problem is not to rely on developers to install these libraries and components. Include them in your application's folder structure.

Let's say your application's UI project has a reference to a third-party control library, such as DevExpress or Infragistics. You could require each developer to navigate to a central location download and install the product. And you could mandate that it be installed in a specific location.

TIP   If you absolutely *have* to force developers to formally install a third-party product to run the application, don't rely on them to download it from the internet. You never know when the version you're using will become unavailable for download. Instead, make the installation package available to your developers on a central location (a subfolder in your project's VCS, for instance). And make sure it's crystal clear that the developer must go to that location to install the product in order to continue working.

In our opinion, requiring developers to perform the installation adds unnecessary overhead to a developer's process. A better solution is to take the files that are referenced by your application (and any other supporting files), copy them into your application's folder structure, and reference them at that location.

TIP   Be sure to make all project references relative, not absolute. Not every developer will use the same base folder for all of her projects.

Now your solution is self-contained. All files needed to build and run the application are included in your folder structure. A new developer starting on the project (or an existing developer wishing to test the build process on a fresh version of the code) can get everything they need from one place. No separate installation and no referring to a readme file. You can be assured that all the references work because everything that's being referenced is included in your folder structure.

In addition, you're now insulated against versioning issues with third-party libraries. Even if newer versions of libraries become available, you don't need to upgrade to them until you're ready. As long as you keep a version of it them your VCS, you can guard against backward incompatibilities.

**Challenge your assumptions: Include third-party libraries in your solution**

It may seem counterintuitive, but including a copy of all third-party libraries used by your application (either to execute it or as part of the build process) in your solution tree is a clean way to make sure developers can get up and running fast. This strategy also protects you from versioning issues if later versions of a library become available.

In short: developer friction is greatly reduced by including copies of third-party libraries in your solution. Sure, a bit of hard drive space is lost to duplication, and it's potentially more difficult to upgrade an entire suite of applications to the latest version of a third-party utility. The key word in that last sentence is *potentially*.

But let's examine the benefits. By including copies of all external libraries in your solution, you maintain control over when and if they're upgraded. Your application won't suddenly break one day because someone in another team decided to upgrade a grid control somewhere in a centralized code repository that you were referencing.

In addition, as we've already mentioned, you have the benefit of developers being able to download the code at any time and be up and running without first having to install another package or retrieve the latest version of another project.

This benefit doesn't apply just to new developers. You'll find that existing developers will have no qualms with simply deleting their solution folder and retrieving the latest version of the code should the need arise. And if they can do this with confidence, you'll be surprised at how often the need does arise.

Keep in mind that this guideline is a suggestion, not a rigid life tenet. There may be cases where third-party libraries have dependencies on registry settings or license files in order to be used in a development environment. If you do run into such a library, don't waste time trying to figure out how to incorporate it into your source code repository. A well-crafted readme file at the root of your solution folder is the next best thing.

Next, we'll see if we can organize your folder structure a little better.

### 2.3.2   *The folder structure*

Because you're working on a brownfield application, you'll obviously have a folder structure already in place for the application. And your first intuition will be to use that as the root of your code's repository in the VCS.

It very well could be a good candidate for the root folder. But consider that there may be other code artifacts that you should include in the solution:

- External libraries (as described in section 2.3.1)
- Documents
- Configuration and build files used for deployment and testing
- Other tools and utilities

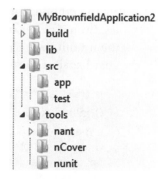

So before we check in, let's take a look at one alternative folder structure in figure 2.7, one that includes both the source code and all other code artifacts.

Figure 2.7 shows one suggested folder structure for your application before you put it into source control for the first time. Note that the source code makes up only one part of it. Table 2.1 describes each folder.

**Figure 2.7    A sample folder structure to facilitate getting developers up and running quickly**

**Table 2.1    Description of folders in the folder structure**

| Folder name | Description |
| --- | --- |
| Build | Contains artifacts related to the automated build process. We'll discuss this folder's purpose in more detail in chapter 3. |
| Docs | Stores any documents *directly related to the code*. All other documents should be kept in some form of content management system outside the application's code repository. |
| Lib | Contains all third-party libraries required to run the application itself (as described in section 2.3.1). |
| Src | app—Contains the source code for the application. |
|  | test—Contains source code for your test projects. Don't worry if you don't have any yet. We'll talk about this in chapter 4. |
| Tools | Stores any third-party tools or utilities that aren't required to run the application but that are necessary for the build process. Examples include unit-testing frameworks, automated build tools, and utilities that provide statistics on code coverage and other metrics (these tools will become clearer in the next few chapters). |

**TIP**    In section 2.3.1, we talked about including third-party libraries with your code in the VCS. These libraries should reside in the lib folder. But simply copying them into this folder isn't going to be sufficient. You'll also need to update your project files so that they reference the libraries in the new location.

Keep in mind that this folder structure is merely a suggestion and is meant as a means to get your team discussing potential issues with your current structure. If your solution already contains test projects in a structure that works for you, by all means don't deviate from something that's working. But if you're considering changing your layout, we'll cover some tips on doing so. And now is the time to do it because moving folders in a VCS can often have repercussions.

TIP    Moving folders and files within a VCS isn't always an easy thing to accomplish. If your code is already in a VCS and you'd like to change the structure to match this one, consider detaching the code from the VCS, modifying the folder structure, and then reattaching it. If you decide to go this route, be sure to test whether your VCS will maintain the file/folder history after the detachment and reattachment.

In this structure, your application's source code would reside in the *app* subfolder within the *src* root folder.

At this point, the easiest thing to do would be to copy the code wholesale into this folder. We prefer the solution (.sln) file in the root folder and updating the references to the projects within it. As we add more noncode artifacts to the solution in later chapters, it will make more sense to have the solution file at the root. Also, having the file at the root makes it easier for developers to find and it works better with some services, such as Team Foundation Server.

### A FINAL NOTE ON THE TOOLS FOLDER

As mentioned earlier, the tools folder should contain utilities and applications that are used as part of your build process. This folder isn't the same as the lib folder. The key differentiating question as to whether a utility or library is a lib or a tool is this: will it be deployed with the application? If the answer is yes, it's a lib; otherwise, it's a tool. Table 2.2 can help you grasp this concept.

**Table 2.2   Distinction between the tools folder and the lib folder**

| Candidates for the tools folder | Candidates for the lib folder |
|---|---|
| Automated build products (such as NAnt) | UI components (such as DevExpress, Infragistics, Telerik) |
| Unit-testing frameworks (such as NUnit, MbUnit, xUnit) | Inversion of control containers (such as Castle Windsor, StructureMap, Spring.NET) |
| Mocking frameworks (such as Rhino Mocks, TypeMock, Moq, Autofac) | Logging frameworks (such as log4net) |
| Code coverage/metrics analysis tools (such as NCover, NDepend) | Object-relational mappers (such as NHibernate, LLBLGen Pro) |
| | Common internal libraries developed by your organization |

TIP    If your company makes use of internally developed libraries that are used by more than your application, treat them as you would any other third-party library: reference them as binaries rather than with a direct reference to the project itself. Including direct project references to them often leads to versioning and compatibility problems. Direct project linking forces you to integrate any time that that team decides to commit code to the repository. Ideally, you'd rather be committing code based on a schedule that you determine for yourself.

That's enough on your project's folder structure. Now let's look at the corresponding folder structure within the VCS itself.

### 2.3.3    *The VCS folder structure*

Now that you've created the ideal folder structure (and updated any assembly references if necessary), you're almost ready to check in for the first time. But first, we need to prep your VCS by creating a similar folder structure within it manually.

> **NOTE**    Even if your VCS allows you to add a project to the code repository directly from Visual Studio, you should still do it manually. As we saw in the previous section, the source code is only part of what goes into the repository. And if you add single items to the VCS directly from Visual Studio, you could potentially be creating a version of the code that won't compile for another developer. Committing noncompiling code isn't something that you want to do. All changes made should be committed at the same time so that other developers will get them as a package when they update from the VCS.

As a general rule, and as figure 2.8 illustrates, your VCS folder structure should match the physical folder structure. But if your VCS supports branching, you may want to consider adding another folder level at the root of your project in the VCS.

Let's consider an example to explain further. At your company, you have three projects you'll be adding to source control:

- MyBrownfieldApp
- YourBrownfieldApp
- TheirBrownfieldApp

In this case, the root level of the VCS will contain three folders, one for each project. Each project folder will contain two folders: branches and trunk. And the trunk folder of each project will store the folder structure described in section 2.3.2.

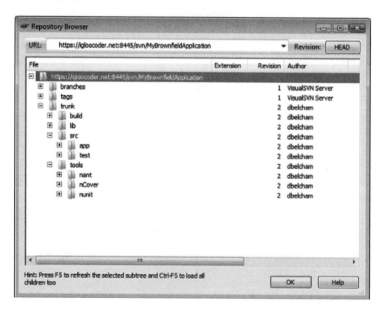

**Figure 2.8  Example of maintaining the same physical file structure in the VCS as you have on a local working folder**

**NOTE** A convention for one popular VCS product, Subversion, is to also create a folder called *tags* at the same level of branches and trunk. This folder provides support for Subversion's mechanism for labeling code. CVS, another product on which Subversion is based, uses the same convention. Figure 2.8 shows this convention in use.

Later, when you've added your code to the repository for the first time, you'll be able to start accessing it through Visual Studio (if the VCS supports it), but the initial structure should be created manually. How you accomplish this depends on the VCS. Typically, there will be some sort of interface to the VCS that will let you browse the repository and create new folders (or projects, as they're referred to in some products).

One of our earlier questions was to ask what should *not* be included in version control. We'll tackle that next.

### 2.3.4 *What not to include in the repository*

The last thing we need to talk about before we check in code to the new structure is which files to *exclude* from the repository.

By default, compiling a project in Visual Studio will create two subfolders in the project folder: bin and obj. Neither of these folders should be included in the VCS repository.

There are two reasons for this:

- They're both created by Visual Studio when you compile the application. They can be generated at any time on demand and there's no reason to include them in the repository.
- Because they change every time you rebuild the application, they'd constantly be checked in and out. In a file-locking VCS, the generation of these files could even prevent you from compiling.

Other candidates for exclusion:

- Developer-specific user settings (such as *.suo, *.csproj.user, and *.vbproj.user files)
- Files added by productivity add-ins for Visual Studio (such as CodeRush or ReSharper files)

There may be an exception to the last item. Some productivity add-ins include settings you want to be applied project-wide to ensure consistency. In this case, you may need to include these files in your VCS repository.

How do you ensure these files and folders are excluded from your repository? The good news is you probably don't need to worry about it. Most VCS products are aware of the common files and folders that should be ignored (such as bin and obj folders), and they'll do so automatically when you check in the code. Figure 2.9 shows a screenshot of the feature from TortoiseSVN.

You can add to this list on a global or application-specific basis, depending on your VCS.

**Figure 2.9   TortoiseSVN, like many VCS tools, allows for ignoring patterns and files.**

**WARNING**   Sometimes third-party libraries will include a bin folder (such as log4net, a .NET logging utility). By default, it won't be included in version control. The lack of inclusion can lead to bugs that aren't obvious at first because they don't appear on every developer's machine. In these cases, you must override the global pattern and include the bin folder for the library explicitly. Better yet, include the third-party contents of the bin folder in your project's lib folder if possible.

Phew! Seems like a lot of work to get your code properly prepared for version control. Although it is, in our experience, this work pays off quickly and several times over for a brownfield project. For instance, now that we've done all this work, the actual check-in process should be a snap. Let's get the code checked in and verified.

### 2.3.5   *The first check-in and verification*

Okay, you now have a folder structure you like, all your dependencies are included in it and appropriately referenced, and you've configured your VCS to ignore any files that aren't user specific. You're ready to add the code back into your VCS.

How your code is checked in depends largely on the VCS you're using. But if you've followed along with our discussion, the act of checking in should be straightforward.

If you're using a VCS product that allows you to work outside Visual Studio, we recommend using it for the first check-in. You're more likely to include the noncode artifacts and any libraries that live outside your source code. Regardless, when checking in be sure to review the list of files being added to your repository to ensure you've caught everything you want and nothing you don't. Also, make sure the files being committed to the VCS are being added to the appropriate location in the VCS repository itself.

If something doesn't look right, stop and think before proceeding. Is your VCS trying to add a file you don't want to include? Maybe you need to cancel the check-in and update your ignore pattern. Are the lib and tools folders not appearing in the list? Perhaps you aren't checking in from the real root of your application.

The underlying message is this: don't just check in the code blindly thinking you'll work out any problems later. Because we see the check-in dialog box so often in a VCS, developers often become numb to the information in it. Pay attention to this dialog box, at least this once. Don't be afraid to cancel the check-in until you've had a chance to review your structure or settings.

Once you're satisfied with the structure and settings and have checked in, you still aren't done. You need to verify that the code will work out of the box. A new developer should be able to retrieve the code from source control, and it should compile and run with minimal effort.

The best way to verify is to actually do it, preferably on a different workstation (virtual or physical) than the one you're working on. Just getting the code isn't enough;

you also need to verify that the code compiles in the integrated development environment (IDE), that all projects load in the IDE, and that any automated build scripts succeed (if you have any). If so, pat yourself on the back. If not, make a note of any errors and tweak your version control implementation as necessary.

**WARNING** Remember, this process is all about reducing developer friction, not causing pain points. Keep a practical eye on the clock while you tweak the process. If you're spending hours trying to automate some element of the "new developer checkout" procedure, consider the tried-and-true readme file instead.

We've provided some tips on getting your brownfield project into a state that reduces developer friction on your team going forward. But we're not done yet. Getting set up is only the first step. You still need to be able to check in code effortlessly. For that, we're going to learn to dance.

## 2.4    *The check-in dance*

Now that you're all checked in, it's time to start working with the versioned code. Although you may be familiar with the process of checking in and checking out, it helps to formalize the process somewhat. Working with a VCS is generally universal to any project, whether it's brownfield, greenfield, or legacy, so this section is applicable to any project.

Even if you're new to using version control, the process may seem intuitive at first. The steps are outlined here and summarized in figure 2.10:

1  Check out the file(s) you wish to modify.
2  Make your changes.
3  Ensure the application compiles and runs as expected.
4  Check in your changes.

Chances are, if you use this process, you're using a file-locking VCS (see sec-tion 2.2.3). The reason this version of the dance is so straightforward relates to the restrictive nature of file locking. Because no one else can modify your files while you're editing them, checking in the code is fairly benign.

However, there's a problem inherent in this process. Even though your files have been locked for editing by other developers, that doesn't mean the rest of the application is stagnant. While you work on your changes, the rest of the team is changing other files. The changes they make may be inconsistent with yours. For example, you may have changed the name of a property and another developer has created a new class that uses that property during the

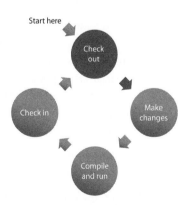

**Figure 2.10    The steps of the check-in dance for a file-locking VCS**

time you were changing it. Because it's a new class, you wouldn't know about it to change it yourself while you were working. When you check in your changes with the new property name, the next person to get the latest code won't be able to compile.

To counter this scenario, we need to add two more steps to the process:

1 Check out the file(s) you wish to modify.
2 Make your changes.
3 Ensure the application compiles and runs as expected.
4 Get the latest version of the application.
5 Ensure again that the application compiles and runs as expected.
6 Check in your changes.

Figure 2.11 shows the same process with the two new steps.

Congratulations on learning to dance.

The new steps, 4 and 5, are included specifically to handle instances when code has changed during step 2, when you're making your changes.

Consider what happens if you omit steps 4 and 5. You check in code that potentially leaves the application in an unstable state. Anyone who retrieves the latest version of the code won't be able to compile.

And that's just unacceptable. Your VCS is the heart of your application. It's the only true source for your code and at any given moment; you have to be absolutely certain that the code in it works. (In upcoming chapters, we'll refine the definition of what it means for an application to *work*; for now, it means the application should at least compile.)

In short, a codebase in your VCS that doesn't compile should be considered the ultimate failure

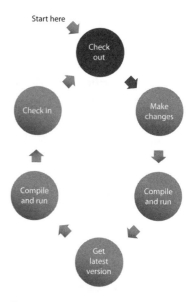

Figure 2.11  **The steps of the check-in dance for a version-merging VCS**

in your process. And worse, if we omit steps 4 and 5 of the check-in dance, we've put the onus on the next person to discover (and potentially fix) any problems that arise. All that person did was get the latest version of the code, and now he's stuck trying to fix someone else's problem before he can even begin to work on his own bugs or features.

So we include steps 4 and 5 for two reasons:

- To ensure that the code in your VCS is (almost) always in a stable state
- So the developer who causes the conflicts is the one who fixes them

We've been discussing the check-in dance with a file-locking VCS. If you've configured your VCS to use the version-merging model, there's a slight modification that's necessary. Here are the steps with the change in bold:

1 Check out the file(s) you wish to modify.
2 Make your changes.
3 Ensure the application compiles and runs as expected.
4 Get the latest version of the application **and merge your changes into it**.
5 Ensure again that the application compiles and runs as expected.
6 Check in your changes.

Notice the additional instruction in step 4. Remember that with a version-merging VCS, anyone could be modifying any file at the same time. While you're working away on Customer.cs, another developer may be modifying it as well. Plus, they may have checked in their changes while you were making your own.

So when you retrieve the latest version of the application to see if it still compiles and runs, you may have a bit of extra work to do. You may have to merge your changes in with the changes made by another developer to the same file. This ensures that the code you check in is stable for the next developer who retrieves the latest version of it.

We'll revisit the check-in dance in the next two chapters when we add continuous integration and automated testing to the mix. For now, let's move on to some more tips on making your VCS work harder for your brownfield application.

## 2.5 Tips for working with version control

In the final section of this chapter, we'll discuss some quick tips on how to use source control effectively at this stage. As we add tests and a continuous integration process, we'll have more to say on this topic. Until then, we have two final tips on working with version control:

- Check in often.
- Decide on a labeling/tagging strategy.

We expand on each of these tips next.

### 2.5.1 Check in often

One of the thoughts that may have occurred to you during the discussion on the check-in dance is "What if I've made a lot of changes over several days? Won't it take a lot of effort to merge those into the appropriate trunk or branch?"

Yes, it will. And as your doctor might tell you, if it hurts when you bend your arm like that, don't bend your arm like that. If it's too much work to merge so many changes when you check in, don't make so many changes each time you check in.

If you're used to hunkering down for a few days to complete a feature, checking in often may require a slight shift in what constitutes "check-in-able" code. Don't wait until you're feature complete before finally checking in. Rather, check in as soon as you have a new piece of code that does something useful. This approach will minimize the amount of merging you need to do when you do need to merge.

The advantages of this practice will become more apparent when we discuss unit tests in chapter 4.

**But I *really can't* check in this feature half-finished**

Real life doesn't always work out the way you want. In a brownfield application, while you're still working out the kinks of your new ecosystem, it may not be practical to check in code as often as you would like. Perhaps the new feature you're working on will break existing code, for example.

In these cases, consider branching your code for the new feature. Branch the code off the trunk and add the new feature there rather than on the main trunk.

There's a great big caveat for this practice: eventually, you'll want this feature incorporated into the trunk. When you do, be prepared for a painful merge. Because of this issue, consider carefully before undertaking a feature branch. Very often, you can still pick apart the code into chunks that can be checked in as a unit.

That said, we still prefer feature branching to going days without a single check-in, if only to make use of the normal benefits of a VCS.

### 2.5.2   *Decide on a labeling/tagging strategy*

Labeling your codebase at regular intervals can be useful. At the very least, you should label every time you deploy to a new environment. That way, if bugs occur you can always retrieve the same version of the code that you deployed, even if you've made changes since then.

Here are some possible options:

- On every check-in (very likely, this is overkill)
- Every night (useful if you create an automated release every night)
- When a particular feature is complete
- When you're about to undertake a large-scale refactoring
- When the major or minor version number of the application changes

In the next chapter, we'll return to labeling when we discuss methods for configuring your continuous integration process to label your codebase and the advantages this practice can have. For now, it's useful to at least sit down as a team and decide if and how you plan to make use of labels in your VCS.

These two tips should get you on your way to making the most of your VCS. Our overarching goal in this section (and indeed, the entire chapter) is to start you down the road of looking for ways to improve your process, starting with version control. In the next chapter, we'll continue the theme and explore how we can smooth out the wrinkles in your build process.

## 2.6 *Summary*

Although VCSs would appear to be a mandatory feature on all software development projects, you'll still encounter projects where a VCS isn't in place. Still other projects will have VCSs that don't offer the capabilities that you need to operate in your environment or development style.

In this chapter, we've started improving your ecosystem by examining your VCS. Here are some of the recommendations we made:

- Ensure you have an efficient way of comparing different versions of a file.
- Examine alternative ways of interacting with your VCS.
- Review how your VCS handles checked-out files and consider moving toward a version-merging model instead of a file-locking model.
- Include any file dependencies your application has with the code in the VCS.
- Restructure the folders in your VCS to account for the fact that it contains more than just code.
- Perform the check-in dance every time you check in code.
- Break down your code changes so that you can check in more often.
- Develop an appropriate labeling strategy for your team.

The short form of this list is simple: examine how you work with your VCS and eliminate any friction your developers have. Don't accept cumbersome processes because you believe no alternatives exist.

Version control systems are the heart of the construction portion of any software development project. In this chapter we provided you with a lot of techniques and ideas that you can implement on your brownfield projects as you grow and improve them. In the next chapter we'll look at tying the VCS into a process that continually builds and verifies your application.

# Continuous integration 3

**This chapter covers**

- Setting up continuous integration
- Closing the feedback loop
- Updating the check-in dance

In the previous chapter, we set up a version control repository to enable all developers to have the latest version of the code. Now we're going to tackle a problem common in all software development projects: integration.

Large software projects are often split into separate components as part of the design, and it isn't until late in the project that the components are integrated into a single cohesive solution. Often, this integration is a massive undertaking in and of itself and may even take several weeks and require changes to existing code in order to make it work.

When you integrate your code regularly as an ongoing part of your process, you discover problems and incompatibilities—pollution—much earlier. This technique, called *continuous integration* (CI), results in more streamlined and automated builds, especially when it's part of the process from the beginning.

Brownfield apps often suffer from many of the problems CI seeks to prevent. Fortunately, it's possible to implement CI when you take on a brownfield project and quickly reap the same benefits you'd see with a greenfield project.

In this chapter, we'll introduce the core techniques of CI and show you how to apply them to a brownfield codebase. If you're not familiar with CI, you'll also discover how to apply it to new or early-stage projects.

Before we go into details on the process, let's look at some other pain points.

## 3.1 Pain points

We've already discussed one of the common pain points you can address through implementing continuous integration. Integrating a project's components at the last minute can be an arduous process. This last-minute integration can be particularly prevalent in brownfield applications because of the way the code weaves together in these projects. It's common to find a small number of large classes in some areas so that it's unavoidable for developers to overlap while they're working, as with a single data access class that has static methods providing all access to the database.

Just consider a team of developers continuously checking in code for months and months. What are the odds that one developer's changes will cause another's to fail? Ninety percent? One hundred percent?

Let's say we're working on an application and one developer, Huey, is working on a screen that requires a grid. As a diligent developer, Huey knows the company has a license for a third-party grid and incorporates that into the application. He installs the grid, adds a reference to it from the project, and checks in the code.

Now consider another developer, Lewis. Lewis comes in the next morning and retrieves the latest version of the code. And because Lewis doesn't have the grid installed, the code won't compile. All of a sudden, Lewis needs to do some investigative work before he can even start on his day's work. See Figure 3.1.

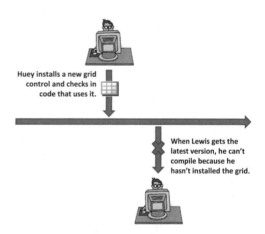

Huey installs a new grid control and checks in code that uses it.

When Lewis gets the latest version, he can't compile because he hasn't installed the grid.

**Figure 3.1 Adding a component to version control that requires developers to install something first is a source of friction.**

Here's another scenario. Consider this class:

```
public class Person

{
    public string FirstName { get; set; }
    public string LastName { get; set; }
    public DateTime Birthdate { get; set; }
}
```

In this scenario, let's say Michael wants to refactor the class so that the `LastName` property is called `Surname` as the team attempts to better match how the business thinks of the object. He changes the property and diligently updates all references to it in the rest of the code.

Now assume another developer, Jackson, has been working (not quite as diligently as Michael) on a screen to edit the `Person` class. He finishes the screen and checks in the code, but forgets to get the latest version before doing so. As such, his code uses the now-defunct `LastName` property and is incompatible with Michael's recent changes.

The next person to retrieve the latest version of the code will have a problem. The application no longer compiles. So she'll have to wear the detective hat as she attempts to find out why the application won't compile.

These are only a couple of the problems that CI can solve. Now let's take a look at what CI is and how it can mitigate these problems.

## 3.2   *What is continuous integration?*

In Martin Fowler's seminal article on the topic,[1] he defines CI as follows:

> Continuous Integration is a software development practice where members of a team integrate their work frequently, usually each person integrates at least daily—leading to multiple integrations per day. Each integration is verified by an automated build (including test) to detect integration errors as quickly as possible. Many teams find that this approach leads to significantly reduced integration problems and allows a team to develop cohesive software more rapidly.

If you aren't familiar with the practice of CI, this can seem like a lofty goal. The key to the process is the *automated* build, whereby the application can be built in its entirety automatically and at any time. Once an automated build can be achieved, CI becomes a process that can be scheduled, launched manually, or launched based on some external event (a common one is to launch the CI process each time code is checked into the source code repository).

---

**Culture shift**

As you read this section, bear in mind that the challenges behind CI are more cultural than technical. Incorporating CI into your process may require some adjustments in your team's mentality. Few people like to be reminded constantly when they've made mistakes. Early in a brownfield project, you may encounter resistance as the CI process reports issues on a regular and frequent basis, because developers aren't used to having their work double-checked on every check-in.

Countering this resistance is a question of changing your mindset. The point of CI isn't to identify more problems. All it does is identify existing problems earlier, before they reach the testing team or the client. CI won't find all of them, of course, but it does add an important safety net. In our experience, you'll find that safety net adds to the confidence level of your development team and keeps them focused on code rather than process.

---

[1]  http://martinfowler.com/articles/continuousIntegration.html

The ultimate reason for CI is to find problems quickly. We call this "closing the feedback loop."

### 3.2.1 The feedback loop

It's inevitable that problems will arise in your code. Whether it's a bug or a configuration issue or an environmental problem, you won't get everything right the first time. With many brownfield projects, in just glancing over the defect list you may find a lot of issues that could have been fixed if the team had had a dedicated process to integrate all the code together on a regular basis before releasing to the testing team. Furthermore, when combined with automated tests and code metrics (see chapters 4 and 5), CI becomes a powerful tool in your toolkit.

Most of the time, these problems are compilation errors and are discovered by the development team. If your code doesn't compile, that's a problem. But you get feedback on it almost instantly courtesy of Visual Studio. The IDE tells you right away that your code has something wrong with it, and you fix it.

Imagine that you built your application, compiled it, and released it to the customer without ever running it. It would almost certainly fail and you wouldn't have a happy client. Generally speaking, having your client discover errors is a bad thing.

To guard against this issue, most developers will run the application locally before handing it off. They'll open it, run through some test cases to see if it works, and then pass it on when they deem it working. If any major issues pop up during their quick tests, they think "Phew! Glad we discovered them early."

### 3.2.2 Closing the feedback loop

That's the basic idea behind the feedback loop. It's the amount of time between when a problem is created and when it's discovered. In the worst-case scenario, the client discovers it. In the best, it never leaves the development stage. Many brownfield projects suffer from a wide feedback loop. Given that problems will occur, we'd like to discover them as soon as possible; we want to close the feedback loop. If we don't, the problem will only grow as it progresses to the client, as shown in figure 3.2.

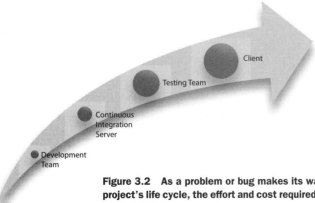

**Figure 3.2   As a problem or bug makes its way through each stage in a project's life cycle, the effort and cost required to resolve the bug increase by an order of magnitude.**

Closing the feedback loop is essentially why we have testing teams in place. They act as a buffer between the development team and the client. One of their primary objectives is to discover problems before they reach the client.

CI is, in effect, a way to close the feedback loop for the project team. Instead of being informed about bugs days, weeks, or months after they were created, from either the testing team or the client, feedback surfaces within minutes. Because CI becomes a way of life on a project, problems that arise are dealt with immediately.

As we said earlier, one of the key aspects of CI is automating your build process. We'll look at that process next.

## 3.3    *Automated builds and the build server*

Automation is one of the cornerstones of CI (and indeed, our entire industry). Without automation, CI is almost impossible. You should strive to automate as much of the build process as possible, from compilation, to testing, to releases.

Theoretically, automation could be accomplished with batch files. You could create one to retrieve the latest version of the application from version control and compile the application. This batch file could then be scheduled to run, say, every 10 minutes. After each run, it could send an email detailing the results of the test.

> **NOTE**    Remember in chapter 2 when we went to the trouble of setting up your folder structure so that it was self-contained? We'll let you in on a little secret: that wasn't just for the benefit of your new developers. It also makes your CI process run that much more smoothly.

A batch file satisfies the definition of CI, if not the spirit. Luckily, there are a number of tools available to make this automation easier than creating batch scripts manually. (The appendix lists some of the tools available to assist with automating your build.)

> **WARNING**    The CI process doesn't replace your QA department. Never forget that compiling code only means the application passes a few syntax rules. Similarly, passing tests means only that the code is meeting the expectations of the tests as they were written. These are *not* the same thing as doing what the users expect. Quality assurance is still required for the big picture, to make sure everything works well as a whole.

The CI process requires a separate machine to act as the build (or integration) server. This machine resembles the production environment as closely as reasonable, save for any software required to automate the build.

The purpose of the build server is to act as the mainline. The automated build process could run and pass on any number of developers' machines, but until the build successfully runs on the build server, the application isn't considered to be in a stable state.

Furthermore, a failed build on your build server is a serious offense. It means that at that exact moment, your application doesn't work in some fashion. If development were to stop right then, you wouldn't have a working application.

Don't let the fact that it's called a *server* scare you. A spare developer box in a corner of someone's office is usually sufficient to act as a build server. The important criteria are that it not be actively used by anyone and that it reasonably resemble an end user's configuration.

The build server should be free of any special software, especially development IDEs (such as Visual Studio) and third-party installations, if possible. That isn't a hard-and-fast rule because you may find it necessary to install, for example, database software to store databases that are created and dropped during integration tests.

> **No server? No problem!**
>
> If resources are tight or require an unholy amount of bureaucratic red tape to request, another option is to use virtualization. You use software (such as VMware Workstation or Virtual PC) to set up one or more instances of your environment running within an existing system.
>
> Even if you have the option of unlimited hardware, virtual machines offer benefits as build servers. They're easily created and readily disposable. Plus, they can be rolled back to a known state quickly. The primary concern with the build server's performance is that it doesn't slow down your development efforts. As a result, virtualization is a viable (and in many cases, preferred) alternative to a dedicated computer.

The reason a clean machine is preferred is that development machines can get polluted by the various tools, utilities, and scripts we like to install, uninstall, and reinstall. By using a clean computer as the build server, we can often discover environmental issues like, for example, an application that contains an errant dependency on the Visual Studio SDK.

Before we look at the details of an automated build process in section 3.5, let's assume we have one in place somehow. How will this affect your check-in dance?

## 3.4 An updated check-in dance

In chapter 2, we talked about the check-in dance:

1 Check out the file(s) you wish to modify.
2 Make your changes.
3 Ensure the application compiles and runs as expected.
4 Get the latest version of the application.
5 Ensure again that the application compiles and runs as expected.
6 Check in your changes.

After adding a CI process to the application, we need to add one more step:

7 Verify that build server executes without error.

The updated dance is shown in figure 3.3.

The reason for the additional step is that you aren't truly finished until the build machine is able to compile and test the application. You may have forgotten to add a class or a new third-party library to version control, for example. Such an error will be caught when the build machine attempts to compile the application.

As you'll recall, this is one of the scenarios from the introduction to this chapter, where there was no CI process and Huey had checked in a new component that required an installation. The problem didn't manifest itself until the next developer, Lewis, retrieved the latest version of the code. That next devel-

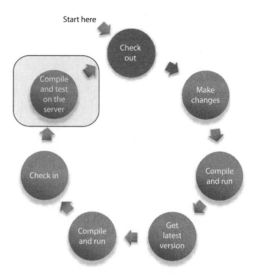

**Figure 3.3   After adding continuous integration, you need to add a step to the end of the check-in dance to allow the CI server to do its work.**

oper may be retrieving the latest version as part of his check-in dance, which means he has changes that need to be checked in. Instead of being focused on committing his changes to the version control system, he must deal with tracking down a missing reference before his code can be checked in.

Note that with most automated build software, step 7 of the check-in dance is performed automatically for you by the build server. There's no need for you to do it manually. The build server would be configured to trigger this step whenever a change is made to the source code repository. But even so, your work is still not done after you complete step 6. Rather, step 7 becomes

   7  Wait until you receive confirmation from the build server that there are no errors.

You don't continue coding until you know that your changes have not broken the build. This approach saves you from having to roll back any changes you make while the build is going on. Presumably, your process takes only 2 or 3 minutes at the most, so you usually aren't sitting idle for long. Plus, this practice is more of a guideline than an actual rule. In reality, most developers don't like to stop their rhythm after checking in code. In the beginning, when you are new to CI, this is a good guideline to adhere to. As you gain more confidence and check in more often, don't be too draconian about enforcing this rule.

### 3.4.1   *Breaking the build*

If your changes have broken the build, you have some work to do because there are three important rules to follow when there's a broken build:

- Nobody shall check in code when the build is broken, unless it is specifically to fix the build.
- Nobody shall retrieve the latest version of the code when the build is broken.
- He who broke it, fixes it.

A broken build is a serious issue, at least on the build server. It means that the application won't compile, has failing tests, or is otherwise in a state that's unstable. As such, there's no sense in retrieving code that doesn't work or checking in unrelated code that could exacerbate the problem. The final rule is a matter of convenience. The person who checked in has the most knowledge about the problem and is in the best position to get the team back on track. He or she is allowed to enlist help, but ultimately the person whose check-in caused the problem should spearhead the effort to fix it.

There's one final note on steps 1 and 2 of the check-in dance, now that we're implementing a CI process: local developer compilation and testing of the application should be done in the same way it's done on the build server. That probably means performing these steps outside the Visual Studio IDE via some form of batch script. As mentioned in section 3.3, the build server should be free of IDEs if at all possible so it won't be using Visual Studio to run the build. Besides, compiling the application in Visual Studio doesn't lend itself well to automation.

Instead, if your build process involves executing a build script to compile the application, you should do the same to locally compile the application as part of the check-in dance. If you use a batch file on the build server to run your tests, use the same one on your local machine. If you use an automation tool, such as NAnt, Rake, or pSake, use the same tool locally before checking in.

The reason should be obvious: if you use a different process than the build server to compile or test your application, you run the risk of errors occurring on the build server that don't occur on your local machine. These errors could be caused by differences in configuration, which files are included in the compilation process, which assemblies are tested, and any number of other things.

## Challenge your assumptions: Don't build in the IDE

There are a number of reasons that you may not want to build your application in your IDE. First, consider that Visual Studio performs a number of visual tasks to report the progress of the compilation. Each of those updates takes time, and when you're working with a large codebase, or with a large number of projects in the solution, that time adds up. Compiling at the command line provides only a bare minimum of updates to the developer. As a result, compilation may be faster.

Also consider that you want to build your application locally in the exact same way as it will be built on the CI server and for release. If your CI server is building the application using a build script, IDE-based compilation can't provide the same level of confidence that all is well.

> **(continued)**
> Make the Alt-Tab keystroke out of Visual Studio and into the command-line window. The speed increase in your build process and the increased confidence in your local codebase may surprise you.

With that in mind, running the automated build locally is necessary only when you're doing the check-in dance. However you and your fellow developers may wish to compile the application and run the tests during the normal development process, that's entirely left to personal preference.

With all of this information now at hand, let's revisit one of our pain point scenarios from section 3.1.

### 3.4.2    *Removing the pain: a check-in walkthrough*

Recall the changes that Michael and Jackson made in our scenario from section 3.1. Michael had changed the LastName property to Surname. Jackson added code that used the LastName property but didn't get the latest version of the code before checking in. He skipped step 2 of the check-in dance and the problem fell to the next developer to discover and possibly fix the error.

Now let's assume we have an automated build process in place. As soon as someone checks in code, it will do the following:

1  Get the latest version of the application
2  Compile it
3  Notify the team via email of the result

As soon as Jackson checks in his code, our automated build process kicks in and promptly fails the second step: compiling the code. The team gets an email that the code is broken and we've even configured the process to let us know who made the last check-in—in this case, Jackson.

Our rules for broken builds now come into play. Michael, Lewis, Huey, and the rest of the team stop what they're doing. Maybe they make their way to the coffee station for a refresh. More often, they saunter over to Jackson's cubicle for some good-natured ribbing. Perhaps they bestow upon him some symbol indicating he was the last person who broke the build, for example, a rubber duck (the "fail duck"). Jackson, alert to the lighthearted mockery about to befall him, realizes he forgot to get the latest version and quickly makes the required change. It's a quick fix and before the first person has set foot in his cubicle, he's made the change and performed the proper check-in dance. He can now await his fate with a clear conscience.

The point is, amid all this camaraderie, the problem is discovered almost immediately after it was caused. As a result, it is fixed in very little time. That's the power of CI.

Also, note that despite your best efforts, it *is* still possible to break the build, even when performing the check-in dance. It's a matter of timing. During the time between

> ## CI and team dynamics
>
> We've made light of the social aspects of Jackson's plight, but they're an important side benefit of CI. Without CI, Jackson's error would go undiscovered until someone else needed to get some work done. Maybe that person would sit and grumble about the uselessness of the rest of the team and fix the problem, not even bothering to bring up the incident. Or perhaps she would confront Jackson with a trite "your code is broken" and walk away. Neither is the path to a healthy team relationship.
>
> But when the build is monitored by a nonjudgmental third party (the build server), we've found that this often adds some levity to a team's dynamics and helps them work better together. In past projects we've worked on, a failed build is an occasion for team members to get up and walk around and engage in some lighthearted jibes. Assuming it doesn't happen often and the target doesn't take it seriously, this camaraderie is a good thing because along with the problem being fixed right away, the team is bonding at the same time.

when you get the latest version and the time you check in, someone else may have made changes. See figure 3.4.

**Figure 3.4  During the time between when you get the latest version and check in, someone else may have checked in code.**

Although no one is at fault in this case, it results in code that doesn't work in the version control repository. Again, the sooner you discover this, the sooner it can be fixed and you can return to your work. In practice, this scenario doesn't happen often, and when it does, usually the changes don't conflict. Also, many version control systems will recognize and warn you if this situation arises.

One of the major benefits CI and the check-in dance offer is that they get your team into a good rhythm of coding. Edit, build, get, build, commit, integrate...edit, build, get, build, commit, integrate... As you can see, there is rhythm in simply saying the words. We call the rhythm derived from this process "the metronome effect."

### 3.4.3  The metronome effect

Musicians with particularly harsh childhood piano teachers may not appreciate the analogy, but it's helpful to think of the CI process as a metronome. Like a good metronome, it helps set and keep the rhythm of a project.

The rhythm of a project is primarily defined by how often you check in code. If developers check in sporadically and sparingly, such as every week, the project has a slow rhythm. But if each developer checks in regularly (say, three or four times a day), the project moves along at a good tempo.

The combination of a good CI process and an edit-merge-commit version control system encourages the practice of checking in at a regular pace. Since we get near-instantaneous feedback from our CI system on whether the code we've just checked in works, we've removed an important pain point: the pain of checking out code that doesn't work and the subsequent investigation of problems introduced by other people. If the automated build is executed on every check-in, any errors in the code will be flagged almost immediately after they are checked in.

This immediate feedback alone drastically improves our confidence in the code and, just as importantly, allows the VCS to fade into the background so that we aren't afraid to get the latest version of the code. And with a CI process in place, each check-in is a reminder that the project is still in a stable state, further increasing our confidence.

Whereas the CI process *allows* you to check in more frequently, an edit-merge-commit VCS will *encourage* it because of the check-in dance. Part of the dance is to retrieve the latest version of the code and merge your changes into it. If there's a conflict (if you have made changes to the same section of code as another developer since your last check-in), you need to manually examine these changes and decide which ones to keep—not an easy process and one made more difficult if there are many conflicts.

By checking in several times per day, you minimize the chance of these conflicts occurring as well as the impact when a conflict does arise. Check-ins are no longer a monumental event that requires an afternoon to merge your changes with the rest of the codebase.

One of the keys to achieving a regular check-in rhythm is not to wait until a feature has been completed before checking in. That practice is a throwback to the days when the source code repository was viewed as a collection of mini-releases and each feature was considered a unit of work. Developers were of the mindset that there was no benefit to be gained checking in code that half-worked.

### What does *working* code mean?

This outdated view of version control is rooted in the definition of what it means for code to *work*. Traditionally, your code worked when it included a complete and tangible feature for the client to see—a good perspective for a client, but not for a developer. For you, pieces of code work simply if they do what you want them to do.

As we progress through this book, you'll find that our definition of *working code* will change. At the moment, it means that the code compiles because that's all our CI process is checking for. In the next chapter, we'll expand on this and include automated testing. So *working code* will then encompass code that compiles and passes the automated tests. Later, we'll include software metrics.

Once you're able to produce working code at will, you can drop the antiquated notion that you have to wait until an entire feature is complete before checking in. That's what labels are for in your VCS.

Instead of working to less-frequently reached goals, developers are encouraged to check in often. A good rule of thumb is to check in as soon as you've completed a slice of code and it's covered completely by automated tests (more on this in chapter 4).

With a proper CI process in place, an interesting side effect occurs. The application is, at any given moment, releasable. What we mean by *releasable* is that we're confident that the application can be put into a testing or production environment and that it will function within it. Although not all features may be complete, we have confidence that the ones that do exist work.

Having the team ticking like a diligent metronome reduces the friction associated with integrating code. Initially, you may be wary of checking in code for fear that you'll break the build. Although breaking the build in the CI environment isn't optimal, it's serving its intended purpose: early identification of issues. We've found that once the team gets used to the idea, a check-in becomes almost a nonevent. The frequency of check-ins becomes a part of your physical habit as well as a foundation for your confidence in your work.

Hopefully, we've made clear the benefit of incorporating a CI process into your brownfield application. Now it's time to get back to the practical application of it and examine the steps involved in the CI process.

## 3.5 Setting up a CI process

There are three general steps to setting up a CI process for an application:

1 Compile the application
2 Run automated tests
3 Create deployable releases

These steps may not seem like magic at first glance. In fact, they correspond to a subset of the steps in the check-in dance discussed in section 3.4. A developer compiles his code, tests it, then "releases it" (checks it into the source code repository). Each step builds incrementally on the others, as shown in figure 3.5.

**Figure 3.5  The three basic steps of an automated build. Each of the incremental steps builds and relies on the previous.**

The difference is that each of these steps is completely automated as part of the build script. You should have a process that, once completed, can be scheduled at regular intervals or executes based on some external event.

You don't need to wait for the build server to perform these steps; the process can also be launched manually. Indeed, we encourage you to do so on your local development machine. This approach treats each developer's machine as its own build server in a way. And it's helpful to think of them as such because it gets you into the habit of running the build process locally in the same way it's executed on the build server. In this way, you minimize the chance of problems being elevated into the source code repository.

**NOTE**   Running the build script locally, and often, increases the speed of the feedback loop to its maximum. Within seconds of adding or modifying code, each developer can know if they've introduced any issues into the application.

Over the course of this section, we'll present code snippets in NAnt format. NAnt is a popular open source utility used to automate the build process. It's XML based and started as a port of the Ant build utility for Java. You don't need to be familiar with the syntax to understand the examples.

A word of caution before we describe these in more detail: when implementing CI into a team that's not familiar with the process, consider introducing each of these three steps individually rather than all at once. Introducing all the steps at once can be overwhelming and can quickly demoralize a team.

Let's look at an example of what we mean by incremental introduction of the steps. In this example, the build process is based on an NAnt build file. On the server, we've installed TeamCity,[2] an application that allows us to monitor our version control system and launch the NAnt build script whenever someone has checked in code.

The first thing we do is modify the build file so that it compiles the application. This typically means one developer modifies the build file on her local machine according to section 3.5.1.

When she gets it to a state where it will successfully compile the application, the developer updates the build server with the new build file and verifies that TeamCity can successfully execute the build file and compile the application. After that, each developer updates his or her local copy of the build file and verifies that it executes successfully locally.

**NOTE**   This movement of updating the build file from the change initiator to the build server to the rest of the development team needs to be effortless. The best way that we've found to push changes to the team and build server is to include the build file in source control. As you'll see in section 3.6, adding this build component to source control elevates the build script to first class status in the project.

We then repeat the process for step 2 once the team is comfortable with the automated compilation's correctness. One developer modifies the build file so that it now executes the tests in addition to compiling the application. (See chapter 4 for more on automating tests.) He then updates the build server and the rest of the team updates their local copies of the build file.

Finally, we do the same for step 3. Processes to automate the release of the application are added to the build file and distributed to the team.

Alternatively, if a developer were to modify the build file to implement the steps all at once, there's a greater chance that the build won't work completely when it's moved to the build server. As with any work that we do, we must test and verify the execution

---

[2]  See http://jetbrains.com for information on how to install and configure TeamCity.

of the build script. If too much automation has been included all at once, it can be difficult to track down the changes needed to make the build process work correctly.

Let's look at each step in the process in more detail.

### 3.5.1 Compile the application

The following NAnt target will compile your application according to how it is set up in your solution (.sln) file using the Debug configuration:

```
<target name="compile"
    description="Compiles using the Debug Configuration">
    <msbuild project="src\Moo.sln">
        <property name="Configuration" value="Debug" />
    </msbuild>
</target>
```

❶ NAnt target

❷ MSBuild task

In this snippet, we use a target ❶, which is NAnt's way of organizing pieces of work (similar to methods in a class). We use the built-in `<msbuild>` task ❷ to compile the application using MSBuild.

That's all there is to it. Granted, our choice of tool has helped somewhat, but at its core, compiling the application is a pretty benign event.

#### VERSIONING THE APPLICATION

While you're setting up the compilation of the different assemblies, it's advisable to have the process automatically version those files. In .NET, versioning of assemblies is handled through attribute values in the AssemblyInfo.vb or AssemblyInfo.cs files, depending on whether you're using Visual Basic or C#. Build scripts tools, like NAnt, usually offer a way to automatically generate the AssemblyInfo file with contents that are determined during the build process. The alternative is to read in the file, modify it, and save it again.

Autogenerating an AssemblyInfo file lends itself to having your CI and build processes assign a version number to the assemblies being compiled. Using the capabilities of the build script tool and including the autogenerated custom AssemblyInfo file will achieve this for you. All that's needed is a way to create or determine the version number that should be used.

If possible, try to have your CI tool (such as TeamCity, Hudson, or CruiseControl.NET) generate this version number. Most will generate a build number that you can then use in your application's version number. Alternatively, there are ways to configure the build process to pull the build number from your VCS itself to incorporate into your application's version number. In this way, your CI process can not only compile the application, but version it as well.

---

#### Version number as a safety check

In environments with lax or nonexistent release processes, developers often migrate code to testing, and possibly even production, from their machines at their own whim. This strategy is particularly common in brownfield projects.

*(continued)*

To counter this issue, have your build process default the application version number to 0.0.0.0. That way, when a developer builds the application locally, it will be tagged with this version number. But if the build server compiles it, it will overwrite the default and apply the normal version number.

This method of versioning an assembly doesn't prevent a developer from accidentally deploying an assembly she compiled locally. But if a locally compiled assembly does somehow make it to a test server, it will be that much easier to identify from the 0.0.0.0 version number.

While we're on the subject of automating our compilation, let's take some time to consider the options available to us now.

**COMPILING OUTSIDE VISUAL STUDIO**

In section 3.5.1 we created a task that compiles the application in the same way Visual Studio does. But now that we're automating the process, we don't necessarily *need* to do it the same way.

Consider the following task, which compiles all the C# files in a given folder (including files in a subfolder) into a single assembly using the csc.exe command-line compiler:

```
<csc target="library" output="${compiled.assembly}" debug="true">      ① csc
    <sources>                                                            task
    <include name="BrownfieldAppRoot\**\*.cs"/>      ② File
  </sources>                                            inclusion
  <references>
    <include name="${thirdparty.nhibernate}"/>       ③ Required
  </references>                                          references
</csc>
```

NAnt calls out to csc.exe ① to compile certain files into an assembly as defined by the ${compiled.assembly} variable. The code tells us which files to compile into the assembly ②. In this case, it's all .cs files in the project directory, including subfolders. Finally ③, we have to tell csc.exe which external assemblies we're referencing. In this case, we have a reference to an assembly specified by the ${thirdparty. nhibernate} variable.

It may seem strange at first to compile your carefully layered application into a single assembly. Haven't we been told for years to keep our application logic in separate layers to make it easier to maintain?

Using csc.exe or vbc.exe, as shown earlier, offers you the ability to control the contents of your final compiled assemblies at a much more granular level than using the solution and project files you normally see in Visual Studio. Making this transition allows you to view Visual Studio's Solution Explorer window as a file organizational tool, one to help you keep the structure organized while you're developing. But you may want to deploy the application differently, based on your physical layering instead. This approach takes away the pressure of trying to squeeze your logical or physical layering into the solution/project way of thinking. (We'll come back to layering in chapter 8.)

The lack of solution/project alignment doesn't mean that we've abandoned structure altogether. Instead we're placing the files into folder structures that make hierarchical sense when we're working in the editor. We still must align our compilation of these files with the deployment needs of our application and environment. Depending on your situation, this strategy can allow you to compile your application into, say, one assembly or executable per physical deployment location.

---

**Challenge your assumptions: Solution Explorer isn't a designer for layering your application**

When we first began learning to incorporate logical and physical layering in our applications, we were taught to distinguish the separate layers by creating separate projects in our Visual Studio solutions. We ended up with solutions that had projects called MyApp.Data, MyApp.UI, MyApp.Business, and so on. Although this approach works, it also taught us to think that the IDE, and more specifically Solution Explorer, is a tool for designing *both* the logical and physical layering of our applications.

Instead of suffering this in the name of "We've always done it that way," we suggest that you look at Solution Explorer merely as a tool for organizing files. Create projects when code concerns require you to, but don't let your logical and physical layering dictate them. Instead, let namespacing and folder structures in one project delineate the layers.

For example, it often makes sense to separate your application into a UI layer, a business layer, and a data layer in Visual Studio. But if this is a Windows Forms application being distributed to the client, why do you need to deploy it as three separate assemblies? Why not roll it all into one to make deployment easier? (Yes, yes, we've heard the "What if you need to update only a single component?" and "What if you want to reuse the component in other apps?" arguments. Without getting into lengthy counterarguments, we'll sidestep those questions. Our point is that the option is there and should be considered.)

When it comes time to build your application, use a scripting tool, like NAnt or MSBuild, to compile the raw code files into assemblies as you'd like to deploy them. The results may include many files for each physical layer that you're deploying to. Also consider the possibility that creating one file per physical layer may be the simplest option available without harming the execution of the application.

---

If you're thinking that this drastic difference in structure and compilation could cause significant and painful integration, you could be right. You could be right if you aren't using the automated build script to continually integrate the code (in this case, integration is the act of compiling) on a frequent and continual basis. This painful integration, above all other things, proves the worth of making an automated build script that can be run easily, frequently, and locally by developers. If that build script can quickly provide positive and negative feedback to the developer, problems resulting from the difference in compilation and structure between the script and the IDE will be addressed often and before they become a problem for the entire team.

### Tales from the trenches: Building the hard way

On one project we were on, the build process was manual. It wasn't an easy build, either. The Build Person (when you have a title for a task, it should be immediately noted as a pain point) had a script that ran close to 20 tasks long. On top of that, about four of those tasks resided in a loop that had to be performed for each and every client the company had.

When the count of clients reached five, the pain of creating a release for any or all clients began to mount. By the time there were 15, it was almost unbearable. The "script" was nothing more than an infrequently updated document that had been printed and hung on the Build Person's wall. Although it outlined the steps required to create a release package for each client, the intricacies of the process were lost on all other people in the company.

So the Build Person slogged on in his own version of torture. Each execution of the "script" took over an hour and a half of a tedious manual process involving copying files, changing references, incrementing assembly version numbers, and compiling assemblies, among other things. As you can imagine with such a manual process, problems were frequent.

Each client's release package had to be manually, and independently, verified just to make sure that the assemblies could talk to each other. The result was a significant, and unnecessary, burden on the testing team. In the end, this process was one of the more obvious friction points between the testing and development teams.

Looking back on this project, we should've recognized the pain that could've been solved by automating such a tedious process. We didn't know about build tools at the time, but all we needed was a batch script that could be executed from the command line. Although we learned a lot from this project, one of the biggest lessons was that we should never have a manual/error-prone process for something as important as creating release packages for our clients.

Now that we've discussed the nuances of and options for getting an automated build script to perform compilation, let's look at the next step in the build process: the execution of automated tests.

### 3.5.2    *Run automated tests*

Once your build process is successfully compiling the application on the build server, the next step is to incorporate tests into the mix. This includes both unit and integration tests.

**NOTE** This section is a precursor to chapter 4. You may want to skim and come back to it after you've had a chance to read the next chapter. We've included it here because we feel it's important to have a CI process in place as soon as possible to close the feedback loop, even if the only thing it does at first is compile the application.

For the moment, we'll assume your solution already contains unit tests and integration tests. If not, chapter 4 goes into more detail on how to set them up. If necessary, you can create a project with a single dummy test for the sake of setting up the CI process.

The following snippet is an example of a simple NAnt target that will execute NUnit (a unit-testing framework) against an assembly that contains automated tests:

```
<target name="test" depends="test.compile">
    <exec program="nunit-console.exe"
        basedir="${dir.tools}\nunit\bin"
        workingdir="${dir.compile}"
        commandline="${dir.compile}\MyProject.Test.dll
            /xml=${dir.compile}\MyProject.Test-Results.xml"
failonerror="true" />
</target>
```

**❶ Target with a dependency**
**❷ Shell out task**
**❸ Failing on test errors**

The target shown here executes the nunit-console.exe application with appropriate parameters. It depends on another target, test.compile ❶, which will compile the test project into an assembly called MyProject.Test.dll. We shell out to nunit-console.exe ❷ to perform the testing.

When it has completed the execution of all the tests that it can find, NUnit will return a success or fail indication. We highly recommend that you make any failure within NUnit reflect as an overall failure of the build script—shown here ❸ with the `failonerror` attribute. If you don't, your build will still be successful because it's contingent only on whether NUnit was able to run and not on whether all the tests passed.

Setting up automated testing can include many different types of tests and tools. At the core are pure unit tests that only execute and verify isolated segments of code through unit-testing frameworks like NUnit. It's also possible to launch integration, acceptance, and UI tests from your build script. By their nature, these tests usually take more time to execute and can be more difficult to set up and run. Tests of these types shouldn't be relegated to second-class status, but their slower nature does impose a penalty on the velocity of the feedback loop that the developer is involved in. Section 3.7.1 addresses how to deal with long-running tests in your CI process.

Now that we've addressed testing in our build scripts, the final step in the build process is to create releases.

### 3.5.3 Create deployable releases

Now that your CI process is both compiling and testing your application, your developers are able to get into a rhythm, as discussed earlier. But there's still one step left in the program: you must be able to create a releasable package of the application automatically at any given time.

What constitutes a *releasable package* depends on your scenario. In determining this definition, start with your current release process and try to automate and verify as much of it as possible.

If the release process for your application involves handing a Microsoft Installer (MSI) file to another team for server or client installation, you should strive to have your automated build create that MSI file. Other times you'll work on an application that's deployed using Xcopy capabilities. Your release, in that case, will probably be a file folder that can act as the source for the Xcopy to use.

Note that releases and deployments are two different things. A *release* is the deliverable that will be used during a deployment. A *deployment* is the act of installing a release into an environment.

A release is something that you can create every time you check in code. There's benefit to doing so even if you don't end up using many of the releases. It takes up a bit of disk space, but this problem can be mitigated with an appropriate retention policy on your releases. In exchange, you can have a deployable package at your fingertips at any given moment.

We'll talk a little more about the releases folder in the next section.

### Automating deployments

While you are in an automatin' kinda mood, consider automating the deployment process as well as creating releases. Whether this involves deploying an updated one-click installation for a Windows application or deploying a web application to the test environment, there's value in having a process that can be done with minimal intervention in a repeatable way.

Even after you automate the deployment process, it's not often a good idea to deploy the application as part of every check-in, at least at first. If your team is in a rhythm of checking in often, many of the check-ins will result in no noticeable change to the testing team and, worse, could potentially create an acceptance testing environment that's considered buggy.

Instead, create a CI process that runs the deployment process on a separate schedule, say, nightly or weekly. Or create one that's launched manually whenever your team feels you have a package worth deploying.

In any case, deployment affects more than just your development team. We advise you to discuss deployment with your testing team with regard to the schedule and manner of deployment. If the schedule doesn't work for them, expect to see an increase in complaints, often in the form of defect reports that say "This feature doesn't work" when a change was either expected and not deployed or not expected and deployed.

Regardless of what's to be distributed, you'll still need to automate the process of building that package. There are a thousand ways to release software. Automating the simple ones may require only that you copy files from one location to another. More complicated scenarios may require you to zip files, stop and restart a web server, recreate a web application, or update a database.

## Tales from the trenches: A tale of two release processes

In the past, we've worked on projects that have varied levels of maturity in the creation of their release packages and the process of deploying that code to different environments. In one case, we participated in a project where every production deployment was frenetic, bordering on chaotic.

That project had multiple testing environments, some solely dedicated to the development team, available for releases to be tested in. Unfortunately, testing in these environments was limited to verification of the application's functionality, not testing the deployment process. The result was that release packages, and the accompanying written installation scripts, were first tested the day of production deployment.

When issues surfaced, not all fixes were applied back to the artifacts used to create the release package. What was the result? We saw the same issues on many subsequent installations. Eventually someone would be involved in multiple releases and they'd get frustrated with having seen the same thing over and over, so it would be fixed. But because many people rotated through the responsibility of supporting the infrastructure team, many recurring issues were seen only once per person and quickly forgotten.

To contrast that tale of pain, we also worked on a project that had a mature release and deployment practice. Employing CI and automated build scripts, we created every release in an identical manner. Every time the CI server executed, the release package was created. In fact, we mandated that installation into any server environment had to be done only from a release package created by the CI server's automated process.

On top of having practices that promoted consistency, the team was engrained with the belief that release packages needed thorough testing well before production installation. We made extensive use of different testing environments to iron out the minutest of issues we encountered.

Two situations occurred that proved the effort and diligence were well deserved. The first was a new-to-the-project manager who required input for scheduling a production release. He stated, "Let's schedule one week to do the production installation." The team's collective response was "Give us 5 minutes." Too aggressively confident? Perhaps.

Proving that our confidence wasn't misplaced, we arrived at work on a Monday morning to find out that the least experienced team member had installed the software to production the previous Friday. Although we knew that this day was coming, nothing had been formally confirmed or conveyed to the development team. The installation went so well that this developer said, "It only took a couple minutes." On top of that we had yet to receive any help desk tickets during the 3 days it had been installed.

*(continued)*

Well-practiced release creation and dedication to practicing production installations can pay huge dividends in how your project and team is perceived by management and the clients. In our mind, the week that you release your software to production should be the most anticlimactic week in your project.

Setting up and verifying automated releases and deployments can be time consuming and tedious. But putting in the effort to achieve this level of CI brings a great deal to a team by reducing the amount of time that you spend conducting releases and deployments. Because your CI process has been practicing releases and addressing any issues that surface immediately, the ease and stability of each release to a client will portray your team in a positive light. We all know it's never bad to look good to the client.

You may have noticed a distinct lack of specifics for brownfield projects in this section. The good part about implementing CI is that it can be done at any time in a project's life cycle. Whether you're just starting out or already have a well-loved application in place, adding CI to the mix can be little more than automating what your team does every day—compiling and testing the application.

While the setup of CI can occur at any point in the life cycle of a project, there are some helpful conventions that impose more effort on a brownfield project than one that's greenfield. In the next section, we'll examine how applying some of these conventions can introduce change to the folder structure of a brownfield application.

## 3.6   *Build components*

When working on an automated build process, you'll create a number of components that will be used in the process. At a minimum you'll have a build script file. You may also end up with supporting files that contain scripts for database creation and population, templates for config files for different testing environments, and others. These are files that you want to have in source control. Because these files are related only to the build process, we recommend that you organize them in a separate folder, as shown in figure 3.6.

In addition, you can create a project or solution folder within your Visual Studio solution to hold these files. See figure 3.7 for an example.

As you can see in our sample folder structure, we have subdirectories to store different types of files. The config folder stores any configuration files that will be included

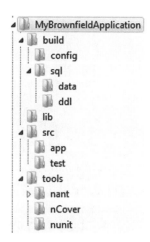

**Figure 3.6   Keep the build components separate from your code and third-party libraries.**

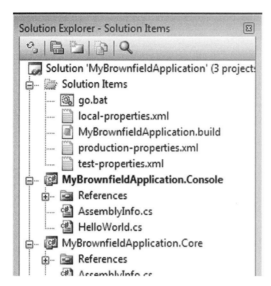

Figure 3.7 Build components can be stored in Visual Studio in solution folders or even separate projects for ease of use. Note that solution folders don't map to physical folders.

in your release package. This folder also includes any templates that you have that are used for the creation of configuration files.

## Environment templates

Templates are a great way to add environment-based configuration values to your project's automated build process. They are akin to .ini files that contain variables with values specific to a certain environment.

For example, your main build script could make reference to a database connection string stored in a variable. When you initialize the script, you could tell it to load the variables from the appropriate template based on which environment it was building for (development environment, test environment, or production).

Examples of variables that make good candidates for environment templates include database connection strings, logging configurations, and third-party service endpoints.

We also show a separate sql folder, which includes folders for data and DDL (data definition language, the scripts that create or alter your tables). The purpose of the sql folder is to have a repository for any SQL scripting artifacts that you may have for the creation of your release. The data and DDL scripts are separated primarily for file management reasons. The DDL folder would hold all scripts needed to create a database, its tables, their keys and relationships, and any security entries needed. The data folder contains all the scripts for priming the database with any initial data the application needs, such as lookup values and application configuration settings.

Keep in mind that this structure is merely a recommendation. Our goal isn't to impose a rigid folder structure for you to copy in your own brownfield application. Rather, we hope to get you thinking about your application in a different way, as more than just code. Our recommendation is based partially on simple organization of the files, concepts, and tools. It's also based on the need to make the build script as simple as possible.

Your build script should create two additional folders in your local source tree. When compiling the code into assemblies and executables, you'll need to put those compiled files, or build artifacts, somewhere. Having your script create a compile folder is a good way to keep the results of the build process separate from the raw code and build components. After you add automated testing, the compile folder can also be used as the working directory for the testing.

The second folder that you may want to have your build process create is a release folder. Here you can store the deployable releases we mentioned back in section 3.5.3. Figure 3.8 shows a sample structure.

**Figure 3.8   Example of creating a release archive in your folder structure**

**NOTE**   If you automate your releases into a folder such as the one in figure 3.8, it'll look like this only on the build server. There's no need for developers to store the various releases of the application on their local machines. In fact, if you have the build script automate the versioning of your application (as discussed in section 3.5.1), the only folders they should see are Latest and v0.0.0.0.

Neither the compile nor the release folder should be added to your VCS. The contents of the compile folder can be re-created at will so there's no need to include it. As for the release folder, you should archive its contents, but that's best handled through a separate nightly backup process, not your VCS.

You should also consider a retention policy as well because the build process could potentially create dozens of archives per day. As a general rule, keep the release that was most recently deployed to the acceptance testing environments (and possibly the one that was deployed prior to that as well).

From the start of creating your automated build scripts, through the files that will be required for compilation and on to the archiving of the final releasable assemblies, there are a number of things that will be considered build components. Maintaining a flexible and reliable folder structure sets the foundation for allowing you to achieve a clean, efficient, and maintainable build process all while increasing the speed of the feedback loop.

Continuing to narrow our focus, we'll now turn our attention to the details of your CI process.

## 3.7    *Tweaking the CI process*

Now that you have a basic CI process in place that builds, tests, and creates releases, you can get back to developing and ignore the build process, right? Well, if you've read any technical books at all, you should know by now that the answer to any question that ends in "right?" is always no.

You should tweak the build process from time to time. Perhaps you have added a new tool that needs to be compiled into the test assembly in order to run the tests. Or maybe you've changed the structure of your application and the compilation order needs to be modified. Or you've added a web service and you need to incorporate it into the releasable package.

Whatever the case, you'll find that your build process must be revisited whenever you do something out of the ordinary.

Now's the time for us to examine some common situations that will require you to tweak your build process.

### 3.7.1    *Handling long-running tests*

The final step in our modified check-in dance is to stop what you're doing until you receive confirmation that the build completed successfully. But what if your tests take 10, 15, even 30 minutes to run? Perhaps you have a suite of tests that primes and cleans up a testing database before and after each test. As you can imagine, this action occurring in hundreds or thousands of tests can extend the length of the test run into minutes or even hours.

In these cases, it isn't practical to expect developers to wait around until the tests have completed. We need to relax the restrictions somewhat and consider how we can modify the build so that developers can get back to work quickly after a check-in but still be reasonably confident that the application is being properly tested.

You should consider this problem for two different testing locations: locally and on the build server. As a developer, you should be able to run the automated build script locally without having to wait more than a few minutes. If the local process takes any longer, many developers will have a natural tendency to avoid running it. This reluctance could lead to fewer check-ins and, thus, lower confidence in the code.

One way to overcome the friction caused by long-running tests is to separate the build process into two parts. The first part compiles the application, executes the unit tests, and performs a release of the software. This process should always execute quickly.

The second part of the process is similar to the first, except that it would also execute the slow-running tests.

These two test execution paths (the fast and the slow) should be exposed from the build script separately so that they can be accessed and executed by the local developer as well as the CI server. The ability to access the different testing executions has to be frictionless. A common solution is to embed the execution of the script into separate command-line batch files, one for each of the paths.

The CI server can be configured so that it executes the fast build every time a developer checks in code. If the fast build completes successfully, it should trigger the slow build. With this implementation, you don't have to wait until the integration tests have completed. Once the compilation and unit tests have run successfully, you can be reasonably confident enough to begin working on your next task. The confidence stems from the fact that your unit tests have passed and that the integration tests are more environmental. If any of the tests fail, chances are it's an issue with your infrastructure or network rather than your code. This may not always be the case, but it's a trade-off you should consider in the name of developer productivity.

Incidentally, while the slow build process is running, other developers shouldn't have to wait for its completion to perform their own check-in process. If another developer checks in code while the integration tests are still running, the CI process should queue up another test run for the integration tests to execute as soon as the current run completes. Many CI software applications offer this capability natively. If you have, or have the potential for, a large number of slow-running tests, software that can easily be configured to handle build queuing can be vital to ensuring that all types of builds and tests are run as often as possible without impeding the developers.

### 3.7.2   *Architectural changes and additions*

From time to time, your projects are required to make major architectural changes or additions. As a result of these changes, your deployments and releases are altered. Often the change of a deployment strategy will affect the compiled structure of the application.

All of these things will likely require you to change the build script. When that happens, you'll see the benefits of having a well-factored build script. Changes and additions should be easy to apply in isolation and with limited effect on the surrounding build process.

Like the initial creation of the build script, making changes and additions requires verification. Like compiling and releasing code within a continually integrating environment, working in the build script requires local execution, testing, and verification. In this case, testing and verification would be for the compilation and release package for the application.

### 3.7.3   *Labeling the build*

Another useful tweak is to label or tag each build. This labeling can, and should, be done automatically by the build process. Most VCSs allow for this, and most automated build tools will plug into this ability as well.

We've already discussed one way of labeling the build in section 3.5.1 when we talked about having your build process version your assemblies. Versioning your assemblies can be useful in identifying issues resulting from deploying the wrong version of your application.

Another way to label your application is in the version control repository. You can handle this process in many ways. Some CI tools offer this ability so that the code is automatically labeled whenever it's retrieved for compilation. If your tool doesn't offer this capability, build scripting tools can perform this operation.

Many build scripting tools have built-in integration with various VCSs. When this is the case, you can add labels to the VCS with a simple call from your build scripting tool of choice.

It's possible that your VCS doesn't have labeling support in either your CI server software or your build scripting language. If so, you can, as a last resort, use your build scripting language to call out to a command shell. At the command shell, you can then execute a console tool for your VCS and use its functionality directly to perform the labeling.

When applying a label to your code repository, be sure to include the version number generated by the CI process. Another good idea is to apply an appropriate label to the repository when the application is deployed. This can be invaluable in pinpointing the origin of bugs, especially ones that were thought to have been fixed.

We haven't provided an exhaustive list of CI tweaks. Some of them may not even be necessary on every project. Although our primary goal was to give you an idea of some useful adjustments you can make to your build process, we also wanted to get you thinking outside the somewhat prescriptive steps we've provided. CI is a good first step in evaluating your brownfield project's ecosystem because there are so many ways you can tweak it to get some quick wins. While you are working, always be on the lookout for friction that could be resolved by automating it in your build process.

## 3.8   *Summary*

Continuous integration is an extremely beneficial practice when implemented on any project, brownfield or otherwise. It helps to build some much-needed confidence within the development team, allowing the team to trust the state of the code residing in the version control system. Developers will be able to look at the status of the CI server and immediately determine if the codebase is in a correctly compiling, tested, and deployed state. That, combined with the use of a check-in dance, should allow developers to never worry that getting the latest version will make their local codebase unusable.

The combination of CI and frequent code check-ins should have a near-immediate effect on your brownfield project. It will create a metronome effect that will get team members into a natural rhythm for the day-to-day work on their project. Often this will have a tremendous effect on the team's confidence, which may have been shattered by the pain of having to fix others' mistakes on a regular basis.

In this chapter we also refined the check-in dance to reflect the way that we work in a CI environment. The check-in dance looks like this:

1  Check out the file(s) you wish to modify.
2  Make your changes.
3  Ensure the application compiles and runs as expected.
4  Get the latest version of the application.

5 Ensure again that the application compiles and runs as expected.

6 Check in your changes.

7 Verify that build server executes without error.

Implementing the core of CI can be a fairly simple task. The process of creating the automated build scripts that are run on the integration server, as well as locally by individual developers, can take more time. Take these tasks on incrementally. The work-to-benefit ratio weighs heavily in favor of the benefit side of the equation. Go forth now, and build…continuously.

In the next chapter, we'll build (no pun intended) on our ecosystem by adding automated testing into the mix to increase our confidence even further.

# Automated testing

### This chapter covers
- Increasing confidence
- Evaluating existing tests
- Integrating existing tests
- Automating test execution

We're now three chapters into a book on software development and we have yet to write any code. We have a good reason: many brownfield applications become contaminated because the proper foundation wasn't laid out before the team, past or present, started coding. On other projects, it *was* laid out, but subsequently ignored in the face of growing deadlines and spiraling requirements.

This chapter continues that theme. Now that we've gone through the first chapters and the source control, build, deployments, and releases have been automated, it's time to look at our testing strategies. Perhaps the project already has some degree of unit testing. Maybe the project has no unit testing at all; you appreciate its relevance but haven't implemented any due to a lack of time. Finally, it's possible that the project has no unit testing and there's strong opposition to its use on the project.

Whatever the case, over the course of this chapter we'll continue laying groundwork for the eventual code changes in later chapters. We'll start with a discussion on why we write tests before delving into the various types. By the end, we hope to convince you not only that you can't live without tests but that implementing them isn't nearly as cumbersome as you first thought. The first step is understanding what issues you may be seeing in your projects. For that, let's look at some of the common pain points that relate to automated testing.

## 4.1    Pain points

It isn't hard to come up with examples of pain caused by a lack of tests. Take any large application, pick an outstanding bug, and ask a developer to fix it. In such cases the pain will often manifest itself physically on the developer's face.

Any time you write a piece of branching logic into your application, which is common in the form of `if/else` and `switch` statements (or `select` in Visual Basic), how is each branch verified to work as expected? Do you manually configure the application to run each branch independently, taking the time to personally interact with it while this happens? If so, how long does that verification process take you? After you have verified that the logic is working as expected, how do you perform regression tests on those scenarios 10 minutes, 10 hours, 10 days, or 10 months from now?

Figure 4.1 shows how branching logic can quickly get out of hand.

Let's consider another example. After writing a number of small, interrelated components, you'll eventually need to verify that they work together. Now is when you find out if the address retrieval component works with the email construction component. Again we (and you should) ask, "How do I test this? Is the process time consuming? Does it depend on the consistency of human interaction? How will it be repeated the next time that regressions need to be run?"

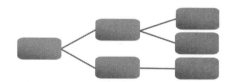

**Figure 4.1   An example of branching logic within your code. Each path through the code represents a potential point of failure and should be tested.**

These two pain points, verifying the correctness of your code and ensuring components work together, apply when developing new features. What about once the application has moved into maintenance mode and has bugs?

**NOTE**    Maintenance of the application doesn't begin once it has been released into production. From a developer's perspective, each line of code you write enters maintenance mode immediately after it's written.

The act of fixing bugs, at any point in the application's life cycle, can be a pain point in and of itself. To repair the bug, first you need to be able to reproduce it. Typically, this means launching the application and navigating to the screen where the bug occurs. Often, preconditions need to be met, such as appropriate data in the database.

Then, as you fix the bug you must continuously launch the application, navigate to the screen again, and test the latest code you've done. Depending on the complexity of the bug, you could spend most of your time in the application rather than in the code. Even when the bug is fixed for the specific scenario you tested, an exhaustive test to make sure it hasn't introduced other bugs is usually deferred, or handed off to a QA/testing team.

You may have noticed that we're dancing around the solution for these pain points: automated tests. We'll remedy that shortly, but first let's move on to the underlying motive behind automated tests.

## 4.2 Living in fear of change

Confidence. It is one of, if not *the* primary reason for tests of any kind. Without tests, all we have to go on to prove that our application does what it's supposed to is the gut feelings of the development team. A large codebase without tests is akin to a trapeze artist with no net. Most of the time, things hum along smoothly, but when something goes wrong, such a spectacular failure it is.

Once an application reaches any substantial size, the lack of tests starts to have an impact on your attitude toward it. It starts with a slight hesitation when the client requests a new feature. Then words like *spaghetti* and *minefield* start to enter the project's lexicon.

As the brittleness of the codebase increases, you begin to fear change. Designers, business analysts, testers, and management join with the developers in their hesitation to modify areas of the application. Eventually it will get to the point where users find workarounds for major bugs because they either fear the ramifications of reporting them or have just plain lost confidence in the development team. Even small codebases suffer from a lack of confidence. Let's look at a hypothetical case.

Let's assume we have an online restaurant locator service, and it's expanding outside the United States into the Caribbean, specifically the Bahamas. In order to ease the transition, they've purchased the data for all the local restaurants in the country and imported it into their system.

One of the first things you discover is that the Bahamian users are complaining about the screen used to find local restaurants. On this screen, users enter their address and the application displays a list of participating restaurants in the area on the screen.

Now there's something unique about Bahamian addresses: there's no zip code or postal code. Instead, the code for the post office that services each address is baked into the address itself. But like 90 percent of applications built today, we've made the zip code a required field on our search screen.

It's an easy enough bug to fix. We modify the search parameter screen so that the zip code is optional and diligently test to make sure the database allows nulls for the field.

## Tales from the trenches: The pinnacle of fear

We worked on a project with one particular module that was the source of a great deal of fear. At one point, the business rules changed and this module needed to be altered. When this requirement was mentioned to the team, developers, analysts, testers, and management began to show the signs of fear. People stuttered while trying to discuss the pending change. Noncoding solutions were suggested. Many team members literally broke into an anxious sweat.

Instead of diving straight into a solution, we decided to spend time researching the current state of the affected code. The reason for the fear quickly became apparent. Although there were many things wrong with the code structure, the root of the fear was driven by a lack of reproducible test scenarios. With over 100 code execution paths, the testing required to manually verify the complete set of code executions was unmanageable. Many scenarios were being missed or ignored, which resulted in the release of many new and/or regression defects.

After some work, automated tests were created for all the code execution scenarios. Subsequent requests for change from the business were met with far less trepidation by the developers. Over time and a number of releases without regression defects, management, analysts, testers, and the business clients gained confidence as well.

Soon, however, we start getting reports of errors in the search *results* page itself. It seems the mechanism in which we locate restaurants involves looking up the user's zip code, retrieving the coordinates for it, and finding restaurants within a certain radius. And now that the zip code is optional, this service is failing spectacularly for our increasingly annoyed Bahamian patrons.

Now, one might argue that you didn't do your due diligence when incorporating the new postal codes—and one would be right. After all, when doing something as major as accommodating a whole new country, it should be obvious that it would affect the page that searches based on location. But perhaps the developer who fixed the bug didn't think that page searched based on zip or postal code. Or maybe the application is much bigger in scope and the developer made a valiant effort to catch all the scenarios but developers are only human and it was the end of the day and he had a bit of a cold and...

The point is, if every developer did comprehensive testing of bug fixes and didn't miss any possible scenarios, there wouldn't be any bugs in the first place.

What this contrived example illustrates is that fixing one bug can often introduce others. Often the new bugs are in areas you might not even have realized were related. For example, you might not imagine a lot of pain involved in fixing a bug in a timesheet entry system whereby we don't allow entries after noon on the cutoff date. But what if we move the server from Toronto (where all the employees are) to Bangladesh and forget to account for the shift in time zones?

The underlying argument of this discussion is that without tests, you'll eventually become hesitant, then reluctant, then outright fearful about fixing bugs or adding features to the codebase. You become afraid that even the slightest modification to a seemingly benign business rule will have far-reaching implications. We have yet to meet a single developer who enjoys having bugs he thought were fixed come back to haunt him in some other form.

It's not just the development team that needs confidence in the application. If you're afraid to work with the codebase, you can imagine how the management team and the client and users feel about it. It takes only one bad experience to create animosity between the business and the IT department. This animosity and distrust can reach the point where, when an application is needed, the customer will go outside the company to have it built. Needless to say, rebuilding such a relationship takes a long time. It is possible, though, so let's take a look at some of the techniques.

### 4.2.1 Regaining confidence and control

We slid down a slippery slope a little at the end of the last section. Automated tests are not the be-all, end-all of your relationship with your clients (the end-all perhaps, but certainly not the be-all).

Let's revisit our earlier scenario on zip codes in the Bahamas and change the parameters a bit. Now assume we have a full suite of unit and integration tests backing up our code. We hit the reset button, go back in time, and move into the Bahamas again for the first time with no changes to the application other than automated tests.

As before, say the system fails when customers try to enter an address with no zip code. But now, instead of diving in and fixing the code right away, we write some tests to expose the bug. We start with a unit test that creates an account with a typical Bahamian address, which fails, as we'd expect it to.

---

**Challenge your assumptions: Write a test before fixing a bug**

When you're tasked with fixing a defect in a brownfield system, what's your first step? Do you search out a person who you know worked on that area of the application and can provide you with some background? Do you just start debugging the code as you attempt to reproduce and resolve the reported issue?

Chances are that you're working in a large codebase with areas you're not intimately familiar with. Because of that, you'll probably have to spend some time narrowing down the area where the bug resides. Once you know approximately where the problem is, you can begin to use our recommended technique: writing a test.

If you've adequately narrowed the point of failure, you should be able to write a test that exposes the bug. That is, don't write a test that passes. Instead, write one that tests what you *want* the code to do but what it isn't currently doing. Write a test that *should* pass but doesn't.

> *(continued)*
>
> Sure, it seems odd to intentionally create this failing test, but what you're doing is preparing for the bug fix. You're creating a harness that will confirm when you have the application working correctly. The test serves not only to notify you when you've done enough to resolve the issue, but it also will stay on as part of your testing suite to ensure that no future changes to the code will create the same bug again.
>
> There's a caveat: sometimes the code exists in a state that makes it hard to write a good test prior to fixing a bug. You may look at it and think that you have to refactor until it's testable. If these are your thoughts, hesitate. By performing that refactoring, what would you introduce? Do you have sufficient tests available now to verify that your refactoring was successful? If not, do you want to introduce the risk of more defects at that point in time?
>
> So do the best you can. Any verification that you can provide to yourself after working on the bug will be better than none.

So we write the code to accommodate the new address format and the test passes.

We're not done yet, as we haven't run the new code through its paces in integration tests yet. This task shouldn't be too difficult; presumably, we already have integration tests that run the gamut for a test account using a U.S. zip code. We have tests that go through our location process end to end with a standard U.S. address. All we need to do is run through our suite of integration tests using a Bahamian address instead.

And lo! We get a failure. It seems that when we get to the test that retrieves the data from the web service based on the zip code, we get an error: *unrecognized zip code*. We can now write a test to expose this bug and fix it before going any further.

There's something subtle at play here. Notice that in both the no-test and the full-test scenarios, we haven't changed anything to do with how we address either bug. The code to fix it is identical in both cases. All we've done is shifted when and by whom the bug was discovered. Rather than releasing the code after fixing the first bug and having paying customers discover it, we've found it ourselves and can now fix it as part of the current release cycle. We've closed the feedback loop.

**NOTE**   Recall the feedback loop from section 3.2 in chapter 3. By having tests in place for your application, you increase the speed with which bugs are discovered. This is a good thing. Your application has bugs. If you can find them quickly, there's less chance they'll still exist when the application is released to an unsuspecting public.

Every step further away from the developer a bug is allowed to travel without being found increases the cost of repairing the bug.[1] The best way to minimize this cost is to catch defects in the application at development time. Automated tests can help with

---

[1]  This concept is taken from *Code Complete, 2nd Edition* (Microsoft Press, 2004), by Steve McConnell.

that job. Better yet, running these tests means we can announce with confidence that we haven't introduced any new bugs while fixing something.

Back to our example whereby we have a full suite of tests and you breathe a little sigh of relief that the integration tests saved you while the management team congratulates you on a job well done. Chances are the client won't offer you any kudos for not introducing unforeseen bugs, but when it comes time to have another application built, at least they won't say, "Whatever we do, don't call the IT department."[2]

Although this kind of confidence is a benefit derived from automated test suites, there are other reasons to use them as well. Let's spend some time looking at them.

### 4.2.2   The need for tests

The point of this discussion is that your application needs tests. Here are a few reasons why:

- To ensure bugs aren't repeat offenders
- To ensure new development is of an acceptable quality
- To preserve and build on the confidence the various parties have in the applications
- Most importantly, *to increase the speed of the feedback loop*

However, ours is a brownfield application and possibly one of substantial size. If you don't have any tests in place, we're not so unreasonable as to assume you'll halt all new development and bug fixes for the next 3 months so that you can retrofit unit and integration tests into your code.

But tests should always be near the forefront of your mind going forward. No new code should be checked in without being supported by tests. If you're fixing bugs, have at least one test in place to ensure that the same bug does not get reintroduced inadvertently when another one is fixed. And new features don't get added if they aren't adequately covered by unit tests.

**NOTE**   Bugs are expensive and should be fixed once and only once. Writing a unit test to first expose the bug, then to verify it has been fixed, is a good way to ensure it doesn't recur.

In this way, you ensure the important parts of your application are the focus for your tests. Yes, if there are currently no bugs in a section of code, it will never be covered by tests. But then, if there are no bugs, one might argue it doesn't need tests.

So with that as our rallying cry, let's turn our attention to specific types of tests, starting with unit tests.

## 4.3   Types of automated tests

We have no desire for this section to be a comprehensive discussion of techniques and practices for writing tests. There are entire books on the subject, including Roy

---

[2] With credit to Steve Martin from the movie, *Roxanne*

Osherove's excellent *The Art of Unit Testing*.[3] Instead of delving deep into the subject, we'll give a brief overview of the two types of unit test to set the context, and then in the next section, discuss them within the context of a brownfield application. For the most part, however, we'll assume you're familiar with the concept of unit tests in general, if not the implementation. One key point to remember about your automated tests (unit or otherwise) is that they're a strong form of documentation. Well-written tests that pass will provide invaluable feedback to future developers about how you intend the codebase to work.

> **What's a unit?**
>
> The key to writing unit tests is defining the unit that's being tested. In general terms, this is simply the smallest piece of code that can be tested.
>
> The smallest piece of code that can be tested isn't always obvious. If you're testing whether a property on a class can be set properly, there isn't a lot of ambiguity. But if you're testing whether someone's account was created successfully, things aren't as obvious. Are you testing whether it was added to the database successfully? Whether it was sent to an account creation service? Whether the new account can be successfully retrieved (which may or may not be from the database)?
>
> The good news is that practice makes perfect and help is only a web search away. Although you may experience early pain when defining your units, take heart that it does get easier with practice.

Assuming you're able to define the unit to test, the next step is to test it. There are two broad ways of doing this testing, which we'll discuss next.

### 4.3.1  *State-based tests*

The most basic and intuitive type of test is state based. In state-based tests, you verify that the state of an object, an object property, or a variable is as you expect it to be. Most often you do so by executing code in a method, followed by verifying some result. Depending on the code being exercised, the result may be a value returned from the method call. Other times you may verify values associated with an object.

State-based tests have no knowledge of the inner workings of the code being exercised. All we know is that it performs some action and we know what effect that action should have. As the name implies, the state-based test is based on the state of an object before and after an action is taken (see figure 4.2).

**Figure 4.2  State-based testing doesn't require any knowledge of the code under test.**

---

[3]  Roy Osherove, *The Art of Unit Testing* (Manning, 2009)

Let's look at an example. Listing 4.1 shows a sample state-based test using the NUnit unit-testing framework.

**Listing 4.1   State-based test**

```
[Test]
public void Full_name_should_concatenate_first_and_last_names()
{
    Customer customer = new Customer();      ❶ Set up
    customer.FirstName = "Jimi";          ←─┘    data
    customer.LastName = "Hendrix";

    string expectedFullName = "Hendrix, Jimi";  ❷ Execute
    string actualName = customer.FullName();  ←─┘ code
                                                     ❸ Verify
    Assert.That(actualName, Is.EqualTo(expectedFullName));  ←─┘  results
}
```

As you can see in listing 4.1, there are three components to this simple test. First, ❶ shows the setup of information that is required to execute the test. Following the setup, ❷ highlights the execution of the code that we're testing. Once the code under test has been executed, ❸ shows where the test verifies that the output is as expected.

> **Challenge your assumptions: Naming your tests**
>
> Don't be afraid to be verbose when naming your tests. You're not designing an API, nor are you creating methods that will be called by anything other than an automated testing framework. The main criterion for a good test name is that it should be easy for a developer to read and understand what the test is doing without having to parse the code. Better yet, a test name should enlighten the reader on the functionality of the application and, more precisely, the specific code under test.

In listing 4.1, we're testing to ensure that the `FullName` method for `Customer` will concatenate the `FirstName` and `LastName` as we expect (LastName, comma, space, FirstName).

**NOTE**   We have no hint as to how the `FullName` method does its job. All we know is that it returns a string. Maybe it uses string concatenation, maybe it uses a `StringBuilder`, or maybe it sends the data off to another service. All we care about is that it returns a string and should be in a certain format.

Although listing 4.1 is a simple test, it's important. With this test in place, if we ever decide to go back and alter the code in the `Customer` class, we can be reasonably confident that the `FullName` method will still behave as expected.

When this test fails, one of two things has happened: the output of the `FullName` method has unexpectedly changed, or the business requirements of `FullName` have changed, making this test no longer correct.

State-based tests are often referred to as *black box tests* because we see the inputs and verify the outputs, but the inner workings are a black box to the test. In contrast, interaction tests know how the code they're testing works. We'll look at interaction tests next.

### 4.3.2  Interaction tests

An interaction test is one where we test how two or more objects interact with each other. It's best described after looking at an example.

Listing 4.2 shows a simple example using the Rhino Mocks framework. Don't worry about the syntax or the explanations too much; we'll clarify them shortly.

**Listing 4.2  Interaction-based test**

```
[Test]
public void Loading_order_should_retrieve_order_from_repository()          ◁
{
    var mockRepository = MockRepository.Create<IOrderRepository>();        ◁
                                                             Create a mock
    int orderId = 123;                                           object  ❷
    mockPollOrder.Expect( m => m.FetchById( orderId ) )    ◁
        .IgnoreArguments()                                Set      Define test
        .Repeat.Once()                          mock expectations  objective  ❶
        .Return( new List<Order>( ) );                         ❸

    var orderService = new OrderService( mockRepository );  ❹  Execute
    orderService.Load( orderId );                          ◁       code
}
```

In listing 4.2, the object we're testing is an `OrderService` ❶. Specifically, we're testing the effects of placing an order. What this test tells us is that when we call `Load` on an `OrderService` object ❹, we expect the `FetchById` method ❸ to be called on an `IOrderRepository` object ❷ that's passed into the `OrderService` object through the constructor call.

For developers new to interaction testing, there's a lot to take in with this example. Like many interaction tests, it makes use of mock objects, which are proxy objects that take the place of real implementations. When we run this test, the mocking framework will autogenerate a class that implements the `IOrderRepository`, and then create an instance of the autogenerated class.

The reason we go through this exercise is because we don't care how `IOrder-Repository` works *in the context of this test.* We're concerned with testing only the `OrderService`. Whether `FetchById` goes to a database, the file system, or a web service is irrelevant for the purpose of this test. All we care about is that the `OrderService` is going to call this method at some point.

So we create a mock implementation of `IOrderRepository` that we can manipulate in a way that facilitates our test. We set expectations on which calls the `OrderService` will make on the `IOrderRepository` object when we exercise our test.

In this way, we test how the `OrderService` *interacts* with its dependencies (the `OrderRepository`).

### The Rhino Mocks syntax

In listing 4.2, you can see a number of things that are part of the Rhino Mocks framework. The first is the `MockRepository.CreateMock<T>` syntax, which will create a mock object that we can manipulate for our test. The returned object is a fake object that implements the `IOrderRepository` interface.

After creating the mock object, the next Rhino Mocks–specific syntax is the `Expect (m =>...)` call. Here we make assertions about what we *expect* to happen during our test. This code doesn't execute at this time; it's recorded so that we know how to react when the `OrderService` makes this call.

One of the nice things about Rhino Mocks is that its fluent interface for expectations is easy to understand. In this example we're stating that we expect a call on the `OrderRepository`'s `FetchById` method. When that call happens, we don't care about the argument being passed to the `FetchById` method, but we do expect that it will only be called one time. And when it's called, we'd like it to return an empty `List<Order>()` object.

If you're interested in learning more about Rhino Mocks, we suggest you look through the resources at www.ayende.com. Also, *The Art of Unit Testing* gives a good overview of Rhino Mocks as well as other mocking frameworks.

You don't necessarily need to use a mocking framework to do interaction tests. You could create the fake objects manually (for instance, a `FakeOrderRepository` that implements `IOrderRepository`) if you're having a hard time wrapping your head around the concept. This approach can be a good way to try out interaction tests without having to dive in head first. It doesn't take long before you start experiencing pain from hand-rolled fake objects. In our experience, switching over to true mock objects sooner rather than later will save you more time over the long run.

Although far from a comprehensive discussion on interaction tests, this section has provided a quick introduction to set the stage for our later work on adding these tests to our codebase.

### Specification-based tests

Another type of test that's gaining momentum is specification-based tests or, more commonly, specifications.

A specification is a way of describing tests in a more natural language. In the agile world, specifications flow directly from the user stories. In conjunction with unit testing, the developers (in conjunction with the business users) write specifications about how the application should behave. Developers then write code with the goal of satisfying those specifications.

Specifications are written in support of an overall business requirement. Here's a sample specification for the code that we're testing in listing 4.2:

**(continued)**

```
As a Customer Support Representative,
I can save an order,
So that the order can be fulfilled by the restaurant.
```

The "As a/I can/So that" syntax is important because it lends itself to automated frameworks as well as reporting tools so that the gap can be closed between developer and business user. Indeed, we encourage you to write specifications alongside the business user.

Writing specifications, like unit tests, takes practice. If you feel you'd like to try your hand at them, we suggest using them for new code only, rather than trying to retrofit them over existing code. They're generally more useful for outlining behavior that hasn't been written rather than verifying the correctness of existing code. For the latter case, state-based or interaction tests would be better suited.

That's about as wet as our feet are going to get on the theory behind unit tests. It's time to get practical and determine how to apply automated testing to an existing codebase. We'll start by addressing any existing test projects you may already have.

## 4.4    (Re-)integrating existing test projects

Your application may already contain unit tests. Perhaps the previous team had good intentions and started out ensuring all code was tested, but then they fell by the wayside in the face of mounting time pressures. Another possibility is that partway through the previous version of the application, it dawned on someone that unit tests might be a Good Thing and a halfhearted attempt was made to retrofit some in.

Whatever the reason, many brownfield applications will include a test project that's incomplete at best and incorrect at worst. If you're among the lucky ones, the existing tests will even pass, assuming they haven't been ignored, commented out, or just plain removed from all the compile configurations in Visual Studio.

The underlying steps we'll follow to revisit this test project are outlined in figure 4.3.

With that, let's look at your current tests.

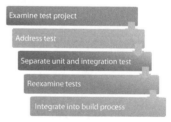

**Figure 4.3   Steps to integrate an existing test project back into your process**

### 4.4.1    Examining existing test projects

The first step in analyzing an existing test project is simply to see if it compiles. If the testing project isn't currently part of your standard solution structure, leave it that way and work in a new solution for now. At this point in our analysis, the testing project (or projects, as it's not uncommon to find more than one) will be volatile. Keep in mind we now have a continuous integration (CI) environment going. Adding instability into the environment of all the other developers would potentially impose a great deal of friction on them if we start breaking the build.

Getting test code to compile in isolation sounds well and good; all you have to do is go in and fix things until the project compiles, right? There's that word *right* again. In this case, it means there are other things to think about once each test is compiling.

First, is the test project worth compiling? Are the tests valid? The tests probably haven't been maintained for some time, so it's possible that they no longer make sense in terms of the current code structure. Worse yet, the test code may look technically applicable, but business requirements may have changed so that the code is no longer relevant.

There are three things you can do with an invalid test:

- *Delete it*—If the test is no longer technically appropriate, delete it from the test suite. If you've started at the front of this book, you'll already have this code in a version control system (VCS), which will allow you to retrieve it if the need ever arises. (Hint: It never does.)
- *Refactor it*—If the test is still potentially relevant, consider refactoring it. The problem with this approach is that it's often faster just to delete the test and start from scratch. From personal experience, refactoring existing tests can be an arduous mental exercise. It often spirals into confusion about what should be tested, when, and in what manner. As a general rule, save yourself the headache and start fresh if you're thinking of refactoring.
- *Ignore it*—Most testing frameworks have attributes that will allow you to keep the test in the suite but not have it execute during a test run. These attributes can be useful if the test still has business value but is currently failing and needs reworked.

### Don't ignore your tests

Don't ignore your tests for too long. Ignored tests are like rotten apples in a box. If you have one, pretty soon you have two, then six, and then fifteen. Before long the stink they cause will catch your attention. What do you do when one day you realize that you have allowed 10 or 20 percent of your tests to become ignored? At that point you're back where you were when we started this chapter: analyzing your test suite, fixing outdated tests, and deciding if you should keep them, ignore them, or delete them. Why bother going through this effort if you're going to perpetuate this kind of analysis work for yourself?

The simple rule is that tests can't be ignored for long.

It's surprising how many test projects have been omitted from the overall solution simply because it became too much work to keep the code in sync with the application's code. Test projects like this are at the extreme end of staleness. If you haven't already done so, take the time to get the tests compiling, review them, and rewrite or purge them as required.

Once the tests are all compiling, the next step is simply to add the test project back into the solution. Because you've already read chapter 2, you're using a VCS and the addition of the test project should be distributed to the rest of your team the next time they retrieve the latest version from it.

Now we come to an important step. Watch what happens when developers start to retrieve the latest version. Is the automated build now broken? Does the test project add friction to the developers' work in any way?

If the answer to either question is yes, pull the test project back out as fast as you can. You need to address the issues, then add the project to the solution again. It's important to act on the appearance of this (and, indeed, any) friction. If you ignore it, people will adapt. And they'll probably adapt in ways that are detrimental to the project's overall well-being.

For example, let's say we add the test project to our solution and it includes a pre-build command that copies a file into the testing directory. And suppose that in some circumstances, like, say, when the application is running in Internet Information Services (IIS), the file is locked and can't be copied. The prebuild command will fail intermittently, not allowing the project to be built.

In this scenario, we've added significant friction to one or more developers' work. Now they have to remember to shut down the application in IIS while they're compiling. Perhaps this leads to them not running the application in IIS anymore and using the built-in Cassini web server from Visual Studio. This could lead to issues when the application is deployed in IIS because you don't use it regularly while developing the app.

This is the type of workaround you want to avoid. You're changing a developer's behavior to deal with an issue that should've been corrected early on: you should remove the test project at the first sign of friction, fix the problem, and then reintegrate the test project.

**TIP**  Don't allow friction to remain in your work process long enough for you to find a workaround for it.

Analyzing existing tests and reintegrating them into the project can be a tedious first step. Once it's done, your work isn't over. Just because you have added back existing tests to the project, nothing says that those tests are valid. Even if all of the reintegrated tests are running and passing, they may not be verifying the code under test correctly. In the next section we'll look at how we can review those tests and determine whether they're working as we need them to.

### 4.4.2   *Address existing tests*

Assuming that you have been able to reintegrate the test project, you now have all your production and testing code in one environment. With all the tests compiling

and included in the solution, the next step is
to start adding tests, riiiiiight?

Well, yes, the next step *is* to start adding
tests, and we'll go into that later in the chapter. But at the same time, you should do
something else in parallel: review the existing tests.

Regardless of your path to get here, you
have tests from the past in your solution now.
One of the questions for you and the rest of
your team is, "How valid or correct are the
existing tests?" Just because you have tests
doesn't mean that they're providing any value
to you.

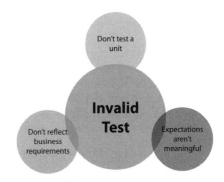

**Figure 4.4   There are many reasons a test
may be invalid.**

Unit tests can be invalid or incorrect for any number of reasons. In general, an incorrect test is any unit test that gives the illusion of validating a piece of code but doesn't
provide any significant or meaningful verification of the code it's exercising. Tests like
these provide a false sense of security. They build confidence that's misplaced and set
to crumble. These aren't good traits for a project or a codebase to have.

Although you may not be able to determine all the reasons that unit tests can be
incorrect, they'll fall into three broad categories, as shown in figure 4.4:

- They don't test a unit.
- The expectations aren't meaningful.
- They don't reflect business requirements.

Let's examine each of these categories.

### TESTS THAT DON'T VERIFY A SINGLE UNIT

The first category, tests that don't address a unit, means your test is verifying more
than one single unit—for example, a test that checks whether a customer is valid, then
checks to see if it was saved to the database.

That we consider this "incorrect" may seem confusing. After all, we need to test
how the pieces work together, don't we? Of course we do. But the problem with tests
like these is that they usually present several code execution paths that require
verification. More paths to verify mean more permutations in your test. More permutations mean more test configuration. And more test configuration means brittle tests.

Instead of trying to test multiple things in a single test, it's much easier to test each
piece (or execution path) separately. Then you can have a separate test altogether
that verifies how the pieces interact with one another. One effective method is to test
each unit of code thoroughly by itself using state-based tests. This approach will allow
you to verify that the results are as you expect for each of the code paths. If the unit of
code being tested is small enough, the setup required to exercise all the execution
paths will be quite manageable.

Many brownfield applications will contain integration tests that claim to be unit tests. These are usually easy to spot. They are long-winded and have complicated set-ups compared to what they're testing. Often they span multiple layers of your application and even connect up to a database or read a configuration file. In any case, these aren't unit tests. But neither are they to be discarded outright. More likely, they are integration tests, which we'll discuss later. Evaluate them to see if they qualify as valid integration tests, and if so, move them to your integration test area.

You still need to verify that the pieces of code will interact with one another as expected. This point is where interaction testing and mocking frameworks come into play. Again, because the unit of code under test is smaller, configuring the tests for each permutation of interaction should require minimal coding effort.

Getting a brownfield application to the point where you can adequately test inter-actions between pieces of code can take some time. To effectively do interaction test-ing, you must have clearly defined seams and logical layers (we'll discuss layering in chapter 8) in your code. Without this, interaction testing can be enormously frustrat-ing to the point of being impossible.

If you find tests that require a lot of setup before the code under test is executed, this can be a sign of poor tests. It can also be a sign of code that doesn't adhere to the single responsibility principle (discussed in chapter 7). If this is the case, the solution is to refactor the existing code into smaller pieces (units) and write both state- and interaction-based tests for all of them.

### TESTS THAT DON'T SET MEANINGFUL EXPECTATIONS

Even if you're testing a cohesive unit of code, the tests may not be of any value. As you can see in listing 4.3, a test can pass, but not fully test the execution of the code it's exercising.

#### Listing 4.3  Expectation lacking meaning

```
[Test]
public void VerifyMenuItemImport()
{
    string sampleItem =
            "Item(Name:Chicken Vindaloo, Price:$11.95, Category:Entree)";

    IImportMenuItem menuItemParser = new ImportMenuItemParser();
    MenuItem menuItem = menuItemParser.For(sampleItem);

    Assert.That(menuItem, Is.Not.Null);
}
```

The expectations and assertions that our tests make should be clear and rigid when-ever possible. In listing 4.3, the intent of the code being exercised isn't clear enough. All we know from this test is that the method call should be returning a non-null MenuItem object. Think about this for a second. What's the minimum amount of code that you need to write to make that test pass?

The code in listing 4.4 will pass our test. But few would agree that it's valid code. The code in listing 4.4 is probably wrong—we all can guess that—but the test in listing 4.3

isn't explicit enough to give us confidence to say that it's definitely wrong. Based on the name of the test alone, it would be easy for us to get a warm, fuzzy feeling that everything was okay.

**Listing 4.4   Minimum code to pass test**

```
public class ImportMenuItemParser : IImportMenuItem
{
    public MenuItem For(string itemToBeParsed)
    {
        return new MenuItem();
    }
}
```

So what *would* give us that confidence then? We have to write a test that sets the minimum expectation that we have for the code as clearly as possible. In this case we expect to have a MenuItem returned to us that has a Name, Price and Category. The first thing we need to do is change the name of the test to reflect our goal (see listing 4.5).

**Listing 4.5   Intention-revealing test name**

```
[Test]
public void ImportMenuItemParser_Should_Transform_Input_Into_MenuItem()
{
    string sampleItem =
        "Item(Name:Chicken Vindaloo, Price:$11.95, Category:Entree)";

    IImportMenuItem menuItemParser = new ImportMenuItemParser();
    MenuItem menuItem = menuItemParser.For(sampleItem);

    Assert.That(menuItem.Name, Is.EqualTo("Chicken Vindaloo"));
    Assert.That(menuItem.Price, Is.EqualTo(11.95));
    Assert.That(menuItem.Category, Is.EqualTo("Entree"));
}
```

That's better. You now can say with much more certainty that the ImportMenuItem-Parser must parse the input string and assign values from it into the properties on the MenuItem object. The minimal amount of code required to make this test pass has changed significantly. If we were to exercise the code in listing 4.4 with the test in listing 4.5, the test would fail.

Vagueness in testing, such as we just displayed, tends to be rampant in brownfield applications. Over time, developers may have become frustrated with the complexity of testing their codebase. Instead of refactoring the codebase so that it adheres to principles like single responsibility and separation of concerns (see chapter 7), they've relaxed their testing discipline. Not only has this increased the fragility of the test suite, it has also reduced its effectiveness. This is a classic sign of a brownfield application and is a direct cause of the contamination that defines it.

**TESTS THAT DON'T REFLECT BUSINESS REQUIREMENTS**

Another set of tests that are prime candidates for deletion are those that are no longer testing functionality that meets business requirements. Like the code that these tests are exercising, they've been forgotten. The code may work fine, the test may pass, and the test may be testing all the right things, but the code being tested may not be used in the application in any meaningful way. In fact, it's not uncommon for the tests to be the only place in the application that calls the code being tested.

Of all the incorrect test types that you're going to search for in your brownfield application, tests that don't reflect business requirements will be the hardest to find. Until you have knowledge about the application's inner workings, you won't be able to recognize that these tests aren't calling useful code.

Most likely, you'll find them by accident. You'll probably stumble into a piece of long-retired code, delete it, and then find that one or more tests will no longer compile.

These tests aren't hurting anything by existing. At worst they're inflating your code coverage statistics (see chapter 6). At best, they're protecting a unit of code that you may, on some mythical day, start using again. It's our opinion, however, that if you encounter code that's no longer being used in the application, you should delete it. You may feel that you'll need it at some point, but that's your VCS's job: to maintain that history and keep it hidden from you on a daily basis. Code and tests, in this circumstance, are adding to the maintenance workload that your project is creating. Deleting them helps a little in reducing that load.

TIP    We suggest not going out of your way to search for tests that test irrelevant code. The reward-to-effort ratio is far too low. As you refactor the application, you'll come across these tests, and they can be deleted at that time along with the defunct code.

In this section we explained that as part of addressing existing tests, you'll identify and categorize tests as either unit or integration tests. Because these serve different purposes, let's look at how we can separate them for easier management.

### 4.4.3   *Separate unit tests from integration tests*

The final step in the process of adding inherited unit tests back into the solution is to segregate true unit tests from integration tests. We'll talk later in this chapter about what defines integration tests, but for now think of them as tests that execute more than one unit of code at a time. Because integration tests run slower than unit tests, separating them can reduce test execution friction. We talked a little about how to overcome this in chapter 3.

Physically separating these two types of tests is usually a good practice. By "physically," we mean into entirely separate folders or even separate assemblies. Having integration test classes intermingled with unit test classes in the same folder will make it more difficult to separate the two of them in the build script for your CI process, which is something that might become necessary at some point during the project.

Why would we want to do this? Well, integration tests run much slower than unit tests. It's their nature. They're testing how components, such as your code, databases, and web services, integrate. Instead of forcing the developers to always run slow integration tests, split them so that the option of running the slow tests can exist. Having a process for developers to run only unit (fast) tests when appropriate can help to increase the speed at which they work.

So at the very least, we recommend creating two folders at the root of your test project: one for integration tests and the other for unit tests (see figure 4.5). Within each of these folders, you can use whatever subfolder or file structure you like. But as long as they're separated at some root level in the file system, they can be easily separated within the build script should the need arise.

Another option is to have one test project for integration tests and one for unit tests. Although this will work, this solution is overkill. It's effectively the same as segregating the tests into separate folders in one project. So unless there's a technical need for the two types of tests to be separated (and compiling them into separate assemblies isn't one of those needs), it's easier to keep the tests within a single project.

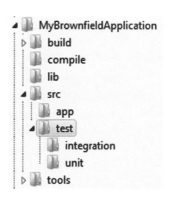

**Figure 4.5  Physically separating unit and integration tests in the folder structure allows for build scripts to easily create separate testing assemblies.**

### Tales from the trenches: Testing at a snail's pace

We joined a project that had a reasonably sized suite of unit and integration tests. As development continued, developers began to complain that the amount of time to run the automated build script, which included test execution, was slowing down their development progress.

In this case, the script took over 30 minutes, sometimes over 40, to execute completely. If one unit test failed during execution of that script, developers would have to fix the problem and rerun the build script, which cost them another 30 minutes of effective working time.

When we looked at the tests, it was apparent that unit and integration tests needed to be separated. A semblance of separation existed, but some integration tests existed in the unit-testing folders, and vice versa. After taking some time to whittle through the tests and moving those running slowly into the integration area, we set about altering the build script.

Instead of developers running one script to execute all tests, we configured it to execute the script for unit tests alone, integration tests alone, or both combined. By allowing the developers to run the fast tests at times, we cut the wait time for test execution from 30 to 40 minutes every time down to 5 to 6 minutes most times. In the end, the team still complained that 5 to 6 minutes was too long to wait, but at least we had them working at a much faster pace and we could concentrate on trying to improve the speed.

Regardless of how you organize your tests, you should always be looking at the tests as a way to expose current or potential future issues in your code. As we move into the next sections, we'll talk more about this.

### 4.4.4  *Reexamining your tests*

We've gone through a lot of techniques for identifying tests that you may want to include, exclude, and eliminate from your brownfield test suite. While you're going through this process, there's one thing that you should be watching for at all times. Look for areas of brittleness in the test suite. When you're writing tests, note the ones that take a lot of effort to write. When tests are failing, watch for areas that seem to be breaking on a regular basis and gather information about the points of failure.

That information is something that you should file away and look to address in the future. It may be useful when making code design decisions like creating or modifying the logical layers in the code. Having gone through the test re-inclusion exercise will have given you some idea as to what areas of the application should be attended to and in what order. Tests are client code to your application. Looking at it from the point of view that a client would will give you a different view of the code's state.

> **TIP**  Any code that you write will have a client. At a minimum this client will be a developer (most likely you) who is writing tests to exercise the code. Possibly, the client will be a developer who's consuming the code in another part of the application. On the far end of the spectrum, the client could be a developer who has purchased your third-party utility or control and is adding it into their application. Writing code with the concerns of your client in mind will increase its usability and readability. One effective technique for achieving this is test-driven design (see section 4.6). Because it's concerned with creating and designing code from the code client's perspective, and doing so before writing the actual code, you'll be writing code as a client on a regular basis.

Writing code from its consumer's perspective is a good practice. Unfortunately, writing code this way doesn't provide verification that the code written is functional. Because automated tests are one of the clients for your code, executing those tests can provide some of that verification. Let's spend some time on this topic now.

### 4.4.5  *Executing the tests in your build script*

Having completed a review of the inherited tests (and reworking as necessary), the final step of the process of reintegrating existing tests to your brownfield application is to have the build process execute them. By adding the execution of the tests to the automated build process, you're ensuring that every time the build script is executed, either by a developer on their local machine or on the CI server, the suite of tests is executed as well.

If you've followed our advice from chapter 3, you'll already have an automated build script in place. So the next step is to add a task to the script that will exercise your tests. How this is implemented will depend on the CI software and unit-testing framework you're using (and even then, there's often more than one way of skinning this cat). Here's a simple NAnt target that will execute all tests within a given assembly using NUnit:

```
<target name="test" depends="init">
    <nunit2 failonerror="true">
        <formatter type="Plain" />
        <test assemblyname="${build.dir}/${test.assembly}" />
    </nunit2>
</target>
```

The sample uses the `<nunit2>` NAnt task to execute all unit tests within the assembly, `${test.assembly}`, which is defined elsewhere in the build script.

An integral part of this sample is the `failonerror` attribute. This means that if *any* of the tests fail, the entire build will fail. A failing test has the same status as a compile error. A broken test is the sign of something unexpected in your code, and it indicates that the build process doesn't have confidence in the compiled code. If the automated build script doesn't have confidence in the compilation, you shouldn't either. Code compiled with failing tests shouldn't be deployed to any environment, test or otherwise.

**NOTE**  We can't recommend strongly enough the importance of ensuring that the overall build fails if one or more tests fail. It may seem harsh at first, but it indicates that a written expectation (your failing test) hasn't been met. When expectations aren't being met, the application isn't working as you'd desired. In this regard, failing tests are as serious as a compilation error because the application isn't functional in this state.

With your unit-test suite being executed during your build process, you've completely reintegrated the inherited tests. You now have a suite of tests that have been vetted for correctness and verified to pass. Along the way you'll have removed some tests that weren't providing you with any benefits and modified some to provide more than they did before.

Overall, you've increased your confidence in the codebase, and that's what's known in the industry as a Good Thing. You could stop here and still be much better off than you were at the beginning of this chapter. We're certainly breathing a little easier.

But there's much more to do. There are ways to further increase the confidence that the developers have in the quality of the product. That, in turn, will increase the confidence that QA, management, the client, and other groups have in the product as well. As that happens, your project will become much more enjoyable to work on. Because that's something we all want, let's look at what we have to do to add new tests to the project.

## 4.5   *Adding a new test project*

For those applications that don't yet have a test project, you haven't been forgotten. In this section, we'll walk through the steps for adding a new test project and integrating it into the CI process.

And, thankfully, there isn't much you need to do. The steps are a subset of integrating an existing test project, except that you have to create the project first.

So first let's create a Class Library project in your solution with an appropriate name (such as MyApplication.Tests). Next, add a reference to the unit-testing framework you're using.

**NOTE**   Recall from chapter 2 that the unit-testing framework files you reference, along with all their dependencies, should be stored within the tools folder of your root application folder. To find the files you need to include, check for a subfolder called *bin* in the folder where you installed or unzipped the unit-testing framework. Most frameworks will store everything you need within this folder, and it's a matter of copying the entire thing into your tools folder. Because you'll probably end up with more than one tool, we also recommend an appropriately named subfolder (such as NUnit, MbUnit, or xUnit).

After adding the project, create two folders in it: one for unit tests and one for integration tests. As mentioned in section 4.4.3, it is helpful to have unit tests and integration tests physically separated so that they can be compiled, and ultimately executed, separately if need be.

With the two subfolders created, we can already skip to the end and add the test project to the CI process. This is done in the same way as outlined in section 4.4.5: you add a step to the CI process to exercise the tests in your test assembly (the code snippet in section 4.4.5, which shows a sample NAnt task for integrating NUnit tests into the automated build, applies for new test projects as well as existing test projects).

**NOTE**   You may find that after integrating your new test project into the automated build, the build fails because there are no tests to execute. If this is the case, just write a test. Any test. If you can pick off one that makes sense from your code, that would be an ideal starting point. Otherwise, create a class called `DeleteMe` and add a test that asserts that $1 + 1 = 2$. The important part is to get the tests executing in the CI process as quickly as possible. After that, any additional tests will execute with this safety net in place.

As with the existing test project scenario, make sure the build is configured to fail whenever one or more tests in your test suite fail. Once that is done, we can start adding new tests to the codebase.

## 4.6   *Writing new tests*

By this point, you should have a test project in place with all the tests within it being executed as part of your automated build in your CI process. We now have the framework in place to write some new tests.

One of the key parts in the definition of a brownfield application is that the codebase is in active development. As part of that work, we expect that there will be refactorings as well as completely new features added. And as we've mentioned before, it's difficult to have confidence in code if it isn't being tested. After all, how can we be sure that modifying existing code or adding new code won't break something?

As you might expect with two different scenarios (writing new code vs. modifying existing code), there are multiple ways to approach the test writing. First, let's look at writing new tests when you're modifying existing code. It's this scenario that will offer the most challenges.

### 4.6.1   *Tests on existing code*

Modifying existing code to add new or changed functionality is much like fixing bugs. It's likely you're going into an area of the application that may not be covered by tests at all. Making changes with confidence in that scenario is hard to do. So how do we resolve that?

The scenario we discuss here is slightly different than when you fix a bug. Here, we're adding a new feature or changing existing functionality. It's a subtle difference but the method to attack it, testing, is the same. You should never make a change to code until there's a test in place first to prove that your change will be successful when you're done. Don't worry about testing the current functionality; it's going to go away. Instead, create tests that verify the functionality you *intend* to have after making your changes. Write a test as if the code is already doing what you want it to do. This test will fail, but that's good. Now you'll know when your modifications are done: when the test passes.

Let's look at a simple example to explain what we mean. Say you have a service that retrieves the display name for a customer, as we do here:

```
public string GetDisplayNameFor( Customer customer )
{
    string format = "{0} {1}";
    return String.Format( format, customer.FirstName, customer.LastName );
}
```

Because ours is a typical brownfield application, there are no tests for this method. For now, we're fine with this because no bugs have been reported as yet.

Now, the client says that they'd like to change the format of the customer's name to LastName, FirstName. After searching through the code, we zero in on this function and…then what?

This is a benign change, so you'd probably just change the format string and be done with it. But let's rein our instincts in for a moment and try to make sure this issue doesn't come back to haunt us.

Instead of diving into the code, let's write a test to verify that this function behaves the way we want it to (listing 4.6).

**Listing 4.6   Testing to verify desired functionality**

```
[Test]
public void Display_name_should_show_last_name_comma_first_name( )
{
    MyNameService sut = new MyNameService( );
    Customer customer = new Customer( "Tony", "Danza" );
    string displayName = sut.GetDisplayNameFor( customer );
    Assert.That( displayName, Is.EqualTo( "Danza, Tony" ) );
}
```

Listing 4.6 is a test that verifies that our name display service returns names in the format LastName, FirstName.

You may be asking yourself, "Won't this test fail in the current code?" The answer is, "You better believe it'll fail." The current implementation of this function displays the name in FirstName, LastName format.

But we know we're about to change the current functionality, so there's no point verifying that it's correct. Rather, we want to make sure that the new functionality is correct. And we do that by writing the test first.

By writing the test for the modified functionality first and having it fail, we've now given ourselves a specific goal. Setting it up in this way makes it unambiguous as to when we're finished. We aren't done until the test passes.

For completeness, let's modify the `GetDisplayNameFor` method so that it passes our test:

```
public string GetDisplayNameFor( Customer customer )
{
    string format = "{1}, {0}";
    return String.Format( format, customer.FirstName, customer.LastName );
}
```

We run the tests in our automated build and voilà: the tests pass. We can now commit both the tests and the newly modified code to our source code repository.

### The reality of testing existing code

Our example was just shy of being utopian (read: unrealistic) in its simplicity. In many cases, maybe even most, it will be nearly impossible to test existing code in isolation in this manner. Perhaps you have a single function that (a) retrieves a connection string from the app.config, (b) opens a connection to the database, (c) executes some embedded SQL, and (d) returns the resulting `DataSet`.

If you need to modify such a function in any way, you're looking at a fairly significant refactoring just to get this one piece of code properly layered so that you can test each of its tasks.

In part 2 of this book, we'll go into layering in more detail as well as various other techniques for teasing apart your code to facilitate testing.

In the end, you achieve the modified functionality you wanted, confidence in that functionality, and the ability to perform ongoing regression testing for that functionality if anything changes. Instead of just adding the changes that the client needs, you've added long-term reinforcement as well.

With our existing code covered (so to speak), we'll now talk about approaches for testing against new code.

### 4.6.2  Tests on new code

When you're working on your brownfield application, you'll run into one more new-test scenario: that glorious time when you get to write all new code, such as a new module for your application. More likely than not, you'll be tying into existing code, but you'll be adding, not modifying, most of the time. It's like your own little greenfield oasis in the middle of a brownfield desert.

Compared with testing existing code, writing tests for new code should be a breeze. You have more control over the code being tested and chances are that you'll run into less "untestable" code.

There are two ways to write unit tests for new code: *before* the new code is written or *after*. Traditionally, test-after development (TAD) has been the most popular because it's intuitive and can be easily understood.

Writing tests before you write your code is more commonly known as test-driven design (TDD). We won't pretend this topic is even remotely within the scope of this chapter (or even this book), but since we have your attention, it's our opinion that TDD is worth looking into and adopting as a design methodology.

**Test-driven design**

Although it has little bearing on brownfield application development specifically, we can't resist at least a sidebar on test-driven design. It's worth your effort to evaluate it at your organization and try it on a small scale.

Using TDD allows for the creation of code in response to a design that you've determined first. Yes, folks, you read it here: TDD is about designing first. Unlike some schools of thought, this design process doesn't usually include UML, flow charts, state diagrams, data flow diagrams, or any other design tool supported by a GUI-driven piece of software. Instead, the design is laid out through the process of writing code in the form of tests. It's still design, but it's done in a different medium. The tests, while valuable, are more of a side effect of the methodology and provide ongoing benefit throughout the life of the project.

Let it not be said that it's an easy thing to learn. But there are a lot of resources available in the form of books, articles, screencasts, and blogs. Help is never more than an email away.

Whether you choose to write your tests before or after you write your new code, the important thing is that you write them. And execute them along with your automated build.

As we mentioned, writing tests against new code is similar to how you'd do it in a greenfield project. As such, it's a topic best left for a book more focused on unit testing.

Now that you've mastered creating unit tests in different scenarios, it's time to move on to integration testing.

## 4.7    *Integration tests*

Testing code in isolation is all well and good for day-to-day development, but at some point, the rubber is going to hit the road and you need to know that your application works on an end-to-end basis, from the UI to the database. That's the role of integration tests.

> **NOTE**    In the context of integration tests, *end-to-end* extends from the database on one side up to, but not including, the user interface on the other. We'll look more at the user interface in the next section, but for now, consider integration tests as "subcutaneous" tests: ones that start right below the surface of the UI.

When unit testing, we often create mock or fake objects to take the place of anything that is extraneous to the object we're testing. By creating and using mock objects we don't connect to a database or read a configuration file. Rather, we create objects to mimic these actions so that we can test the real logic.

But the time will come where you want to make sure that you *can* connect to the database to retrieve the data you want or that you *can* read the configuration file and that it's returning the information you expect. More than that, you want to make sure that the Save method on your web service will do everything from start to finish, regardless of how many components are involved: populate it with defaults, validate the object, save it to the database, return the new ID, and so on. And although your unit tests can verify that each of these tasks works in isolation, it isn't until the integration tests that we can be totally confident that a task works in its entirety.

Integration tests are often easier to write than unit tests. They don't require a lot of thought with respect to how your components interact. The setup for the tests is usually a lot of busy work to configure databases and web services and such. It's often not trivial, but it's intuitive.

A good candidate for starting your integration testing is your data access layer. During unit testing, you usually try to abstract the database to such an extent that you don't even care if it exists. But at some point, you'll need to verify that you can, in fact, connect to a database somehow, whether it's with a direct DbConnection or through an object-relational mapper tool (more on those in section 4.9). At the very least, you need to verify that the permissions are appropriate in your database, which isn't something that's easily tested in a unit test.

**Challenge your assumptions: Let your users write your acceptance tests**

There's an increasing desire to incorporate an application's users into the software development process. An extension of this idea is to have your users actively involved in writing the acceptance tests that drive out the application's behavior. We've already touched on this in the sidebar "Specification-based tests" earlier in this chapter.

One way to encourage such collaboration is through the use of a tool that facilitates this kind of interaction. One example of such a tool is FitNesse.[4] With it, users and developers collaborate in defining what the software does as well as the tests that will define whether the software does what it purports to do.

Regardless of whether you use such a tool, it's not a replacement for anything we define here. Its strengths lay more in the acceptance testing phase of an application. As with any tool, your individual team dynamics will decide whether it has any merit.

Because unit tests require small segregated components for testing, and brownfield applications tend to have few of these, integration tests can be easier to add to existing projects. Adding integration tests to brownfield applications isn't quite the same ordeal as adding unit tests. The reason is that no matter how convoluted your objects are underneath the covers, you typically test at a higher level. The fact that your mammoth method reads a configuration file, connects to a database, and executes embedded SQL doesn't matter to the integration test. All the setup required to make that work would need to be in place regardless of how the application is layered.

Writing integration tests for a brownfield app is almost identical to doing it for a greenfield app. In both cases, you write the tests after the code is completed. The difference is that in a greenfield application, you'd presumably write your integration test as soon as possible. In a brownfield application, the code has been in place for some time and you're essentially retrofitting integration tests into it.

As with unit tests, you don't necessarily need to add integration tests to existing code just for the sake of it. But similarly, you *should* add integration tests whenever you modify existing code.

**Challenge your assumptions: Execute the integration tests separately**

Integration tests can add considerable time to your automated build process. Almost invariably, this extra time results from accessing external resources (such as a file, a network resource, a web service, or a database). Typically, integration tests open the resource, use it, and then close it again. There's no room for caching in an integration test (unless that's specifically what you're testing).

In chapter 3, we discussed a method of chaining the running of your integration tests after your unit tests. Remember when we suggested that you work to segregate your unit and integration tests? Here's where that effort pays off.

---

[4] http://fitnesse.org

As we mentioned at the start of this section, we're looking at integration tests as being subcutaneous in nature, right below the UI. Having tests that exist immediately below the UI doesn't, however, mandate that there's no need for testing at the user interface level. Let's take a look at this type of testing now.

## 4.8   *User interface tests*

The thorn in the side of any automated build process is the thing that users most identify with for the applications: the user interface. It's just not that easy to mimic clicks on a screen in an automated fashion.

In many ways, the jury is still out on how far you take testing of the user interface. On the one hand, a properly layered application won't have any test-worthy logic in the UI. Using patterns like Model-View-Controller and Model-View-Presenter (see chapter 10), the UI code becomes a series of events that call other, more testable code. Indeed, if you have a method in your `Controller` class called `UpdateJob` and it's fully tested with unit and integration tests, there's little to be gained by testing the `click` event for a button that calls this method.

Because ours is a brownfield application, we can't assume our UI is sufficiently thin that UI tests are totally unnecessary. And with the rise in popularity of JavaScript libraries and Ajax, web UIs are becoming increasingly feature-rich so that they can have complex business and validation logic in them.

In addition, UI testing frameworks have become more mature and easy to use, and many have strong communities where you can get help when you run into trouble. These are valuable advantages because as we've said several times, if a process causes friction with developers, they'll avoid it.

One possible consideration with UI testing is that the UI can be volatile, especially for new features. Converting a `ListBox` to a `RadioButtonList` is no longer as trivial a task as it was before you had a full suite of tests covering the page.

Whether or not your application needs UI testing will be a judgment call, like anything else. Most of the time, UI tests aren't as necessary as unit and integration tests, especially if you're able to apply comprehensive integration tests close to the UI surface. But if you find that a lot of bugs are being discovered due to UI interactions, UI testing is definitely something worth considering. As always, be sure the tests are integrated into your automated build process and that any failures in them will cause the entire build to fail.

It's possible to write your own tests to mimic the UI. In many cases, it could be as simple as instantiating an object representing the form you want to test and calling methods or raising events on it. There's usually much more to this process than that (like ensuring it's using the proper configuration and handling dialogs), but for simple forms it's a viable option.

We also mentioned the use of UI testing frameworks. Some popular ones are Watir/WatiN (Web Application Testing in Ruby/.NET) or Selenium for automating web browsers, and NUnitForms for automated Windows Forms applications. In addition, projects such as JsUnit allow you to test your JavaScript in isolation of the UI.

Bear in mind that everything comes with a cost. UI testing isn't trivial to automate, especially in a CI environment. For example, automating a web application may require the testing framework to physically launch Internet Explorer, Firefox, Opera, Safari, and Chrome (see figure 4.6)—which means that all these browsers need to be installed on the CI server. And browsers were meant to be interacted with. All it takes is a single alert call in your JavaScript to launch a dozen browser instances on your CI server over the course of a day.

All this testing can seem overwhelming at first. You may have started this chapter thinking "Yeah, I know we need to unit test but I don't know how to get started." Now, your head is swimming with integration tests and UI tests (and shortly, database tests).

Don't get too wrapped up in the implementations of these tests. One of the nice things about automated testing in a brownfield application is that anything you do is almost always useful. Pace yourself while you're getting started, and as always, keep your eye on the pain points. You'll be an expert tester in no time.

In the meantime, let's see what we can do about testing your database.

**Figure 4.6   Many considerations are involved when you're testing a web interface, not least of which is the fact that you must test on all major web browsers.**

## 4.9   *Managing your database*

Most applications require a centralized database of some fashion. And this fact can be a source of friction with developers, especially if they're all accessing the same database. Having more than one developer actively developing against the same database is akin to both of them trying to write code on the same computer against a single codebase. Eventually, two people will be working in the same area at the same time.

And even if they don't, at some point you may need to alter the schema. Perhaps a column has been added or you need to modify a stored procedure while you're modifying a feature. If others are working against the same database, they could have problems because they're using the modified database schema with an older version of the code, at least until you check in your changes.

Integration tests and automated builds add another level of complexity to this equation. Chances are your integration tests are adding, modifying, and deleting data from the database. Woe betide any developer trying to work against a database when integration tests are running against it.

The advice here shouldn't be a surprise: each developer should have his or her own copy of the database if it's logistically possible. Ideally, the local database would run locally on the developer's own machine, but the next best thing would be a separate instance running on a server elsewhere.

By having individual copies of the database, you not only eliminate the risk of having an updated schema with outdated code, but you can also run the integration tests at any time without fear of interfering with anyone else.

**NOTE**   It should go without saying that you should have separate databases for each environment as well. For example, you don't want your quality assurance department working against the same database as your user acceptance testers. And no one should be looking at the database used by the CI server for the automated build.

Having many different databases floating around your development project introduces a management and maintenance problem. Let's look at how we can mitigate the risks that it introduces.

### 4.9.1   Autogenerating the database

When executing your integration tests, it's best if they run against a clean copy of the database—one built from scratch and populated with appropriate initial data.

If you don't start with a clean database, you tend to end up with data-dependent tests that fail sporadically due to issues with the data. For example, perhaps your integration tests insert a record into a customer table using a known customer ID for the sake of testing various aspects of the data access layer. If you don't remove this data after you've done your tests, you'll get a failure the next time you run the tests as they try to insert the same customer with the same ID. This issue wouldn't occur in production and yet it's causing problems during testing.

So it's a good idea to include in your build process a task that will create the database, initialize it with test data, and drop it (see figure 4.7). There may even be cases when you want to do this process several

**Figure 4.7   The process for running integrations tests against a known set of data**

times within a single test run. For example, if you don't want to use the same test data across the whole suite of integration tests, you may drop, re-create, and populate the database for each functional area of the application. Incidentally, dropping and re-creating a testing database is one reason why integration tests can take much, much longer to execute than unit tests.

There are a number of ways to accomplish this sequence of events. The most obvious way is to do it yourself. Creating, populating, and dropping a database are all functions that can be done through SQL queries, and most database applications provide a command-line interface for executing queries against it. With this method, the task in your automated build simply needs to execute a series of command-line calls.

This approach may be adequate for small applications, but it can become cumbersome very quickly. You must manage every aspect of the process, from the data definition language (DDL) scripts, to the data loading scripts, to the commands that execute them.

Luckily, there are other options that make this easier, though in our opinion, still not entirely friction free.

If you use an object-relational mapper tool (described in chapter 10), it may offer the ability to autogenerate your schema, dropping the existing database automatically. That still leaves you with the task of populating the database if that's something you need to do.

A number of third-party applications and frameworks are available that can help you manage your database. Some are geared toward the process of promoting your application between environments, but they can be easily adapted to an automated build process. Examples of products in this area include

- Microsoft Visual Studio Team System for Database Professionals
- Red Gate's SQL Toolkit
- Ruby on Rails Migrations
- NDbUnit (a library for putting a database into a known state)

Once your application has an existing version of its database in a production environment, the requirements for how you manage changes to that database's structure and content change.

### 4.9.2    *Dealing with an existing database*

Because ours is a brownfield application, there's a good chance a database already exists in production. In that case, you no longer have the luxury of being able to deploy the database from scratch. Now you have a versioning issue in database form; how do you manage all the changes made to the database after it's been rolled out?

Again, you could manage changes yourself, keeping track of modifications to the schema and creating appropriate ALTER TABLE scripts in your VCS. But you almost certainly will run into problems when you make a change to the database, and then need to propagate that change to the other developers—not an impossible task, but certainly unpalatable.

> ### Challenge your assumptions: Migrations for database management
>
> Just because the application is written in .NET doesn't mean you can't look to other languages for help. After all, only the application itself is deployed, not your CI process.
>
> Ruby on Rails Migrations allows you to more effectively manage changes to your database schema among your team and makes it easier to roll out these changes to the various environments. And if the thought of learning a new language is off-putting for the sake of database management, consider how much time it takes to version your SQL scripts.

Third-party vendors can come to the rescue here as well, offering tools for comparing one database schema to the next, generating appropriate scripts, and even executing them.

Databases offer some unique challenges to testing. The volatile nature of business data doesn't lend itself to the consistency required for automated testing. Be sure you give your database testing strategy some serious consideration because it's easier to add pain to your process than remove it.

## 4.10  Summary

Phew! Things are getting hectic all of a sudden. We've covered a lot of ground this chapter and we finally started looking at some actual code.

As usual, we started off examining some pain points of working on a project that doesn't have any automated tests. From there we looked at how automated tests can vastly improve the confidence everyone feels in the codebase. By writing tests to expose bugs before we fix them, for example, we close the feedback loop between the time a bug is written and the time it's discovered.

We talked quite a bit about unit tests, differentiating between state-based tests and interaction-based tests. The latter often require the use of mock or fake objects, but they often require less configuration in order to focus on the specific unit being tested. We also recommended separating your unit tests from your integration tests to avoid potential problems in the future.

After that, we examined any existing test projects that you may have had in your project and what to do with any invalid tests in them (refactor them, delete them, or ignore them). Then it was on to the automated build process and how to incorporate the test project into it.

For those applications with no existing test projects, we talked about how to create one and integrate it into the build process, which is essentially the same process as for existing test projects.

Then it was on to writing new tests. Again, it isn't necessary to write tests on existing code until you're addressing a bug or adding a feature that involves the code. At that time, you should write the test assuming the code does what you *want* it to do rather than verify that it acts like it currently does.

We talked briefly about unit tests for new code before moving on to integration tests with respect to brownfield applications. Then it was on to user interface testing before we closed with some thoughts about how to manage the database during your test process.

We now have a solid foundation. Our version control system is in place and the continuous integration process is humming along. Now that we've added a test project for unit and integration tests (and possibly user interface tests) and we have a process in place for writing tests going forward, our confidence is probably higher than it ever has been for our lowly brownfield application. And we haven't even started writing any real code for it yet.

In the next chapter, it will be time to analyze the codebase to see if we can figure out which areas are in need of the most work. After that, we'll talk about how to manage the defect-tracking process, and then it'll be time to dive into the code!

# Software metrics
# and code analysis

5

---

**This chapter covers**

- Defining software metrics and code analysis
- Looking at common metrics
- Automating the generation of metrics

---

It's almost time to start ripping apart the code—and you probably could start doing that right now. With source control, continuous integration (CI), and automated tests in place, there's nothing stopping you from skipping ahead to part 2—except perhaps curiosity and a desire to do things correctly. You still have that desire, right?

But we encourage you to be patient just a little while longer. This chapter's topic will be interesting if only because it may show you a little too much about yourself. Specifically, we'll see if you have any latent obsessive-compulsive characteristics when it comes to monitoring code statistics for your application.

We'll forego our traditional "Pain points" section for this chapter because metrics don't address any pain points directly. Rather, they can provide you with a way of identifying pain points caused by other problems.

By the end of this chapter, you should have an idea not only of what metrics can show you, but how you can make effective use of them in your brownfield application. We'll start with what software metrics are and why we need them, which should help put them in perspective.

## 5.1 What are software metrics and code analysis?

It's often forgotten that our industry is a branch of computer science, and like all good sciences, results should be measured. Software metrics are some of those measures. They include measures like the number of lines of code, the number of classes, or the depth of inheritance.

With these metrics, you can perform analysis on your code. The two types of code analysis are *static* and *dynamic*. Let's define each one.

### 5.1.1 Static code analysis

Static code analysis is performed on code without executing it. These metrics can be gleaned by looking at the code (or, more likely, parsing it with a tool). Common examples are lines of code, class coupling, and cyclomatic complexity. Each of these examples will be covered, as well as some others, later in the chapter.

As you well know, code doesn't sit idle. The fact that it executes offers another dimension of analysis that you need to consider: dynamic code analysis.

### 5.1.2 Dynamic code analysis

As you can probably guess, dynamic code analysis is performed while the code is executing. An example of dynamic analysis is code coverage. Code coverage is a measure of which pieces of code were exercised during an execution run against the application.

Other common examples are analyzing memory usage and checking for memory leaks. Often, these can't be done unless the code is executing.

Later we'll talk about some metrics of interest, but first let's put code analysis in context.

### 5.1.3 Why do you need code metrics?

By and large, the answer to this question is, you *don't*. Or at least, you *may not*.

Your project could very well survive without code metrics. In our opinion, they aren't quite as critical as, say, automated tests. For a good many projects, particularly small- to medium-sized ones, a comprehensive suite of tests may suffice if you have the right team in place.

But they provide a lot of value, particularly for brownfield applications. Often when you start on a brownfield project, the sheer size of it can be overwhelming. At this point in the book, you've done a lot of work in the ecosystem. You've added a CI process and integrated automated tests into the build.

But now you're nearing the point where you'll start diving into the code. There's a monolithic thing staring us in the face and the question becomes, where do you start?

As this is a brownfield book, everyone knows by now that the code is in need of some love and you probably have a sense of the magnitude of the task ahead. But should you start by tearing apart dependencies? Or should you start by tackling the monstrous `if` statements in your validation logic? Maybe you should start by figuring out why users are reporting so many bugs in the accounting module?

Code metrics can help you answer these types of questions. By analyzing the statistics, you can see which classes have the highest coupling, for example, and perhaps implement some form of dependency injection (see chapter 9) to reduce it.

You're closing in on part 2 of this book, where you'll start learning techniques for working with the code. Code metrics can help us determine which techniques to apply and where to apply them.

Over time, metrics can also help you spot trends in your code. Downward trends are usually the ones you're most interested in, but upward trends are often noteworthy as well.

You can also use defect reports for code analysis. There will be more talk of defects in the next chapter, but the basic idea is that you relate each defect to a section, or module, of the application. Then you can spot trends, such as whether a certain module has an abnormally high number of defects, and examine them as potential locations for refactoring.

Finally, you could even use static code analysis to enforce architecture constraints. For example, you typically don't want your UI layer to talk directly to the data access layer. With a static analysis tool, you could set up your automated build to break if such a dependency is created. It's arguable whether the cost of setting this up in an automated build is worth the benefit, but it's an option if you're starting out on a brownfield project with an inexperienced development team.

Knowing the different types of analysis and some of the situations that they're useful for, you can begin to look at some of the specific metrics that are commonly used.

## 5.2    Some metrics of interest

As you can imagine, there is a large number of software metrics, some more useful than others. Some are obvious (such as number of lines of code, or LOC) while others may require some investigation (such as the vaguely named Maintainability Index). In this section, we'll briefly discuss some common ones.

This section is hardly meant to be an exhaustive analysis of the various code metrics available. But we'll give you a good baseline for when you start refactoring code in part 2 and provide a nice background for why you'll be making certain changes.

Let's start with what we call the Three CC's: code coverage, cyclomatic complexity, and class coupling.

### 5.2.1    Code coverage

Coverage is one of the most common code statistics you'll encounter because it's intuitive to grasp both the concept and its benefits. The idea is that you start your

**Figure 5.1   Code coverage utilities are useful when attached to your automated test process. Here, the code coverage tool monitors the test utility to see how much of your application code is exercised by the tests.**

application and the code coverage tool will monitor all code that's executed during the session. Afterward, it will produce a report on which code was executed (or *covered*) and, more importantly, which code wasn't.

Code coverage has limited use for any reasonably sized application. At least, neither of us would want the task of thoroughly exercising each and every function of an application, including edge cases, during a single manually driven session.

The real power of code coverage comes when you combine it with unit and/or integration tests. In this scenario, you don't hook the code coverage tool up to the application. Instead, you wire it up to the automated test harness you're using to exercise your tests. When done this way, the code coverage tool doesn't monitor the application; it monitors the automated test utility. This utility runs the tests in your application, which in turn execute your application code.

At the end of the test run, the code coverage tool produces a report indicating which areas of the application code were exercised by the tests and, again, which areas weren't executed at all. Figure 5.1 shows the connections between the tools and the assemblies.

With this setup, you get a useful metric that tells you what percentage of the code is covered by unit tests. More importantly, you can get an actionable report that tells you specifically which areas of your code have *not* been exercised by your unit tests.

Code coverage is typically displayed as a percentage. For example, 60 percent coverage means that 60 percent of your application code is being executed by your automated tests. As a dynamic code analysis, it can be applied at different levels; application, class, and method are the most common.

Simply executing and exercising aspects of your code can provide confidence in the correctness of the code. If you're exercising your code through the execution of automated tests, the analysis assumes that your tests are providing correct and positive confirmation (see chapter 4 for more on that). What this analysis doesn't provide you with is insight into the structure of your code and its maintainability, changeability, and replaceability. For this let's look at the other CC's.

### 5.2.2   *Cyclomatic complexity*

Cyclomatic complexity is, as its name implies, a measure of complexity. Specifically it checks for how complex an application is internally. It's determined by measuring the number of paths, or cycles, through your code. if statements, for loops, switch statements (`select` in VB), and conditional checks (`and`, `or`, and `not`) all increase the cyclomatic complexity of an application.

For example, the method in listing 5.1 has a cyclomatic complexity of 3.

**Listing 5.1   Method with a cyclomatic complexity of 3**

```
function void Process( Job job )
{
    switch ( job.status )
    {
        case ( JOB_STATUS.NEW ):
            ProcessNewJob( job );
            break;
        case ( Job_STATUS.CANCELLED ):
            CancelJob( job );
            break;
        default:
            UpdateJob( job );
            break;
    }
}
```

**❶ Possible execution paths**

In this method, each `case` statement ❶, along with the default path, represents a possible path through the code.

Cyclomatic complexity is somewhat related to code coverage in that it tells you how much work you'll need to do to fully cover your code. If you have a high cyclomatic complexity, there are a large number of possible execution paths through your code, which means that much more testing is required to cover them all. On top of the increased difficulty when testing, methods and classes with higher cyclomatic complexities are inherently more difficult for a person to understand. Although not always a direct corollary, high and concentrated cyclomatic complexities decrease the readability and maintainability of the codebase.

### Are you sure it's three?

Depending on the tool you use, it may show a cyclomatic complexity of 4 for listing 5.1. That's because some include the "default" branch. This is the case where you don't go through the `switch` statement at all. If that sounds esoteric to you, it does to us too.

The real answer to this question is, it doesn't matter what the answer is. The important thing is that you measure your statistics consistently and set appropriate thresholds to meet.

On their own, numbers don't have any meaning. It's only when they are taken in context that they tell a meaningful story. For example, a cyclomatic complexity of 7 doesn't necessarily mean you have a problem. But if every other method is hovering around 3 or 4, that 7 may need to be looked at.

As with any statistical measure, if you don't set the proper context you won't get a clear picture.

Note that removing cyclomatic complexity isn't necessarily your end goal. Many business rules are complicated, plain and simple. If there are 15 possible ways to calculate someone's paycheck, you aren't going to remove the complexity of this process in your application. The most you can hope for is to move the code around until it's more manageable and easier to maintain.

Although cyclomatic complexity can indicate code that will be difficult to maintain, maintenance usually imposes a need to change on the codebase. The next CC addresses the ability for a codebase to absorb change with minimal impact.

### 5.2.3 *Class coupling*

Class coupling is another common metric. It describes how tightly coupled your classes are to each other. In other words, how dependent are your classes on other classes?

There are different levels of coupling, but let's look at two types: afferent coupling and efferent coupling. Like the words used to describe them, there isn't much difference between them. From the perspective of a given class, afferent coupling asks this question: how many classes depend on me? Efferent coupling asks the reverse question: upon how many classes do I depend? Figure 5.2 shows the difference.

Usually, you want your classes to be loosely coupled. For example, your classes shouldn't depend on concrete implementations of other classes. You should shoot for a low value for your coupling statistics.

Higher coupling usually indicates a codebase that will be resistant to change. It's not that you won't be able to change that codebase, but the change you try to make will usually require significant ancillary changes. This outcome is also known as the ripple effect. It's this ripple effect through the code that you want to minimize for the sake of maintainability. You've worked on a change to a system where you believe the impact will be minimal, but once we're set into it, the tentacles of change start to reach further and further. We've all been there. The ripple effect is one of those code problems that can cause significant maintenance nightmares and, ultimately, high costs. Unfortunately, this effect happens far too often in brownfield projects.

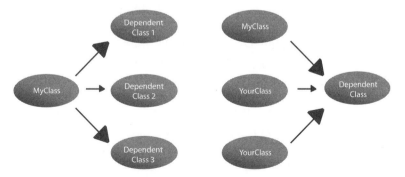

**Figure 5.2  Efferent coupling (left) tells you how many classes your class depends on. Afferent coupling (right) shows how many classes depend on your class.**

In part 2, and especially chapter 9, we'll discuss specific methods of reducing class coupling. Hint: Your classes should rely on interfaces more than they should concrete classes.

Once you've determined the likeliness of these ripples occurring when changes are attempted in your code, you need to know why that is. One of the reasons can be a lack of cohesion in the classes.

### 5.2.4   *Cohesion*

Somewhat related to coupling is cohesion. If a class is highly cohesive, its functions and responsibilities are closely related. If the class's responsibilities are more disparate, it's said to have low cohesion.

Experience has shown that an application that has a large number of low-cohesion classes often is harder to maintain than one with more cohesion. Low cohesion leads to cases where seemingly small changes must touch a lot of classes, leading to a more fragile environment. In addition, classes that aren't cohesive tend to be harder to understand, and you end up spending a lot of time navigating through various classes trying to find the code that's relevant to the task you're working on.

Despite efforts to quantify it, cohesion is more subjective than other metrics. The reason is that *closely related* can mean different things to different people. For example, is it more cohesive to group functions by horizontal layers (data access, business logic, UI) or by vertical slice (all functions related to adding a customer, all functions related to searching for orders, etc.)?

Also, how finely grained do you make your classes? A single class called DataAccess isn't going to win any cohesion awards, but on the other end of the spectrum, should you have a class for each possible database call?

Despite this ambiguity, there have been attempts to measure cohesion, or at least guide you toward better cohesion. Figure 5.3 shows a dependency matrix from the software tool NDepend (described later) which can be a useful indicator. There are also a few academic formulas designed to help assess cohesion, but in our experience, cohesion tends to increase naturally as you tackle other, more measurable metrics and introduce better coding practices in general.

Examples of classes with low cohesion are the ubiquitous classes called Utility, StringFunctions, Global, or something similar. These classes typically contain numerous useful little utility functions that can be used application-wide. With the release of extension methods in .NET 3.5, these classes have become that much more prevalent.

Web services are often weakly cohesive as well. Often, methods are grouped together into a single web service for the sake of convenience to reduce the overhead of having to create references to multiple services.

The argument for high cohesion isn't to say that you should throw away your HelperMethods classes or break out your web services into individual classes. Like with most other metrics, it's impractical to eliminate low cohesion entirely. You can only learn to recognize when it's causing a problem in your application.

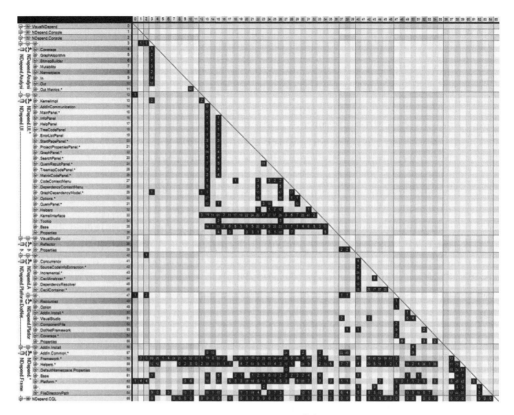

**Figure 5.3  A dependency matrix (shown here from NDepend[1]) can help assess cohesion. Squares around the diagonal suggest higher cohesion.**

As has been mentioned before, there isn't one metric that provides all the answers. With cohesion, there's a possibility that some of the measures can be somewhat more subjectively applied. As you'll see in the discussion of the next metric, even the terms themselves become more subjective.

### 5.2.5  *Distance from main sequence*

Part of the appeal of the distance from main sequence metric is that you get to use terms like *zone of pain* and *zone of uselessness* in conversation. In fact, it's a combination of two other metrics: abstractness and instability.

Abstractness and instability should be intuitive. Abstractness (abbreviated *A*) measures how many of your internal types are abstract (or interfaces) compared with the total number of types. It ranges between an assembly with no abstract classes or interfaces (A = 0) and one where there are no concrete classes (A = 1).

Instability is a comparison of efferent coupling (the number of types on which the assembly depends) to the total coupling. The following formula demonstrates this

---

[1]  www.ndepend.com

concept in mathematical terms (*Ce* stands for efferent coupling, and *Ca* stands for afferent coupling):

$$I= \frac{Ce}{(Ce + Ca)}$$

In less theoretical terms, instability is just a measure of how stable the assembly is, as you'd expect from the name.

From the formula, you can see that a high efferent coupling will increase an assembly's instability. Intuitively, if your assembly depends on a lot of other assemblies, it means you may have to alter it if any of those dependent assemblies change. Conversely, a high afferent coupling means a lot of assemblies depend on this one, so you're less likely to change it and break those dependencies. Your assembly is more stable in the sense that if it's refactored, a lot of code will be affected. Instability is also measured on a range of 0 (stable) to 1 (instable).

A theoretically ideal assembly will have its abstractness and instability total to 1. The assembly is said to have a good balance between abstractness and instability in this case. When A + I = 1, this is known as the *main sequence.*

With this background behind us, the distance from the main sequence (abbreviated *D*) is just what it sounds like: how far is your assembly from this idealized main sequence?

This concept is easiest to see with a graph, shown in figure 5.4.

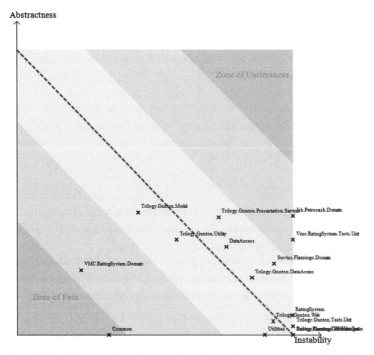

**Figure 5.4   A graph of the distance from the main sequence taken from NDepend. Notice the Common assembly nestled in the Zone of Pain indicating that it contains a high number of concrete assemblies and that many assemblies depend on it.**

Notice the two labeled areas. The Zone of Uselessness indicates that your assembly is abstract and instable. This means there are a lot of abstract classes or interfaces that are highly dependent on external types, which is, as you would expect, pretty useless.

At the other end of the spectrum, you have classes that are concrete and have a lot of other assemblies relying on them. There are many types that depend on your classes, but your classes are concrete and, therefore, not very extensible. Hence, the Zone of Pain.

None of us wants the legacy of their code to be useless or painful to work with. Although the exact formula and the exact ratio number is calculable for this metric, we suggest that it be used as a delta metric. We don't care so much about the exact value of the metric, but how it changes over time along with code changes. If during one month of development effort you see that a specific module has moved closer to the zone of pain, it should be an indication that a problem may be lurking.

Continuing with our trend to quantifiable, but subjective metrics, let's take a look at an identifier that the development community is perhaps far too enamored with. The shocker is that it's based on one of the pillars of object-oriented programming.

## 5.2.6   *Depth of inheritance*

This metric shows how many levels, or how deep, a particular class goes in its inheritance hierarchy. It's a measure of how many base classes a particular class has. This metric is often referred to as a depth of inheritance tree (DIT).

Classes with a high depth of inheritance are generally more complex and harder to maintain than those with a lower depth. The reason is that as you increase the depth, you add more and more methods and properties to the class. But by the same token, it also means inherited methods will likely be reused more often by derived classes.

Use caution when basing decisions on this metric. More than the other metrics that have been mentioned, this metric isn't meant for hard rules such as "No class will have a DIT higher than 5," for example. Inheriting from `System.Web.UI.UserControl`, for instance, automatically means you have a DIT of 4.

Instead, this metric should be used to flag *potential* trouble spots. If a class has a DIT of 7, it should certainly be examined closely for a possible refactoring. But if upon close inspection you can justify the hierarchy, and if a better solution isn't available, you should feel no guilt in leaving it as is.

Now that you've learned about a number of individual metrics, let's take a look at how they can be used in combination.

## 5.2.7   *Maintainability Index*

This metric has an intuitive and seductive name—*intuitive* in that it's a measure of how maintainable the code is—and *seductive* in that there's some quantifiable way to measure what's inherently a qualitative metric.

The formula for the Maintainability Index looks like this:

$$MI = 171 - (5.2 \times 1n(HV)) - (0.23 \times CycCom) - (16.2 \times 1n(LOC))$$

In this equation, *HV* is the Halstead Volume (a measure of the code's complexity weighted toward computational complexity), *CycCom* is the cyclomatic complexity of the code, and *LOC* is the number of lines of code. An optional component has been omitted that's based on the number of comments in the code.

---

**Lines of code antipattern**

One metric that's often brought up is the number of lines of code in an assembly, a class, or the application as a whole.

This metric is an easy one to comprehend. You simply count the number of lines of code (LOC). Of course, it's easy to inflate your physical LOC count artificially so typically, when talking about LOC, reference is being made to *logical* lines—the number of lines of code as the compiler sees it.

We're calling it out here because it's rarely of any use within a brownfield project. It's mostly a throwback to the 1980s when programmers were paid by the LOC. These days, the number of lines of code one has written is typically used only in a sort of perverse version of "pissing for distance" when egos are running hot. These days, it has some value as a means of comparing similar projects, but for our purposes, LOC isn't a metric that produces anything actionable.

The simple fact is that there are many ways to code almost every piece of code. If one method of solving a problem has more LOC than another, it doesn't explicitly mean that the code with the large LOC count is better. Many other factors, such as readability, maintainability, and correctness, play a much more important role than the number of LOC.

In today's world of productivity utilities, code-generation tools, and autoformatting templates, LOC isn't an informative indicator of anything other than possibly how much typing you've done. It's mentioned because it's often brought up by people bent on assigning more value to it than is necessary.

---

The complicated and seemingly random nature of this formula should raise some concerns as to its usefulness, especially when determining something as subjective as how maintainable an application is. Indeed, the data that was used to determine this formula predates .NET by a half decade or more.

If the statistical package you're using includes this metric (like Visual Studio Code Metrics), it may be of academic interest. Its day-to-day usefulness is limited, which brings us to our next topic: becoming a slave to the statistics.

## 5.3  *Becoming a slave to statistics*

It's easy to get wrapped up in code metrics. For example, there are many opinions on what constitutes sufficient code coverage. Some say you should strive for 100 percent code coverage. Others say that's not only an inefficient goal, but it's an impossible one in most cases. They would suggest that coverage of 75 percent may be more adequate and appropriate for your needs.

Regardless, once you wire code metrics into your build process, you may be surprised at the effect it has on you and some of your team members. Once you have a baseline level of statistics, developers may become draconian in maintaining it.

The extreme version of this is when the development team is so concerned with the statistics that they act with them specifically in mind, regardless of whether it's for the good of the project.

For example, assume you've implemented your automated build so that it fails when your code coverage goes below a certain level, say 80 percent. Let's also say your code currently sits at 81 percent coverage.

One day, during a massive refactoring, you discover that there's a whole section of code that's no longer needed. The problem is that this code is 100 percent covered by unit tests. And the codebase is small enough so that when you remove this code, the overall code coverage will drop to 79 percent, thus failing the build.

You can handle this situation in one of three ways:

- Roll back your changes so that the useless code remains but the code coverage remains above 80 percent.
- Retrofit some tests on existing code until the code coverage returns to 80 percent.
- Lower the code coverage limit.

If you choose either of the first two options, you may be taking your love of statistics too far. The reason for having a code coverage limit in place is to discourage any *new* code being checked in without corresponding tests. Remember from chapter 4 that our recommendation was to write tests on new or changed code only. But in this situation, that hasn't happened. From an overall maintainability standpoint, you're doing a good thing by removing unnecessary code. The fact that code coverage has gone down is a valid consequence of this.

The correct thing to do is to choose the third option: lower the code coverage limit so that the build doesn't fail. This way, you can still check in your changes but you don't need to focus on a superfluous task, like adding unit tests specifically to maintain code coverage. Yes, you've lowered your code coverage limit, but you've maintained the underlying intent of the metric.

This example underscores a larger point: avoid having your automated build process be dependent on any particular statistic, whether it's code coverage, class coupling, or some other statistic. Unless you're using a metric to enforce an aspect of your architecture, you shouldn't have the build fail when a statistic drops to a certain level.

One reason for this has already been mentioned: there may be valid reasons for a drop in the metric. But more fundamentally, the practice keeps developers too focused on code metrics when they should be concentrating on the code.

## Tales from the trenches: Tracer bullets

When first joining a large brownfield project, we had a number of options to choose from to get ourselves comfortable with the codebase and the issues we may have inherited with it. One of the techniques we could've used was to wade through the code in the development environment, but we would've missed large portions of both the codebase and the architecture. Instead, we took our first look at the code through the eyes of metrics.

After running a code metrics tool (in this case, NDepend) against the codebase, we had a much better idea of the areas we should look into further. These were portions of the application that were flagged as being highly coupled and possibly having excess complexity. Once we'd seen the general groupings of issues, we had a rough idea of where in the application possible problems *could* crop up. Note that we said *could*. In effect, what we'd done by gathering metrics on the codebase was to start firing tracer bullets.

For those unfamiliar with the term, *tracer bullets* are ammunition rounds that have been modified to include a pyrotechnic component that lights when the round is fired, making it easy to see in flight. By reviewing the trajectory of the round, shooters can adjust their aim to be more accurate.

Using code metrics as tracer bullets allows us to get a rough idea of where issues exist in the codebase. We can use the information we gather as a tool to help direct our changes so that development effort can be properly focused to achieve the project's end goals (quality, maintainability, replaceability, reversibility). The primary goal of tracer rounds, and metrics, isn't to inflict direct hits. Instead, we use them to refine our efforts.

In our project, we combined the metrics we gathered with current and past information from our defect-tracking system (see chapter 6) to refine our knowledge of the issues that the project was facing. Based on that combined information, we were able to refine the development efforts. The tracers we fired pointed us toward a quality and stability issue in the system.

Once we'd performed this ritual a couple of times in the project, we slightly shifted the focus of what we were gleaning from the metric reports. Instead of looking for specific numbers on certain metrics, we shifted to reviewing the delta in each metric that we felt was important to achieving our goals. For example, we felt that coupling was causing significant code stability issues on the project. Instead of saying that we wanted to achieve an efferent coupling value of, say, 2 in a certain module, we looked at the change from one salvo of tracer bullets to the next. Because we were actively working to improve coupling, we expected to see it lowering with each iteration. If we noted that the value didn't change or had increased, we immediately flagged the metric for investigation.

For us, using metrics as a guide and a delta measurement proved to be an effective way to gain a strong understanding of the direction that our coding efforts needed to take. By themselves, the metrics didn't indicate this. The true value came from combining metrics, their deltas over time, defect entry–based information, and the knowledge of the end goal we were trying to achieve.

In short, software metrics are there for guidance, not process. It's useful to monitor them at regular intervals and make decisions and adjustments based on them, but they shouldn't be part of your day-to-day activities. We'll expand on this idea later in this chapter after you've learned how to provide easy access to the analysis metrics through integration with our build process.

## 5.4 Implementing statistical analysis

Now that you've been warned not to focus on statistics, the natural progression is to outline how to automate their generation.

Here comes the bad news: unlike most of the tools covered so far, the most common tools used to perform statistical analysis on your code aren't free. But for the optimists in the crowd who need a silver lining, with a commercial product comes technical support, should you need it. And there still exists the stigma in many organizations that if the tool is free, it has no place on the company servers.

For code coverage, the de facto standard for .NET applications is NCover, which only recently became a commercial product. The older, free version is still readily available, though it predates .NET 3.5 and doesn't work completely with the new features. Visual Studio Team System also includes a code coverage utility, but it isn't as easily integrated into an automated build as NCover is.

For the rest of the code metrics, you could use the Code Metrics feature in either Visual Studio Team Developer or Team Suite. At present, both calculate five metrics: Maintainability Index, Cyclomatic Complexity, Depth of Inheritance, Class Coupling, and Lines of Code. At the time of this writing, Code Metrics is available only for Visual Studio 2008.

Alternatively, NDepend will provide the same statistics plus several dozen more,[2] and it's available for earlier versions of Visual Studio. NDepend also provides more reporting capabilities to help you zero in on trouble spots in your code. Like NCover, NDepend is a commercial product requiring purchased licenses.

Both NDepend and NCover are easily incorporated into an automated build and your CI process. Both come with tasks that can be used with NAnt or MSBuild, and there are plenty of examples of how to weave the output from each of them into popular CI products, like the open source CruiseControl.NET or JetBrains' TeamCity.

### 5.4.1 Automating code coverage

As mentioned earlier, code coverage is useful primarily as a mechanism for evaluating how well your code is covered by tests. The implicit dependency here is that both your application and the test project(s) should be compiled. Therefore, the process that needs automation consists of these steps:

1  Compile the application.
2  Compile the tests.
3  Execute the code coverage application against the unit-testing utility, passing in the test assembly as an argument.

---

[2]  www.ndepend.com/metrics.aspx

If you've made it this far in the book, steps 1 and 2 should already be done in your automated build, leaving only automation of the code coverage application. Any code coverage utility worth its salt will have a command-line interface, so automation is simply a matter of executing it with the appropriate parameters.

Notice that two applications are being executed in step 3. Code coverage utilities usually involve connecting to a running application so they can monitor the methods being covered. Recall from chapter 4, you connect up to the unit-testing application to execute our unit and integration tests while the code coverage utility watches and logs.

Listing 5.2 shows a sample NAnt target that will execute NCover on a test assembly.

> **Listing 5.2   Sample NAnt target executing NCover for code coverage**

```
<target name="coverage" depends="compile test.compile">
    <exec program="${path.to.ncover.console.exe}">
      <arg value="//w &quot;${path.to.build.folder}&quot;" />
      <arg value="//x &quot;${path.to.output.file}" />
      <arg value="&quot;${path.to.nunit.console}&quot;" />
      <arg value="${name.of.test.assembly}
/xml:${path.to.test.results.file}" />
    </exec>
</target>
```

Notice that a dependency has been added on the compile and test.compile targets to ensure that the application code and the test project are compiled before executing NCover.

### Code coverage: Two processes for the price of one?

As you can see from the sample target in listing 5.2, you end up with two output files: one with the test results and one with the code coverage results. This is because you actually are executing your tests during this task.

You don't technically need to execute your tests in a separate task if you're running the code coverage task. For this reason, many teams will substitute an automated code coverage task for their testing task, essentially performing both actions in the CI process. The CI server will compile the code, test it, and generate code coverage stats on every check-in.

Although there's nothing conceptually wrong with this approach, be aware of some downsides. First, there's overhead to generating code coverage statistics. When there are a lot of tests, this overhead could be significant enough to cause friction in the form of a longer-running automated build script. Remember that the main build script should run as fast as possible to encourage team members to run it often. If it takes too long to run, you may find developers looking for workarounds.

For these reasons, we recommend executing the code coverage task separately from the build script's default task. It should be run at regular intervals, perhaps as a separate scheduled task in your build file that executes biweekly or even monthly, but we don't feel there's enough benefit to the metric to warrant the extra overhead of having it execute on every check-in.

Also note that NCover is being connected to the NUnit console application. That way, when this task is executed NCover will launch the NUnit console application, which will execute all the tests in the specified assembly. The test results will be stored in the file specified by the `${path.to.test.results.file}` variable (which is set elsewhere in the build file).

Now let's see how we can automate other metrics.

### 5.4.2 Automating other metrics

Automating the generation of code metrics is similar to generating code coverage statistics: you execute an application. The only difference is the application you execute and the arguments you pass.

The following snippet is an NAnt task that will execute code analysis using NDepend:

```
<target name="code-metrics" depends="compile">
    <exec program="${path.to.ndepend.console.exe}">
      <arg value="${path.to.ndepend.project.xml.file}" />
    </exec>
</target>
```

Unlike the code coverage task, this one depends only on the `compile` target, which means the application must be compiled before the task can be executed. Doing so ensures that the metrics run against the current version of the code on the machine. Also note that NDepend includes a custom `<ndepend>` NAnt task that can be used as an alternative to `<exec>`.

---

**Why separate code coverage?**

Some of you may be asking why we're singling out code coverage for special attention.

Conceptually, there's no reason why code coverage should be treated any differently than other metrics. One could make an argument that it's a more useful metric (or at least an easier one to understand), but it's just another statistic.

The reason is tool availability. At the time of this writing, NCover is the standard for code coverage for all intents and purposes. Until recently, it was a free tool, which helped make it somewhat ubiquitous. That, and the intuitive nature of code coverage, has pushed code coverage to a level of heightened awareness.

By contrast, utilities that generate other metrics, such as NDepend, aren't as prevalent. Whether it's due to the fact that these tools have a cost associated or whether the underlying statistics aren't as readily actionable as code coverage, the fact remains that tools are commonly used for code coverage, but not so much for other metrics.

---

This task may seem on the sparse side considering the work to be performed. For example, there isn't even an argument for the output file. The reason is the implementation details are hidden in the argument, the NDepend project file. This file contains details of the metrics you'd like measured, the output XML file, and any Code Query Language (CQL) statements to be executed. CQL is an NDepend-specific querying language that allows you to raise warnings if metrics don't meet a certain standard. For example, you could fail the build if, say, your afferent coupling was higher than 20.

A full description of the NDepend project file is outside of the scope of this book. Our goal is to show how you could automate such a tool in your build file. As you can see, it's as simple as executing an application.

But before you start integrating code metrics into your CI process, we have some opinions on the topic that you should hear.

### 5.4.3   *Metrics with CI*

Now that you've briefly read about incorporating code coverage into your CI process and we've touched on our opinion about this topic, let's expand on that concept with this question: how do you integrate code metrics into your CI process?

The answer is, you don't.

You don't generate code metrics on every check-in the same way you compile and test your code. Generating statistics can be time consuming, and the incremental value of doing it on every check-in is minimal. And as mentioned in section 5.3, you risk encouraging bad habits in yourself and your development team.

Instead, consider having a separate (but still automated) process specifically for analyzing your codebase. It could be scheduled to run once a week or twice a month or some other interval or only through manual triggering, but make sure it's a large enough one that you can see meaningful changes from one run to the next.

The task will be closely related to your CI process. For example, the NAnt targets you use to generate statistics will likely sit alongside the targets that compile and test the applications. But they won't execute as part of the regular check-in process. Rather, you can create a separate task that executes these targets on a schedule rather than on a check-in trigger.

When you do this, you can start monitoring trends in your application. For example, if your code coverage increases at a steady pace, then starts slowing (or even dropping), that's a sign of something that needs attention.

We'll provide a more in-depth discussion on trending in the next chapter when we're looking at defects.

In the beginning, you may want to monitor the metrics more often, if only for the psychological effect you'll achieve in seeing the numbers improve early in the project. As the code progresses, the improvements will become more marginal and you'll get into a rhythm that increases your stats naturally. It's still a good idea to monitor them on occasion, just to make sure you're still on track. But at that point, you're looking more for discrepancies. Checking your metrics should be a matter of comparing them to the trend to see if they're in line. If so, move on. If not, do your investigative work to see if corrective action is necessary.

Before closing, and since there's space available, this is a good spot for a quick discussion of other tasks that could be automated in your build process.

## 5.5  *Other tasks for automation*

Code metrics aren't the only things that can be automated. As you can probably tell from our NCover and NDepend examples, you can automate any application, provided it can run unattended.

Just as with code metrics and tests, you'll need to decide not only whether the task is important enough to automate, but also whether it should be incorporated into your CI process. Start with the assumption that any task other than automated unit tests should be excluded from your CI process unless you're feeling friction because of its omission.

Here's a list of processes that could be automated (along with suggested applications for performing the operation):

- Generating documentation from XML comments (Sandcastle or Docu)
- Enforcing coding standards (FxCop or StyleCop)
- Check for duplication in your code (Simian – Similarity Analyser)
- Code generation (CodeSmith or MyGeneration)
- Data migrations, test database creation (SQL Data Compare/SQL Packager, SQL scripts)

You should be on the lookout for tasks that can be automated, even if it's simply executing a batch file to copy files from one place to another. The benefits of reducing the possibility of errors and keeping yourself focused on useful tasks should be readily apparent.

Like with CI in chapter 3, our goal with this brief section was twofold: to give you some ideas as to what to automate but also to kick-start your thought process. Is there anything you have to do manually and by rote to build your application? In many brownfield applications, the answer is yes. Often regular tasks creep into the build process without us realizing it. At one point, maybe you decided to generate documentation from the code. Then you did it again, then again and again until it became part of the regular process. Surely someone thought "Why am I doing this?" but has anyone thought, "Why aren't we automating this?"

## 5.6  *Summary*

The honeymoon is over. We spent the better part of chapter 1 convincing you that working on a brownfield application is an exciting endeavor. Working through the next chapters, you've made some tremendous headway by installing a CI process, automating your tests, and setting a foundation for future development.

But now you've been hit with a dose of reality. In this chapter, you took your first hard look at the state the application is in. You examined some code metrics, such as code coverage, class coupling, and cyclomatic complexity, and learned how to automate them.

When you take your first look at the statistics for the software metrics you've entered, the initial numbers might be overwhelming. And let's face it: there's no encouraging way to say "We're neck deep in the zone of pain."

Like the tortoise, slow and steady wins the race. You read about using the reports to zero in on problem areas and to identify refactoring points that will give you the most bang for your buck. Once they've been singled out, all that's left is how to deal with them. That's where part 2 comes in.

In part 2, we'll talk extensively on various techniques that will make the software more maintainable. Coupled with the tests you're writing for all new code, you'll find that the numbers become more palatable on their own without requiring a directed effort to, say, reduce coupling.

There's one final chapter before we dive into some code. This one involves managing the defects and feature requests that come in from your testing department and users. Between the code metrics and the defect/feature requests, you'll be able to make informed decisions on how to convert this brownfield application into something manageable.

# Defect management 6

**This chapter covers**

■ Exploring types of defects

■ Reviewing your brownfield project for defects

■ Understanding the anatomy of a defect

■ Achieving Zero Defect Count

On the majority of software projects, most of the effort is put into the construction tasks required to create something tangible. We focus on the analysis, design, and coding that produces the software. Inevitably during that effort, you'll make errors and incorrect assumptions that lead to defects. How you react to these defects is an important factor in the health of your project.

Projects have a wide range of techniques, both explicit and implicit, that they employ to disseminate information about defects. The techniques will vary, from word of mouth to tools that enforce formalized workflows. Regardless of the technique, every project needs to have a process for managing defect information.

There's ample opportunity for friction and pain points to surface in the defect-tracking process. In brownfield projects, it's common to see large backlogs of defects that haven't been addressed in many months (or at all). Defects that have been lingering in a backlog for any amount of time will be of questionable quality and should be reviewed. The effort required to determine the quality of a defect creates friction in the resolution process.

On some projects, you'll step into the fray only to find that nobody from the development, testing, or client teams knows what defects even exist. There's a difference between having no defect-tracking tool and having no defect-tracking process. It's possible to stay on top of defects without a tool, but you can't do it without a process.

Similar to the contaminated code aspect of a brownfield project, it's likely you'll inherit a backlog of unresolved defects when you're starting. Reducing the backlog effectively is a significant pain point when you're first starting a project—especially when you take into account that many teams don't consider defect fixes to be "real work." Although this chapter is about managing defects, we'll use it to frame an important discussion on how to counter the defects-are-beneath-me mentality.

Trends, recurring scenarios, and specific pain points can be identified by gathering defect-related information. Because pain points are one of the things that you can identify using defect information, why don't we discuss the pain points that can impede effective defect gathering?

## 6.1   *Pain points*

Joni walked into the meeting room full of hope. She was taking a look at the defect list for the first time and her co-worker, Mitchell, was going to lead her through it. Mitchell sauntered in with a stack of papers covered in Post-It notes.

"What's all that?" asked Joni.

Mitchell dropped his pile on the table with a flourish. "That," he said, "is my personal defect list."

Joni looked at the stack of papers with growing dread. "I thought we had a tool in place to keep track of them."

Mitchell scoffed. "Pfft, that thing is so out of date it's almost retro. I stopped using it when I started seeing active defects logged against version 1.2. We're on version 5. So I keep my own personal list."

Just then Pearl poked her head into the meeting room. "Mitch, sorry to bug you. I'm going to take the defect where the user can't log in on stat holidays."

Mitchell started rummaging through his pile. After a few moments, he looked up. "I don't have that one with me. I think Bailey was going to tackle it…actually, now that I think about it, that one was fixed a while back. Here, try this one." And he hands Pearl a well-weathered pink Post-It.

Now, there are some obvious problems with this company's defect tracking. First, although they have a system in place, it has been allowed to decay. So the team has had to work around this situation by coming up with their own inefficient system. Furthermore, there's no real way to track the progress of defects in their system. One also wonders how the testing team or the client even reports them.

Without a good defect-tracking process, you lose confidence in the application—a situation that inevitably affects the overall quality (see figure 6.1). Your team rarely sees the results of fixed defects; they see only more and more of them being reported. After all the effort you've put into building confidence with a functional version control system (VCS), a continuous integration (CI) process, and automated tests, it would be a shame to have it fall apart during defect tracking.

So let's take a look at how you can manage the inevitability of defects. We'll begin with a breakdown of the various kinds of defects.

## 6.2 Types of defects

In section 6.1, you read about one of the classic pain points with defect tracking on brownfield projects: the current tracking tool simply isn't fulfilling the project's needs. An easy way to determine if this is the case is to answer this question: Is the team using the

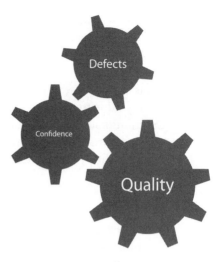

**Figure 6.1 Your policy toward defects will affect both your project team's confidence and the overall quality.**

tool? If the answer is no (or one of its cousins: "not really," "kind of," "we used to," or any answer that starts with "well…"), frustration and angst are bound to grow between testers and developers (in both directions) as well as between the client and the team.

Assuming there's a system in place, it's only as useful as the entries within it. With brownfield projects in particular, you'll find different classes of defects that aren't useful— "defective" defects, as it were. This definition includes defects that

- Have been resolved but not closed (languishing entries)
- Are incomplete
- Are duplicates of existing defects or were tested against an incorrect version of the application (spurious entries)
- Are feature requests in disguise

Figure 6.2 shows each of these types.

Each of these defect types has its own nuances, reasons for existing, and special attributes. To understand how to deal with their existence, we first need to look at each type in more detail.

### 6.2.1 Languishing entries

Languishing entries are defects that were entered at some point in time, probably justifiably, but have never been resolved in the

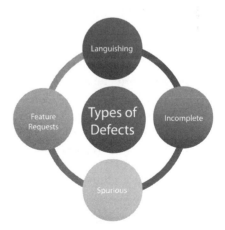

**Figure 6.2 Defects come in many flavors: languishing, incomplete, spurious, and feature requests.**

tracking system. Languishing defects may have been correctly resolved by the technical team, closed as nondefects by the testers or client, or just never attended to.

A backlog of languishing defects can indicate a couple of things. It might mean that the team or client has lost interest in using the software and hasn't updated the status of the defects. Perhaps the software is cumbersome to use, or the team doesn't see any value to updating the status, or the culture of the team is such that they believe this mundane task is beneath them.

There are other reasons defects could languish, but regardless, their existence is a sign that there's a problem with the defect-tracking system or the process for managing defects.

### 6.2.2   *Incomplete entries*

No matter the age or freshness of the defects in your system, they're only as useful as the information that each one contains. Many project team members (and clients) are notoriously lax in providing fully fleshed-out details within a defect entry. Examples include *cannot log into the system* or *printing error.*

Although it may seem like overkill to provide so much information at the time of defect creation, memories fade over time. Testers, developers, and clients may not have enough information to accurately work on the defect or search for past occurrences. The pain from this problem usually isn't felt in the initial phases of development, testing, and release of software. It sneaks up on a team over time and quietly wreaks havoc on the efficiency of the process. We discuss the makeup of a good defect entry in section 6.5.

### 6.2.3   *Spurious entries*

Of all the types of defects, none are more frustrating for a team member than those that add work without providing any tangible benefit. Spurious defect entries do just that. On brownfield projects that have a historical backlog of defects, there will undoubtedly be defects that aren't really defects.

There are a few reasons why an entry could be spurious. Two people may have recorded the same defect (duplicate entries). The wrong version of the application may have been pushed to the test team and they logged defects against an incorrect version. The defect could simply be nonreproducible.

Regardless of the reasons behind their creation, this type of defect is sometimes referred to as a *ghost*, meaning one that you spend time chasing but can never find.

### 6.2.4   *Feature requests*

These defects are another favorite for development teams. They're feature requests masquerading as defects. For example: *The Save button doesn't send an email confirmation to the customer* or *There's no way to print an invoice.* These are fundamental pieces of functionality that the application should provide but doesn't.

At some point, all projects seem to acquire feature requests as defects. Depending on the software development methodology you follow (waterfall, agile, or something else), they often lead to arguments about scope and schedule. Being able to distinguish between defects and feature requests isn't easy; sometimes it's downright political. As a result, it's common for this type of defect entry to turn into a languishing entry.

You can tell a lot about a team by its attitude toward defects. In our experience, defects, and the mechanism of tracking them, regularly cause pain on projects, brownfield or not. Although some of the issues can be institutional, and much harder to resolve, significant gains can be made by attending to the defect-tracking and -management processes. Let's look at what to expect during the initial review of your brownfield project's defects.

## 6.3   *The initial defect triage*

Many brownfield projects treat defects as a separate project stage. Often defects are recorded as the team concentrates on the ongoing development effort, but they aren't addressed right away. Instead, defects are allowed to pile up unattended with the intent that "We'll fix them before the next release."

This mentality is often a precursor to becoming a brownfield application. It can lead to hundreds or even thousands of existing deficiencies that have never even been acknowledged, let alone reviewed. Under these pretenses, defects become stale quickly. You'll probably find yourself in this situation when starting on a brownfield project.

---

**Tales from the trenches: The worst-case scenario**

On one project, our first two months of work were consumed by managing the enormous defect backlog and the effort required to work through those defects. This project was one that had yet to go to production and at the time had over 700 open defects logged against it. As we worked through the defects, we had to be efficient in all the aspects of defect triage, information gathering, and resolution that you'll read about in this chapter.

Luckily, we had a sizable development team that could take care of fixing the issues. Unluckily, we had defects that were over 2 years old, whose original enterer had left the project, were logged against drastically changed modules, and/or were unclearly documented. As you can imagine, a lot of time was spent on defects that were no longer valid. This effort was required so that the developers, testers, management, and client could regain confidence in the system's functionality and correctness.

In the end we managed to survive the 2 months dedicated to this task (immediately prior to production release). Beyond the skills to work through a defect mess such as the one we encountered here, the biggest thing we learned is that although Zero Defect Count (discussed in section 6.6) seems impossible to achieve, it's far better than the alternative that we'd just encountered.

*(continued)*

After the mass defect resolution, we stated (not asked) to our management that the development team would be, from that point forward, working under a policy of Zero Defect Count. They laughed at our naive idealism. For the remaining 10 months on that project, we worked hard, every day, to fix defects as quickly as they were entered in the tracking system. During that time, we rarely had more than a couple dozen open defects at any one time. On top of that, we were able to maintain our new feature delivery velocity.

So believe us when we say that we've been there and done that. If you're embarking on this journey, we feel for you—really, we do—but we also know that you can succeed. Heck, if we can, there's no reason you can't.

When you join a brownfield project, you'll inherit all its defects. How should you manage such a large number of items? When analyzing them, you'll have to determine their worth to the project. But unlike reviewing existing tests (section 4.4), the analysis of defects is going to involve more than just the development team. The testers and business representatives should be included in this process. They're the people who best understand the expectations that weren't met when the defect was created.

## Come prepared for the long haul

There's no sense sugarcoating. Unless your idea of a good time is sitting around with a group of people for possibly several hours discussing the minutia of a few hundred bugs, analyzing defects with your team won't be a fun task. Nothing causes the psychosomatic sniffles like a 3-hour defect bash.

Going through defects en masse is an arduous task and will take its toll—not just because of the length of the meeting required to go through them but because of the ever-increasing sense of dread you feel as you slowly become aware of the sheer numbers of defects.

Use whatever you can think of to keep the analysis meeting productive. Bring in pizza, take breaks, create a soundtrack that plays in the background (one obvious suggestion for an opening song: "Also Sprach Zarathustra").

One pitfall to watch for: it's easy to overanalyze the early defects, leading you to short-shrift later ones when fatigue sets in. If you find this pattern occurring, shake things up a bit. Switch meeting rooms or take the team out for coffee (or something stronger). Schedule another meeting if you have to, but in our experience, the team's attention span gets shorter and shorter with each successive one.

When viewing historical defects the first time, the goal is to get through them quickly. Don't spend a lot of time analyzing why a defect exists or how you'd solve it.

Depending on the number of defects you have in your backlog, you may not have time to get all the information for each one. The meeting is about deciding three things about each defect:

- What can and can't be done about it?
- Who should do it?
- How important is it to fix it?

With that in mind, there's one of three things you can do with a defect during triage: close it, assign it to the testing team, or assign it to the development team, as summarized in figure 6.3.

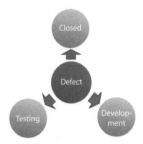

Chances are the only ones that can be closed are spurious defects. You may also encounter, and be able to close, defects that have been unconsciously resolved—ones that have been fixed without realizing it. These defects are a relief in the triage process; most will require more work before being resolved.

**Figure 6.3　In the initial defect review, the goal is either to close the defect or assign it to the development or test team.**

Defects that can't be closed need to be assigned. Again, you don't want to use this time for drawn-out design discussions. There are two possible assignments: the development team or the testing team. If you can easily reproduce the defect and the testing team or client confirms that it's still a valid defect, it goes to the development team. Otherwise, it goes to the testing team to investigate further. Their responsibility is to provide further information on the defect, such as steps to reproduce it or clarification about the business functionality that's not being met.

---

### Bring the testers and client

It's important to include the testing team and the client at the initial defect review. They will be invaluable in determining context around many of the defects. Without them, there's a definite risk that some defects will be closed erroneously due to misinterpretation.

If the client isn't available, use a client proxy. A client proxy is a person who has detailed knowledge about the business domain and has been empowered to act on behalf of the client. Although they may not be rooted in the business on a day-to-day basis, they either have historical context to work from or the ability to quickly gather contextual information from the client.

A client proxy won't have all the answers. There will be times where she has to return to the client for clarification and possibly even decisions. Effective client proxies are trusted by both the business and the project team to accurately represent the needs of the client and thus they've been given the authority to act on behalf of the client.

During the initial review, you'll attempt to reproduce several of the defects. Because you're working with a large backlog of defects, efficiency is important. Dealing with difficult-to-reproduce defects significantly decreases your triage velocity.

Backlog defects will, by nature, be hard to reproduce. The longer a defect is left unattended, the more likely there will be too little information to reproduce it. It's also possible that the application has been altered and the behavior seen in, or around, the defect has changed. Your defect resolution efforts will run into both of these situations.

One of the primary reasons that the defect can't be reproduced is that the information contained in the defect report either isn't clear or is incomplete. If the defect's creator is at the meeting, it's possible that you'll be able to get quick clarification from him.

There will be times when you engage the original defect creator in a discussion and he isn't able to provide you with an immediate answer. Like you, the originator of the defect probably hasn't worked with it for some time. It's entirely possible that they may not remember the scenario, the intricacies of the business, or the goal of that portion of the application. Instead of working with speculation, assign the defect in question to them so they can take their research offline. The time spent doing better research on the situation will provide you with a far better solution and, ultimately, a better software product.

If you have to hand the defect off to another person for further research, take the time to note on that defect entry what you've done to that point. This note will help the person doing the research as well as the person who has to reproduce it next. That may be the next developer assigned to resolve the defect, or it could be the tester who's working to prove the fix that the development team implemented.

In the end, if the defect truly isn't reproducible by all efforts, don't be afraid to close it. Be sure to document all your efforts in the event the defect arises again in the future.

After working your way through the defect triage, the real work begins. Your testers have their assignments and you, the development team, have yours. Next, we'll see how to plan out your work.

## 6.4   *Organizing the effort*

Your first obstacle when working through a large defect list will be one of scheduling. Rarely is the project going to have the luxury of assigning the entire development team to the defect backlog at one time. Even if management makes a commitment to quality, they always seem to dictate that the project must continue moving forward with new features while the team figures out a way to work the defect backlog simultaneously. As figure 6.4 shows, working on defect analysis in parallel with ongoing development is possible, but pieces of the analysis become more difficult.

**Figure 6.4   New feature development and defect resolution will almost always occur in parallel.**

As stated in previous sections, defect analysis regularly requires the input of the business, testers, and the original creator of the defect for a full understanding. If the development team is paralleling the defect analysis with ongoing development, it's a safe guess that the rest of the project team is also going to be working on the ongoing development while they're being asked questions from the defect analysis. And although your team may be prepared to handle the parallel work, the other project members may not have had the same pep talk. As a result, information gathering from those groups may be slower than you'd hope.

Because this type of delay can occur, it's important to involve the entire project team at the beginning of your defect effort to ensure you can get through the backlog with some efficiency. Be sure your testers and the client know that you'll be calling on them about new features *and* existing defects. That way, they don't get the impression that the development effort is fragmented and unfocused.

### 6.4.1 *Tackling the defect list*

If there was one thing that could be designated as "nice" about a large defect backlog on a brownfield project, it's that you're not starved for choices. There are a lot of defects to choose from. If you have outstanding questions with other team members who are busy, your team can carry on with other defects and return when answers are provided. Although not an ideal workflow, this technique can be effective when attention is paid to the outstanding questions.

The reason this workflow isn't ideal is that it's better to start and complete each defect as a single contiguous piece of work. One of the reasons that a large defect backlog exists is precisely the mentality of "We'll get back to those when we have time." Don't let this mentality infect your effort to eliminate the backlog. Be diligent in your pursuit of the needed clarifications. Be persistent to the point of annoyance when requesting information from other teams.

**WARNING**    It can be a dangerously fine line to tread between annoying and persistent, but it can be effective in small doses. If you're consistently determined near the start of a project, you'll establish that this effort is important and that you aren't going away until it's done. The biggest risk you run is that other groups on the project team will shut down communications rather than deal with you—which is why we suggest parsimonious use of this tactic and that it's always practiced with politeness and gratitude.

While working on the defect backlog, set milestones for the project to aim for. Depending on the size of the backlog, you may have a milestone of completing the analysis of the first 100 defects. Not only are these goals good for the morale of the backlog analysis group, but they also provide the backlog team with reminders to thank the other groups and people on whom they've been leaning during the process. Regardless of the size of the milestones, or even if you use them, it's important to remember to include other contributors in the process. They should receive their just dues as well as seeing, and hopefully buying into, the group's effort in increasing product quality. It's another small and subtle step that can be used to create a project-level culture of quality.

### 6.4.2   *Maintaining momentum*

No matter the level of commitment to quality the team has, working on defect analysis can be a tedious and draining experience. If you keep the same group on defect analysis for any amount of time, their morale will decline and, with it, the quality of defect resolutions. If you're in a position where some developers are doing ongoing development in parallel with the defect resolution team, try swapping teams out at regular intervals.

One way that we've handled this inevitable decay in morale was to swap different people into the defect analysis role at the end of new feature iterations (see figure 6.5).

This technique helped maintain a steady analysis rhythm for the team. It also made it easy to include information in verbal or written reports for management, who will certainly want to know how the effort is proceeding. The most obvious result of this method of managing the work is that fewer people will be working on the ongoing development effort. In some situations, this approach may not be feasible.

**Figure 6.5   Swapping team members regularly from defect resolution to new features helps keep morale from flagging.**

Another method that has worked well for us is to tack on a defect-resolution task at the end of each ongoing development task. With this technique, once a developer has finished a task assigned to her, she can then grab three or five defects off the backlog.

In this scenario, the analysis effort tends to proceed in fits and starts so it's much more difficult to know the speed at which the work is proceeding. In the end, the effort usually spreads out over a longer time frame when using this approach, but it also promotes the idea that defects are everyone's responsibility.

Although both of those techniques have drawbacks, they do provide one significant benefit: collective code ownership. Everyone is responsible for fixing defects, which will help ingrain the belief that anyone can work on any part of the application. Collective ownership is an important aspect of your commitment to quality.

Regardless of the techniques you implement when resolving your existing defect backlog, make sure to pace yourself. The most important task is to resolve defects correctly, and the size of the list is the second-most important factor. Some defect backlogs are intimidating and need to be handled in smaller pieces. Don't be afraid to take on only what the team can handle at one time. Any amount of progress is positive. In section 6.6, we'll talk about the concept of Zero Defect Count, which is a goal to strive toward. This goal will provide a lasting positive effect with regard to the quality of your project.

> **Challenge your assumptions: Collective ownership**
>
> Collective ownership promotes the concept that all developers feel responsible for making all parts of the application better. More traditional thoughts on code assignments create silos, where a very few people are responsible for one small portion of the application. As a result, you end up with the data access guy, the web services guy, the UI guy, and so on. None of those people will feel comfortable entering someone else's code.
>
> Regularly you hear the phrase "hit by the bus" on projects—which is kind of morbid but appropriate. People are talking about the risk associated with having one person responsible for a critical portion of the application. Silo'd code responsibilities promote a hit-by-the-bus mentality. Instead of dispersing the risk, the risk is being concentrated and focused into very small areas.
>
> Collective ownership doesn't mean that all developers must have the same level of understanding across the codebase. Rather, it implies that the developers are all comfortable working in any place in the application at any time.
>
> If you want to increase the ability of your team to react to changes or defects, collective ownership is one of the best methods to employ. You need time and team discipline to implement it, but the long-term benefits are remarkable.

Regardless of the method you're using while working through your defect list, you'll almost certainly encounter one particular type of defect regularly: spurious defects. This topic warrants a little special attention.

### 6.4.3 *Dealing with spurious defects*

While you're working to reproduce a defect, it may become clear that the entry isn't a problem with the system. In fact, a defect entry may not be a problem at all. It may be a misunderstanding of system or business functionality, or it may simply be wrong.

Analyzing spurious, or false, defects will absorb more time than any other type of defect in your backlog. Not only do you spend time trying to verify that the defect exists, but you also need to validate that the defect is spurious in order to justify it to the testing team and/or client. It's not enough to declare that the defect doesn't exist; you must also be confident in stating that the functionality in question is fully correct. You don't want to be on the receiving end of the oft-quoted cynicism, "It's not a bug, it's a feature."

As a result, false defects are difficult to accurately identify. You need to have a clear set of criteria for falsity. There are three reasons for a defect to be considered false. Meeting any one of these criteria indicates that you have a spurious defect:

- The behavior explained in the defect doesn't exist in the application.
- The assertion about the expected functionality in the defect explanation is incorrect.
- The details of the defect are duplicated in another defect.

There are a couple of reasons leading to the first criterion. The defect's creator could've misdiagnosed the application while they were using it. Or the application's expected functionality could've changed since the time that the defect was created.

The second criterion will be more common than the first on most brownfield projects. Defects that have been sitting idle for months or years will be fixed without anyone realizing it. Sometimes they're fixed by proactive developers. Other times they'll have been fixed by developers too lazy to update the defect-tracking system. It's also common that the application has organically evolved and the "defective" functionality has either been removed or changed in such a way that it no longer contains the same defect.

The only way that defects in this category will be found is through manual review of the defect backlog. The interesting thing with these defects is that when reviewing them, the client or client proxy interaction is usually quite quick. When presented with the scenario, people with knowledge of the business will quickly realize how incorrect the perceived functionality was. Consequently, the defect is marked as spurious and filed away with no further action needed.

The third criterion should be obvious. If defects aren't often addressed in a timely manner, it's inevitable that some duplication exists. But before dismissing a defect as a duplicate of another, be sure it *is* a duplicate. "Received an error while printing" and "Print output is incorrect" aren't the same thing.

Regardless of the reasons for a spurious defect, take care to note the logic behind it. Like nonreproducible defects, spurious defects need to have clear and complete reasoning for them. Except in rare cases, you're probably persisting defects to a system to provide a historical context to your team, the client, or the maintenance team. Spurious defects become valuable if they can clearly state why the application should *not* work in a certain way. By recording these facts, you're creating a learning project and in the bigger picture a *learning company*,[1] meaning that lessons learned are retained for current and future members to build on.

A common type of defect you'll encounter as you work through your backlog is one that's actually a feature in defect clothing. Although these defects partially fall into the spurious category, they do deserve their own area of discussion. We'll talk about these, the most emotionally charged of the defect types, next.

### 6.4.4   *Defects versus features*

Ah, the age-old debate. The question of defect versus feature has raged since the first quality review of a software application. In the days since, there have been two sides to the argument. On one side stands the software development team who says, "It's not a bug because we built the functionality based on the knowledge provided to us at the time." On the other side are the quality reviewers (testers, QA, clients) who simply state, "It's not what we want or need and therefore it's a bug."

---

[1]   Author Jeffrey Liker coined this term in his book *The Toyota Way* (McGraw-Hill, 2004).

Being in conversations that take either of those tones can be frustrating because both sides are, essentially, right. It's important to remember at all times that the application is being built to service the needs of the client. If something isn't working the way they need or want it to, you need to address it. Whether you call it a defect or a feature is moot (see figure 6.6).

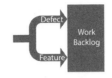

**Figure 6.6  The question about whether something is a defect or a feature is moot. The work still ends up in the backlog either way.**

That said, the difference between bug and feature is important. It's common for clients to log feature requests as defects in the hope of forcing the project team to address them with immediacy. It's possible to talk all day on the futility and underhandedness of this practice, but it will occur nonetheless.

Brownfield applications, in particular, are susceptible to features masquerading as defects. The state of the project over time has deteriorated to the point where budget and timeline constraints have forced management to deny requests for new features. In response, the client tries their hand at logging a feature request as a defect, sees a few of them get attention that way, and now has a new technique for getting work done.

The problem that the client doesn't see is that their feature requests as well as their defects are probably being prioritized at the same level. So defects may or may not get fixed before new features get added, or vice versa. In either case, chances are that the client isn't getting their most desired work done first.

Having a conversation to discuss the finer details of defect versus feature and the criteria that distinguish one from the other often isn't going to be fruitful in a brownfield project. This is especially true when there's a large backlog of defects as well as a client pushing new features in as defects. In our experience, convincing the client of the difference isn't going to change their opinion about the work they want done. All you'll do is further feed a belief that the project team isn't interested in serving the needs of the business. You also run the risk of breeding a lot of developers with Hero Programmer Syndrome (see chapter 1, section 1.3.3).

Instead of discussing the nuances of defects and features, we've had success by involving the client in deciding the work priority. Sit down with her and discuss the work that's in the backlog regardless of whether it's a defect or feature. Once she has some understanding of the remaining work, get her to prioritize the work effort. Have the client rank each outstanding work item and defect from highest to lowest. Then, simply empower her to choose what the team works on next.

**NOTE**  Prioritization won't be a onetime event on any project. Priorities change, so you should review them on a regular basis. If you haven't yet reached a point where the team has a strong culture of quality, hold these prioritization meetings frequently. Once you've started a good rhythm whittling down the backlog of open defects, and the client has started to believe in the process of fixing defects as soon as they appear, you'll find that work prioritization will only be required when the team is resetting for another concerted effort.

You'll derive two significant benefits from this kind of collaborative prioritization. First, the client will realize she can't have everything all the time. She'll become aware of the choices that need to be made and that although some tasks will bubble to the top of the work list, others will fall to the bottom through her valuation of each one.

## Challenge your assumptions: Numerically incrementing priorities

Traditionally defects have been assigned priorities from a list of values that may include High, Medium, Low, and any number of others. When prioritizing, it's common for defect owners to want their defects to be assigned the highest level of priority possible. The result is a list of defects that are all listed as Urgent or High. Once priorities are assigned in this way, the prioritization values have become meaningless. What's the most important defect from a list of 50 that have been categorized as High?

A useful technique we've used in the past is to assign defects a numeric priority. If you have 50 defects, assign each one a number between 1 and 50 and don't allow any of the numbers to be reused. Then, each defect is appropriately ranked with respect to the others.

At times this type of prioritization will require hard decisions. When two defects appear to be of equal importance, how do you assign them to different levels? Don't give in to well-intended deviations from the no-repeated-values rule—they lead straight back to a situation where all items are High priority. Instead, take the time to make a decision on the appropriate value. Ask yourself, "If the product absolutely had to be delivered with only one of these items being addressed, which would it be?" (Hint: the answer can't be "both.")

The second benefit of this style of collaborative prioritization is that the client will become more closely integrated into the planning effort for the project. Over time, she'll see and understand the ramifications of her requests and the project team will come to respect those requests much more.

As the client and the team work on prioritization, you can then start to involve the client in your estimating process. A client who understands the project's prioritization process, plus the work effort estimation that happens, will become a great ally when the project has to make hard decisions about scheduling.

In the end, though, regardless of what tools or techniques you employ in the defect-versus-feature battle, remember the key point that project teams are there to create software that meets the needs of the client. If a request is presented as either a defect or a feature, and the business does need the request filled, you have an obligation to address that business need in some fashion.

We've talked a great deal about reviewing existing defect entries and how to address them. Now let's outline the components of a good defect entry.

## 6.5    *Anatomy of a defect entry*

In section 6.2 we touched on the fact that a defect may not be the epitome of clarity or completeness. We've found, in our experience, that these are a common problem on many projects, brownfield or not. Well-meaning team members will create a defect that doesn't contain enough context or detailed information that the next person reading it can understand the intended idea. As a result, defects make too many trips between people as clarification is added. Usually the need for frequent clarification isn't a technical problem; it's a communication issue. Team members aren't communicating well with one another.

> **Challenge your assumptions: Fear not the face-to-face conversation**
>
> Many developers prefer disconnected discussion when communicating. Our comfort zone tends to be one where we can craft our thoughts carefully before responding. Email is a fantastic example of this disconnect. So is adding questions or requests for clarification into a defect-tracking system rather than taking a walk to someone else's office to ask them directly.
>
> Performing conversations in person or over the phone will be rewarding both personally and professionally. Face-to-face conversations provide all parties with the opportunity to clarify their impressions on the subject matter. It gives all parties the chance to more deeply explore aspects of the discussion that may lead to more meaningful information in the end. On top of that, face-to-face conversations usually take a fraction of the time that the write-reply-reply-reply... pattern provided through email does.

We've all seen defects where all that's recorded is a summary similar to "Customer Edit screen doesn't work." For the consumers of this defect, the problem isn't stated in a clear enough manner that they can effectively begin to diagnose any problem. Perhaps the only thing that they can do is open the Customer Edit screen to see if it displays an obvious error. For all they know, the end user could be claiming that the screen should have a label that reads "Customer #" instead of the value "Customer No.". Regardless, defects with too little information lead to inefficiencies and, ultimately, project risk.

Figure 6.7 outlines the characteristics of an ideal defect (as it were).

Although the traits outlined in figure 6.7 may seem simple, it's amazing how rarely these values are found in a logged defect. Let's look at each of these traits in detail in the hope that you can improve the quality of defects entered in your system.

**Figure 6.7   Concise, clear, complete, constructive, and, ultimately, closed are the traits of a good defect entry.**

### 6.5.1   *Concise*

Conciseness generally applies only to the defect summary. In most cases, this is the only part of the defect you'll see in defect reports. For that reason alone, defect summaries should be concise.

Being concise will be vitally important on a brownfield project that has hundreds of defects. You'll be referring to the defect list regularly both in reports and in conversation. A concise summary can become a good mnemonic for the defect when you discuss it with other developers.

Given that, rewriting defect summaries en masse after the fact has limited value. As with many tasks you could do when reviving a brownfield project, rewriting summaries is nothing more than a make-work project. If you plan to refer back to them often in the future, there may be enough long-term value in doing this work. You'll need to gauge the needs, timelines, and resources available on the project before taking on a piece of work requiring this level of effort.

### 6.5.2   *Clear*

Clarity tends to conflict with being concise. In brownfield applications, it's not uncommon to find defects that have summaries consisting of little more than a statement like "Tab order" or "Save broken." Although such statements may be concise, they're far from clear.

Instead of a summary that has limited informational value, try increasing the summary to be a simple statement outlining the scenario. A summary of "Tab order" would be clearer if it read "Edit Customer tab order fails leaving Address Line 1." When you look at the summary, you understand the situation surrounding the defect. Better yet, it's a more effective mnemonic for developers who are quickly scanning the defect list on a regular basis.

Furthermore, when you fill out the details for a defect, be sure to remove any ambiguity. Now is not the time to practice your shorthand. This rule applies when you're entering details on how to reproduce it and when you're expanding on how you fixed it as well. Entering text like "Clicking Save doesn't work" isn't useful if a Save button, menu item, and toolbar icon all appear on the same screen.

### 6.5.3   *Complete*

The phrase "The devil is in the details" seems tailor-made for defect reports. The details are the core of any defect. Nothing is more frustrating than opening a defect report and finding either incomplete information or no details at all.

Working with defects doesn't have to be futile because of poor defect details. There's also no point in directing blame to people because everyone has entered a poor defect detail at least once on a project. On a brownfield project, there's the very real possibility that the person who entered the defect is no longer part of the project team, and the ones who are around possibly can't remember the details because the defect is so stale. Regardless, defects lacking necessary detail need to be supplemented before they're resolved.

Probably the single most important piece of information that needs to be included in all defect details is guidance on reproducing the defect. Depending on the complexity of the defect scenario, this guidance may range from something as simple as "Open the Customer Edit form" to a complicated set of steps that outlines the ancillary data that's required, the steps to first put the system into a specific state, and then the steps required to generate the defect. Regardless of the complexity, we can't stress enough the value this information provides. Without this information, the people responsible for fixing and retesting the defect will be guessing and not able to do their jobs adequately.

In combination with step-by-step detail for reproducing the defect, it's also important to include a clear description of the defective behavior observed at the time it was generated. Once someone has gone through the process of reproducing the defect, there must be some way for them to distinguish what it was that triggered the defect's creation. In some situations, this information may be as simple as "Error dialog is generated." In others, it could be some incorrect interpretation of the business rule, such as "Selecting Canada as the country doesn't change the list of states to a list of provinces."

As a corollary to outlining the incorrect behavior, it's also useful to include a description of what *should* have happened when you reproduce those steps. This level of detail isn't always necessary. ("Application should not crash" doesn't add much value to a defect.) But whenever there's room for interpretation, try to remove as much ambiguity as you can. Pointing out how it failed is only half the defect. Describing how it should succeed is the other half.

Enhance the description of the false behavior with whatever additional information is available. Screen shots can be invaluable. If an error was generated, gather the error message details, stack trace, log entries, and anything else that may be generated when it was thrown. If entering certain inputs causes incorrect data to be displayed, collect screen shots of both the inputs and the resulting incorrect data. Any information that can be provided to bolster the claim of false behavior makes resolution quicker and clearer.

Once the defect has been resolved, details of the decision or action taken should be entered. Don't go crazy and start cutting and pasting code into the defect. A brief explanation that says, "Added support for saving to PDF" will let the testers know what to look for when verifying that it's been fixed. If done correctly, the details can also provide feedback to testers on what other areas of the application may have been affected by the resolution.

Also, if the defect wasn't acted on, be sure to include an explanation. Preferably you'd include something more substantial than "Didn't feel like it," but a resolution like "Discussed with the client and they have a workaround. Was decided that the cost of fixing would be prohibitively high at this point" makes it clear that you've taken steps to address the defect.

By the end of at defect's life, it will have the following components in its detail section:

- Steps to reproduce the scenario
- Data and supplemental files needed to reproduce it
- Description of the incorrect behavior that was observed

- Description of the correct behavior that was expected
- Summary of the actions taken when resolving the defect

Although there are other pieces of information that you may want or need to track in defect details for your project, these are the core components. Without them, the efficiency of the team will decline. Their absence will also create a future where older defects are meaningless when reviewed.

### 6.5.4  *Constructive*

Carrying on our analysis of a defect entry from figure 6.7, a defect report is useful for more than just a record of bugs and how you solved them. Defects can provide valuable insight long after they're closed. This is true only if you can glean that insight from them in bulk. Typically, you'd provide the ability to review defects in bulk by individually classifying them.

Defect classification is nothing more than a way to group or categorize similar defects together. There are a number of ways that you can classify defects. It's fairly common to classify based on severity (ranging from "minor UI issue" to "crashes the host computer") and the area in the application that the defect was found.

If you're looking to implement defect classification, first figure out what information your project needs or would benefit from. Just because other projects classify based on application area doesn't mean that the same information would be helpful on your project.

Developers on a brownfield project should be interested in classification on past defects and certainly on all new ones. Summarized classification data can be used to gain insight into problem areas of the application, code fragility, code churn, and defect resolution success rates.

---

**Recognizing code churn**

Code churn is a count of the number of times that lines of code have changed. It can be determined by looking at the number of lines of code that have changed in an area (method, class, etc.) of code. It's also possible to calculate code churn by counting the number of times that an area of code has changed.

The metric will indicate whether an area of code is highly volatile and thus more prone to defects being generated. As with any static analysis metric, numbers that indicate an acceptable threshold are gray and, in this case, depend on the size of the code area that is being observed.

We suggest that you take code churn as an indicator that further and deeper investigation is required instead of as a sign that action absolutely must occur. In some projects, high code churn in areas may be acceptable although in other situations, it may not. Rather than giving you hard values to strive for, we suggest that you go by intuition and not use code churn automatically as a metric to trigger immediate action.

Unlike with defect summaries, back-filling defect classifications can be valuable. The categories and tags you assign to a defect can (and should) be reported against to help guide your effort and mark your progress. We'll talk more about defect reporting in section 6.7.

### 6.5.5  *Closed*

This portion of a defect is an obvious one but worth including in our discussion. Always remember that your goal is to (eventually) close the defect in some manner. Most often, closing a defect is done by fixing it. We've talked about other reasons it could be closed as well: it's a duplicate, it's incorrect, it isn't reproducible, and so forth.

Very often in brownfield applications, the goal for many developers isn't to close the defect so much as it is to "get it off my plate." A common tactic is to focus on one small point of clarification so that you can reassign it to the testing team. After all, if it's not assigned to me, it's not my problem, right?

This is small thinking. In the next section, we'll talk about using the defect list to instill a culture of quality in your team. Without that culture, defects can constantly be juggled back and forth between the client, the development team, and the QA team without any real work being performed on it.

> **The deferred defect**
>
> Another type of defect that often lingers in a backlog is one that is deferred. A defect may be deferred for many reasons. The work to fix it may not be proportionate to the benefit. You may be waiting on the purchase of a new third-party product that addresses it. It may be a feature in defect's clothing that's on the radar for a future version of the application.
>
> Whatever the reason, get these off your defect backlog somehow. With most tracking systems, you can set its status to *deferred* or something similar. This type of status assignment is acceptable only if you can easily filter them out whenever you generate a list of open defects. It's cumbersome to scan through a list of backlog defects and always have to mentally skip over the deferred ones.
>
> If your tracking system can't filter easily, move the defect to another medium, even if it's a spreadsheet called DeferredItems.xls.

The desire to simply rid yourself of assigned defects needs to stop. Any open defect in the system should be considered a point of failure by the entire team. You must make every effort to resolve a defect as quickly (and correctly) as possible. Instead of punting it over the wall to the QA team to find out what they mean by "The status bar is too small," try a more drastic tactic: talk to them. Get the clarification you need by phone or in person. Don't let the defect linger so you can beef up your progress report by saying "Addressed 14 defects" where 6 of them were reassigned for clarification.

On the surface, a defect entry seems a simple thing. But as we've shown here, there's more to it than you might think at first glance. Defect entries that aren't concise, clear, complete, and constructive will take longer to move to their ultimate desired state: closed.

Creating a mind-set that values the importance and existence of defects is one of the signs of a mature development team. It takes great humility to publicly accept that you erred. It takes even more maturity to readily act to rectify that error. Now is a great time to look deeper into this kind of team mind-set.

## 6.6    *Instilling a culture of quality*

You're at a unique point in your brownfield development cycle. You've consciously recognized that improvement is necessary and (provided you've read chapters 1–5) you've made some effort to do so. You've also started a concerted effort to knock down your defect backlog, and in the coming chapters, you'll also get deeper into pure development topics.

In some ways, you're starting anew with your development effort. The pragmatist in you knows that although you've been working on your ecosystem, you haven't stopped all development on the codebase. But nonetheless, you're standing at a crossroad.

One path is well trod. It's the one that will lead you down a road you've traveled before. You'll take some detours, but for the most part, it's the way you've always done things and it will inevitably lead you back to this same crossroad.

The other path may be unknown but is fraught with possibility. Unfortunately it's a much less-traveled path and it's full of obstacles that will try to get you to veer from it. It's the path leading you to a culture of quality.

Hmmm…a little more evangelical than we had in mind but the sentiment remains. Rather than continuing on down the path that led you to brownfield territory, you should start thinking, as a team, about your commitment to quality.

No one is suggesting that you're not committed to quality now. But are you? Can you honestly say you have never compromised in your code just to meet a deadline? Have you not once looked at some questionable piece of code that another developer (or even you) has written and decided, "I can't deal with this now. I'm going to leave it as is and make a note of it for future reference"? Have you not, after trying several times to get clarification from the client for some feature, just given up and forged ahead based on assumptions, hoping no one would notice?

Of course you have. So have we. You die a little on the inside when you "have" to do these things, but it always seems like the only choice at the time, given the remaining work.

But because you're embarking on a fairly major undertaking to improve your codebase, make some room in your schedule to ingrain and reinforce your commitment to the quality of your application.

**NOTE**    The entire project team, not just the developers, has to be part of the commitment to quality. If the development team members are the only ones not willing to compromise, they'll quickly become a pariah of your organization through their incessant nagging.

What we mean by committing to a base level of quality is this:

- You'll always do things to the best of your ability.
- You won't stand for workarounds or even defects in your code.
- You'll actively and continuously seek out better ways of improving your codebase.

Note that this isn't a ceremonial commitment. It requires dedication from every member of the project team, from developers, to testers, to management, to clients (see figure 6.8). Each one of these people has to commit to quality at a level where any person on the team will gladly help to answer questions on an outstanding defect or feature at any point in time. If this communication breaks down at any level, plan for much slower defect resolution and lower quality overall.

**Figure 6.8  Remember that the development team is only one part of the overall project team.**

Let's tie commitment to quality back to our discussion on defects. One key way to initiate your commitment to quality is to work toward a policy of Zero Defect Count, which we'll talk about next.

### 6.6.1    Zero Defect Count

Most project teams submit to the idea that there will always be defects. They believe that defects are an ever-present cost of development.

But there's a problem with this mind-set. If you believe there will always be at least one defect, then what's the problem with there being two? Or five? Or twenty? Or five hundred? By accepting that defects are inevitable, you also accept that they'll accumulate and, more importantly, that they can be ignored for periods of time. Every so often, such a project will switch into defect-fixing mode and the team is tasked with working down the open defect list as quickly as they can.

Some teams have reasonable control of this phenomenon. Other teams lack the discipline necessary to minimize the impact of the accepted open defect list. Those projects end up with open defect counts in the hundreds or thousands. Usually they have no solid plan to resolve the issues beyond "We'll fix them before we release." Although this type of posturing may placate some people in management, others will see the amount of debt that the project is accumulating on a daily basis. Like financial debt, defect debt is a liability and liabilities have risk associated with them. A high or increasing number of open defects adds to the overall risk that the project will fail.

If open defects are a risk, each one resolved is a reduction in risk. Ideally you'd like to have mitigated all the risk associated with defects. To do that, you must have zero open defects.

Now, when you read "zero open defects," you're probably thinking it's an idealist's dream. And on projects that have a traditional mentality, where it's okay to carry open defects, you'd be correct. But if you change that mentality so that carrying open defects isn't acceptable, it becomes a more realistic possibility.

Zero Defect Count may seem like an impossible goal to set, but it isn't when the team strives for it on a daily basis. We've been in meetings with management where we've stated that our teams will work under the one overriding guideline of zero defects. And in those meetings we've been laughed at by every attending manager.

Their skepticism is rooted in their belief that this guideline means the team will turn out software with zero defects on the first try. We know release software without defects isn't possible. Achieving zero defects isn't about writing perfect code the first time. It's about making quality the foremost concern for the team. If code is released and defects are reported, the team immediately begins to work on resolving those defects. There's no concept of waiting to fix defects at some later point in time. Defects are the highest-priority work item on any developer's task list.

Attending to defects immediately doesn't necessarily mean that all work stops on the spot while the defect is investigated. The defect can wait until a developer has reached a comfortable point to switch their working context. Ideally, the developer can complete their current task entirely before working on a defect. Realistically, they'll work on that current task to a point where they can confidently check in their code (see section 2.5.1 in chapter 2 about avoiding feature-based check-ins) and then quickly transition to defect resolution. As a result, defects may not be addressed for a few hours and possibly a day, but preferably no longer than that. If defects haven't been attended to after half a week, the culture of quality on the team needs improvement and reinforcement.

On a brownfield project, a number of preexisting issues must be resolved before Zero Defect Count can be attained and sustained. The first, and probably the most obvious, is the current defect backlog. In section 6.4, you read about techniques and realities of working through a backlog. Until you've eliminated the defect backlog, there's no chance of attaining Zero Defect Count. Once you've eliminated the backlog, the project is at a point where it can begin to build a Zero Defect Count culture. Hopefully, by that time you've instilled a culture of quality in the team so that the concept isn't so far-fetched.

### ACHIEVING ZERO DEFECT COUNT

Like the growth of any cultural phenomenon, a culture of Zero Defect Count takes time to develop. Developers are geared toward driving to work on, and complete, new features and tasks. Defect resolution often subconsciously takes a back seat in a developer's mind. The best way we've found to break this habit is to have champions on your side: team members (leads or peers) who are adamant that defects need immediate attention. But having team members who proclaim the immediacy of defects and then go off and resolve all the defects themselves are of no use when creating the team culture. The entire team needs to be pushed to collectively resolve defects in a timely manner.

A simple and effective method to create collective urgency is to hold daily standup meetings specifically for defects. These meetings should be quick (unless your project is generating a daily defect count that's significantly higher than the number of team members) and requires nothing more than a brief update by each developer on what defects they're currently attending to. Our experience shows that meetings of this nature are needed only for a short time and defect reviews can then be rolled into the standard daily standup meeting. The purpose of the specific standup for defects is to reinforce the importance of defects to all team members at the same time.

Note that this technique is most effective with a team that has a relatively strong sense of self-organization. For teams that don't have that self-organizing instinct, guidance from the top will be in order. Having a single defect supervisor is one approach to solving the problem of a reluctant team. The person in charge is responsible for ensuring that the defects are being addressed at an overall team level or is tasked with assigning defects out to specific individuals and verifying that they were resolved. Both options can work, but it will take a strong person who is well respected by his or her peers to succeed in either. Our experience has shown that it's this type of team that's the most difficult to convince and convert. Accomplishing a culture of Zero Defect Count in this situation is going to require time and patience.

## Tales from the trenches: Zero Defect Count in action

In section 6.3 we told you about our experiences with a worst-case scenario. We mentioned that we transitioned the project into one that lived by the Zero Defect Count principle. We won't kid you: making this transition wasn't easy to achieve on that brownfield project. The culture of the project, and the corporation itself, was that software development proceeded until it was determined that enough features were available for a production release, which was then followed by a "stabilization period" in which as many defects as possible would be resolved prior to the release. Our desire to change this mentality to one of Zero Defect Count sent ripples through management quickly.

Having seen the problems inherent in the big bang approach to stabilization, we knew there was no other way to turn around the client's opinion of the team—which wasn't a very high one given how the defect count grew. Rather than taking the bureaucratically correct steps of proposing the change to Zero Defect Count, we decided a more dictatorial approach was required for such a drastic change in culture for developers and testers. So we stated in our release wrap-up meeting that we were going to move the team to a culture of Zero Defect Count. Management scoffed, developers were stunned, and testers aged almost instantly. Once we explained the premise and the approach we were to take, we at least got buy-in from the testers. Management remained skeptical until we'd shown many consecutive months of success.

*(continued)*

The key for success was getting the development team to commit to fixing defects as quickly as they appeared in the tracking system. Naturally, developers would much rather be working on new feature development than defect resolution. So we made it the responsibility of the developer leads to ensure that defects were assigned to developers between each new feature task that they were assigned. Because we had a large team of developers, we never asked a single developer to completely clear the current defect backlog because we needed to ensure, for morale reasons, that everyone on the team was pulling their weight on defect resolution.

In addition to ensuring an equitable distribution of defect work, we denied attempts by developers to pass a defect off to "the person who originally wrote that part of the system." We prevented defect pass-offs for a couple of reasons. First, collective ownership is a powerful concept when trying to achieve extremely high levels of quality. Second, we wanted to instill a culture where resolving defects was exponentially more important than assigning blame for creating them.

After a few months, we'd changed the culture of the entire development team to one where Zero Defect Count was as important as meeting our deadlines. Developers wouldn't look for new feature work until they could prove to the developer leads that they'd resolved some defects. Management of the Zero Defect Count policy disappeared and it very much became a culture.

As we said, this transition wasn't easy. Developers griped about having to fix defects for quite some time. Like any cultural change, time and persistence paid off in the end.

Zero Defect Count is a part of an overall culture. It's a decree that a team must live and die by. When they do, zero defects will seem the norm and your project will feel much healthier. It's by no means an easy task to achieve, but the rewards, in terms of both project and psychological success, can be amazing. A team that works in a Zero Defect Count environment has more confidence and a penchant for quality that bleeds into other areas of its work.

One of the obstacles you'll face in moving to Zero Defect Count (and in moving to a culture of quality in general) is skepticism from the stakeholders, especially if the defect backlog is particularly large. Many of them will have heard this song before and will be tough to convince. In the next section, we'll see how we can address that.

### 6.6.2   *Easing fears and concerns from stakeholders*

Working through the open defects on a brownfield project can be an arduous and lengthy process. Many project members may perceive it as a giant time sink and won't buy into the process. There will be scoffing at the beginning. Clients may wonder why attention to quality hasn't happened in the past. Project managers may be concerned it will affect deadlines and morale. A common lingering concern is that after all the effort expended changing the culture and fixing defects, the project will be back in the same situation it's in now, with a large open defect backlog. Some team members may have even gone through more than one "defect bash" in the past.

Addressing this fatalism starts with a mind-set change. You must appeal to your newly defined commitment to quality. And you must do it every single chance you get. Ignore the skepticism and stay focused on the larger goal. Most projects have either explicit or implied levels of quality for them to be deemed a success. Follow this mantra: a large backlog of open defects is a *huge* risk to that success. If you can convince yourself and your team that this risk is large and does exist, the rest will eventually come.

Defects should be considered a personal affront to your team—like your code has physically thrown up on your keyboard and the only way to clean it is to resolve it in such a way that it never comes back.

When you treat defects like that, the stakeholders will recognize your commitment to quality. In our experience, clients respond well when you take defects seriously. They get the sense that you're committed to giving them the highest-quality product you can.

Similarly, project managers are usually quick to see the link between quality as a metric and project success. But you may have trouble convincing your manager to allow defects to take such a high priority in your task list. If so, convince your manager to let you try the process for at least 3 months (preferably 6). Even if there's no substantial improvement in that time, at least the seeds have been sown that quality is something you're thinking about. But by the same token, if there's no substantial improvement in 3 months you have to consider that maybe a more drastic approach is necessary, such as a change in the project team's makeup.

Also, be aware that reviewing, triaging, and replicating historical defects has a high per-defect resource cost. Addressing historical defects takes more effort than addressing them as soon as they're reported—which means as your backlog drops, and as you become more adept at the defect-resolution process, it becomes much easier to maintain a base level of quality as you go.

With all this talk of how to manage defects, it makes sense to discuss how a tracking system fits into the mix.

## 6.7    *Working with a defect-tracking system*

Throughout this chapter, we've talked about defect tracking, the anatomy of a good defect, the process to dig a project out from under the weight of a defect backlog, and other things. In all of that, there hasn't been any time spent talking about the tools that you can use to manage defects. Defect-tracking systems have been mentioned, but not in specific detail.

If you were hoping to get great insight into the one killer defect-tracking system that will bring peace, harmony, and glory to your project, you're reading the wrong book. We're not going to discuss the specifics of any defect-tracking systems that are on the market partially because we're still on the hunt for that divine defect tracker ourselves. Instead, our focus is going to be on the tool's interaction with your team and project.

It seems that every project has some sense that they need to be logging and tracking defects. Unfortunately, defect tracking is often treated as a second-class citizen. It's a necessary evil in the software development process. We've regularly seen projects that have defect-tracking systems that were obviously implemented with little or no thought to the purpose they fulfill for the project. They were there because every project needs bug-tracking software.

Most companies would never implement business-critical software without due analysis or careful thought. You know that the by-the-seat-of-your-pants acquisition and implementation plan is rarely successful, yet this approach is still done with defect-tracking systems.

The results are pretty obvious on a brownfield project. When you ask about certain areas of the software, people respond with statements like "We never use that." Worse, there are projects where the defect-tracking software has been completely abandoned because the project team couldn't work with it without imposing significant overhead to the process. If any of those situations apply, it's fairly obvious that the system was implemented without first knowing what the project team needed or how they worked.

Here's one example: if the project doesn't have the concept of a module, don't impose one onto the team simply because the defect software requires it. It would be a needless classification that would allow for careless or sloppy entries in the system. Additionally, you've imposed another step in the process of the defect creator. Instead of seamlessly moving from one required piece of data to another, defect creators have to know whether they should skip this one specific data entry point.

**WARNING**    A well-configured defect-tracking system will work seamlessly in your process and won't be a source of friction (though its contents might). You can accomplish this type of process integration through well-planned and carefully researched implementation of a tool.

Even after you've implemented a defect-tracking system that works well within your process, you may have to do some convincing to get everyone to use it. Brownfield projects may have people who have been worn down by the workflow required in the past. You'll need to get them on board to make the system work.

If a project team has started to grow any amount of team-based code ownership and quality standards, your argument will be easier. Don't focus on the fact that the tracking system is where defects are found. Instead, point out how the system can be used to better analyze problem areas within the application. Show your team how reporting from a defect-tracking system can improve their ability to remedy areas of questionable quality.

Implementing a defect-tracking system that collects meaningful and relevant information is only half of the workflow you require. Simply entering data into a system doesn't make it useful to the team. The use comes from your ability to retrieve that information in a way that adds value to the project team. It's at this point you should start to think of how to report on that data.

**Challenge your assumptions: Do you really need defect tracking?**

The common assumption on software projects is that a software-based defect-tracking system is mandatory. Is it really, though? On a brownfield project, you may have no choice but to use a software system for tracking defects. The size of the backlog may dictate some way to supplement the collective memory of the team.

But if you've inherited a small defect backlog, or if the team has worked its way out of the defect backlog, perhaps you don't need a software system. If you're working in a Zero Defect Count environment and have open lines of communication, maybe email is enough to track defects.

It's possible to run an entire software development project, with high levels of technical and business-related difficulty, without formal defect-tracking software. We've done it successfully in the past. Although arguments can be made that risk, pain, and friction will appear without a system, consider that those arguments may derive from speculation based on experience from past projects. Always determine if the recommendation to drop defect tracking will work for your specific project. Sometimes it will; sometimes it won't.

## 6.8 Defect reporting

Everyone who opens a defect-tracking system reads reports filled with defect data. The report may be as simple, and informal, as an Open Defect Listing filtered by your username. Defect-tracking systems, like any system having data input, are not overly useful if the data can't be viewed and aggregated in a meaningful way.

Reporting on defects is much more useful to the development effort than printing out a list of the open defects. On brownfield projects, there will usually be existing data in the defect-tracking system. You may have worked through reviewing and resolving a defect backlog. Now that you have all that information, what can you do with it?

We've already mentioned the most common daily report, Open Defects Listing for a User. This list is where developers will go to select work from their work queue. If you've been able to instill a strong sense of team code ownership, the report may not even be filtered by the developer's name. Instead, developers will be running an Open Defects Listing for the entire project and picking items from it to work on.

For brownfield projects, you can glean some important information from your defect list through trending data.

### 6.8.1 Trending data

When you're reviewing reports, it's common to get trapped in the current-point-in-time details of the data. Although looking at the specifics can provide good information to the reader, trending data tends to be more informative on brownfield projects. The importance of trending data is especially high when you're first starting on a project where there's historical data.

Trending of defect data isn't difficult to do provided you have sufficient useful data. Most trend-based reporting that we've used is possible with the standard data that most projects collect on defect entries. Two particular pieces of data are worth further discussion: module and version number.

### TRENDING BY MODULE

Having defects categorized by module (application area) is a common practice. The module category is a quick and easy way for the person attempting resolution to determine where to start in their work. It also provides a method for the project team to determine which modules need the most immediate attention based on the current number of open defects in each module. But these two options aren't the only useful pieces of data that you can get when trending by module.

When talking about trending based on associated module, we mean observing the explicit change and rate of change over time in the number of defects assigned to a module. You monitor the number of defects in a module at set intervals and note the difference at each interval. You may also want to generate these reports for new defects only, defects from all time, or defects that remain open at the end of the interval.

Figure 6.9 shows a simple graph of the number of defects per module over time.

In all of these reports, the information you'll get tells you how the project is changing. A steady increase in the number of defects in a module over time may signal the code is becoming too difficult to change or maintain.

Another piece of trend data that can provide valuable insight is the average number of times that a defect is returned as not resolved. If there's a trend upward on this value, it may be a sign that the project team is slipping on its commitment to quality and Zero Defect Count. It could also be a sign that the development team isn't communicating with the client very well.

Trending reports seem rarely to be included out of the box with many defect-tracking applications. In fact, in some cases you have to supplement the system with custom reporting. Other times, you may be just as well served by a gut feeling of the trend based on a regular review of a snapshot report.

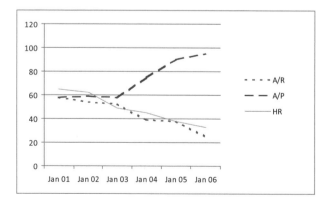

**Figure 6.9  A sample graph showing number of defects per module over time. Note that the increasing defect count in the A/P module indicates it could use some attention.**

In the end, trending of defect data doesn't come with a hard-and-fast set of guidelines of the actions you should take. This information should be used to *support* decision making, but not to drive it. Just because there was an increase in new defects logged on a certain module, it doesn't necessarily mean that the module requires significant rework. It may just be an indicator that all developers were actively working in that area of the application during that time.

The final use of reporting in defect-tracking systems that we're going to cover concerns software releases.

### 6.8.2 *Release notes*

Depending on the project, there may be a need to provide information about the changes to the software when it was released. Commonly known as release notes, these can be valuable at the start of a brownfield project to show progress to your client and provide a starting point for your testing team.

One of the main sections in your release notes should be a list of resolved defects. If you have to generate this list by hand, it can be a hassle. So it makes sense to leverage the defect-tracking system to create a list of these resolved issues.

Unfortunately, this effort almost always adds some form of overhead to your process. To generate a report of resolved defects for a release, you must link defects to a release number. In most cases, you'll need to add another field to the defect report that the resolver must enter when updating it.

Although this change may seem trivial, each additional data entry point will increase the time spent on the defect. People will forget to enter the value, or they'll enter the wrong value, and they'll do it on a regular basis. It may not be frequent, but it will happen. Usually, the best you can hope for is that it doesn't happen often enough to warrant any special action. Depending on the capabilities of your tracking system, try to make it as easy as possible for users to enter this information correctly. If a few mistakes slip by, it's not the end of the world.

Because this type of reporting requires data entry on each defect, we don't recommend that you try to backfill the existing entries in the defect-tracking system. First, it would be a tedious and monotonous job that we wouldn't wish on even the most annoying intern. Second, you won't know what value to put in for any historical defect without doing a lot of research. That time is better spent elsewhere.

In any case, historical release notes provide little value. The releases have already been sent out to the client. There should be no desire to resend the release just so that it includes release notes. Most likely the release notes for past releases will never be created, and certainly they'll never be used by the client. If you need, or want, to create release notes on your brownfield project, do it for future releases.

There you have it. Reporting on your defect-tracking system can provide some benefits to your project. If you're a developer looking to improve code, don't forget to trend the defects by module and release. When you have the opportunity, use your defect-tracking system to generate information that will be sent to the client. Traceability back to your system when a client is asking questions is a great asset in convincing the client that you're on top of the situation.

## 6.9    *Summary*

Defect tracking is an oft-maligned part of projects. Management demands it as a necessity. Systems are installed and turned on without any thought to how they integrate with the project team or what process they're using. Everyone complains that entering defects sucks and then they proceed to perpetuate the problem by creating entries that are either incorrect or incomplete. The development team despises it because they end up having to do detailed research to supplement the entry just so that they can begin resolving the issue. Once defects are resolved, they're forgotten as relics of the past.

We've seen all of this occur on projects and none of it has to. With some thought and analysis, defect-tracking systems can be configured to work effectively for a project and still provide rich information to the project team, in both the present and the future. Analysis shouldn't be limited to the configuration of an already chosen system. The project team should take the time to determine if the project's practices and procedures even require a defect-tracking system. Sometimes nothing may be needed. Don't fight it. If it works, let it happen.

If a brownfield project does have a defect-tracking system, be wary of the backlog of open defects. Be wary in the sense that you can't avoid them and that the team will be addressing them sooner or later. Because backlog defects are inherently stale, working the backlog sooner will be your best option.

Work that backlog until it's completely cleared and then maintain a policy of Zero Defect Count. Succeeding with that policy will, at first, take effort both to work the incoming defects and to put the codebase into a state of higher quality. Work to make Zero Defect Count a cultural force on the project. If quality is naturally high because of the way the team works, it's one less thing that needs to be managed.

No matter the effort put into the quality of a system, defects will occur. Having the team address defects immediately will make their resolution much easier. Some of those defects may be feature requests masquerading as defects. This type of feature/defect isn't a problem per se, but it can affect the scheduling of work on the project. If you catch feature requests that appear in this manner, don't turn them down outright. Instead, put the power in the hands of the client. Have them prioritize the feature request against all the other outstanding work and defects. Not only will this type of prioritization ensure the requests aren't lost, but at the same time the instigator or client will feel that their request has been attended to.

Brownfield applications that have existing defect-tracking systems can be a trove of analytical data. Don't forget to use it to track information and trends in the past development effort. It will guide you to places that may need attention to prevent future catastrophic meltdowns.

Don't treat defect tracking on a project as a second-class citizen. Embrace it as an area to improve, like so many other things on a brownfield project. It will take time, but the end goal of an efficient and effective project can't be achieved without finding and resolving the friction points in the defect-tracking system.

Thus ends our journey into your project's ecosystem. Starting with the next chapter, we'll look at your application's code, beginning with a topic near and dear to our hearts: object-oriented fundamentals.

# Part 2

# The code

Our ecosystem is done! We've come a long way and, more importantly, significantly increased our confidence for what lies ahead. And what lies ahead is the subject of part 2.

We now shift our focus to the actual code of your application. Over the next few chapters, we'll discuss many ways you can effect change in your code to make it more maintainable and easier to change. We won't provide an exhaustive list of all the changes you could possibly make. But we'll focus on topics that, in our experience, will give you a lot of bang for your buck in a brownfield application.

We'll start by getting back to the basics in chapter 7. Here, we'll review what it means to be object oriented and get you in the right frame of mind for future changes. We'll go over some common principles that will be the basis for many of the code changes in the subsequent chapters.

Chapter 8 builds on this foundation by looking at how to layer (or, more likely, *re*layer) the application. Our work on automated unit tests will bear some fruit as we discuss how to use these tests to isolate the layers in our applications.

Chapter 9, "Loosen up: Taming your dependencies" will be an interesting topic. Here we'll look at how to tease apart the dependencies of your classes to reduce your coupling and increase the maintainability of your code.

In chapter 10, we'll look at patterns for the user interface, specifically Model-View-Controller and Model-View-Presenter, and how best to take advantage of them in a brownfield application.

Chapter 11 is at the other end of the application. Here, we'll move to the data access layer. You'll see strategies on refactoring your data access, including how an object-relational mapper can abstract away the database and provide you with a reusable and testable data access strategy that's receptive to change.

In chapter 12, we delve into integration territory. We talk about how to work with external systems and how we can manage our interfaces with them to reduce our exposure in the event they change.

Finally, in lucky chapter 13, we close with some encouragement on how to keep the momentum going to ensure the project doesn't lapse back into brownfield contamination.

# Bringing better OO practices to the project

**This chapter covers**

- Reviewing components of OO languages
- Using OO principles in brownfield apps
- Other useful practices for maintaining code

Most programmers can recite the four foundational components of an object-oriented (OO) language by rote. But when was the last time you stopped to think about them explicitly while you were coding? Are you using objects to their full advantage? Or do you create a few domain objects and encase them in procedural logic? Be honest—there are no wrong answers.

A good many brownfield projects fail to take advantage of basic OO principles. Often, the principles are ignored completely. This isn't necessarily a bad thing, but...well, that's not true. The quickest path to a brownfield application is to ignore OO principles and write large volumes of procedural code wrapped in a couple of classes.

ASP.NET applications are often excellent examples of poor OO design due to the nature of the ASP.NET pipeline. It's common to have large methods performing complex business logic, or even data access, directly in the code-behind for an ASP.NET page. This code usually sits alongside the same code that determines how to render UI elements on the page. As we'll see in chapter 10, not only does this practice break the single responsibility principle (discussed later in this chapter), but also it's fragile and nearly impossible to test in an automated way.

Let's look at some code to illustrate. Listing 7.1 shows a sample `click` event from an ASP.NET code-behind class.

---

**Listing 7.1  Sample ASP.NET `click` event**

```
public void listBoxSearch_Click( object sender, EventArgs e )
{
    string searchTerm = textBoxSearchTerm.Text;
    searchTerm = parseSearchString( searchTerm );        ❶ Gather inputs
    int countryId = listBoxCountry.SelectedValue;
    DataTable searchResults = SearchApplicationDb         ❷ Retrieve search
        .GetSearchResults( searchTerm, countryId );
    gridSearchResults.DataSource = searchResults;         Bind results
    gridSearchResults.DataBind( );                        to page

    string searchCriteriaText = getSearchCriteriaText( );  Display search
    labelCurrentSearch.Text = searchCriteriaText;          criteria on page
}
```

---

At first glance, listing 7.1 may seem benign. It's short, easy to understand, and the complicated work is delegated to other functions. But as we'll see from the principles in this chapter, it violates more than one OO principle, including abstraction, the single responsibility principle, and encapsulation.

Furthermore, this code is almost impossible to test in an automated fashion. The search results are retrieved using a static call to a data access class ❷. Plus, we're parsing out a search string ❶, which is almost certainly something that should be tested in isolation. The code itself exists in a web form's code-behind, which means we'll likely need some ASP.NET infrastructure in place just to run it, let alone test it.

So chapter 7 may seem like review at first, but it's actually foundational. Everything we talk about between now and the final chapter will be steeped in the concepts we discuss here.

We start with the very first thing you learned about object-oriented design.

## 7.1   OO fundamentals

Don't worry, we haven't suddenly handed off ghostwriting this book to a Comp-Sci professor. We're well aware that you know the stock interview answer to "What are the fundamentals of OO?"

But we're going to mention them anyway as the first step in our journey into fundamentals. Like many good principles, they're worth reviewing from time to time to make sure you keep them in the back of your mind. After all, it's easy to fall into the trap of writing procedural code and calling it an object just because it's wrapped in a class.

> **Object-oriented versus procedural code**
>
> The difference between object-oriented code and procedural code is often over-looked. Just because your methods are wrapped in a class doesn't mean you're being object oriented. You can still write procedural code in an object-oriented language. We've already done it in the lone code sample you've seen so far in this chapter, listing 7.1.
>
> Objects aren't limited to physical concepts like animals and vehicles and beverages. `EnglishLanguageParser`, `TaskScheduler`, and `DataCollector` could be valid objects as well. These examples are more abstract concepts that perform some function rather than represent a real-world thing with arms and legs and wheels and ingredients.
>
> As you read through this chapter and review your code, ask yourself, "Is this procedural code in OO clothing?" at regular intervals. As you become well versed with the ideas in this chapter, you'll find that question easier to answer, especially if you get into the habit of regularly testing your code.

Without further ado, the foundational principles of object-oriented programming are

- Encapsulation
- Inheritance
- Abstraction
- Polymorphism

Although they're only four of many object-oriented concepts, these are considered to be the foundation of an object-oriented language. As foundational concepts, these four tenets will be built upon in all the programming techniques that are discussed in part 2 of this book. So before getting into the other concepts, let's have a quick refresher on these four principles.

### 7.1.1 *Encapsulation*

Encapsulation is the process by which you shield the implementation details of an object's functions from outside callers. For example, when you call a method, `Find-DocumentsNamed(name)`, you don't care how the class finds the documents. All that matters is that it does what it claims to do.

We feel encapsulation is the most overlooked of the four principles. Evidence of poor encapsulation litters code. In the most egregious cases you'll find things like forms or web pages having intimate knowledge of data access details such as connection strings or SQL queries.

Instead of being privy to those details, the screens should know only that they're calling some method on a class to return data to them. How that code performs the data retrieval should be hidden from the screen itself.

Many of the principles we discuss later, such as single responsibility, are based heavily on the idea of encapsulation.

### 7.1.2  *Inheritance*

Inheritance is the mechanism by which we create classes that are more specialized versions of other classes. These subclasses inherit properties and methods from their parents and often implement additional behavior or override existing behavior.

You know this definition already. You know that `Mammal` inherits from `Animal` and that `Dog` and `Cat` both inherit from `Mammal`. And you've no doubt seen countless examples of how each mammal implements the `Speak()` method through the magic of `Console.WriteLine()`.

Inheritance is probably the most easily understood of the OO principles. You've likely written, or at least encountered, an `EntityBase` class in some form that implemented an `ID` property. All other identifiable entities inherited from this class and, with it, the ID property.

It's nearly impossible to work in .NET without inheritance. ASP.NET pages automatically inherit from `System.Web.UI.Page` and user controls from `System.Web.UI.UserControl` (which, in turn, inherit from `System.Web.UI.Control`). And although it's possible to create a custom exception that doesn't inherit from `System.Exception`, that's the…ummm…exception rather than the rule.

Inheritance is often overused. In chapter 5, we talked about the depth of inheritance metric as one to be aware of. In many brownfield applications, it's not uncommon to see a large inheritance tree where each class in the tree adds a bit more functionality until the top level has such a large number of functions (new and inherited) that the original intent of the base class is lost.

Using inheritance to create a "pure" object structure tends to be an academic exercise that hurts an application more than it helps. In the case of the ubiquitous Animal > Mammal > Cat, Dog example, if the application has no need for an Animal abstraction, then don't create it. Later in the book you'll see places where it may appear that we're inheriting when we should be maintaining the simplicity of the inheritance tree. We talk more on the importance of keeping things simple in the last section, and we come back to inheritance when we discuss useful OO principles in section 7.4.

### 7.1.3  *Abstraction*

Abstraction can be a tricky concept to pin down because the term *abstract* is used in different contexts (for example, *abstract classes* in C#). From the perspective of object-oriented programming, it's the method in which we simplify a complex thing, like an object, a set of objects, or a set of services.

An API is an abstraction in some form. Take any namespace from the .NET Base Class Library and that will be an abstraction. The `System.IO` namespace, for example, is an abstraction of your system's I/O functions. It's further subdivided into other abstractions like `System.IO.Compression` and `System.IO.Ports`, which are more specialized cases of I/O. This subdivision is also called a *lower level of abstraction.*

Abstraction is an important concept in OO design. Many of the principles we discuss in section 7.3 are rooted in it, such as the single responsibility principle and the dependency inversion principle.

### 7.1.4  *Polymorphism*

Related to inheritance is polymorphism. We know we can inherit subclasses from base classes. Polymorphism allows us to use subclasses as if they were base classes. This means we can call methods on a subclass without having to know exactly what type it is.

The canonical example of polymorphism is the `Speak` method on an `Animal` class, as shown in listing 7.2.

**Listing 7.2  Polymorphism example**

```
public abstract class Animal
{
    public abstract void Speak( );
}

public class Dog : Animal
{
    public void Speak( )
    {
        Console.WriteLine( "Bark" );
    }
}

public class Cat : Animal
{
    public void Speak( )
    {
        Console.WriteLine( "Meow" );
    }
}

public void MakeAnAnimalSpeak( Animal animal )    ❶ Method with base
{                                                     class parameter
    animal.Speak( );
}

public void MainLine( )
{
    MakeAnAnimalSpeak( new Dog( ) );    ❷ Calling method
    MakeAnAnimalSpeak( new Cat( ) );
}
```

In this example, we have a method, `MakeAnAnimalSpeak` ❶. We don't care what type of animal it is; we just know that it can speak. In the `MainLine` method ❷, we call `MakeAnAnimalSpeak` with a couple of different subclasses of `Animal`.

Polymorphism is used prolifically throughout the .NET Framework. One example is the `ToString` method, which behaves differently depending on the type of object you're calling it on. `ToString` is defined on `System.Object`, from which all classes derive. So we know we can always call it on any object, but how it behaves depends on its implementation within a particular object.

We hope that's all we need to say on OO fundamentals. We'll continue with the assumption that you agree that OO programming is good. And while we're talking about desirable characteristics of our code, let's turn our attention to some overarching "-abilities" we'd like it to have.

## 7.2   Code "-abilities"

Although the basic tenets form the bedrock for our development, there are some more general "-abilities" or "attitudes" you should strive for in your code. You should always keep these underlying goals (see figure 7.1) in the back of your mind as you work. They're important to brownfield applications because it's the lack of them that has led to your reading this book.

### 7.2.1   Maintainability

We start with the granddaddy of all abilities: your code absolutely must be maintainable. If it's not—well, forgive us for not feeling too badly about it because it will lead to more people purchasing this book.

**Figure 7.1   Five "-abilities" that help lead to a maintainable application**

At all times, you should ask yourself the question, "Will the next person who looks at this code be able to easily figure out what it's doing?" And bear in mind, the next person could be *you*, a year from now.

---

### Coding for the next guy: An extreme position

Taking the idea of maintainability to the extreme, Damian Conway puts it this way in his book *Perl Best Practices: Standards and Styles for Developing Maintainable Code* (O'Reilly, 2005): "Always code as if the guy who ends up maintaining your code is a violent psychopath who knows where you live."

---

The reason maintainability is so important is because your code spends the vast majority of its life being maintained. In some respects, it enters maintenance mode as soon as it's written. It makes sense that we'd want to make it as easy as possible to work with during the maintenance phase.

How you make your code maintainable is essentially the topic of the remainder of this book. From the OO design principles, to layering, to inversion of control containers, the primary reason we discuss these topics is so that our code is easy to work with.

In fact, the rest of the "-abilities" essentially follow from the idea of making your code more maintainable, starting with readability.

## 7.2.2  *Readability*

Readability is sort of a catchall category for a few related ideas. The overall intent is that you should make your code easy to read. Readability encompasses both low-level things, like appropriate variable and method names, as well as higher-level concepts, like ensuring that developers can easily understand your code at a meta level. That is, they should be able to look at a class and quickly determine its function as well as its boundaries. It's just as important to understand what a class *doesn't* do as what it *does* do.

**NOTE:**  If you stop to think about your day-to-day activities when writing code, you'll discover you don't spend that much time *writing* it. Most of the time, you're reading, and more importantly, trying to understand it, especially in brownfield applications. So it's reasonable to put effort into ensuring it's readable.

For a brownfield application, there are a couple of easy things you can do to help out. First, gone are the days when variables needed to be named x and y to save space. If your variable represents a collection of customer objects, called it customerList or listOfCustomers or customers—not custList or list or myList or li. The compiler doesn't care what your variables are named. But the person reading it does. You can achieve a quick win for little effort by renaming unclear variables.

The same idea applies to method and property names. To a new developer, a method called DoCalc() isn't nearly as meaningful as CalculateMinimumTemperature( ).

If you're concerned about carpal tunnel syndrome when typing out long method names, keep in mind that the available IDEs and productivity tools make it easier than ever to access and navigate your code without having to type the names out in full.

Another way to make your code more readable is to consider using a fluent interface. First coined by Eric Evans and Martin Fowler, the term *fluent interface* refers to a way of having methods build on each other in order to make the code read better.

Fluent interfaces fit into a fairly small niche. They don't necessarily lend themselves to widespread use but can be useful in specialized areas. We've already talked about them in the context of mocking in chapter 4. Listing 7.3 shows another example.

**Listing 7.3  Sample fluent interface**

```
imageTransformer
    .From( selectedImage )
    .Using( pixelsPerInch )
    .With( bilinearResampling )
    .ResizeTo( width, height );
```

In listing 7.3, it's clear what the code does, even if you have only a vague idea of the domain. This clarity results from the fluent interface as well as from the variable and method names.

Good fluent interfaces can be tricky to build—which is another reason their focus is narrow. As you may have noticed, the "transition" methods in listing 7.3 (such as From,

Using, and With) don't make much sense on their own. They're designed specifically to be used in a fluent interface. This narrow focus makes the overall API rather chatty, which can confuse matters if the object is used for other, nonfluent purposes.

Nevertheless, fluent interfaces have their place and, when applied appropriately, can add much readability to your code.

Our next "-ability" deals with how testable your code is.

### 7.2.3  *Testability*

*Designing for testability* comes from microelectronics. You design your code specifically so that it can be tested in isolation, free from any other distracting variables. It's a simple enough goal and one that forms the foundation of science. If a theory can't be tested, it's not a valid theory. We should try to maintain the same rigor in our coding.

Chances are, your brownfield application contains many classes that weren't designed for testability. You may have discovered some of them already if you attempted to write automated tests for them after chapter 4. For example, if you need to set up a connection to a live database, ensure an app.config is in place, and start a web service in order to test a certain method, it was clearly not designed for testability.

A testable class is one that you can test with a minimum of infrastructure. We'll discuss a number of design principles that can help achieve testability. We've already danced around one when we discussed mocking objects in chapter 4: we ensure our class depends only on interfaces that can be stubbed or mocked during testing so that we can focus solely on the behavior being tested.

### 7.2.4  *Extensibility*

Whenever possible, you should allow developers to extend your code easily. You don't know how your code will be used in the future and there's no need to account for every possible scenario. But you should make it easy for others to add behavior to your code if they need to.

Extensibility isn't as easy as it looks. Simply converting all your private methods to public isn't the road to a more maintainable application. Later in this chapter, we discuss the open/closed principle (OCP), which deals with extensibility in detail and describes methods for achieving it in your code.

### 7.2.5  *Reversibility*

Reversibility means that you design your code so that any design decisions you make can be reversed easily. The concept may seem counterintuitive at first. Why would you write it if you planned to reverse it later?

But the flexibility to reverse your design decisions is critical to maintainability. How many times have you agonized over a piece of code to get it just right because you knew it would be impossible to change later? (This feeling is often called *Framework Builder Anxiety.*)

Instead, consider designing with an eye for reversibility. As Martin Fowler in his paper "Is Design Dead" put it: "If you can easily change your decisions, this means it's less important to get them right—which makes your life much simpler."[1]

This axiom is true in life—in general. For example, what if, after purchasing a house, you had the option of selling it back to the original owner for its current market value with no questions asked, even years after you purchased it? The house-buying process would be a lot less stressful because it wouldn't matter if you didn't like it or your personal circumstances changed.

The same goes with code design. If you make reversible decisions, there's no need to ponder the far-reaching ramifications. Any discussions can be countered with "We can change it later if we have to."

Reversibility has some bearing on brownfield applications because, in many cases, you'll be at the business end of a previous irreversible decision. You'll often encounter a bad design choice that can't easily be changed. If you decide to tackle the task of reversing the irreversible, make sure you learn from the original design and don't replace it with a similarly irreversible one.

Let's look at an example of an irreversible design decision in listing 7.4.

**Listing 7.4  GetData method**

```
public static DataSet GetData( string storedProc, string tableName,
        params object[] parameterValues )
{
    DataSet ds = SqlHelper.ExecuteDataset(m_connectionString,
        storedProc, parameterValues);
    DataTable table = ds.Tables[0];
    table.TableName = tableName;

    switch (storedProc.ToLower())         ◁──  ❶ Branching
    {                                               based name

        case "twi_get_artists_and_tours":
            ds.Tables[1].TableName = "Tours";
            ds.Relations.Add("Artist_Tour",
                ds.Tables[0].Columns["ArtistID"],
                ds.Tables[1].Columns["ArtistID"]);

            return ds;
    }

    return ds;
}
```

There are some interesting decisions made in this design. First, it's a public method that assumes the caller knows which stored procedure to retrieve and that does specific tasks depending on the name of that stored procedure ❶. What if we later decide to retrieve this data directly from the database using SQL or an object-relational mapper? What if

---

[1]  www.martinfowler.com/articles/designDead.html#id59803

the structure of the data returned by the `twi_get_artists_and_tours` stored procedure changes? All of these factors impact not only this code but also the code that calls it. Not a happy place to be when you're in the data layer.

### 7.2.6   *Adaptability*

Related to the idea of reversibility is adaptability. It's guaranteed that your code will change over time. Requirements change, bugs are fixed, new features are added. Even migrating from one .NET Framework to another brings about new ways of doing things. When writing your code, you should keep this aspect of its maintenance in mind and make sure that you can change things without massive rework.

Encapsulation is an easy way to accomplish adaptability. Another is through the use of design patterns like the Adapter and the Façade.

---

#### Design patterns

Throughout the book, we mention design patterns, like *Adapter* and *Façade* above. Patterns are a sort of developer shorthand for ways to solve a particular problem. For example, when we say "We can use a Strategy pattern," what we mean is "We can encapsulate the underlying algorithm so that the client can swap in different implementations at runtime" (see listing 7.9 later in this chapter for an example).

Patterns can help you focus your thinking when it comes to attacking a problem. You could be talking about how to solve a problem with someone else and they'll say, "Would X pattern be useful here?" Whether or not it's useful, it's sometimes a good way to change your thinking about a problem if it's giving you trouble.

Design patterns can be powerful when discussing them with other developers but only if your audience is familiar with them. And even then, it doesn't hurt to be clear. Sometimes developers may have different ideas on how to implement certain patterns.

Similarly, be careful you don't go pattern crazy, which can occur if you start seeing places to put patterns where a simpler solution may be more viable. Always go back to the maintainability of the application. Often the simplest solution is the best one.

Because we don't want to focus too much on the use of patterns, we don't devote any more than a sidebar to the overall concept. We talk about patterns from time to time and briefly explain any that we bring up, but they're typically in support of another concept.

There are several excellent books on patterns. We suggest starting with *Head First Design Patterns* (O'Reilly, 2004) and then moving on to both *Patterns of Enterprise Application Architecture* (Addison-Wesley, 2002) and *Design Patterns* (Addison-Wesley, 1994).

---

The Adapter pattern is a method of converting one interface into another. It's used when a client is expecting one interface but the system it's connecting to provides a different one.

The Façade pattern is slightly different in its intent. It simplifies a set of interfaces into a single interface that's presumably easier for the client to use.

Both patterns can be particularly useful to brownfield applications. They allow us to move our code into a more testable state without affecting other areas we haven't addressed.

We're not done describing useful code principles just yet. In the next section, we go a little deeper and talk about some principles that apply to object-oriented programming.

## 7.3 Useful OO principles

Now that we have a handle on the core concepts and underlying goals, we can expand on them with some useful principles that will help guide us as we add new features and refactor existing code.

As with the OO fundamentals, none of these principles are new. Although they aren't generally as well known, many of them have been around for over 20 years in one form or another. For more in-depth discussions on some of them, we encourage you to read *Agile Principles, Patterns, and Practices in C#* (Prentice Hall PTR, 2006).

### 7.3.1 Favor composition over inheritance

In section 7.1, we talked a lot about the dangers of relying heavily on inheritance. It can give you a nice warm feeling to use inheritance often because somewhere, in the deep recesses of our mind, we feel like we're making Professor Bate, who taught us Computer Science 101, proud. We're avoiding duplication by putting our reusable code in a base class.

But in many cases, inheritance is a short-term solution to a problem. It often leads to a dense inheritance tree that can be hard to maintain—a phrase that should set off very loud, very annoying alarm bells.

The reason inheritance can become unmaintainable is that when you need to change the behavior of a method at the top of the hierarchy, rippling effects occur all the way down.

Coming up with an example showing the deficiencies of inheritance isn't difficult. Take any object that has behavior—say a DinnerPlate class. And some of our plates are decorative, so we create a DecorativeDinnerPlate class with a bunch of new behavior associated with it, like CountryOfOrigin and SnobFactor.

Later, we add mugs to our application. So we create a Mug class. Pretty soon, we discover that some of our mugs can be decorative as well, so we create a DecorativeMug class, also with CountryOfOrigin and SnobFactor properties.

As this point, we discover that we've duplicated quite a bit of code between DecorativeMug and the DecorativePlate. It's clear we'll have to create new base classes called Dish and DecorativeDish and derive our DecorativeDinnerPlate and DecorativeMug classes from them.

But what if we then start offering decorative rugs? Or decorative glassware? And what if some of our plates, mugs, rugs, and glassware are hand-crafted and some aren't? Soon, we end up with an inheritance hierarchy with classes like `HandCrafted-DecorativeMug` and `FactoryMadeDinnerPlate`. See figure 7.2 for a taste.

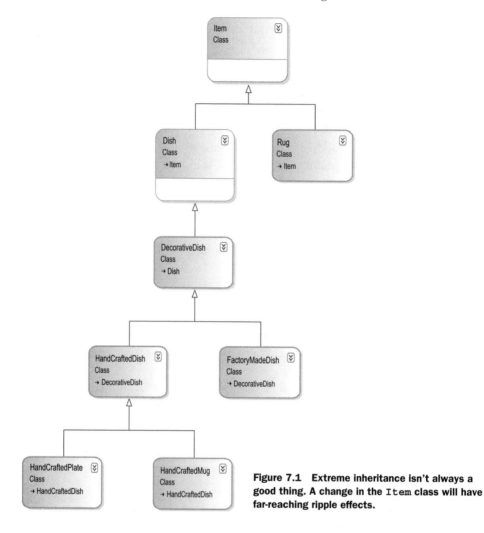

**Figure 7.1   Extreme inheritance isn't always a good thing. A change in the `Item` class will have far-reaching ripple effects.**

Instead, we should separate out aspects of the objects into classes. We create classes called `DecorativeUse` and `RegularUse` as well as an interface, `IUse`. We do the same for an `IManufactureMethod` interface. Then, our `DinnerPlate` and `Rug` classes look like listing 7.5.

**Listing 7.5   Classes that use composition rather than inheritance**

```
public class DinnerPlate
{
    IUse Use { get; set; }
    IManufactureMethod ManufactureMethod { get; set; }
```

```
    }
    public class Rug
    {
        IUse Use { get; set; }
        IManufactureMethod { get; set; }
    }

    public class Tester
    {
        public void CreateSomePlatesAndRugs( )
        {
            DinnerPlate regularFactoryMadePlate = new DinnerPlate( );
            regularFactoryMadePlate.Use = new RegularUse( );
            regularFactoryMadePlate.ManufactureMethod = new FactoryMade( );

            Rug handMadeRegularRug = new Rug( );
            handMadeRegularRug.Use = new RegularUse( );
            handMadeRegularRug.ManufactureMethod = new HandMade( );
        }
    }
```

We can now add new behaviors easily as well as new objects that can make use of whatever behaviors are relevant. For example, we may want to include an IFabric interface on the Rug class but not on the DinnerPlate class.

In effect, we've switched from using inheritance to using composition. We have a flat structure but we extend the classes by *composing* behaviors for them. By composing our objects with these behaviors, we allow for much more flexibility than if we'd used inheritance.

### 7.3.2 *Separation of concerns/single responsibility principle*

If you learn nothing else from this section, remember the single responsibility principle (SRP) and the notion of separation of concerns (SoC). SoC is the process by which we break down the functionality of an application into distinct modules that don't overlap. It's a critical concept that we revisit often.

SoC is abstract; there's no guidance on *how* to separate the concerns or even how to define the concerns. A concern is simply an area of interest in the application. And by and large, your definition of a concern may not match someone else's.

The single responsibility principle can help. It's a more concrete concept that states "A class should have only one reason to change." (*Agile Principles, Patterns, and Practices in C#*)

The key to this definition is "reason to change." Often the reason to change can be hard to pin down. For example, you could argue that a class called PrintFunctions needs updating only when the application's printing behavior changes, and therefore, it doesn't violate SRP. Conversely, you could say that the class is handling the printing of jobs *and* the printer configuration screen. Thus, it *does* violate SRP.

The scope of your application will define what a "reason to change" is. It could be that the PrintFunctions class is a façade over a third-party printing subsystem, in which case the only thing wrong with it is the misleading name. Or it could contain half a dozen disparate print-related functions, none of which depends on any others, in which case consider breaking up the class. For example, perhaps you separate it into a `Printer-Configuration` class, a `Printer` base class, and a couple of entity-specific subclasses (such as `JobPrinter` and `CustomerPrinter`).

Listing 7.6 shows a class that does too much.

**Listing 7.6    Class with too many responsibilities**

```
public class PrintFunctions
{
    public void ResetPrinter( )
    {
        // ... code to reset printer
    }

    public void SendPrintCompleteEmail( PrintJob printJob )
    {
        // ... code to send email to the person who printed
    }

    public void PrintToFile( Document documentToPrint, string filename )
    {
        // ... code to print document to file
    }

    public void PrintToPrinter(Document documentToPrint, Printer printer)
    {
        // ... code to print document on printer
    }

    public void SetPrinterConfiguration( Printer printer,
            PageSize pageSize )
    {
        // ...
    }

    public void SetPrinterConfiguration( Printer printer,
            PageSize, ColorScale colorScale )
    {
        // ...
    }

    public void SetPrinterConfiguration( Printer printer,
            ColorScale colorScale )
    {
        // ...
    }

}
```

The code in listing 7.6 has a lot of responsibilities. It's resetting printers, printing to printers, printing to files, and making configuration settings.

Listing 7.7 shows the same class with the responsibilities delegated.

**Listing 7.7 PrintManager with one responsibility**

```
public class PrintManager
{                                                    Class with notification logic  ❶
    private IPrintNotifier _printNotifier = new EmailNotifier( );    ◄─┘
    private IPrintConfiguration _configuration =
        new DefaultPrintConfiguration( );           ◄─┐   Class with config-
    private IPrintDestination _destination =        ❷  uration logic
        new PrintFileDestination( DEFAULT_PRINT_FILE );
    private IDocumentPrinter _printer = new Default( );    ◄─

    public IPrintNotifier PrintNotifier { get; set; }
    public IPrintConfiguration PrintConfiguration { get; set; }
    public IPrintDestination Destination { get; set; }
    public IDocumentPrinter Printer { get; set; }    Class with
                                                     printing
    public void Print( PrintJob printJob )           functionality  ❷
    {
        _printer.Print( printJob.Document );
        _printNotifier.Notify( printJob.Sender );
    }
}
```

The code in listing 7.7 is leaner than the previous version. That's because it doesn't deal with extraneous functions like emailing the sender or setting the configuration. All that has been moved to other classes like DefaultPrintConfiguration ❷ and EmailNotifier ❶.

By default this class will print to a file, but the client can override it with another destination if it wants. Ditto for the print configuration. This class is concerned only with the print action (and even then, that's delegated off to an IDocumentPrinter object ❸).

It should be obvious why this class is easier to maintain than the previous version: it doesn't do very much. Its sole responsibility is to print documents. If we change how printers are configured, we don't need to touch this class. If we add a new method to notify senders that a print job is complete, again, we don't need to change this class. This class changes only if the printing process itself changes.

### Don't forget to decouple

Although the class in listing 7.7 has been reduced to a single responsibility, it's still highly coupled. It contains a lot of default objects. For instance, by default it will notify senders by email if a print job is complete. This behavior can be overridden, but if someone is relying on the fact that emails are sent out and we decide to change to Short Message Service (SMS) notifications, we'll have some broken code.

In short, this code is still rather dependent on a lot of other objects. In chapter 9, we talk about how to break those dependencies.

## SRP AND BROWNFIELD APPLICATIONS

In our opinion, moving your application to be more SRP oriented is the best road to making it more maintainable. With each class responsible for one, and only one, piece of functionality, the classes tend to be much smaller and more manageable. Granted, you'll have many more classes than you may be used to, but this issue can be mitigated through careful organization of your solution structure and by taking advantage of code navigation abilities in Visual Studio, or a third-party add-in such as JetBrains' ReSharper or DevExpress' Code Rush.

In any case, the benefit—a less coupled, more cohesive application—far outweighs any trauma you may feel at having too many files. In addition, you'll usually find that code that adheres to SRP is easier to maintain because the classes are easier to change. By definition, classes with a single responsibility have only one reason to change—so when that reason arises, it's easy to determine where the change needs to be made.

Unfortunately, brownfield applications are often notoriously coupled and when you're staring a 6,000-line method in the face, single responsibility often gets relegated to the status of "would be nice but I have *real* work to do."

In addition, in chapter 4 we advised against writing new code without backing tests. Writing fully tested new code 100 percent of the time can seem like a lofty goal if you're facing a bug in a method that spans four printed pages. It's often difficult to implement tests on code without having to refactor first. In his book *Working Effectively with Legacy Code*, Michael Feathers calls this the Legacy Code Dilemma: "When we change code, we should have tests in place. To put tests in place, we often have to change code."

This conundrum most often manifests itself when you want to break up a piece of code into separate pieces of responsibility: we're separating dependencies into individual classes.

The reality is that unit tests may not be possible. And when that's the case, you need to tread lightly when you need to modify the code. If you can't write a unit test (and you should be *very* sure that you can't), chances are it's because the code has a lot of external dependencies that need to be set up. In this case, an integration test may be possible.

If an integration test is possible, your work is much easier. Now you have a safety net for when you perform the real work. You can start breaking out the dependencies into separate classes/responsibilities and know that you're not breaking anything.

In addition, as you separate responsibilities, you can also write unit tests for them along the way. Even though you have an integration test backing you up, you still want unit tests for individual classes because they're run more regularly. The last thing you need is to have someone break one of your new classes and not have it caught until the integration tests are run overnight.

Another important concept is the open/closed principle.

### 7.3.3 *Open/closed principle*

The open/closed principle is an important one for brownfield applications because it directly addresses how stable an application is. It states that "Software entities (classes, modules, functions, and so on) should be open for extensibility but closed for modification."

This idea seems contradictory, but in practice, it's easy to achieve. Let's consider an example. Listing 7.8 shows an `OrderRepository` class with a `FindBy` method. This method will return an `IEnumerable` list of `Order` objects based on some criteria.

**Listing 7.8  `OrderRepository`**

```
public class OrderRepository
{
    IEnumerable<Order> FindBy( OrderedDateFinder dateFinder )      ◄─┐   Concrete class
    {                                                                  as a parameter ❶
        foreach ( Order order in _orders )
        {
            if ( dateFinder.Matches( order )
            {
                yield return order;
            }
        }
    }
}
```

Notice that the `FindBy` method ❶ takes an `OrderedDateFinder` class. Without knowing its implementation, we can probably deduce that it will find all orders with a specified `OrderedDate`.

The issue with this code is that it depends on a concrete implementation of `OrderedDateFinder`. For example, suppose the requirement for `FindBy` changes so that we want to find orders by `FilledDate` rather than `OrderedDate`. And assume `OrderedDateFinder` is used elsewhere in our code so we can't change its implementation.

To accomplish this new requirement, we need to create a new class, `FilledDateFinder`, and change the signature of `FindBy` to take that class instead of `OrderedDateFinder`. We need to modify `OrderRepository` to accommodate a change in the client code. This code isn't closed for modification.

Let's backtrack a bit and assume our class looks like listing 7.9 instead.

**Listing 7.9  `OrderRepository` that's closed for modification**

```
public class OrderRepository
{                                                          ❶  Abstraction as
    IEnumerable<Order> FindBy( IFinder finder )      ◄─┘      a parameter
    {
        foreach ( Order order in _orders )
        {
            if ( finder.Matches( order )
```

```
            {
                yield return order;
            }
        }
    }
}
public interface IFinder          ➋  Abstraction
{                                      definition
    bool Matches( Order order );
}
```

In this version, FindBy ➊ takes an interface, IFinder ➋, rather than a concrete class. The code that calls it can pass in whatever object it likes as long as it implements that interface. If we want to find orders by OrderedDate, we create an OrderedDateFinder and pass it to the FindBy method. Later, if we want to find orders by FilledDate, we create a FilledDateFinder and pass it instead.

This code is now closed for modification. If we change how we wish to find the orders, there's no need to modify this code.

By the same token, we've also allowed this code to be extended in an infinite number of ways. Searching for orders based on OrderedDate or by FilledDate no longer becomes an either/or operation. We can implement *both* Finder classes. Alternatively, we could implement a CustomerFinder that searches all orders with a particular customer, or an OrderedInTheLastMonthFinder, or an OrderedOnASundayIn2007Finder. However you wish to filter your orders, the solution is simply an IFinder away.

Keep in mind that interfaces aren't the only way to achieve abstraction. Listing 7.10 shows a much more concise alternative that takes advantage of the .NET Framework to do much of the work for us.

**Listing 7.10   Abstraction using Predicate<T>**

```
public class OrderRepository
{
    IEnumerable<Order> FindBy( Predicate<Order> finder )
    {
        return _orders.FindAll( finder );
    }
}
```

In listing 7.10, we use the Predicate<T> class to achieve the desired extensibility. Listing 7.11 shows how you could call this class in .NET 2.0.

**Listing 7.11   Abstraction using anonymous delegate**

```
public IEnumerable<Order> GetOrdersByFilledDate( DateTime filledDate )
{
    IEnumerable<Order> orders = _orderRepository.FindBy(
        delegate( Order order )
        {
            return order.FilledDate == filledDate;
        }
```

```
    )
    return orders;
}
```

Going further, in .NET 3.5, we could call this method using lambda expressions, as in listing 7.12.

**Listing 7.12  Abstraction using lambda expressions**

```
public IEnumerable<Order> GetOrdersByFilledDate( DateTime filledDate )
{
    IEnumerable<Order> orders = _orderRepository
            .FindBy( o => o.FilledDate == filledDate );
    return orders;
}
```

In both listing 7.11 and listing 7.12, we achieve extensibility using a base class, `Predicate<T>`. As long as we provide the `FindBy` method a class that inherits from this class, we can retrieve orders in any number of ways. But `Predicate<T>` also allows us the flexibility of providing a delegate, which means we no longer even need to create a class to perform our searches. This technique can be useful if we want to create many simple, one-off search criteria and still provide the flexibility of allowing search classes for more complex cases.

### Maintainable for whom?

If you're new to predicates, delegates, and lambda expressions, you may be questioning the maintainability of listings 7.10 through 7.12. After all, if the team is just switching from a .NET 1.1 environment, they may view these listings as hieroglyphics.

New language features always bring about a certain amount of trepidation, especially to managers under tight deadlines and who aren't confident in the team. There's a certain comfort to following the tried-and-true way that has worked in the past and where you can always find developers to maintain the code.

Although there's certainly a balancing act, you shouldn't shy away from a framework feature just because it's new. It relates back to one of our underlying themes in the book: if it eases friction, do it.

Listings 7.10, 7.11, and 7.12 allow us a tremendous amount of flexibility with little code. The sacrifice is that the person reading the code has to understand how predicates, delegates, and lambdas work. The benefit is that once those three techniques are understood, developers have another tool they can use elsewhere in their day-to-day work. Not such a bad trade-off.

The open/closed principle is usually achieved, consciously or not, through the use of design patterns. All of the examples in this section use the Strategy pattern. We encapsulated the filtering algorithm into an interface, which allowed us to swap out implementations of it at runtime.

Two other patterns that can be used to achieve OCP are the Template Method and the Decorator pattern. The former involves creating an abstract class with a method that makes calls to other abstract (or virtual) methods. It's up to subclasses to implement or override the base class's abstract/virtual methods in order for the template method to execute appropriately.

A Decorator is a class that wraps another class and adds behavior to it. Note that this is different than inheriting from a base class. Instead, the Decorator implements the same interface as the base class, and you typically pass the class you're decorating into the Decorator's constructor. Listing 7.13 shows an example of using a Decorator to add auditing capabilities to a class without having to edit the original code.

**Listing 7.13   Sample Decorator**

```
public interface IVacationCalculator                      ◄─┐   General
{                                                          ❶  interface
    int GetVacationDays( Employee employee );
}

public class RegularEmployeeVacationCalculator : IVacationCalculator   ◄─┐
{
    public int GetVacationDays( Employee employee )
    {                                                      Implementations ❷
        return 10 - employee.VacationDaysUsed;                of the interface
    }
}

public class ExecutiveEmployeeVacationCalculator : IVacationCalculator  ◄─┘
{
    public int GetVacationDays( Employee employee )
    {
        return 25 - employee.VacatioDaysUsed;
    }
}

public class AuditableVacationCalculator : IVacationCalculator   ◄─┐
{
    private IVacationCalculator _calculator;               Decorator class ❸
    private IAuditor _auditor;

    public AuditableVacationCalculator(
            IVacationCalculator calculator, IAuditor auditor )
    {
        _calculator = calculator;
        _auditor = auditor;
    }

    public int GetVacationDays( Employee employee )
    {
        _auditor.AuditVacationDayRequest( _calculator, employee );
        return _calculator.GetVacationDays( employee );
    }
}
```

The AuditableVacationCalculator ❸ is our Decorator. Notice that it implements the same interface, IVacationCalculator ❶, as RegularEmployeeVacationCalculator and `ExecutiveEmployeeVacationCalculator` ❷. It also takes another `IVacation-Calculator` instance (the object it decorates) in its constructor. It can be used to decorate any other vacation calculator, including another `AuditableVacationCalculator` if you want to audit things in more than one way. In this way, Decorators can be chained together to add increasing levels of functionality to a group of classes without ever modifying the original code.

### Naming in patterns

Notice that our `AuditableVacationCalculator` class doesn't include the word *Decorator* in its name. This omission was a conscious decision. There's a tendency to indicate the use of a pattern by using its name explicitly in the class name. It's our opinion that incorporating the name of the pattern in the class name should be avoided if possible. It tends to clutter up the name of the class with developer jargon rather than focusing on the actual behavior of the object. Also, the implementation of the class may change at some point and you don't want that implementation tied to any particular pattern because of a poorly chosen name.

To summarize, in some cases, the pattern name may help make the class's intent clearer, but in our experience, it's better to name objects based on their responsibility rather than their implementation.

The Decorator is essentially a textbook definition of OCP. The class being wrapped remains closed for modification, but its functionality is extended through the use of a Decorator.

Also, the Decorator is an example of favoring composition over inheritance (see section 7.3.1). In listing 7.13, we added auditing functionality to the vacation calculator without affecting any base classes. In effect, we compose an auditable vacation calculator from an existing vacation calculator.

There's much more that could be said about the Decorator, Template Method, and Strategy patterns, and we encourage you to learn about them so that you can recognize their use and, more importantly, when to use them appropriately. But it's time to bring the discussion back to brownfield applications.

#### OCP AND BROWNFIELD APPLICATIONS

A sure way to fulfill the "contaminated" criterion of a brownfield application is to ignore the open/closed principle. When adding a new feature to a project, many developers' first instinct is to add the code to an existing class in the application, regardless of its suitability. This tendency leads to bloated, incohesive classes that are hard to test and difficult to maintain.

It's not hard to make a class open for extensibility while keeping it closed for modification. The general rule of thumb is this: code (or refactor) to interfaces.

By coding to interfaces, you can easily add new functionality without having to recompile existing code. Remember the `Finder` example in listing 7.9 or the Decorator example in listing 7.13. In both cases, we were able to achieve a greater degree of flexibility and add new functionality because we used an interface rather than a concrete class.

Moving on, we have the principle of least knowledge.

### 7.3.4  *Principle of least knowledge*

Also called the Law of Demeter, the principle of least knowledge is often summarized as follows: Talk only to your immediate friends.

The formal definition is wordier and scientific-sounding. It's easier to understand with examples.

By and large, the principle states that you shouldn't go more than one level deep in the object hierarchy when making method calls. For example, a call like `myCustomer.GetOverdueInvoices()` is valid, but `myCustomer.Invoices.FindOverdue()` is not. The first example makes a call directly on `myCustomer`. The second example goes two levels deep by first making a call to the `myCustomer` object, then calling a method on the result of that call, a collection of `Invoices`.

The reason the second example isn't valid is that we've broken encapsulation. The `myCustomer` object doesn't shield us from the inner workings of its collection of invoices. We need to know both how the `myCustomer` object *and* the invoices collection work. Requiring this level of knowledge is dangerous because if we change how the invoices collection works, we now potentially have to change both the `Customer` class as well as the code that uses it.

To make this class less knowledgeable, we create a method on our `Customer` object called `getOverdueInvoices`. For now, it'd simply return the results of `Invoices.FindOverdue()`, but the advantage is that if we change how overdue invoices are loaded for a customer, we need change only the `Customer` class, not any classes that reference it.

> **Law of Demeter in practice**
>
> Despite the alternate name for the principle of least knowledge, it's by no means a law. Although it can lead to more maintainable software, it can also lead to an interface with a lot of wrapper methods. Furthermore, these methods can start you down a path where you violate the single responsibility principle and separation of concerns.
>
> In addition, there has been much discussion recently on fluent interfaces, a topic we've discussed before. Often, API designers will purposely (and often rightfully) flaunt the principle of least knowledge to make an interface easier to understand and easier to discover.
>
> For example, take the following snippet using version 2.4.6 of the NUnit automated testing framework:
>
> ```
> Assert.That( myValue, Is.Not.Null );
> ```

> **(continued)**
> Clearly, this code violates the principle by requiring you to go through the `Not` object on the call to `Is`. But this bending of the law was a conscious design decision on the part of the designers, and we feel you'll agree that the result is a piece of code that's much easier to understand and thus easier to maintain.

**PRINCIPLE OF LEAST KNOWLEDGE AND BROWNFIELD APPLICATIONS**

Looking at brownfield codebases, you'll usually see that the principle of least knowledge is broken. It's not uncommon to see code that looks like this:

```
MyObject.MyCollection.Add(something);
```

Although this code looks harmless, there are hidden dangers lurking. The `MyCollection` property on the `MyObject` object is likely exposing a `List`, `List<T>`, `IList`, or `IList<T>` as its type. What if we were to change that return type? Now, `MyCollection` may not have an `Add` method available on it (say, for example, if we changed to `IEnumerable<T>`). The result is that our change has a ripple effect through the codebase with regard to the methods that are available off the `MyCollections` property.

Consider this alternative:

```
MyObject.AddSomething(something);
```

The `AddSomething` method, on the `MyObject` class, is now hiding the mechanisms (namely the `Add` method on the underlying `MyCollection` collection) required to add an item. The resulting `AddSomething` method may look like this:

```
public void AddSomething( Something itemToAdd) {
    _myCollection.Add(itemToAdd);
}
```

Now if we're to change the underlying collection type (`myCollection`), and thus the way we may have to add an item to it, we can focus that change in code in one spot.

How does this discussion apply to brownfield refactorings? Well, the biggest benefit is that you're more likely to be able to isolate the changes that you're making within your codebase if you follow the principle of least knowledge. Instead of having to make changes across a wide range of classes with every refactoring, you're more likely to make the change in one spot. Because brownfield codebases will probably have places where the principle of least knowledge has been ignored, you may find it valuable to refactor to this principle before taking on some of the larger refactorings that we talk about later in this book.

In the end, the principle of least knowledge is a tool that will help you isolate changes within your brownfield codebase. The next principle continues on the track of isolating changes and is the subject of an entire chapter in this book, but we introduce it here first.

### 7.3.5  *Dependency inversion principle*

We've already danced around the dependency inversion principle a few times and chapter 9 is devoted almost entirely to it. Robert Martin defines it as follows:[2]

> High-level modules should not depend on low-level modules. Both should depend on abstractions.
>
> Abstractions should not depend upon details. Details should depend upon abstractions.

An abstraction is typically an abstract base class or an interface. So another way to put this principle is this: don't rely on a concrete implementation—use an abstract base class or an interface instead.

That's all we'll say about dependency inversion for now because it will be explained in entertaining detail in chapter 9. Our last concept is interface-based design.

### 7.3.6  *Interface-based design*

Although not technically a principle, interface-based design is an approach that can be useful in brownfield applications, especially in large teams. The idea is that the person who writes the code (the supplier) and the person who plans to call the code (the client) agree on an interface for calling a method. The client agrees to pass in appropriate values to the method, and the supplier guarantees that a specific outcome will occur.

All this talk of *client* and *supplier* and *guarantees* is a bit formal considering the underlying idea is simple, especially since you're usually both the client and supplier. Essentially, interface-based design is one of the core concepts behind test-driven design.

When doing test-driven design, you create the tests *before* you create the code that's being tested. By creating the tests first, you're designing the interface for the code you'll test later.

Let's look at an example. Let's say in our sample application we want a Venue-Booker class and we want it to be able to return all available dates for a booking within a given month.

Listing 7.14 shows one possible unit test that could be written for this as-yet uncreated class.

#### Listing 7.14  Unit test for testing nonexistent code in `VenueBooker`

```
[ Test ]                                                          Fake object  ❶
public void Should_be_able_to_retrieve_available_dates_in_a_given_month( )  ⏎
{
    IVenueRepository fakeRepository = getFakeRepository( );
    VenueBooker venueService = new VenueBooker( fakeRepository );  ⏎  ❷ Class
    DateTime monthAndYear = new DateTime( 2008, 5, 1 );               under test
    IList<DateTime> availableDates =
        venueService.GetAvailableDatesIn(monthAndYear );  ⏎        ❸ Call code
    Assert.That( availableDates.Count, Is.EqualTo( 5 ) );
    Assert.That( fakeRepository.GetAllMethodCalled, Is.True );  ❹ Assertions
}
```

---

[2]  www.objectmentor.com/resources/articles/dip.pdf

In this method, we create a fake venue repository that contains known data ❶. In the next line ❷, we create VenueBooker, which is the class we're interested in testing. Next, we call GetAvailableDatesIn ❸ on the VenueBooker instance. Note that we haven't defined this method yet but we've decided on a signature for it. Finally, we include two assertions that will ensure we've retrieved the appropriate value from our VenueBooker object and that we've called the appropriate method on IVenueRepository ❹.

Let's assume the VenueBooker class and the IVenueRepository interface haven't been created yet. Obviously, the code in listing 7.14 won't compile then. To get the code to compile, we must create a VenueBooker class and an IVenueRepository interface.

But even after we create them, note that we've made a couple of design decisions in this test. We've claimed in the test that there must be a constructor that takes an IVenueRepository interface (whatever that interface may be). We've also dictated that the VenueBooker class must have a method called GetAvailableDatesIn that takes a single DateTime parameter. It returns an object that implements IList<DateTime>.

Furthermore, although it isn't explicitly stated in the code, we can tell from the final line of the test that at some point during the execution of this method, we expect that another method (presumably named GetAll) will be called on the IVenueRepository object that was included in the VenueBooker's constructor call.

With this one test, we've designed a contract for the VenueBooker class and for the IVenueRepository interface. Plus, we've provided some guidance as to how to fulfill this contract. When we create the VenueBooker class, we have an idea of how it *should* work and because the test is in place, we have a built-in mechanism to verify that the code we write *will* work.

One of the reasons interface-based design is so powerful is that it allows us to look at our interfaces from the perspective of the caller. By working from the client down, we're building code that we *know* we'll need. As we've seen from this example, the VenueBooker class had led us to also create an IVenueRepository interface, which in turn, contains a GetAll method. Had we started from the bottom, our design may have looked very different and we may well have coded ourselves into an API that's cumbersome to work with at higher levels.

**INTERFACE-BASED DESIGN AND BROWNFIELD APPLICATIONS**

As we mentioned in the previous section on the principle of least knowledge, interface-based design in brownfield applications is about being able to isolate your changes. When working with a class that has a set of public-facing methods but isn't well written internally, you can apply those public-facing components to an interface and start the isolation process. Then you can change all the places that call that code to work with the interface instead of the original concrete class. By making this change, you've decoupled the consuming code from the implementation of the original concrete class, which will allow you greater flexibility when refactoring.

With the interface in place, you have more flexibility in refactoring the original concrete class. Rather than work with the messy implementation, you can create a brand-new class that implements the same interface but that has an internal structure more to your liking. When the time comes to begin using your new class, you simply need to change the class that's being created (instead of the old class, the code will now create the new class), and very little, if any, of the consuming code will be affected by this change.

Using interfaces is a powerful tool for incrementally applying isolated refactorings to your brownfield codebase. Used wisely, interfaces can save you from the ripple effects that many changes can cause.

That's it for our introduction to design principles. It isn't a comprehensive list by any stretch, but it should be enough to whet your appetite. Before we move on, let's raise a touchy subject: how to introduce these principles into your organization.

### 7.3.7   *Introducing design principles to a team*

It's time we broached a sensitive subject. You may be onboard with learning and applying these principles in your application, but what if you're a lone voice in a sea of dissenters?

There's a good chance you'll meet with resistance when you start proposing all these new-fangled ideas. After all, if the basics of OO design were followed to begin with, chances are you wouldn't be reading this book looking for ways to improve the design of your brownfield application.

When talking about introducing design principles, reactions will vary from skepticism to disinterest to outright hostility. You may encounter junior developers who don't believe they have the capability to grasp such complex topics as SRP. Or maybe your project manager doesn't have confidence in his team and would prefer you dumb down your code so that the team can more easily maintain it.

We've encountered both types of people and more in our careers. And here's our official response to all these arguments: pure and utter crap (though you may want to paraphrase when you talk with your team).

This is a brownfield application. By definition (and granted, it's *our* definition), the application is contaminated by poor design and practices. It's suffering to the point where you need to perform drastic action to make it more maintainable. It behooves everyone involved to consider learning these proven techniques in order not to make the same mistakes. Otherwise, you're left with an application that's simply a different shade of brown.

The principles we've discussed so far aren't magical and they aren't complicated. They weren't thought up in a university laboratory for high-paid consultants to maintain some level of job security. Instead, they emerged from observing real-world applications solving real-world problems. These principles have worked in the past and when rigorously applied, they continue to work and make applications more maintainable.

The fact is no developer is junior enough that she can't grasp them. In fact, that's why they were codified in the first place: to translate the experiences of developers in a way that others can benefit without having to go through the same pain.

In addition, one of the key advantages to the principles we've discussed so far is that they lend themselves to brownfield applications. With the benefit of 20/20 hindsight, you can refactor your design with much more knowledge than you had when you first wrote the code. There are fewer unknowns and there's less chance of making the same mistakes that were made originally.

With that said, you won't be able to convince everybody of their value through sheer force of will alone. Some will believe these are academic meanderings no matter how vehement you are in your stance.

One common argument you'll encounter is that there's no time to bring the team up to speed (or its step-cousin, "We'll worry about that later. Let's just get this project done first."). This position is often rooted in corporate culture. Managers' bonuses are short term; cultivating a strong team of developers is long term.

However you go about introducing design principles to a skeptic, try to avoid turning the discussion into a personality conflict. Easier said than done in many cases, but it's important to always keep a level head and keep the discussion focused on how your position will benefit the project.

Many people, on both sides of the argument, will dig in their heels when faced with a contrary position. If you're one of these people, recognize when you're doing it and consider why the person you're talking with holds the position he or she does. Is it because they've never tried it and don't see the value of it right away? Or do they have a unique perspective of the application and have an alternative pattern in mind that could be just as effective?

In our experience, more people can be won over if you empathize with them and address their specific concerns rather than just repeat your mantra in different ways. (On the other hand, some people are just big jerks.)

Regardless of whether your team is open to trying new things, at some point there will come a time when you have to put your money where your mouth is. How are you going to start introducing these ideas into the code? Or, if you're faced with convincing a skeptic, how can you provide hard evidence of their value?

Here are some ways that can be used to broach the topic of design principles. When to use each one will depend on your particular circumstances.

### DO A PROTOTYPE/SPIKE

Prototypes are an easy concept to grasp—we've all done it in some capacity. You create an isolated coding environment and write some code to test an idea. For example, maybe you take a chunk of the application that's particularly offensive and try to apply the single responsibility principle. Or perhaps you want to test the effect of converting all calls to a service to use interfaces instead of concrete classes (an implementation of the open/closed principle).

You should consider a couple of guidelines when doing a spike or prototype. First, make sure you're isolated from the main trunk (or development branch) of the application. Assuming your version control system supports branching, consider making a branch of the code to create a sandbox. If nothing comes of it, you haven't affected anyone else on the team. But if it turns out to be a successful spike, you can merge your changes into the current development branch and trunk if need be.

Second, time box your spike. Before you start, set a span of time that you think would be reasonable enough to adequately test your experiment. Many an application has been sidelined by a team member saying, "Just one more day and I'll have it for sure."

Whether or not your prototype is successful, always report your findings to the team. Let them know what you liked and disliked about the idea. Perhaps you saw value in the dependency inversion principle but a full implementation would require too large a refactoring this early. It's important to convey your findings to the team so that you can evaluate them on a smaller scale.

Prototypes are useful when you want to test an idea without completely stopping the main work on the application. The prototype can be performed in parallel with regular development by one or two developers.

### LUNCH 'N' LEARN

Holding a lunch 'n' learn can be as simple as scheduling a room over the lunch hour and inviting a bunch of people to talk code. Generally, the topic of discussion is limited to a single principle or pattern you want to demonstrate or talk about. For example, you could talk about the dependency inversion principle and perhaps one person will look into the topic and come up with code samples to lead the discussion.

The important thing is that the person facilitating the discussion doesn't need to be the de facto expert. By all means, if someone has experience, she should be called upon to share, but keep in mind that everyone is there to learn.

---

#### Challenge your assumptions: Why just technical content?

Lunch 'n' learn, or casual classroom learning, is becoming increasingly common in the development community. We've found that there's a belief that the sessions must present dense technical content all the time. We ask you, why not mix it up?

Sure, dense technical content is good to feed to developers (along with pizza and highly caffeinated beverages), but if you mix it up a bit you'll keep people interested in attending. Think about having someone from the testing group present on something that their team is passionate about. Ask another project to present some of their practices to your group. Hold a session that's about keyboard shortcuts for a commonly used tool. Heck, why not have a team member present on some open source tool that they're excited about but that isn't being used on the project?

All these topics provide value to the members of the team, but they may bring a different level of energy to what can become nothing more than a free lunch.

---

Lunch 'n' learns can be effective because you're talking things over as a team. It's as much a social exercise as an academic one. Often, bosses will recognize the benefit of their team taking time out of their day to improve themselves (and by extension, the project) and they'll offer to bring in the lunch. These two aspects can sometimes appeal to developers who are usually more apt to dismiss these new-fangled ideas.

## MENTORING

Mentoring is a useful way of getting someone up to speed on a technique. You sit with a person and implement the practice you wish to adopt with that person.

Mentoring in this way is similar to pair programming in that you're both working on the same problem together. But it differs in the role you play and in the end goal. In pair programming, you both play the same role: a developer. And you're trying to implement some functionality. With mentoring, the goal is to teach and there's a mentor/student relationship instead. Another difference is that pair programming has a stronger emphasis on the pair actively working to prevent erroneous development. With mentoring, it's perfectly acceptable, and even encouraged, to allow mistakes to be made and learned from. The key is that the mentor is there to control the impact that those mistakes can have as well as to give directed instruction and guidance based on them.

In our opinion, mentoring is the most effective way of teaching a technique to a developer. You can offer personalized advice to pointed questions and tailor it to the person you're mentoring.

The downside is efficiency. In a team of 20 people, it's not practical to mentor each developer individually on a full-time basis. With a large team, mentoring is better suited as a supplemental practice to be used to reinforce ideas on a smaller scale, perhaps after a focused lunch 'n' learn event.

## REFACTORING AS YOU GO

The final category is a little clandestine. You don't make a categorical effort to introduce design principles, but as you add features and fix bugs, you refactor in such a way as to introduce them anyway.

### Refactoring as you go: An example

Say you're working on a bug where your Save screen fails when certain inputs are provided—for example, if someone enters a zip code in the wrong format.

As we mentioned in chapter 4, you should make every attempt to write a unit test to expose this bug before you fix it. But in many cases, the code may not be conducive to writing a unit test. Perhaps it has too many dependencies and they make the object you want to test too cumbersome to create in isolation.

In this case, it would help to introduce the single responsibility principle to the code to break apart the dependencies. But rather than calling a meeting to announce what you're doing, you go about your business, tearing apart dependencies until you reach a point where you can adequately test the code and expose the bug.[3] Then you fix the bug and check in the code as you normally would. The technique you used to fix it is almost beside the point.

---

[3] See Michael Feathers' *Working Effectively with Legacy Code* for ways to break apart dependencies to make code more testable.

This method is useful as a supplemental practice only. It shouldn't be your sole method of introducing OO principles to a team. This is because you're introducing good OO principles to the code but not to the team. The code will continue on its path into brownfield-dom and you can only slow its descent.

Instead, encourage your team to refactor as they go after you've provided guidance in the form of mentoring or a lunch 'n' learn. The ideas will be fresh in their minds, and refactoring based on a concept they've just learned will help retain the ideas. As they (and you) gain more knowledge about refactoring, it becomes a much more automatic process.

We'll wrap up this chapter with a few useful acronyms that serve as good guidelines as you refactor.

## 7.4    Adopting a more agile approach

Although we're on the topic of changing fundamentals, now would be an excellent time to examine whether or not your team should consider trying a more agile approach to your coding process.

This section isn't about converting to an Agile (with a capital A) project management style, though we'd certainly encourage that. We're focusing on code. So how can you make your code more agile in the dictionary sense of the word? (Maybe *spry* would be a better word.)

To be agile, your code must be able to respond to change quickly. We all know that requirements change. Being agile means that you can accommodate these changes no matter how late in the project they come. Regardless of the project methodology you use, it helps if your code is adaptive enough to respond in the event you need to make design changes.

With that, let's discuss a few little philosophies you can adopt to achieve this goal. All of them come in convenient acronym format for easy short-term memory retrieval.

### 7.4.1    Keep it simple, stupid (KISS)

Many developers have a natural tendency to overcomplicate design decisions. We often favor clever solutions rather than simple ones.

But complicated code is hard to understand and thus hard to maintain. We refer back to our tenets of readability and maintainability. Yes, your solution may be elegant in its conciseness, but if the code needs to be changed by someone else, it had better be easy to understand. Otherwise, it becomes one of those magical areas of the application that no one wants to touch for fear of breaking something.

One of the easiest ways to make a project unnecessarily complex is through premature optimization. Premature optimization is when we add code to increase performance without first measuring to see if there's a problem to begin with.

Premature optimization is a throwback to the days of yore, when programmers had to be more mindful of things like memory management, network topology, and data access methods. Whether you used a stored procedure or direct SQL had significant ramifications on the usability of your application.

These days, many of these infrastructure issues are sufficiently encapsulated that you don't *usually* need to make design decisions around them. You can design the application the way you would in an ideal environment.

This isn't to say you should ignore infrastructure (or optimization, in general) completely. But if you find yourself saying "What if we're calling this service over the wire?" you should check yourself. It's possible to put that question off until you're in a position to test the performance to see if it warrants attention.

**NOTE** Premature optimization makes sense only if you're in a position to do the optimization in your code at a later time should the need arise. If you're doing significant design of your code at the start of the project (like in the waterfall methodology), you may want to perform a test early on to see if there will be any issues later. Although performance is important, and developers should be conscious of the impact that their code has on it, usually it isn't the primary business concern. As a result, our point is, don't put optimization code into your application until you're sure you need it.

Another related principle is Occam's razor, which is often paraphrased as "All things being equal, the simplest solution is the best." This principle dates back to the fourteenth century and who are we to dispute seven-hundred-year-old philosophers?

### 7.4.2   *You ain't gonna need it (YAGNI)*

This principle is an offshoot of KISS. It states that you shouldn't add functionality to your code until you need it.

Developers often fancy themselves as forecasters. We like to add methods and classes to our project "just in case." For example, say you start writing a data access class that connects to a SQL Server database. But then you start to wonder, "What if we switch to Oracle or DB2 or XML files?" So you go on your merry way parameterizing the code that generates a database connection to accommodate every known data storage format.

Next comes the data retrieval. We're using stored procedures to retrieve data currently. But if we decide to switch to XML files, we'll need to use XPath. Now we need a framework in place to convert our queries into parameterized XPath.

In short, there's a lot of work involved for a scenario that may not occur. Why go through this exercise? Typically, you'll have your hands full implementing just the features the client asked for without including ones she hasn't. And chances are, your client will be much happier if you spent that time bringing the project in on time.

We've already touched on a bit of YAGNI in chapter 4 when we recommended against retrofitting unit tests on existing code until you need to modify it. The reason for this recommendation is, essentially, YAGNI. We assume, in the absence of contradictory data, that the existing code works. So there's no need to write tests for it. But if a bug gets reported, all of a sudden you're going to need tests since we've mandated that tests are required for all code that we modify.

With that said, there's a bit of a balancing act with YAGNI. Taken to the extreme, you could argue that we shouldn't refactor code because it works, so "you ain't gonna need [refactoring]."

Or taking the previous example of accommodating other data stores, perhaps there's a company-wide mandate to convert to Oracle in 3 months. In this case, yes, we don't need to accommodate any databases other than SQL Server, but it would be negligent for us not to plan for a contingency that's almost certainly going to occur in the short term, possibly even before the project ends.

In short, invoking YAGNI should be balanced with other factors, such as refactoring or future features.

### 7.4.3   *Don't repeat yourself (DRY)*

The final principle is "don't repeat yourself," or DRY. This is an intuitive one and basically means "Avoid duplication of code at all costs." As much as we love our Copy and Paste, it can lead to problems in the long term.

The problems are probably obvious to you. Having more than one version of your code leads to waste and is a maintenance nightmare. Whenever you need to change one piece of code, now you need to remember to change it in other places. And that assumes you know the code was duplicated elsewhere.

DRY is one of the core concepts behind the book *The Pragmatic Programmer* (Addison-Wesley Professional, 1999) by Andrew Hunt and David Thomas. In it, they describe various ways in which code is duplicated and how to counteract them. We won't regurgitate their work here, but suffice it to say that you should always be on the lookout for duplicate code and you should deal with it ruthlessly.

Brownfield applications are often a veritable cesspool of duplicate code, and often you stumble on it at random when addressing some other issue. When you do, make every effort to stop what you're doing and deal with that duplicate code. Don't allow it to survive until the end of the day. It *will* come back to haunt you (if it hasn't already).

## 7.5   *Summary*

This chapter has been a whirlwind tour through about 40 years of computer science knowledge. And we've only given lip service to most of the concepts we've introduced. We'll hammer home many of them in later chapters with more concrete examples. In addition, there are already several excellent books available that cover each of them in more detail. We list many of them in this chapter.

We started the chapter off with a review of the fundamental tenets of object-oriented programming. More than a refresher, this review set the stage for the remainder of the principles in the chapter as well as the remainder of the book.

Following up on the fundamentals was a discussion on some "-abilities" you should keep in mind when you're coding, the main one being maintainability. The ultimate goal of all the other principles (and indeed, this entire book) is to make sure your application is maintainable.

After that, we talked about some useful OO principles that have proven successful in the past. Most of them can be found in Robert C. Martin's book, *Agile Principles, Patterns, and Practices in C#*, which includes many more useful ones. Our goal wasn't to enumerate all existing OO principles but to help you get in the right mind-set for introducing good OO practices into your brownfield application. So we included a section on ways you might introduce them to your team.

We concluded with some overarching philosophies that will help you keep your application maintainable, including KISS, YAGNI, and DRY.

Our focus narrows further in chapter 8 where we discuss ways in which you can layer your application.

# *Relayering*
# *your application*

Now that we've covered some of the fundamentals of software development, it's time to start applying them in larger concepts and practices. The first thing that we're going to look at is the idea of layering your application code. Throughout this chapter you'll see how layering application code makes use of fundamentals such as encapsulation and separation of concerns.

The concept and use of the term *layer* are fairly commonly known in software development circles. For years we've referred to the data access layer (DAL) when talking about how an application communicates with a data repository. Often projects go so far as to move the DAL code into a separate assembly as they physically reinforce the boundaries of that layer.

Developers and architects also commonly discuss the user interface as if it's a separate entity altogether. It's at this point, though, that the practice of layering applications seems to be paid nothing more than lip service. When you enter a brown-field project, it's not uncommon to see that the code in the user interface has intimate knowledge of, and even responsibility for, functionality that has nothing to do with rendering the user interface for the user.

In this chapter, we show how you can work toward implementing a strong layering scheme in an existing brownfield application. The techniques discussed will enable you to increase the speed with which changes can be made to the code. They'll also allow developers to focus on certain segments of the application without having to worry about impacting other areas.

Repairing the layering of an application is the first significant piece of architectural rework that should be done when trying to revitalize a codebase. Relayering isn't something you'll be able to implement in a couple of days. Creating layers in an existing codebase takes time and patience. It can also involve a significant amount of change to the existing code.

Don't let the workload dissuade you. We wouldn't recommend it if there wasn't a corresponding benefit (we'll talk about that as well). For now, let's move on and set the next piece of the foundation to your new and improved codebase.

## 8.1　Pain points

A common pain felt on brownfield projects is one where changes are required but the affected code is spread throughout the codebase. In some cases, changing data access code may require working in the code-behind for an ASPX page, while other times it may be in a class file that's in another project.

Consider the examples shown in listings 8.1 through 8.3 for a page that displays a list of musical artists and each one's upcoming tour dates. Listing 8.1 shows a snippet taken from an ASPX page with a repeater outputting a list of artists.

**Listing 8.1　A repeater displaying a list of artists**

```
<asp:Repeater ID="repeaterBands" runat="server"              ◁┐  Parent repeater
OnItemDataBound="repeaterBands_ItemDataBound">                 ❶  control
    <ItemTemplate>
        <div>
            <%#DataBinder.Eval( Container.DataItem,
                "ArtistName" ) %></div>
        <asp:Repeater ID="repeaterTours" runat="server"
                OnItemDataBound="repeaterTours_ItemDataBound">      ◁┐
            <ItemTemplate>                                          Nested
                <div>                                              repeater
                    <%#DataBinder.Eval( Container.DataItem,         control ❷
                    "[\"TourName\"]" ) %> -
                    <%#DataBinder.Eval( Container.DataItem,
                    "[\"TourDate\"]" ) %>
                </div>
            </ItemTemplate>
        </asp:Repeater>
    </ItemTemplate>
</asp:Repeater>
```

In listing 8.1, we're using an ASPX repeater control ❶ to show a list of artists. Each item in the repeater also has a nested repeater ❷ for upcoming tour dates for each artist.

Listing 8.2 shows the code-behind for this page. It retrieves a `DataSet` from a service class and populates the repeater from listing 8.1 with it.

**Listing 8.2   Code-behind for the page listing our artists**

```
public partial class WhosOnTour : System.Web.UI.Page
{
    var _dataService = new TourService( );

    protected void Page_Load(object sender, EventArgs e)
    {
        DataSet ds = _dataService.GetArtistsAndTours( );
        repeaterBands.DataSource = ds.Tables["Artists"];      ❶ Load parent
        repeaterBands.DataBind( );                                  data
    }

    protected void repeaterBands_ItemDataBound(
object sender, RepeaterItemEventArgs e)
    {                                                   Load nested ❷
        RepeaterItem item = e.Item;                           data
        DataRowView dataItem = (DataRowView)item.DataItem;
        Repeater repeater = (Repeater) item.FindControl("repeaterTours");
        repeater.DataSource = dataItem.Row.GetChildRows("Artist_Tour");  ◁
        repeater.DataBind( );

    }
}
```

When the page loads, it retrieves the relevant data ❶ and binds the top-level repeater to it. As each item is bound to a particular artist row, the page also binds the nested repeater ❷ to the tour dates.

Finally, listing 8.3 shows another class that does the heavy lifting. It retrieves the list of artists from a database.

**Listing 8.3   Service class that provides the list of artists to the code-behind**

```
public class TourService
{
    public DataSet GetArtistsAndTours( )
    {
        DataSet ds = TwilightDB.GetDataSet( "twi_get_artists_and_tours" );
        ds.Tables[0].TableName = "Artists";      ❶ Source
        ds.Tables[1].TableName = "Tours";           tables
        ds.Relations.Add( "ArtistTour",         ◁
            ds.Tables[0].Columns["ArtistID"],       Relationship
            ds.Tables[1].Columns["ArtistID"] );  ❷ between tables

        return ds;
    }
}
```

In listing 8.3, a `DataSet` is populated with two tables: Artists and Tours ❶. The tables are also connected with a `DataRelation` ❷.

On the surface, there's an apparent separation of responsibility into various layers. The web page (WhosOnTour in listing 8.2) calls to a service (TourService in listing 8.3) that calls to a (static) data access class (TwilightDB).

But it doesn't take too deep a dive to spot some obvious problems. One of the most spasm-inducing is how the repeater in listing 8.1 is tied directly to the column names that are retrieved from the data access class. The TourService is equally heinous by creating a relation between two DataTable objects in a DataSet based on the ArtistID column. If anything changes in the data structure being returned by the TwilightDB.GetData method, there will be ramifications all the way up to the UI.

This hodgepodge of code organization and poor separation of concerns can cause numerous problems for a development team. As you can imagine, developers may struggle to find pieces of code that are included in listings 8.1, 8.2, and 8.3 because those pieces exist in one place for one implementation but in another place when they move to a different part of the application.

What you may also see is a team that doesn't know where to put their new code. These problems manifest themselves in questions such as "Should I put the Customer cancellation logic in the click event or in its own class? There are other screens doing it both ways, so is either all right?" The sense of orderliness may feel lost when you're working in the code.

Before leaving the pain points, we should add a caveat. Creating clearly defined layers in an application won't solve every instance of the pain points outlined here. But having layers will force on you some of the principles that we discussed in chapter 7, such as separation of concerns. It's those principles that will help you to more easily solve the problems that aren't directly addressed through layering. Let's move on and define some of the base ideas of layers as we work our way to a well-organized codebase.

The first topic is a clarification on layers versus tiers.

## 8.2 Tiers versus layers

It's important to distinguish between a layer and a tier. They're often used synonymously (at least when talking physical separation), but for the purpose of this discussion they need to be differentiated.

### 8.2.1 Tiers

The concept of having multiple tiers in an application, at least in the Microsoft space, became popular in the 1990s as a way to explain the architectural requirements of a distributed software system. The growing popularity of the web focused the need to tier applications to accommodate the fact that there were three distinct components in the applications: the user interface, the business logic, and the data storage repository. This architecture is commonly referred to as three-tier, and it was an extension of the previous two-tier (or client-server) architecture, which would usually combine the business and data access layers. Figure 8.1 shows a typical three-tier application.

At the time, the notion of a tier provided quite a few benefits. The use of tiers allowed an application to distribute processing across more than one computer. This architecture became even more prevalent with the increased popularity of web services, which were often constructed over the business logic tier.

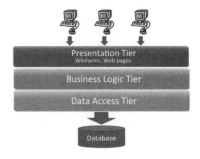

Plus, there was a noble theory that the various layers could be reused across multiple applications. For example, your data access layer could be used by more than one application, and similarly, you could create multiple UIs over your business logic layer. This technique was applied successfully to white papers and demo applications. In the real world, this panacea was a little more sporadic.

**Figure 8.1  Traditional three-tier architecture. The user accesses the presentation tier, which talks to the business logic tier, which talks to the data access tier.**

Since the start of the multitier concept, each tier has often represented a physical separation: the installation and execution of code on physically different hardware. In a three-tier system, that hardware may be a client computer, a middleware (or application) server, and a database server representing each of the three tiers. The definition of a tier has grown to have a one-to-one relationship with a hardware installation.

Although this physical separation of concerns is laudable, it's primitive. Tiers make no space for the separations needed at a more granular level in the code. For example, the middle tier in a three-tier system, the business logic code, encompasses a variety of tasks, such as validation, logging, and business rules. Some of these may even span tiers. This point is where we turn to logical layers to represent the code at that granular level.

### 8.2.2  *Logical layers*

Because physical tiers don't adequately represent all the layering concepts that should be built into applications, there's also a need for the concept of a logical layer. A logical layer has no inherent knowledge of hardware. Its existence is based on your software design and its role is more task based.

The primary difference between logical layers and tiers is that often many logical layers will exist within one physical tier. For example, within your UI tier, you may have one logical layer that's responsible for retrieving data from the business logic tier. Then you may have another layer that will take the data from that tier and convert it into a format more suitable for your UI. Then you could have a further layer that performs some basic validation of this UI object before sending it back to the conversion layer, which subsequently processes it and sends to the layer that communicates with the business tier. Figure 8.2 shows this logical layering within both the UI and business logic tiers.

**Figure 8.2  Very often, a physical tier will contain several logical layers.**

> **"Logical" tiers?**
>
> Although we defined a tier as a physical representation, it was (and is) common to combine physical tiers on the same server; the UI could reside on the same server as the business logic. In this case, your tiers behave more like all-encompassing logical layers that are composed of smaller layers. But for the sake of argument, it's still helpful to think of a tier as a physical entity.

A logical layer could also span more than one tier. Tier spanning usually applies to layers dealing with infrastructure, such as logging or error handling. In a traditional three-tier architecture, spanning of tiers was often accomplished through the use of the ubiquitous Utilities project that all other projects referenced. We'll come back to "layers" of this type in section 8.5.

Logical layers are typically focused in scope. We've already discussed one common example: a layer that converts objects from one form into another. This layer is common in applications that use web services, where you're consuming an object that may be of someone else's design. Creating a logical layer to convert it to something more appropriate for your specific needs will help you isolate yourself from changes to that web service. This concept will be covered more later in the chapter, and we'll expand on it in chapter 12.

A logical layer provides two other benefits to your code. The first is a clearer definition of where different concerns, and the related code, should exist in your application. The old adage, "A place for everything and everything in its place," applies nicely here. Each code concept has its place preassigned (the data access layer, or the validation layer, for example) and any code relating to that concept should be located in that place/layer.

The second benefit is a clear separation of the interaction of a layer with its neighbors. Between each layer is a seam, or gap, that needs to be bridged. Bridging the gap between layers requires the creation of contracts, through interfaces, so that both sides of the gap know what's expected. The best way to accomplish this is through the use of interfaces and interface-based design, which we'll discuss now.

## 8.3   *Isolation through interface-based design*

In chapter 7, the discussion of OO fundamentals touched briefly on the concept of interface-based design. To review briefly, this technique defines how two classes will interact with each other through its methods, properties, conventions, or however you wish to interface between these two objects. The expectations of what will be provided to a particular class, and what that class will return given those parameters, are determined by establishing and using an interface.

Once you've established this contract through the creation of an interface, each class, the consumer and the supplier, can go away and work on the implementation independently. The interface has been predetermined and both classes have a clear understanding of the others' responsibilities. All that's left is the implementation.

The reason for bringing up interface-based design here is that it can be useful in helping you define your logical layers. And in doing so, it helps you insulate your code from changes to other parts of the application.

By this point, you may still be a little fuzzy on the rationale behind logical layers. You may be asking, "What's the point?"

Consider what happens when you use a third-party component for some piece of functionality. It exposes certain methods and properties, and you use the ones that provide value to you. How the work gets done behind the scenes makes no difference, as long as it does what the documentation claims.

But do you go through the exercise of testing the methods that you call on the third-party component? The correct answer is no, but truth be told, we've worked with some dicey libraries in the past. Generally speaking, you don't because you assume that the vendor has done its due diligence and tested them for you.

Furthermore, the library is isolated from changes made in your application; you can make any changes you want in your application and they won't affect the methods' internal processing in the external component. Yes, changing the inputs to the methods you call will change the output. but the outputs will be well known (and hopefully well documented). Put another way, any changes made to your application don't require the vendor to recompile its component.

In keeping with our practice of reinforcing fundamentals, we've essentially just defined encapsulation all over again.

You can think of a logical layer as a third-party component to the code that's calling it. As you design the contracts through the implementation of interfaces that will define the layer, it's helpful to do so with an eye toward isolating the layer just as if you were building it as an external library. So in the process of implementing these contractual interfaces, you're isolating your code from other parts of the application.

That's the isolation part. Insulation is a side effect of isolation. The interfaces defined for the interaction between neighboring layers demark the boundaries for the logical layer. As long as the contract is well understood by both the consumer and the producer (where the consumer is the client that calls the contracted code and the producer is the contracted code itself), the boundaries help insulate the layer from external changes. By using an interface, the contract between the consumer and the producer is clearly defined.

Think back to the third-party component. It was insulated from changes to the client (the calling application) by the very nature of the fact that it's an external assembly. There's no technical way that you can change its implementation.

We've talked quite a bit about contracts, which is probably a bit esoteric. In our experience, they're often (but not always) synonymous with interfaces. A contract is an interface with the methods you wish to use in the contract. At some point, you'll need a concrete implementation of that interface, but as long as the inputs and outputs are well defined, the client code can be written against it now for the purpose of compiling and testing. In chapter 9, we'll talk about how to inject a concrete implementation of an interface into a class.

The interfaces that exist as layer boundaries also have the polite side effect of increasing reversibility (see chapter 7, section 7.2.5). Assuming a layer is well defined, isolated, and insulated, you have the option of replacing its code entirely if you so choose. Being able to reverse or entirely replace code in a segmented way is important when refactoring to use well-defined logical layers. The ability to isolate change or replacement of code allows you to work without worry of corrupting ancillary parts of the application. Let's look at how you can accomplish and benefit from this.

## 8.4    *Anticorruption layer*

In the previous section, we talked about isolating layers from one another with well-defined contracts. We mentioned the benefits of not having to alter your logical layer if the client code is changed.

On the flip side, a well-defined contract can help protect the client code from volatility within the layer. Known as an anticorruption layer, it creates an environment where changes within a layer don't affect calling code.

Although anticorruption layers can be used effectively when working within your own codebase, they're most useful when working with external dependencies. Consider a third-party user control like one of the myriad of grid controls available on the market. It isn't uncommon for a project to upgrade from one version of a user control to a newer one. During these upgrades, the user control may have changed in some fashion that breaks your code. When that happens you now have to work through your codebase in order to bring it back into harmony with the external dependency (in this example, the new version of the grid).

Sometimes making those changes can be a trying experience. The user control may be used in several (dozen) forms. This means you'll have to visit each one to make modifications, and that's a violation of the DRY principle discussed in chapter 7.

But what if you'd created a custom wrapper around that third-party control and used the wrapper in each of the screens? What if you'd created your own class that exposed only the functionality you specifically need in your application? And within that class, the methods exposed would simply delegate to the base grid?

Now whenever you upgrade to a new version of the control, the only changes needed are within the wrapper. As long as the public interface for the wrapper stays the same, none of the client code that uses it needs to know that you're using a new control. (In this case, *interface* refers not to an explicit .NET interface but to the public properties and methods exposed by the wrapper class.)

This wrapper is an anticorruption layer. The next time the vendor upgrades their grid control, and you implement it in your application, the ripple effect through the screens won't occur. Instead, the ripple will be contained within the boundaries of the custom wrapper.

There are also some benefits from a testability standpoint. Although it's rare that you'd use a UI control in a class for automated testing, it's sometimes done on file and message dialogs. It may seem odd to do so, but if you wrap the dialog in a well-defined interface, you have much more freedom to test a class that uses it. You can create your

**Anticorruption layers in practice**

Upgrading a user control may not be quite as simple as we've made it out to be. For example, the new version may include functionality that you want and that isn't exposed by your existing wrapper. Now you need to alter the public interface of the custom wrapper. Also, if something has fundamentally changed in how the control (or whatever code you're wrapping) functions, a nice fuzzy interface around it isn't going to hide that.

Although we acknowledge that anticorruption layers aren't always as clear-cut as we'd like them to be, they're still valuable. You may balk at the idea of wrapping a third-party grid control or even a third-party text box, but the benefits far outweigh any trepidation you may feel about a bit of extra code. It may feel as if you're adding extraneous code, but the feeling will pass. Most likely it will pass when you upgrade the control being wrapped for the first time.

own test subclass that implements the interface or mock out the interface with a mocking engine. Testing this logic no longer becomes one of those areas of the application where you say, "Yeah, we *should* be testing it, but..."

**Challenge your assumptions: Wrapping extreme**

Because external dependencies are (by and large) out of our control on projects, we have to mitigate the effect of their changes as much as possible. The same goes for anything external. You can take this to the extreme, and we have in some cases. On some projects we've seen custom user controls created for the most mundane things. A class that wraps the standard `Textbox` control is one example.

In that case, the wrapper did save us some work. When we hit a requirement for a specific type of behavior that the standard text box didn't support, we upgraded from the stock WinForms text box to a new third-party text box control. The process for that upgrade was limited to modifying the custom wrapper that had been created.

One of the important things to note about creating anticorruption layers is that you design them to meet your needs. You are, after all, applying the Adapter pattern onto the external dependency, so it makes sense to adapt it to meet your specific requirements. Creating the wrapper so that it's agnostic to the dependency that it contains is usually best accomplished by using interface-based design. Create an interface that the client code will be able to work with consistently and that provides the encapsulated dependency with all information that it needs. When the time comes to modify that encapsulated dependency, the defined interface with the clients isn't modified unless absolutely necessary. Now the changes to the dependency are hidden from the client code.

**The Adapter pattern**

Our apologies for unceremoniously throwing in the name of a pattern. We promise that this is an easy one to wrap your head around (so to speak).

The Adapter pattern adapts the interface from one class (the methods/properties of a grid control) into another (the interface we create specifically for our application). As you can see, a custom wrapper around a user control is a textbook definition of it. In fact, it is sometimes referred to as the *Wrapper* pattern.

When you're creating anticorruption layers, an effective technique is to expose only the bare minimum required interface. Don't fall into the trap of creating a wrapper for a third-party control and exposing all the properties, methods, and events that the third-party control exposes. If all you need from a grid object is the ability to bind data to it, expose only one method for that purpose. Exposing more than you require will increase the brittleness of your anticorruption layer, which will reduce its effectiveness in shielding the client code from changes. In addition, grid controls are notoriously chatty and wrapping every property is best left to interns or code generators.

Although we've specifically mentioned anticorruption layers in the context of protecting code from changing external dependencies, it's also possible to do the same to your own code. In essence, logical layering and the encapsulation of functionality within each layer is providing an anticorruption effect to its client neighbor layer.

Internal anticorruption layers are effective when dealing with areas of the application that are in a steady state of change. If a piece of your application is regularly modified, and you're seeing ripple effects of those modifications, consider implementing an anticorruption layer to lessen the burden of change on the developers. By creating seams, the anticorruption layer can significantly reduce the impact of the ripples induced by changes.

By segmenting code-behind interfaces, you're also creating another useful effect: seams. Seams are locations in the code where clearly defined decoupling has occurred. An application with interfaces and interface-based design helping to create logical layers will have seams at this point of decoupling. Calling, or client, code that only references the interfaces (contracts) with its neighboring logical layers is decoupled and has an observable seam. See figure 8.3.

Figure 8.3   **A seam is the interface that one logical layer uses to communicate with another.**

Seams provide you with a couple of benefits. The first takes you back to the discussions on automated testing in chapter 4. In that chapter (specifically, section 4.3.2), we mentioned interaction testing.

As a quick refresher, interaction tests are those that verify the interactions with other dependencies that occur within the method under test. Strong logical layers, and their associated seams, can more easily enable interaction testing. Because all the dependencies for a method will have been created to comply with defined interface contracts, you're able to generate mock objects that can take the place of the required dependencies. Being able to do this is one key to effectively and efficiently testing code in isolation.

The second benefit that you'll quickly realize when refactoring a brownfield application is reversibility. As you'll see later in this chapter, you'll be able to first put existing code behind a seam. After that's completed, the next step in your refactoring may be to rework the code that was just moved. Sometimes on brownfield applications the easiest way to do this is to start fresh. Because everything is decoupled due to the use of the newly created interface contract, it's easy to implement a new concrete class that can contain your refactored or rewritten code. Because it's in its own new class, and it must conform to the declared interface contract, you're able to do this work in complete isolation.

### One man's seam...

Some of you may be familiar with Michael Feathers' definition of a seam in his book *Working Effectively with Legacy Code*. He defines a seam as "a place where you can alter behavior in your program without editing in that place." When we talk of seams, it's using Feathers' definition of object seams. That is, we can alter the behavior of the program by providing an alternate implementation of the interface we've used to define the seam. As he mentions, seams are extremely useful for testing, which is one of the reasons for creating them.

Feathers' definition is more general because it includes other methods where behavior can be altered, such as with preprocessor macros and the Java linker. In the .NET world, these aren't nearly as common as object seams.

Having that isolation can be extremely important in providing developers with the ability to create code that's fully tested and verified before they reverse out the existing code with their new implementation. At that point, reversing the existing code becomes a relatively trivial process. The only thing that requires changing in the client code is how the appropriate class meeting the constraints of the interface is "newed up" (how a concrete class implementing the interface is created). If your code is nicely decoupled and using an inversion of control container (which we cover in chapter 9), changing that client code will probably require modifications only in one central spot.

The combination of interface-based design, logical layers, and seams will provide that ability to completely isolate code from different parts of the application. This isolation makes modifying existing code without creating application-wide ripple effects much easier.

Although seams and interface-based design can cleanly isolate segments of your code from each other, there usually are other pieces of functionality that need to cross those seams. Because these components, or modules, cross one or more of the seams that you've created in your application, they tend to be best represented as vertically aligned layers. We'll discuss those now.

## 8.5 *Vertical layers*

Until now, we've talked about logical layers as horizontal concerns within the codebase. Those horizontal concerns perform some functionality specific to a particular tier. For example, consider a layer that prepares objects for serialization across a network to the business logic tier. This layer is a special-purpose layer within the presentation tier.

By contrast, a vertical concern is one that spans more than one tier. Logging has been mentioned as one example. Others include security checks, error checking, performance monitoring, and transactions. All these concerns are applicable across many, if not all, of the horizontal layers that you'd create. That is, logging is an action that could occur at the UI level, in a services layer, in the data access layer, and in the domain model.

Figure 8.4 depicts an architecture with both horizontal and vertical layers. The horizontal layers are grouped by physical tier.

Because of the vertical nature of these concerns, it's hard to fit them into the layering metaphor. But layers are very much a part of the vernacular in software design, so we'll shunt aside our misgivings.

As is the trend in this book, we're going to strongly suggest that you fall back on fundamentals. Like with all other areas of your code, you should fully encapsulate the vertical layers that you create. Good encapsulation will provide you with the ability to walk down many different roads when implementing something like logging in your code.

You can integrate vertical layers into the horizontal layers in a number of ways. The naive way is to sprinkle your code with calls to the vertical layer, as shown in listing 8.4.

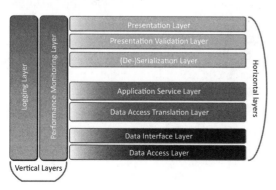

**Figure 8.4   A vertical layer (along the left) will span several, sometimes all, horizontal layers. In this example, the physical tiers are grouped by shades of gray.**

---

**Listing 8.4   Naive vertical layer implementation**

```
public class CustomerServices
{
    public IEnumerable<CustomerListingDto> FetchAll()
    {
        Log.For(this).Debug("CustomerServices.FetchAll called");        ◁────┐

        // ... remaining code to perform fetching

        Log.For(this).Debug("CustomerServices.FetchAll completed");     ◁────┤

    }

    public void Save(CustomerEditDto customerToEdit)        Calls to    ❶
    {                                                       logging
        Log.For(this).Debug("CustomerServices.Save called");            ◁────┤

        //remaining code to perform save

        Log.For(this).Debug("CustomerServices.Save completed");         ◁────┘

    }
}
```

As you can see, sprinkling calls, at the points indicated ❶, through the application code will create noise and clutter in the code. Not only that, but you've thrown separation of concerns and encapsulation out the window in this code.

The method shouldn't be responsible for logging. If you require that every method log information about its state and use, there will be a lot of extraneous lines of code like you see in listing 8.4.

Using this technique also opens the very real possibility that developers will forget to write the necessary line of code that logs the action or that they'll create the line of code incorrectly. Although we believe this is a workable implementation, it isn't optimal in many ways.

---

### Noise and clutter

Noise and clutter in code is anything that distracts the reader from the main thing that the code is doing. One example is comments that state the obvious (like `// Initialize the variable to 0`). Noise can also be caused by lines of code, such as logging entry points, that bear no consequence to the purpose of the code that contains them.

The primary concern with noise and clutter is that the codebase becomes more difficult to wade through. As we mentioned in chapter 7, readability is a primary part of the maintainability of an application's codebase. If the code is cluttered with inconsequential entries, the readability will decline and the maintainability will follow.

That said, reducing noise and clutter can become a religious programmer's battle because of the subjective nature of "noise." There's no simple metric you can use to measure noise and clutter. All we can suggest is that you trust your instincts and do your best to minimize noise in your code.

Ideally, you'd like to remove the logging call line from listing 8.4. You don't want any imposed line noise or clutter in your code, nor do you want to force your developers to remember to insert logging code into their methods. You also want to have all these needs satisfied while still retaining efficient and effective logging. You aren't asking for much, are you?

It's possible to accomplish these lofty goals. One technique is to use aspect-oriented programming.

## 8.6    *Aspect-oriented programming*

Aspect-oriented programming (AOP) is a way of applying separation of concerns to tasks that have traditionally been hard to isolate. Logging is the canonical example because it's common and anyone who's tried it has almost certainly done it the brute-force way as shown in listing 8.4 earlier. But it seems impossible that logging could be separated from the code that needs to be logged.

The promise of AOP is to do exactly that: isolate code that's extraneous to the fundamental functionality of a class. You've already seen how this could be advantageous. Any code that isn't directly related to a method's core purpose is noise. For someone who's scanning it (presumably to solve a problem or add a feature), it's that much harder to determine what it's supposed to do because the logging code needs to be mentally filtered out as you read it.

So the question remains: how can you separate code from a method that seems inextricably linked to it? Let's see what the .NET Framework can do for you.

Here's a trivial class that should be self-explanatory:

```
public class MyClass
{
    public void DoSomething( )
    {
        Debug.WriteLine( "I'm doing some work" );
    }
}
```

As fine a bit of code as we've ever written! We'll leave the creation of a console application to execute this code as an exercise for the reader.

Now, let's say you want to log all calls to any method in this class without having to add logging code to each method. One way you can accomplish this is by using a custom attribute. You'd like the previous code to look like this instead:

```
[Logging]
public class MyClass
{
    public void DoSomething( )
    {
    Debug.WriteLine( "I'm doing some work" );
    }
}
```

The only difference is the addition of the [Logging] attribute to the class. You need to create this attribute and add the ability to log the name of the method being called.

A `LoggingAttribute` class alone won't work. On their own, custom attributes are merely annotations for classes, methods, and parameters. They store metadata but don't do anything intrinsically. You need to do a little more work to execute behavior when the Common Language Runtime (CLR) finds an attribute.

A full explanation of what's involved is beyond the scope of this book, particularly because there are better ways to go about it. But we'll include the code to do so in listing 8.5 for completeness.

**Listing 8.5  Custom logging attribute**

```
[AttributeUsage(AttributeTargets.Class)]
public class LoggingAttribute : ContextAttribute       ❶
{
    public LoggingAttribute() : base("Logging") { }

    public override void GetPropertiesForNewContext(
        IConstructionCallMessage msg)
    {
        var loggingProperty = new LoggingProperty();
        msg.ContextProperties.Add(loggingProperty);
    }
}

public class LoggingProperty : IContextProperty,       ❷
        IContributeServerContextSink
{
    public bool IsNewContextOK(Context newCtx) { return true; }
    public void Freeze(Context newContext) { }
    public string Name { get { return "LoggingProperty"; } }

    public IMessageSink GetServerContextSink(IMessageSink nextSink)
    {
        return new LoggingAspect(nextSink);
    }
}

public class LoggingAspect : IMessageSink              ❸
{
    private readonly IMessageSink _next;

    public LoggingAspect(IMessageSink next)
    {
        _next = next;
    }

    public IMessage SyncProcessMessage(IMessage msg)
    {
        var methodCall = msg as IMethodCallMessage;
        if ( methodCall != null )
        {
            var messageToLog = String.Format(
                "About to call {0}", methodCall.MethodName);
            Debug.WriteLine(messageToLog);
        }
        return _next.SyncProcessMessage(msg);
```

```
    }
    public IMessageCtrl AsyncProcessMessage(IMessage msg,
        IMessageSink replySink) { return null; }
    public IMessageSink NextSink { get { return _next; } }
}
```

As you can see, creating a custom logging attribute isn't trivial. It involves several classes and namespaces from the System.Runtime.Remoting namespace, such as ContextAttribute ❶, IMessageSink ❷, and IContextProperty ❸.

Not only that, but when you're finished, you still don't quite get what you want. To use this attribute, the classes you wish to log must derive from System.ContextBound-Object, as shown here:

```
[Logging]
public class MyClass : ContextBoundObject
{
    public void DoSomething( )
    {
        Debug.WriteLine( "I'm doing some work" );
    }
}
```

With this code, whenever we call DoSomething on a MyClass object, it will output two lines to the Output window: About to call DoSomething and I'm doing some work (it will also output About to call .ctor for the constructor).

You can see the advantage of AOP by what's missing from the DoSomething method. There are no calls to the logging mechanism (in this case, writing to the Debug window), but the method is still logged. When you look through the method, you're no longer bogged down by infrastructure code and you can focus solely on what the method's primary function is.

Having said that, this implementation isn't ideal, which is why we've skimmed over the explanation of the code. First, the developer still needs to remember to tag the class with an attribute. Second, you may not want to log every single method in a class, though the code could be modified to work at the method level.

Finally, having your classes derive from ContextBoundObject is both restrictive and confusing. The derivation from the class is a coupling in itself, which you should avoid if possible. On top of that, a new developer looking at this may wonder why all the classes derive from it. It's not immediately obvious that it's being done to support logging.

**NOTE** Keep in mind that listing 8.5 isn't the only way to roll your own AOP mechanism in .NET. But it's a good starting point and one of the less verbose ones.

Luckily, a number of frameworks are available for .NET programmers to use for AOP, such as Aspect#, PostSharp, and the Policy Injection Block in the Enterprise Library from Microsoft. The main goal of all these frameworks is to encapsulate cross-cutting concerns (vertical layers) in one location. The example of sprinkling logging entries through the codebase functions adequately, but then logging isn't controlled in one location. In fact, it's the polar opposite of being encapsulated in one place: it's strewn throughout the code from top to bottom. And woe betide the developer who wishes to change the signature of *that* method call.

Most AOP frameworks operate under a concept similar to the hand-rolled example version. They intercept method calls and launch code before and/or after the originally expected method call. The interceptor code is what encapsulates the vertical layer or concern, which in this example is the logging. Now all of your logging capability is handled in one central location, the interceptor, and no longer is creating noise in the main classes and methods.

There's an intuitiveness to this approach. It matches the common `OnExecuting`/ `OnExecuted` event pattern used in several places in the .NET Framework. As such, it's easy to learn and we've found developers pick it up easily.

Vertical layers may not immediately jump out at you when you're designing your application. We've harped on logging, which is the canonical AOP example. But almost anything you do in your code that isn't directly related to a function's primary concern could be a candidate. You could use aspects to ensure methods are wrapped in a transaction, to ensure only certain users can execute methods, and even to perform trivial parameter validation (such as ensuring an age parameter is greater than zero).

These are common scenarios, though thinking of them as *aspects* may be new. Be aware of situations where you're creating code that will affect many different layers and address them as cross-cutting concerns from the start. If possible, try to encapsulate the concerns in order to make your code more readable, to preserve the separation of concerns, and to ensure that your code adheres to the single responsibility principle's main tenet: there should be one and only one reason to change any piece of code.

Now that you've spent a lot of time thinking about the structure of the various concerns in your application, you're possibly wondering where the business logic fits into all this. If there are multiple tiers and even more layers in a well-factored application, there has to be somewhere to best locate the information that defines how the business works. We'd like to point you to one of the layers from figure 8.4, but it's not quite that easy, so let's take a look at this from a different perspective.

## 8.7  *Taking a domain-centric approach*

In many brownfield applications, the layering is sporadic and often nonexistent. Some screens may use a business logic service, and others may work directly against a database. A business logic class may be a hodgepodge of methods placed there for no other reason than that the developer didn't know where else to put them.

As you prepare to refactor this code, it's a good idea to think about the overall approach you'd like to take in achieving layered bliss. What's your overall goal in designing the seams and layers? How do you decide where to place functionality in the layers?

We'll be taking a domain-centric approach to this refactoring. You'll refactor with an eye toward the domain that the application was designed to model. If the application is a family tree generator, we'd expect to have concepts like Ancestor and Descendent and Relationship modeled in it. If it's a music library, then Song, Playlist, and Artist should appear.

This concept is abstract so a more concrete (though still fairly high-level) example will help illustrate.

Consider a traditional n-tier web application for a site that manages timesheets for consultants. The user navigates to a page that lists their timesheets to date. The code-behind instantiates a `TimesheetService` object and calls `timeSheetService.Get-Timesheets(consultantId)`, which retrieves the consultant information along with their timesheets.

The `TimesheetService`, in turn, may look like listing 8.6.

**Listing 8.6  Traditional code-behind**

```
public class TimesheetService
{
    public ConsultantData GetTimesheets( int consultantId )
    {
        var consultantData = new ConsultantData( );
        var consultantService = new ConsultantDataService( );
        var consultantDataSet = consultantService
                .GetConsultantDataSet( consultantId );
        var consultant = new Consultant( );
        // Insert code to translate the consultants into a
        // Consultant object

        consultantData.Consultant = consultant;

        var timesheetService = new TimesheetDataService( );
        var timesheetDs = timesheetService
                .GetTimesheets( consultantId );

        IList<Timesheet> timesheets = new List<Timesheet>( );
        // Insert code to translate the timesheetDs into a List
        // of Timesheet objects
        consultantData.Timesheets = timesheets;

        return consultantData;
    }
}
```

The relevant data services would consist of standard ADO.NET code for returning datasets to this class. Figure 8.5 shows how this request might look.

There's nothing magical about this code. Regardless of whether the use of `Data-Sets` makes you cringe, they can be used quite successfully, and have been for several years.

But to a growing number of people (including us), this type of code obfuscates the real reason for creating the application. There's talk of services and datasets and data objects, which overshadow the core objects we're interested in: `Consultants` and

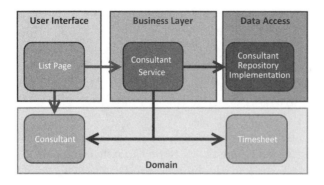

**Figure 8.5   Traditional n-tier representation of a data request. Although we show it here, the domain often doesn't exist as a separate layer.**

`Timesheets`. As it is, we've encountered many applications that don't even bother taking the time to convert the datasets into objects and simply forward them on to the web page for processing. Indeed, Microsoft doctrine and training encourages this.

Instead, some argue that you should start from the core objects that the application is abstracting. You should focus on the domain, rather than the database, the servers, and the programming language.

This approach, made popular by Eric Evans in his book *Domain-Driven Design* (Addison-Wesley Professional, 2003), as well as Jimmy Nilsson's *Applying Domain-Driven Design and Patterns* (Addison-Wesley Professional, 2006), has led to the domain-centric approach we use when we move a brownfield application into layers.

To return to the list of timesheets, we'll sketch a possible way of doing this with a focus on the domain (see figure 8.6).

This diagram doesn't look too different from the traditional n-tier approach. It's almost as if we've combined the business logic layer and the domain.

The major difference is in the direction of the arrows. They all flow into the Domain layer. There's no sense of hierarchy, where a request is passed from one layer to the next.

In this version, the web page holds a reference to a repository, which, in this case, is the `IConsultantRepository`. This interface lives in the domain along with the actual domain objects (`Consultant` and `Timesheet`). The implementation, on the other hand, is stored in the data access layer.

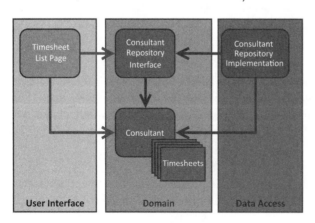

**Figure 8.6   With a domain-centric approach, the domain encapsulates both the business logic and the domain objects.**

**Where do you get your repositories?**

If you're new to the idea of repositories, figure 8.6 may have you wondering, "If I create a `ConsultantRepository` in my client code, doesn't that mean I need a reference to the data access from my UI?" This question should raise some alarm bells.

There are different ways to avoid linking your UI layer to your data access layer. You could use a factory or service locator to create it. (The names are intuitive enough that you should be able to tell what they do—which is good because we don't have the space to go into lengthy discussions of either.)

Another popular (and our favorite) way is through the use of an inversion of control container. We'll talk about IoC containers more in the next chapter.

The salient point is that you can have the best of both worlds. Use a domain interface in the client while the implementation is neatly tucked away in the data access layer.

This is how you're able to use repositories as domain concepts while still divorcing them from the database-specific code needed to implement them. Without getting into too many details of domain-driven design, repositories are responsible for retrieving objects from a datastore and saving them back again. It provides the client code with a well-defined interface (or contract) while still decoupling it from the underlying database technology.

Figure 8.6 is a much simplified version of the architecture we favor. That figure ignores concepts such as logging and data translation services and unit tests. To bring it back to the abstract, figure 8.7 is a more robust depiction of what we're working toward.

Note a couple of things about this diagram. First, notice that the domain is at the center of the diagram. This arrangement is to emphasize its importance and nothing more. This diagram could be flattened into a more rectangular version similar to figure 8.1 at the beginning of the chapter. If we did, you may notice that it's not vastly different from the traditional n-tier architecture.

Second, the Utilities wedge needs some explanation. The code that it represents deals with vertical concerns, such as logging or performance monitoring, that span most

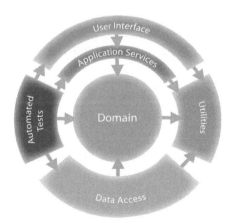

Figure 8.7 The domain-centric architecture we're working toward. It highlights the importance of the domain as the center of the application.

or all layers of the application. Because of this, all aspects of the architecture refer to it. We've already covered vertical layers in detail in the previous section.

The Automated Tests wedge is similar to the Utilities wedge but in the other direction. It needs to refer to each layer rather than be referenced by each one. To use terms from chapter 5, the Utilities wedge has high afferent coupling while the Automated Tests wedge has high efferent coupling.

Finally, the Data Access wedge is kind of an outsider. There are no references to it, save from the Automated Tests. So how (and where) do we instantiate the data access classes? We alluded to this in the sidebar "Where do you get your repositories?" The interfaces for much of the data access classes are kept in the domain. To get concrete implementations, we rely on factories, service locators, and/or IoC containers. In the case of the first two, we'd likely need to add another layer to the diagram. This layer would lie between the Application Services and the Data Access wedges. (Technically, an IoC container takes the place of this layer so using it doesn't obviate the need for it; you just don't need to implement it yourself.) But including it in the diagram would require more arrows and there are already more than we'd like in it.

There's much more that we could say about domain-driven design but, as we noted earlier, there are books that better serve those questions. For now, let's talk about how you can work to implement layering in your brownfield applications.

## 8.8    *Refactoring to layers*

We've covered a lot of concepts in this chapter. Chances are, you've read this far and you're at the point where you're thinking "All well and good, but how am I ever going to implement this in my code?" Well, friend, it's time to cover that very topic.

The normal reaction when implementing a wide-reaching concept like logical layering is to be confused about where to start. The codebase of a brownfield project is usually well established, and picking a spot to start refactoring can be a difficult and risky decision.

On top of that, you may have to decide how to start the refactoring. Like anything major you do with a codebase, refactoring to logical layers and seams is going to introduce some risk. You have to figure out the best ways to mitigate that risk. The remainder of this chapter is dedicated to helping you make these decisions and organize the refactoring as you're undertaking it. Figure 8.8 shows the high-level steps we'll take.

The first step in the process is to choose where to start.

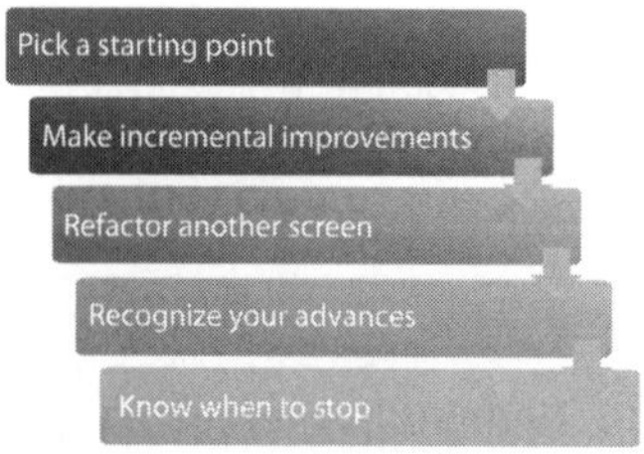

**Figure 8.8   An overview of the steps involved when you refactor your application to use layers**

### 8.8.1    *Pick a starting point*

Not to confuse terminology, but a logical way to begin refactoring to layers is to examine your physical tiers. This approach is typically an easy way to identify where the seams are because you have a physical restriction already in place.

But your true starting point should be with a test, if at all possible. And if that's not possible, make it possible. Only with an adequate safety net should you make sweeping changes like the ones we're proposing. The code already works in a known way. When you're finished, you had better be sure it still works in the same way.

Because ours is a brownfield application, you'll almost certainly run into cases where writing a test for a piece of code seems impossible. It's not. We've already referred to Michael Feathers' *Working Effectively with Legacy Code*. The book has dozens of scenarios to address this specific concern. Indeed, that's its very theme. From "I Need to Change a Monster Method and I Can't Write Tests for It" to "I Don't Understand the Code Well Enough to Change It," you'll be hard-pressed to find an excuse that hasn't been covered.

Once you have a test (or two or five) in place and have identified where to place the seam, you have a choice of whether to work either up (toward the UI) or down (from the UI) from the split. We recommend working down. As you'll see shortly, starting at the UI and working down allows you to thin out the responsibilities of each layer and push the remaining code further for later refactoring.

The process is akin to whittling. You start with a single chunk of code and shave a thin layer off while still leaving a slightly smaller (but still hefty) chunk of code to work on. Once the thin layer has been cleaned up, you go back to the big chunk, shave off another layer, and repeat the process until each layer is manageable. In this way, you make incremental improvements.

### 8.8.2   *Make incremental improvements*

Before we go further: do *not* underestimate the amount of work you'll undertake! We cannot stress this enough. Once you recognize how to layer an application, it's frighteningly easy to start a small refactoring and have it escalate. Often, this escalation happens in small steps so that you don't even realize that the variable renaming you started 6 hours ago has turned into a major overhaul of your data access strategy.

**NOTE**   Don't approach refactoring to layers on a Friday afternoon if you expect to have it done by the weekend.

Incremental improvement is the key to success. In chapter 2, we advocated the mantra *check in early/check in often*. You refactor to layers in the same way—in small, easily reversible steps, backed up by unit and integration tests.

Needing to work this way is why we spent the first six chapters on the ecosystem. The ecosystem is there to help you for just this sort of task. It's designed for the baby-step approach to refactoring so that if anything goes wrong along the way, you'll not only know about it right away, you'll also be able to back out with relative ease.

As a rule of thumb, start with a single screen, preferably a simple one that only reads data. Perhaps use an administration screen that lists users. Examine what it does and how it's currently coded. Try to pick out, and define, a single interface (contract) that will define the first seam between the screen and the layer immediately below it.

**TIP**    Remember to design with an eye toward isolation and testability. This type of refactoring offers a great opportunity to increase the test coverage on the project whether through test-after development (TAD) or test-driven design (TDD) practices. As much as possible, you'd like each layer to be insulated from external changes either above or below it. If you start at the screen level, keep things simple. You aren't re-architecting the entire code for this screen—just the logic for the screen itself.

Ignore the data access and business logic itself for the time being. It will be refactored in due time. Instead, focus solely on the way the screen itself interacts with other components and try to isolate those into well-defined interfaces.

Figure 8.9 shows an outline of how to accomplish this. Here, the first box depicts the original version of the code with no layering. In the first step, you identify a seam to interact with the layer immediately below it.

But notice that you don't refactor the entire block of code to layers right away. Rather, you start with a single seam. You create the contract (interface) and, better yet, you've already got the implementation for it. It's the original block of code you're refactoring. You simply need to move it out into a separate class that implements the interface you're using in the original screen.

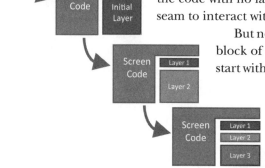

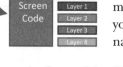

**Figure 8.9   When refactoring to layers, the key is incremental changes—refactoring only a small portion of each screen at a time.**

**NOTE**    The box representing the initial layer in figure 8.9 will probably not be very clean. If you're lucky, it should consist of a simple cut and paste of the original code from the screen you're refactoring, except for any code that's to remain in the UI layer. Your goal here is only to layer the application. Once the layers are defined, you're at a good point from which you can launch further refactorings in isolation later.

Once you've created the first seam of your new layer, you should be at a good stage to check in the code. Again, the ecosystem comes into play and you can run the build script to make sure the application compiles and all tests pass, particularly the one(s) you created before starting your refactoring.

From here, you can apply the same technique to define further layers all the way down the request pipe.

**NOTE**    In figure 8.9, we've depicted each layer as being easily sliced off the one above it. In practice, you may need to use the same technique we did with the screen, where you define a single seam first, and then refactor the rest of the functionality into each layer.

Notice that we're ignoring a huge blob of code in the screen which is visible to the left of the layers in each stage. This is intentional. When you start out, you're working with a single seam in a single layer. The rest of the code can be left as is while you're working out the details of the layers. When finished, you'll have several layers defined but they'll be very thin as you haven't fully fleshed them out yet.

At this point, you can now further refine your layers by moving more code into them from the Screen Code area on the left.

In figure 8.10, you start from the last point in the previous diagram (figure 8.9). You pick out a bit of code to move into Layer 1, thus thinning out the screen code further. As you progress, you whittle away at the code, moving it further and further down the line but leaving pieces of it in each layer as you go until you reach the bottom layer.

**Figure 8.10**
**Further refining the layers**

Notice in both figures 8.9 and 8.10 that the overall size of the code doesn't change. You're always working with the same amount of code. All you're doing is moving it to additional classes (which you create along the way) for the sake of maintainability.

You continue in this fashion until the final refactoring, shown in figure 8.11.

Here, you remove the last vestiges of code from the screen that don't belong there. Until this point, you've been paring away at the code, moving more and more of it out into appropriate layers. When you move the last bit of "lost" code into its appropriate place, you're left with a fully layered architecture, at least for one screen. Now you can move on to the next screen.

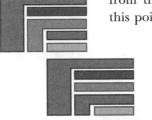

**Figure 8.11  The final refactorings**

Luckily, moving on to subsequent screens is far less work.

### 8.8.3   *Refactor another screen*

So now you've defined your seams and you have an appropriate set of layers for one screen.

As we warned you earlier, you've got your work cut out for you. But don't be discouraged. The good news is that the first screen is by far the most difficult. Not only are you moving code around, you also need to define the layers (and the classes to go into them).

Once the first screen is done, you have two advantages:

- The layers are defined.

- Having gone through the exercise once, you have a better idea of what to expect.

> ### Refactoring large codebases into layers
>
> All of this information about refactoring your codebase to layers can be intimidating, especially if your brownfield project is large. Sure, we've suggested some tips for how you can get started and progress through the refactoring process. Like you, we've taken these ideas and looked at some large projects and thought that we'd never be able to successfully refactor them.
>
> We won't kid you at all. Significant architectural refactorings to large codebases are tough to complete. There's only one reason for that: the sheer amount of code.
>
> If you're taking the slow but steady approach in which you'll work on the refactoring when the team has time, refactoring large codebases into good logical layers will seem to take an eternity. It's our opinion that the larger the codebase, the more dedicated your refactoring effort needs to be.
>
> We've worked on projects like this and we've had success when refactoring to layers. Not all of the individual efforts were successes, but the project results were. The key for us when working on the large codebases was to make it a focused effort. And note that that effort wasn't necessarily by the entire team. In some cases, it was only one person.
>
> Another key factor for our success was working in isolation in the code (for example, through a branch in our version control). We discussed this concept in chapter 2. The isolation allowed us to make radical changes and experiment with ideas while still retaining an easy way to back out those ideas that didn't work.
>
> Don't think that large codebase's can't be refactored, but be aware that they'll impose a significant resource drain on your team. Sometimes, though, the largest codebases are the ones that need these changes the most. Making the effort could well be the best decision you make for the health of the project.

Once the layers are defined, you have a framework to expand on. You won't necessarily reuse the same layers for every screen you work on, but the exercise does help to crystallize your thinking as to what constitutes a good layer in your application.

Working on this size of refactoring one screen at a time can help you better manage both the impact of the changes being made and the size of the current task at hand. The one drawback to this approach is that it can be hard to see all the positive impact that all of your changes are having right away. In the next section, we'll make sure you get recognized for all your hard work.

### 8.8.4 Recognize the advances being made

Although you're refactoring, it can be easy to get mired in the details, particularly if the effort starts to become routine. You may not be recognizing the payoff from all your hard work.

Having appropriate metrics in place can help reveal the benefits of your refactoring. You should notice a drop in coupling as you refactor code out into layers. It helps to take a measurement of this before you start and at regular intervals, if only to see how hard you should be patting yourself on the back.

Informal code reviews are often helpful as well, provided they focus solely on the layering. Having others review your seams and how you've separated responsibility is always a good idea, especially when you've been working on it for some time.

**NOTE** Be sure these layering reviews don't get bogged down in the details of the actual code within the layers. As we've mentioned, once the layers are defined, you can circle back and evaluate the implementations.

It may even be useful to do some early refactoring as a group or at least in a pair-programming session. But keep in mind that the more people involved, the longer it will take to do even the simplest thing. How layers are defined is a subjective topic and people will have different opinions.

Because of the potential size of the entire refactoring to layers task, you'll at some point have to decide when to stop making changes. It's both hard to notice you're in a place where you should stop, and difficult to have the self-control to stop doing the work.

### 8.8.5 Know when to stop

As you can imagine, refactoring to layers is an arduous task. At times, it seems there's no end in sight. The ecosystem you so painstakingly set up in part 1 certainly will start to pay off in spades now. With every minor shaving of code into a layer, you can run your automated build and know instantly if there's a problem. Consequently, the task becomes easier as you go and it's common to get into a good rhythm once the initial layers are defined. Furthermore, if you're generating metrics at regular intervals, you'll have feedback on your progress.

But there will come a time when enough is enough and you'll need to stop, or at least pause, your efforts. Usually, it's some external factor, such as an upcoming critical release or a new feature receiving higher priority. Other times, it may be the realization that the section you're working on is adequately layered and there are other refactorings that will provide a bigger win for the effort.

Whatever the case, at regular intervals you should step back from your task and take stock of the situation. Ask yourself if there's still value in continuing or if there are other tasks that are more important. Resist the urge to finish off "just one last thing" if the team is asking you to move on to something else.

Relayering your application isn't an easy task. Throughout the process, you'll second-guess yourself, often wondering if you're making any progress or just making things worse. Although these steps can be done by one person, it helps to work on these steps collaboratively with the team (or through pair-programming) to avoid getting mired in minutiae. This is especially true when you're first starting out and are unsure what makes a "good" layer in your brownfield project.

## 8.9   *Summary*

Layering is the first application of your recently found OO fundamentals. It's an important topic for brownfield applications because there layering is typically nonexistent, sporadically applied, or poorly defined. In this chapter, we explored the concept of a physical tier and how a layer fits in with this concept.

Next, we reviewed the definition of interface-based design and how it's fundamental in defining layers. We discussed how a well-defined contract (interface) can provide an anticorruption layer around code to help isolate it from external changes.

After that, we examined vertical layers and dove briefly into aspect-oriented programming as a mechanism to handle cross-cutting concerns such as logging and performance monitoring.

We then talked about the benefits of taking a domain-centric approach to refactoring before diving into an explanation on how to start your refactoring, how to measure your progress, and when to stop.

In the next chapter, we'll expand on one of the ideas we touched on here. Specifically, how can we break apart the dependencies in code so that we can properly layer the application?

# 9

## *Loosen up:*
## *Taming your dependencies*

**This chapter covers**

- Using the dependency inversion principle
- Understanding inversion of control
- Testing and inversion of control
- Implementing dependency injection

In chapter 8, we talked about how to layer our application. During that discussion, we brought up the notion of using interfaces to represent the contracts we define between layers. In this chapter, we'll expand on this idea and outline ways to manage the interdependencies between those layers.

As always, we'll tie this discussion back to brownfield applications. But first, let's look at some of the issues inherent in highly coupled code.

## 9.1    Pain points

Problems arising from dependencies can be subtle. They don't usually appear when you first write the application. But as your project moves into brownfield territory, they become more and more prevalent. We'll look at one scenario that demonstrates this, but rest assured, there are many circumstances where you'll notice problems due to dependencies.

One of our developers, Dean, is working on a piece of code. It's for a web application where users sign in and write movie reviews. The code in question is a service that spell-checks the movie reviews for the user before submitting them to the database. Listing 9.1 shows the code.

**Listing 9.1    A service that spell-checks movie reviews**

```
public class MovieReviewService
{
    private SpellCheckDictionary _spellCheckDictionary;

    public MovieReviewService( )
    {
        _spellCheckDictionary = new SpellCheckDictionary( );
    }

    public IEnumerable<DocumentPosition> SpellCheckReview( string review
  )
    {
    IList<DocumentPosition> errors = new List<DocumentPosition>( );
    IEnumerable<String> words = ParseWords( review );
    foreach( string word in words )                        Parsing   ❶
    {
    if ( _spellCheckDictionary.IsCorrect( word ) == false )
    {                                                      ❷  Check
        errors.AddRange( GetAllPositionsOf( word ) );          spelling
    }
    }
    return errors;
    }
}
public class SpellCheckDictionary        ❸  Spell checking
{                                            logic

    private WordDictionary _dictionary;
    public SpellCheckDictionary( )
    {
        _dictionary = new WordDictionary( );
        _dictionary.LoadFrom( ConfigurationManager    ❹  Dictionary
.AppSettings["dictionaryFile"] );                         loading
    }

    public bool IsCorrect( string word )
    {                                                ❺  Word
        if ( IsWord( word ) == false ) { return true; }   verification
        return _dictionary.Contains( word );
    }
}
```

In listing 9.1, the review is parsed into individual words ❶. If a word is misspelled ❷, every instance of this spelling of the word is added to our error list. The SpellCheck-Dictionary class ❸ does the dirty work by checking spellings against a known dictionary. In this case, the word dictionary is being loaded from a file as specified in the application config file ❹. The implementation of the `IsWord` method ❺ isn't shown here, but presumably, it determines if this is an actual word and not, say, a number or an acronym.

The code for `ParseWords` and `GetAllPositionsOf` have been omitted for the sake of space. The former parses the review into individual words and the second returns a list of the position of each instance of the misspelled word in the review. `Document-Position` is a class that stores a location within the review. It has properties to define the starting point of the position and the length.

Notice how `SpellCheckDictionary` is loaded ❹. This class creates a `WordDiction-ary` object and loads it from a file. We've omitted the details of how this task is accomplished because they aren't important. It's unlikely that the file contains every word in the English language, but perhaps it contains locations of various other files, each containing a fragment of the dictionary being used. Whatever the case, all you need to know is that the dictionary is loaded using the `LoadFrom` method and that the method takes a string parameter representing a filename.

This code is in production and working well and the application thrives. It's doing so well that the company decides to expand and allow users to post reviews in Spanish.

The good news is that we've partnered with another company that provides a Spanish dictionary list via a web service. So we don't have to maintain a file ourselves as we do with the English dictionary.

Our language expert, Martin, is put in charge of creating a Spanish spell-checker, and he does so in listing 9.2.

**Listing 9.2   Updated `SpellCheckDictionary` with support for Spanish**

```
public abstract class SpellCheckDictionary          ◁──┐   Abstract
{                                                    ❶  base class

    protected WordDictionary _dictionary;

    public virtual bool IsCorrect( string word )
    {
        if ( IsWord( word ) == false ) { return true; }

        return _dictionary.Contains( word );
    }
}

public class SpanishDictionary : SpellCheckDictionary
{
    public class SpanishDictionary()
    {
        _dictionary = new WordDictionary( );         ❷  Web service
        _dictionary.LoadFromWebService( );    ◁──┘      loading
    }

}
                                                     ❸  Inheritance of
public class EnglishDictionary : SpellCheckDictionary  ◁──┘   base class
{
    public class EnglishDictionary( )
```

```
    {
        _dictionary = new WordDictionary( );
        _dictionary.LoadFrom( ConfigurationManager
.AppSettings["dictionaryFile"] );
    }
}
```

In the version in listing 9.2, `SpellCheckDictionary` ❶ is now an abstract base class. The new `SpanishDictionary` class, unlike the `EnglishDictionary`, loads its word list from a web service rather than a file ❷. Furthermore, our original `EnglishDictionary` class ❸ now inherits from the new `SpellCheckDictionary` base class.

Note that, for the sake of brevity, we haven't specified how we load the `Spanish-Dictionary` from a web service. We should provide it with some details (for example, the URL), but we'll ignore that for now and assume the method can get what it needs.

This code is a problem for our movie review service in listing 9.1. That code is creating a `SpellCheckDictionary` in its constructor, which is tied to the original (English) version of the class. So Martin decides to accommodate the change with a constructor parameter, as shown in listing 9.3.

**Listing 9.3  Updated `MovieReviewService` to accommodate new languages**

```
public class MovieReviewService
{
    public IList<DocumentPosition> SpellCheckReview( string review,
string language )
    {
        SpellCheckDictionary dictionary;          ⬅─┐  Object
        if ( language == "en" )                   ❶  creation
        {
        dictionary = new EnglishDictionary( );
        }
        else
        {
        dictionary = new SpanishDictionary( );
        }
        IList<DocumentPosition> errors = new List<DocumentPosition>( );
        IList<String> words = ParseWords( review );
        foreach( string word in words )
        {
        if ( _spellChecker.IsCorrect( word ) == false )
        {
            errors.AddRange( GetAllPositionsOf( word ) );
        }
        }

        return errors;
    }
}
```

In the previous iteration, we created our `SpellCheckDictionary` in the `MovieReview-Service`'s constructor. That was fine when we had only one possible dictionary. But now this service needs to check reviews against whatever language is provided to it. Thus, we create our `SpellCheckDictionary` in the `SpellCheckReview` method directly ❶ and do away with the constructor altogether.

You can probably tell that, as new languages are brought in, this code will get cumbersome very quickly. For example, if we decide to offer our spell-checking services in French, we'll likely need to extend the `if` statement or convert it into a `switch`. Listing 9.4 shows how this can get out of hand.

**Listing 9.4    Our implementation of new languages**

```
    public IList<DocumentPosition> SpellCheckReview( string review,
string language )
  {
      SpellCheckDictionary dictionary;
      if ( language == "en" )
      {
      // Create English dictionary
      }
      else if ( language = "es" )
      {
      // Create Spanish dictionary
      }
      else if ( language = "fr" )
      {
      // Create French dictionary
      }
      else if ( language = "de" )
      {
      // Create German dictionary
      }
      {
      // Need to handle when an invalid language is provided
      }
      // ... rest of the code …
  }
```

The salient point is that as new languages are added, the code in listing 9.4 becomes increasingly fragile. The reason for the fragility is that the code depends on more and more classes. If you recall from chapter 5, as the number of classes this code depends on increases, its efferent coupling increases. As it stands now, the `MovieReviewService` class already has a dependency on three classes: `EnglishDictionary` and `SpanishDictionary,` as well as the `SpellCheckDictionary` base class.

You may be asking how this is a pain point. Dependencies seem innocuous enough. After all, what's the worst that we've done here? Added an `if` statement so that we create the correct `SpellChecker` class?

But let's say we want to differentiate between Canadian English and U.S. English and we want to use the existing `EnglishDictionary` class to do so. We specify which English variant we're using in the constructor of the `EnglishDictionary` class so that it can make the appropriate adjustments internally.

## Challenge your assumptions: Recognize intimate knowledge

If you started to read this sidebar with the hopes of some racy innuendo, we're sorry to disappoint. Instead we're going to continue discussing software development practices.

When you look through code that's tightly coupled, one of the first things you'll notice is that one class explicitly creates other classes internally. When you see a class that contains code that's "newing up" another class, it's said that there's *intimate knowledge* of class creation. The code creating the new instance of another class must deeply understand the correct way to create a valid instance of its dependency. Looking for lines of code that contain the new keyword is one simple technique that can help to identify areas that have intimate knowledge.

As an example, if a class has a single parameter constructor, then anywhere that a new instance of this class is created, the calling code must understand what's to be passed into the constructor. In some situations this required knowledge may seem benign. But what happens when the constructor parameter is abstract or an interface? Now the calling code must completely understand how to select and create or reference the object instance that should be provided.

If you're creating objects in this manner in one location for the entire application, it doesn't carry such heavy ramifications. But if you're creating these objects in numerous locations in the code base, any change to the behavior of the class will cause significant pain. Any changes to the logic required to "new up" a class cause a ripple effect throughout the codebase.

This behavior is the side effect of classes having intimate knowledge of how to create instances of other objects. As it pertains to dependencies, intimate knowledge is a direct result of tightly coupled code.

Because we've changed the constructor of EnglishDictionary, the MovieReview-Service code will now require modification. Similarly, any changes to the Spanish-Dictionary class require at least a look at the MovieReviewService to see if it needs to be changed as well. Ditto for any other SpellCheckDictionary classes we create that are included in the service. In short, changes we make to *any* of the SpellCheck-Dictionary classes require us to review the MovieReviewService code and possibly update it.

The point we're dancing around is one of responsibility. What's the role of the SpellCheckReview method? Certainly to check a review for spelling mistakes as the name implies. But what else?

As we pointed out in chapter 7 in the section on the single responsibility principle, the answer should be *nothing*. The SpellCheckReview method shouldn't display a list of review errors. It shouldn't save the errors in a database. And that method certainly shouldn't be determining which spell-checking class needs to be created in order to properly check the review. Nor should it determine which dictionary to use because that isn't part of its job. Yes, the SpellCheckReview method *uses* a dictionary, but it shouldn't have to determine which one.

Instead, wouldn't it be nicer if someone else was responsible for selecting the appropriate SpellCheckDictionary? Wouldn't it be cleaner if, when a problem came up loading the SpanishDictionary, for example, you didn't have to look through the MovieReviewService code to see if it was doing something wrong? Rather, you could have a separate class that handles loading the spell-checker and you could zero in on that when a problem arises.

This idea is the essence of the single responsibility principle. The MovieReview-Service is responsible for checking movie reviews for spelling mistakes against a dictionary. When we first started, it had only one dictionary to check against so the MovieReviewService kept that dictionary close at hand.

When adding new languages, we added to the service's responsibilities by forcing it to find a dictionary first. Doing so gave the MovieReviewService another possible point of failure. What if the service can't find an appropriate dictionary? What if a dictionary changes? All of these things now affect the MovieReviewService when it should be concerned with only one thing: where are all the misspelled words in this review?

### What's in a name?

One thing may have occurred to you during this increase in responsibilities: Movie-ReviewService isn't a good name to describe what the class does. If you thought that, have someone give you a pat on the back.

We purposely chose a vague name to illustrate a common problem in brownfield applications. Often, a name is chosen early on when a class is given a bucket of responsibilities and we have no clear idea what they are.

In our case, at the time of creation, we didn't consider that we'd be checking reviews in languages other than English. Maybe it crossed our minds (possibly at the same speed as the deadline we were working toward), or maybe we simply didn't think we'd work in other languages. So a MovieReviewService class to handle spell-checking and possibly other tasks seemed like a good idea.

One of the things you should consider during this chapter as we break apart dependencies is naming. As we strip down our classes to their base responsibilities, are we sure their names properly reflect their intent? Perhaps SpellCheckingService would be a more descriptive name.

One naming-versus-responsibility indicator is the use of the words *and* or *or* in class names. For example, assuming a class named SpellCheckAndPersistService works as advertised, it's obvious that it has multiple responsibilities in it and should be split into at least two classes: one for spell-checking and a second for persisting. This isn't a hard and fast rule, but it's a good indicator.

Better yet, with the industry's penchant for overloading terms like *service*, we may want to change the name to SpellChecker to reduce the ambiguity further.

This has been a rather verbose pain point but necessarily so. Dependency issues don't generally announce themselves as you write code. As your application evolves into brownfield territory, your classes often become more and more dependent on other classes, and you may not see it happen unless you take a step back to review.

Before we go any further with our discussion on dependencies, it's a good idea to review the dependency inversion principle from chapter 7.

## 9.2    *The dependency inversion principle*

In chapter 7, we introduced the dependency inversion principle, originated by Robert C. Martin:

> High-level modules should not depend upon low-level modules. Both should depend upon abstractions.
>
> Abstractions should not depend upon details. Details should depend upon abstractions.

Let's clarify a couple of points. High-level modules are ones that perform a task at a more "meta" level than a low-level module. They'll generally contain the algorithm for a task and leave the details of that algorithm to a lower-level module.

For example, our MovieReviewService in listing 9.1 is a high-level module. It spell-checks reviews. But it leaves the details of the implementation to an individual SpellCheckDictionary class, the low-level module.

Modules are usually defined as high- or low-level based on their relationship to another module. For example, our MovieReviewService could be considered a low-level module compared to another class that encompasses a higher level of functionality. Say, for example, you have a class that's responsible for gathering reviews from the user, spell-checking them, and then saving them to a database. This class may use the MovieReviewService as one of its low-level modules.

As a result of this hierarchy of high- and low-level modules, there's a tendency to start dealing in abstractions that allow us to effectively and elegantly maintain code in the appropriate locations. To talk about that, we need to distinguish between the two common methods of abstraction in .NET: abstract base classes and interfaces.

### 9.2.1    *Abstractions: abstract classes versus interfaces*

The term *abstraction* in the dependency inversion principle may be fuzzy. In .NET, this abstraction is almost always either a base class (often an abstract one) or an interface.

In our example, the SpellCheckDictionary class from listing 9.2 is an abstraction. It's an abstract base class and the EnglishDictionary and SpanishDictionary classes that inherit from it are concrete implementations.

The problem is that our high-level module, MovieReviewService, doesn't depend on the abstraction. Or rather, MovieReviewService doesn't depend on it exclusively. Instead, it depends on SpellCheckDictionary *as well as* the low-level modules. And we've already discussed a problem arising from that specific scenario: every time you change one of the low-level modules, you need to examine the high-level module.

Alternatively, you could've defined an interface with a method, `IsCorrect`, on it. The `EnglishDictionary` and `SpanishDictionary` classes would then implement that interface. In this scenario, both classes would have to implement the `IsCorrect` method.

The choice of whether to use an abstract class or an interface as your dependency is an interesting dilemma. MSDN Framework Guidelines currently favor abstract classes over interfaces, primarily because you can add a virtual method to an abstract class without breaking existing clients. This might be a concern if you're working on a framework or an API that is constantly evolving and is used by several clients.

On the other hand, we feel interfaces give you more flexibility than abstract classes do. You can vary the dependency that's passed to the high-level class in more ways than you could with an abstract class. For example, you could use composition to build up your low-level module with a Decorator pattern (see chapter 7). As long as the resulting class implements the appropriate interface, it can be used in the high-level module.

At the time of this writing, the debate continues as to which is more suitable. In general, we prefer interfaces for their flexibility. But in a large team with a volatile API, there's certainly reason to consider using an abstract class, at least until the API is a little more stable.

Regardless, in both cases, abstractions allow code to ignore the exact implementation that it's working with and instead focus on the functional interactions. Somehow you must provide the correct abstraction to that executing code. Traditionally, this is the crux of coupling issues.

### 9.2.2 *Inversion of control*

Another term you'll often hear in conjunction with the dependency inversion principle is inversion of control. Indeed, these terms are often viewed as synonymous. Although that's technically not true, in most discussions, the distinction is moot.

Inversion of control is a larger concept of which dependency inversion is one part. It deals with the concept of control flow in general and not just high-level and low-level modules (dependencies). That's about as deep as we'll get on the subject because it's a little too academic for this book. There are more ways of achieving inversion of control than using dependency inversion, but we mention the term here because it will inevitably arise in our discussions on dependency inversion, as will the term *dependency injection* (discussed later in section 9.4).

Dependency inversion is best understood with an example. Let's take a look at one now.

## 9.3 *A sample dependency inversion*

The dependency inversion principle describes not only what you *shouldn't* do, but also what you *should* do instead. Both the `MovieReviewService` (the high-level module) and the individual `SpellCheckDictionary` implementations (the low-level modules) should depend on the abstraction (the `SpellCheckDictionary` base class).

Listing 9.5 shows a revised `MovieReviewService` with the concrete dependencies swapped out for abstractions. We've also taken the opportunity to rename the class to be more accurate. The overall change is minor from a lines-of-code perspective, but pretty drastic for our maintainability. We'll discuss it after the listing.

**Listing 9.5    Updated service with concrete dependencies removed**

```
public class SpellChecker
{
    ISpellCheckDictionary _dictionary;

    public SpellChecker( ISpellCheckDictionary dictionary )          ①  Constructor
    {                                                                   injection
        _dictionary = dictionary;
    }

    public IList<DocumentPosition> SpellCheckReview( string review )
    {
        IList<DocumentPosition> errors = new List<DocumentPosition>( );
        IEnumerable<String> words = ParseWords( review );
        foreach( string word in words )
        {
        if ( _dictionary.IsCorrect( word ) == false )
        {
            errors.AddRange( GetAllPositionsOf( word ) );
        }
        }

        return errors;
    }
}
```

In listing 9.5's version of our SpellChecker, no dictionaries are created. Instead, the code relies on an object that implements ISpellCheckDictionary being passed in via the constructor ①.

Listing 9.6 shows the updated SpellCheckDictionary base class. We've omitted the two Spanish and English derivations because they haven't changed from listing 9.2.

**Listing 9.6    The base SpellCheckDictionary and interface**

```
public interface ISpellCheckDictionary            ①  Interface
{                                                     abstraction
    bool IsCorrect( string word );
}

public abstract class SpellCheckDictionary : ISpellCheckDictionary
{
    protected WordDictionary _dictionary;                    Interface use  ②

    public virtual bool IsCorrect( string word )
    {
        if ( IsWord( word ) == false ) { return true; }
        return _dictionary.Contains( word );
    }
}
```

Listing 9.6 is nearly identical to the SpellCheckDictionary from listing 9.2 except for the inclusion of a shiny new ISpellCheckDictionary, which has become our new abstraction. Also notice that SpellCheckDictionary is an abstract class ②, and it implements the `ISpellCheckDictionary` interface ❶. Nothing says you can't do both if it helps your overall maintainability.

Compare listing 9.6 to the changes from listing 9.3 through listing 9.5. This update isn't trivial; it's a breaking change (that is, this change will break any code that consumes it), but not because the classes have been renamed. (In fact, renaming the class is a trivial change with the ability of both Visual Studio and other third-party tools to rename classes and propagate the change throughout the application.)

No, the major breaking change we've made is that we can no longer create a `SpellChecker` class with a default constructor. The caller *must* create a `SpellCheckDictionary` and pass it to the `SpellChecker` class. By making this change you've essentially dictated to future developers that that the `SpellChecker` class can't be considered valid unless it's been provided with a class implementing `ISpellCheckDictionary` during its construction.

This requirement isn't a bad thing. You may argue that we've just moved the crux of the dependency to a new class. Well, you'd be right. Somewhere, some class is going to need to know how to create the correct dictionary object to provide to this class.

But that code shouldn't be here in `MovieReviewService`. As mentioned before, this class isn't responsible for creating dictionaries, but only for spell-checking reviews against a dictionary. Somewhere else in the code, there will be a class that *is* responsible for creating dictionaries. Creating dictionaries will be that class's sole responsibility as well.

At this point, there are probably some questions going through your head. Let's tackle the obvious one.

### 9.3.1 Why invert dependencies?

With the new constructor restriction in mind, why did you go through this exercise? What was wrong with the original implementation? So you had to update our `MovieReviewService` class if we need to add more languages. How often does that happen anyway?

These are all practical questions. After all, in chapter 7, we mentioned the YAGNI principle: don't write code until you need it.

In chapter 5, we discussed a useful metric to monitor on a regular basis: class coupling. To review, efferent coupling is measured by the number of classes on which a given class depends. You generally want this to be low. Our `SpellChecker` class originally depended on four classes when it was still called `MovieReviewService`: `SpellCheckDictionary`, `EnglishDictionary`, `SpanishDictionary`, and `DocumentPosition`. Figure 9.1 shows the dependencies just for the dictionary objects.

**Figure 9.1 Dependencies for our sample classes. Each gray arrow represents a dependency on another class. The dashed arrows indicate that the dependency is based on inheritance.**

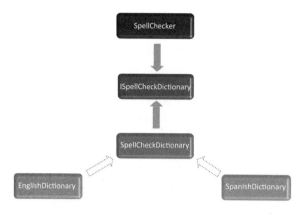

Figure 9.2   **After introducing an interface, we've reduced the number of dependencies and changed the direction of one. More importantly, `SpellChecker` now relies on only one interface.**

We included the dependencies for the dictionaries (the dashed arrows) for completeness. We're not as concerned about these dependencies because they represent an inheritance dependency, which isn't one we need to remove.

Again, you can imagine what this diagram looks like as you add more and more languages. Despite the fact that you've encapsulated some of the logic within the `SpellCheckDictionary` base class, the `MovieReviewService` class is still dependent on any dictionary class it wants to use.

By contrast, the version in listing 9.5 depends on a single class: `DocumentPosition`. The other dependencies have been rolled into the `ISpellCheckDictionary` interface. See figure 9.2. (Again, we've omitted the dependency on `DocumentPosition` because it's outside the scope of this discussion.)

This looks much better. In figure 9.1, `MovieReviewService` depended on three dictionary objects. In figure 9.2, `SpellChecker` depends on a single interface. Furthermore, as we add new dictionaries, that fact won't change. `SpellChecker` will continue to depend only on the `ISpellCheckDictionary` interface.

Still not convinced? Let's look at an area we've been ignoring: the impact on your testing.

### 9.3.2   *The testing impact*

So far, we've talked about refactoring our dependencies to reduce coupling. But how does that ultimately help you? To that end, let's examine the impact your change will have on the code's testability.

How are you testing the original `MovieReviewService` class? When you go through the process of adding French spell-checking, how can you be sure you aren't breaking any existing functionality with respect to English and Spanish spell-checking? What happens if you add French capabilities, and then discover that the English reviews aren't being processed correctly?

Perhaps you've never worked on a project where adding new features broke existing features. If that's the case, you'll have to take our word for it. It happens from time to time.

In chapter 4, we went through the process of adding automated testing to our project. We also made the proclamation that any new code you write should have corresponding tests. So whether or not the MovieReviewService class was tested before, the minute you add a new language to the process, it must be tested again.

But in order to test it, you must have an app.config set up pointing to the English dictionary file you're using. Even more cumbersome is that in order to test the Spanish dictionary, you'll need to connect to a web service somehow. Assuming you're using a third-party service, your test is now dependent on the fact that you can connect to it.

All these prerequisites are required to see if the SpellChecker class is able to collect up errors in a given review. In our opinion, that's far too much overhead in order to set up what should be a simple test.

We won't show this test because, quite frankly, we became physically ill when we tried typing it out. Instead, consider listing 9.7, which shows a unit test written against our updated SpellChecker class from listing 9.5.

**Listing 9.7   Test fixture to verify the functionality of SpellChecker**

```
[TestFixture]
public class SpellCheckerFixture
{
    [Test]
    public void Should_collect_errors_in_a_review( )           Known test review   ①
    {
        var reviewToBeSpellChecked = "review with incorrectWord in it";
        ISpellCheckDictionary dictionary =
        new FakeSpellCheckDictionary( );

        var spellChecker = new SpellChecker( dictionary );       ②  Execute code
        var errorList = spellChecker.SpellCheckReview(              under test
            reviewToBeSpellChecked );

        Assert.That( errorList.Count, Is.EqualTo( 1 ) );
        Assert.That( errorList[0].Word, Is.EqualTo( "incorrectWord" ) );
    }

    internal class FakeSpellCheckDictionary : ISpellCheckDictionary
    {
        public bool IsCorrect( string word )           Fake class for testing  ④
        {
        if ( word == "incorrectWord" )                 Implementing          Verify
        {                                         ⑤  expected results      results  ③
            return false;
        }

        return true;
        }
    }
}
```

There seems to be quite a bit going on in this test, but the behavior it's testing is simple. Here's a summary of what this test does:

1 Retrieves a known test review ❶. It contains a word spelled *incorrectWord* in it.

2 Feeds this review into the SpellChecker class ❷, which will check it against a fake dictionary of our own design ❹.

3 Makes sure the error list that comes back from the SpellCheckReview method contains a single error and that the incorrect word is *incorrectWord* ❸.

Before going into details, notice first how little you needed to do in order to prepare the SpellChecker class for testing. Compare this with the setup you'd need to provide for the original version. There's no web service to configure and no configuration file to provide.

Instead, you can zero in on exactly what this class is responsible for: collecting spelling errors. (One might even call this its single responsibility.) Everything else, such as loading and configuring the source dictionary, is handled elsewhere.

Also, the dictionary's behavior isn't of interest to you in this test. That's why you can create a fake one for our SpellChecker ❹. Its methods do the bare minimum required in order to test the SpellChecker. For example, you instruct the fake dictionary ❺ to return false from the IsCorrect method if the word it's checking is spelled *incorrectWord*.

The meat of the test happens when we create the SpellChecker object. It's here ❷ you create the class under test and execute the method under test, respectively. The question is still often asked: what exactly are we testing in this situation?

When you're first looking at interaction tests, this is a valid question, so let's spend some time talking about it.

### 9.3.3   *What are we testing?*

If you're not used to breaking out responsibilities for your classes at a granular level, listing 9.7 may seem like a useless test. It's not checking the spelling of the review in the normal sense; it's using a review we created against a fake dictionary that we also created. If we gave it the misspelled word *mitocondrial,* this test would still pass because the test is checking only for instances of *incorrectWord* in the review.

Other burning questions: how will the SpellChecker perform with a real dictionary object? And how do you know you can load your dictionaries properly and work with them?

These questions are valid and absolutely should be addressed, but not by this *particular* test. In this test, all you care about is whether the SpellChecker can collect errors from a review given a dictionary. Any dictionary.

How is a spelling error defined? This code doesn't care. That's the dictionary's problem. As long as it's able to tell you if a word is incorrect or not somehow, you can go about your business testing whether the SpellChecker is able to collect those errors into a meaningful list.

In short, you don't care about the inner workings of the dictionary. All you're concerned with is the error collection process of the SpellChecker.

Again, that doesn't absolve you of the responsibility of testing the inner workings of the dictionary. In another test, you'll very much care how it determines what an error is, in English, Spanish, and whatever other language we choose to support. That test (or more likely, suite of tests) will run the gamut of testing actual English/Spanish words against the dictionary.

Similarly, the question of whether your dictionaries load properly can be addressed with another test. You should have tests in place to ensure you can properly load the English dictionary from the config file and the Spanish dictionary from the web service.

As for the question of whether the SpellChecker will work correctly with a "proper" dictionary, that's where integration tests come into the picture. It's all well and good to test each class in isolation, but that's not how the application is going to be run. A good suite of integration tests must be implemented to make sure each component works in conjunction with other components. This isolation is one of the natural side effects of driving code down to the point where each module has one, and only one, responsibility.

### 9.3.4 *The effect of breaking out responsibilities*

Now that you've beaten the SpellChecker's responsibility into the ground, let's follow the responsibility chain through a little further. You'll see what other responsibilities have arisen that have been ignored.

We've talked about the dictionary classes and how they're responsible for determining what a "spelling error" is. Because that's their sole purpose, the responsibility for loading them needs to fall on some other class.

Using dependency inversion, the dictionary classes should depend on some abstraction for this, say an IDictionaryLoader. Then you'd have a ConfigDictionaryLoader and a WebServiceDictionaryLoader. Furthermore, yet another class, say a DictionaryLoaderFactory, would be responsible for creating an appropriate dictionary loader to provide to the dictionary class. That's not to mention a DictionaryFactory itself, which is responsible for creating the dictionary (using the appropriate loader, of course).

If this type of talk is new to you, you may be shaking your head at this veritable explosion of classes and interfaces, none of which do very much. But that's the heart of the single responsibility principle. Classes *shouldn't* do very much. They should do one thing and one thing only. As soon as you add another responsibility, you add to its complexity. Very likely, you're both reducing its cohesiveness and increasing the coupling in your application at the same time.

The increased number of classes is certainly a trade-off to following SRP. But the result is a lot of small, easily tested classes rather than fewer monolithic and complex classes. We started this section asking why you should invert your dependencies. It's taken a while to get to this point but here are the answers:

- To make your classes easier to test in isolation
- To isolate your classes from changes to other classes

**Class explosion**

Let it not be said that you'll reduce your class count by more rigorously adhering to the single responsibility principle. A common reaction when you start breaking apart dependencies is "But I have all these classes and interfaces cluttering up my solution now."

Our response is yes, you do. So what?

The most common complaint about a large number of files in a solution is that navigation suffers. Navigation isn't a code concern, though. It's the sign of a tooling issue. If you're using Visual Studio out of the box, efficient navigation through large numbers of files can be tedious. Shortcuts and context menus are built into Visual Studio that can help with that, but overall inefficient navigation is a sign of a problem with your tool: Visual Studio.

Don't fear: if there's only one thing that you should love about Visual Studio, it's the fact that it has an amazing extensibility framework built into it. As a result, there are numerous add-ins that you can incorporate into your development environment that will greatly aid in code navigation. There are two third-party add-ins (CodeRush with Refactor! and ReSharper) that have become known as productivity tools. Although both do much more than aid in navigation, you'll see a remarkable increase in that department alone.

In the end, you shouldn't compromise your code's design for the sake of your IDE. A development environment is there to aid you in creating code. If it's causing friction, look elsewhere for additional support. Better to change your navigational habits or to enhance your IDE than to leave your code in a less maintainable state.

Before leaving this topic completely, we can simplify our testing even further by getting rid of the fake objects we need to create to satisfy our dependencies. We'll look at how to do that next.

### 9.3.5  *An alternative using mock objects*

There's a way to tighten up the test in listing 9.7 even further by eliminating the `FakeSpellCheckDictionary` altogether. You can do this with a mock object. First introduced in chapter 4, mocking frameworks, such as Rhino Mocks, TypeMock, and Moq, allow you to create stubs for your dependencies. Furthermore, they allow you to control how they react when acted on without the need to create an actual object.

Listing 9.8 shows the same test using Rhino Mocks.

**Listing 9.8   An alternate test using a mocking framework**

```
[TestFixture]
public class SpellCheckerFixture
{
    [Test]
    public void Should_collect_errors_in_a_review( )
    {
```

```
        var reviewToBeSpellChecked = "review with incorrectWord in it";
        var dictionary = MockRepository
.GenerateStub<ISpellCheckDictionary>( );
        dictionary.Stub(
x => x.IsCorrect( "incorrectWord" )
.Return( false) );
        dictionary.Stub(
            x => x.IsCorrect( "" )
    .Constraints( Is.NotEqual( "incorrectWord" ) )
    .Return( true ) );

        var spellChecker = new SpellChecker( dictionary );
        var errorList = spellChecker
.SpellCheckReview( reviewToBeSpellChecked );

        Assert.That( errorList.Count, Is.EqualTo( 1 ) );
        Assert.That( errorList[0].Word, Is.EqualTo( "incorrectWord" ) );
    }
}
```

**❶ Using a stub**

**❷ Setting stub behavior**

Although it may not appear so, listing 9.8 isn't very different from the original version of this test. You replace the FakeSpellCheckDictionary with an object created from the mock repository ❶. This object implements the interface specified, ISpellCheck-Dictionary. Then you tell the mocked object how to behave in different scenarios, much the same way we did in the first version ❷. The first call says, "If, during the course of this test, IsCorrect is called on the dictionary with a parameter of incorrectWord, return false." The second call says, "If, during the course of this test, IsCorrect is called on the dictionary with any parameter that isn't incorrectWord, return true."

As you can see, using a mock framework in this manner is no different than when you created the FakeSpellCheckDictionary yourself.

You could argue that the original version of this test was easier to follow, especially if your team isn't familiar with mocking. That argument is a circumstance of our simplistic and contrived example. In more realistic scenarios, when interfaces are more involved, the power of mock objects becomes more apparent. Just as an example, if you added a new method to the ISpellCheckDictionary interface, you'd need to update your fake object in the first version of this test. In the second, the mocking framework handles that task for you implicitly.

Mock frameworks can be a tremendous help when testing objects with dependencies. But they aren't as easy to grasp initially as concrete fake objects are. They're well worth the time to learn, but be forewarned: it will take time to become proficient in them. We'll revisit them throughout the remainder of this chapter and the book. Before getting to that, we'd like to expand on the underlying concept behind this example. An understanding of dependency injection will pave the way for more advanced approaches for managing your dependencies.

## 9.4 *Dependency injection*

You'll almost certainly encounter the term *dependency injection* during your travels. Dependency injection is similar to inversion of control and dependency inversion, and people will often use these terms synonymously, though differences exist.

Dependency injection is a specific implementation of inversion of control. You've seen it in action already. In listing 9.5, you injected the dependency (ISpellCheck-Dictionary) into the SpellChecker class through its constructor. In doing so, you applied the dependency inversion principle to invert the control of how to find the dependencies for the SpellChecker object.

So to recap the terminology introduced in this chapter:

- Inversion of control is a high-level abstract principle.
- The dependency inversion principle is a means of achieving inversion of control by moving the dependency to an abstraction.
- Dependency injection is a concrete implementation of the dependency inversion principle.

You may be asking yourself why you need to have a specific method for performing dependency injection. Let's look at our SpellChecker class from the perspective of a consumer. Listing 9.9 shows one potential class that would create a SpellChecker.

**Listing 9.9    Class that creates its dependency in the constructor**

```
public class SpellCheckReviewService
{
    SpellChecker _spellChecker;
    public SpellCheckReviewService()
    {
        _spellChecker = new SpellChecker ( new EnglishDictionary() );
    }

    // More code that uses the SpellChecker
}
```

At this point, we're going to reset our example a little and assume that we're dealing only with the English language in our reviews. Later, we'll talk about incorporating others, but until then, the extra language requirement will muddy the waters. Note that the SpellChecker still requires an ISpellCheckDictionary object because you want to adhere to the single responsibility principle. But for now assume the English-Dictionary is the only implementation of ISpellCheckDictionary.

Listing 9.9 shows that when creating a new instance of the SpellChecker class, the consumer (SpellCheckReviewService) will have to know that an EnglishDictionary needs to be provided in the constructor. There's no reason for the SpellCheck-ReviewService to have any knowledge about what's needed to create a new SpellChecker. As soon as you've started to impose that knowledge on the calling code, you've increased the brittleness of this code.

How is the code more brittle? Imagine that you create a SpellChecker in a number of places in the application. Now if the creation requirements of SpellChecker change (for example, its constructor is modified to include a second parameter), you'll have to make changes in many locations throughout your code. This ripple effect isn't ideal from a maintenance point of view.

Ideally, you'd like to create a `SpellChecker` object without having to provide all the necessary goo (the constructor parameters). You'd still like it to be created properly, mind you. But you want someone else to do the work.

Put another way, you want our calling code to look something like listing 9.10.

**Listing 9.10   A class that doesn't require intimate knowledge to create it**

```
public class SpellCheckReviewService
{
    SpellChecker _spellChecker;

    public SpellCheckReviewService( )
    {
        _spellChecker = new SpellChecker( );
    }

    // More code that uses the SpellChecker
}
```

If creating an object without providing its dependencies explicitly were possible, you could eliminate `SpellCheckReviewService`'s knowledge of what's required to create a new instance of the `SpellChecker` class.

For now, let's assume you can create a `SpellChecker` class without providing a dictionary explicitly yet still have a dictionary wired up to the `SpellChecker`. Even then, you're *still* left with a tightly coupled solution: `SpellCheckReviewService` is responsible for the creation of `SpellChecker`.

Referring back to our previous discussion of inversion of control, you should change the `SpellCheckReviewService` to look something like listing 9.11 instead.

**Listing 9.11   Another version that takes an interface in its constructor**

```
public class SpellCheckReviewService
{
    ISpellChecker _spellChecker;

    public SpellCheckReviewService(ISpellChecker spellChecker)
    {
        _spellChecker = spellchecker;
    }

    // More code that uses the SpellChecker
}
```

Just as you did in listing 9.5 with the `SpellChecker` class, you've taken `SpellCheckReviewService` and inverted the control of `SpellChecker`. Rather than relying on the concrete `SpellChecker` class, `SpellCheckReviewService` now depends on an abstraction, the `ISpellChecker` interface.

Put another way, you've altered `SpellCheckReviewService` so that it no longer has a dependency on `SpellChecker`. Instead, you've injected a dependency into the class via the constructor. This process is called dependency injection.

The basic idea of dependency injection is that objects don't explicitly create their dependencies. They're injected into the objects by some external service.

This level of control isn't always easy to achieve. Classes may have many dependencies and each of them may have dependencies of their own, leading to a complex hierarchy of classes required to create the one we're interested in. And as much as we'd like to shirk our object creation duties in individual classes, somewhere along the line, *somebody* needs to create these classes.

One of the underlying ideas of dependency injection is the use of an assembler object to correctly create an object with the appropriate dependencies. (By *assembler*, we mean an object that assembles things, not an object written in assembler language.) In the case of our `SpellCheckReviewService`, you'd use dependency injection to create the `SpellChecker` class (effectively newing it up elsewhere). At the same time, you'd also determine which object to provide to `SpellChecker` to satisfy *its* requirements (the `ISpellCheckDictionary` constructor parameter). Not only will dependency injection provide the correct object type for each of the constructor parameters, it will provide instances of those objects as well. In short, by using dependency injection, we're creating a `SpellChecker` class that's completely ready for use.

---

### Constructor versus setter dependency injection

There are two commonly accepted methods for doing dependency injection: constructor and setter injection.

Setter injection provides dependencies to an object through properties on that object. The object requiring dependencies exposes setter-only properties on itself that allow the calling or creation code to pass in the dependencies for use.

In constructor injection, all dependencies are provided to an object as parameters in its constructor. This method forces an object to be created with all its dependencies in place.

It's possible to combine both constructor and setter injection. Some dependencies are provided in the constructor and others via property setters. Often, people will use constructor injection for *required* dependencies and setter injection for *optional* dependencies, though *optional dependencies* is an oxymoron.

Our preference is to use constructor injection most of the time. We believe it provides a clearer communication of dependency requirements when they're explicitly declared in an object's constructor. When you're reviewing the code, it's much easier to see what's required in order to make a class work if all the dependencies are outlined in the constructor.

In addition, it's too easy to create objects that aren't in a stable state with setter injection. The onus is on the creation code to remember to call the setters on the object after it's created. With constructor injection, it's much harder (though still possible) to create objects without their dependencies wired up.

---

There are a number of ways to implement dependency injection. Two common ones are constructor chaining (also known as poor man's dependency injection) and inversion of control containers. Both techniques have their merits and should be used when appropriate. Although doing constructor chaining for dependency injection isn't as sexy (in programming circles anyway) as using a container, we've used it successfully on large codebases.

### 9.4.1 Constructor chaining

Constructor chaining is a dependency injection technique that requires no external components and doesn't require you to create any infrastructure code. Instead, it makes use of constructor overloading to chain together object constructors. Listing 9.12 shows how to achieve this with our SpellChecker class.

---

**Listing 9.12 An example of constructor chaining**

```
public class SpellChecker
{
    ISpellCheckDictionary _dictionary;

    public SpellChecker() : this(new EnglishDictionary())     ❶ Constructor
{}                                                                chaining

    public SpellChecker( ISpellCheckDictionary dictionary )
    {
        _dictionary = dictionary;
    }
    // ... rest of the SpellChecker code

}
```

In listing 9.12, we've used constructor chaining to perform dependency injection. The first constructor ❶ will call the second one with a default parameter. Now the ideal code from listing 9.10 becomes a reality. You can create a SpellChecker class without having to provide constructor parameters to it and you still get a fully assembled SpellChecker with all its dependencies.

That said, you may have noticed a couple of problems with this technique. First, you have an implementation problem. The SpellChecker can be created only with an EnglishDictionary if you use the empty constructor. You're essentially creating it with default values. If you want to use a different dictionary, you're back to creating a SpellChecker with parameters.

The second problem is that the SpellChecker class is now, once again, tightly coupled to the EnglishDictionary implementation. Not only that, you've also made the SpellChecker class intimately knowledgeable about the method required to create new instances of the EnglishDictionary object. You worked so hard in this chapter to eliminate that dependency from SpellChecker and now you've just idly reintroduced it.

So this implementation isn't quite the end goal you should be looking for. It is, however, a valid strategy for performing dependency injection. Constructor chaining does allow developers to minimize the dependency coupling in the code. Although the code still requires knowledge of how to create your dictionary, it's limited to the constructor of the SpellCheck class.

Constructor chaining doesn't eliminate this coupling completely. To do that, you have to explore the second technique available: containers.

### 9.4.2   Containers

As you saw in the previous section, the constructor chaining technique will leave a residue of coupling within your code. Ideally you'd like to remove this dependency from the code as well. The best way to do that is to make use of an inversion of control (IoC) container.

The purpose of an IoC container is to act as a centralized location from which code can retrieve objects. Not only do containers provide instances of the requested objects, but they also take care of creating and injecting any dependencies required for those objects. If any of those dependencies require further dependencies, those are wired up as well. The container becomes your one-stop shop for objects and their dependencies.

Listing 9.13 shows our `SpellChecker` class as it'd look with an IoC container performing dependency injection.

**Listing 9.13   A class that takes advantage of an IoC container**

```
public class SpellChecker
{
    ISpellCheckDictionary _dictionary;

    public SpellChecker( ISpellCheckDictionary dictionary )         ❶ Only
    {                                                                   constructor
        _dictionary = dictionary;
    }

    public IList<DocumentPosition> SpellCheckReview( string review )
    {
        IList<DocumentPosition> errors = new List<DocumentPosition>( );
        IList<String> words = ParseWords( review );
        foreach( string word in words )
        {
        if ( _dictionary.IsCorrect( word ) == false )
        {
            errors.AddRange( GetAllPositionsOf( word ) );
        }
        }

        return errors;
    }
}
```

You'll notice that listing 9.13 is identical to listing 9.5. As with that listing, only one constructor is required ❶. The difference is that with a container, you don't need to explicitly create the `ISpellCheckDictionary` class that's injected into it. The container will do it for you. Let's take a peek behind the curtain.

When a container creates an instance of the `SpellChecker` class, it has to know what type of object to instantiate and pass in as the `ISpellCheckDictionary` typed parameter. Regardless of what container (third-party or home-grown) you're using, it needs to know what class to use when an `ISpellCheckDictionary` is requested.

In most cases, this request is done through a simple mapping. When you configure the container, you map a requested type to a resolved type. In our example from listing 9.13, the container would map an `ISpellCheckDictionary` to an `English-Dictionary`. That is, when a parameter of type `ISpellCheckDictionary` is requested, the container should resolve it with an instance of the `EnglishDictionary` object.

Configuration of the mapping between the requested and resolved types can take many forms. With some containers, it may be done in XML configuration files, although others may do it in code, using a fluent interface or domain-specific language. Some provide more than one method of configuration. Regardless of the method used to configure the container, that configuration is the trade-off that's made when removing the final couplings that exist in constructor chaining. When you're done, your classes are no longer coupled to concrete implementations, but you also have a little extra code to configure the container. It's an unfair trade-off, but it's unfair in your favor.

**ABSTRACTING THE CONTAINER**

Once you've started using a container to perform your dependency injection, you end up with one remaining dependency: the container itself. Although in most cases using the container will be transparent, you still need to get *some* object at the top of the hierarchy at some point, usually when the application is launched. That means requesting it from the container object explicitly.

A practice that we endorse is to create a custom wrapper that abstracts the container's specific implementation away from your application. Listing 9.14 shows one way of doing this as well as sample client code that calls it.

> **Listing 9.14   Skeleton wrapper for an IoC container**

```
public class ResolveType
{                                          ❶ Resolution
    public static T Of<T>()     ◁──┘          method
    {
        //...
    }
}

public class SomeClientApplicationClass
{
    public void DoingSomeWork( )
{
var spellCheckDictionary = ResolveType.Of<ISpellCheckDictionary>();

    //...
}
}
```

In listing 9.14, we created a `ResolveType` class that exposes a static method `Of<T>` ❶. The `Of<T>` method will call the underlying container itself to resolve the requested type of T. The application will work with this class, not the container itself. As a result, if we decide to switch from one type of container to another, the impact of that change is limited to just the code in the ResolveType class.

### The Common Service Locator

Recently, a project was created called Common Service Locator to provide exactly the abstraction we discuss here. It contains a shared interface for locating services so that you don't need to rely on a direct reference to a specific IoC container.

As of this writing, the project had support for all major IoC containers on the market. Although you may lose some of the advanced features of a particular container, the Common Service Locator provides enough functionality in its "lowest common denominator" form to still be useful.

You can find more information on the Common Service Locator at http://common-servicelocator.codeplex.com.

Here's a final note on our all-but-forgotten SpanishDictionary. Earlier, we cast aside the requirement for multiple language support for the sake of clarity. Once you add multilanguage support, it may not be realistic to assume that we always want to create an EnglishDictionary when requesting an ISpellCheckDictionary object. The more likely scenario is that we'd like to decide at runtime which ISpellCheck-Dictionary object to create.

Doing so is still possible in most third-party containers, and it's certainly feasible to do it if you roll your own container. One way to achieve this goal is to specify to your container that when you request an ISpellCheckDictionary, you shouldn't automatically create a specific object. Instead, you tell the container to call a method on a class that's able to create the object for you. (The class is often a factory class, one whose sole responsibility is to create objects.)

### Third-party or roll your own?

Third-party containers tend to be feature rich with a wide variety of options. But at their core, they're simply hash tables. The key is the interface you request and the value is the concrete type that maps to it.

So don't shy away from creating your own simple container if you have simple needs. Remember, the best tool to solve the problem at hand may be a tool you create. That said, the richness required to handle fringe case scenarios in your application may be best served by a third-party container. In the end, pick what's best for you. And whatever choice you make, remember to abstract the implementation away from the rest of your code to minimize the impact if the time comes to change.

Although this looks easy on paper, keep in mind that the factory class needs to be able to determine which ISpellCheckDictionary object to create. This task often entails setting a property somewhere that the factory class checks. It's not an ideal scenario, but in our experience it's still worthwhile pursuing compared to the alternative of having highly coupled code to maintain.

Now that you've seen examples and we've discussed the nuances of dependency inversion, let's spend some time looking at how you can work with dependency inversion in your existing codebase.

## 9.5    *Dependency inversion in brownfield applications*

Hopefully, we've explained dependency inversion clearly enough that the concept seems relatively simple. You've migrated from a highly coupled MovieReview-Service with embedded dictionaries into a design where you can test each component in isolation.

But this is sample code. The reality is, brownfield applications can be notoriously resistant to separating classes into single responsibilities and, thus, to dependency inversion. Often, the application contains monolithic classes with dependencies on specific databases, config files, web services, and even other classes. Discovering a class's individual responsibility sometimes requires the services of a psychoanalyst rather than a developer. And determining where and how to implement dependency inversion often requires a tea leaf reading.

In reality, refactoring a brownfield application to implement dependency inversion isn't intimidating if done at the right time and using the right techniques. If you have a brownfield application staring you in the face with tightly coupled classes and dependencies, you don't want to start big and you definitely want to have a safety net. Let's start with the safety net provided by automated testing.

### 9.5.1    *Testing for success*

As mentioned in chapter 4, when we were discussing automated testing, unit and integration tests provide peace of mind when refactoring code. If your code is tightly coupled and you plan to refactor out that dependency coupling, do so by first creating integration tests. These tests will act as a baseline to ensure that your changes during the decoupling process won't have any negative effects on the functionality within the code base.

Yes, yes, we can hear your thoughts now. Wouldn't it be nice if you had the time to write integration tests for old code? We agree. Writing these tests will be a long and laborious process.

Here's our advice: write them anyway. Once created, those tests will become a valuable long-term asset for the development team. More immediately, they'll be a valuable asset as you refactor your dependencies.

If you decide that you want to take on the decoupling process without the benefit of a test suite to back you up, nothing is stopping you. We've decoupled applications in the past this way. It's been met with, let's say, "mixed" success. In the more success-ful projects, the failure was visible immediately. In the others, the failures were more malignant and didn't appear until late in the release cycle. Yes, that means that our refactoring efforts introduced some defects into production—which is why we won't work without the safety net of unit and/or integration tests before starting any code changes ever again. But if you're still skeptical, we do encourage you to learn from your own experience. That code-based experience is going to start in one spot and it's going to be up to you to figure out where that spot will be.

### 9.5.2  *The jumping-off point*

Once you've decided if you're going to walk the tightrope without a safety net (or not), it's time to start the refactoring process. Like our example for refactoring to logical lay-ers in chapter 8, refactoring out coupling and dependencies is something you want to do incrementally. As figure 8.8 showed in the previous chapter, you must decouple your dependencies a bit at a time so that you can manage the impact of the changes.

But where should you start? Again, this is a subjective decision. If it's your first time refactoring out dependencies, you'll feel most comfortable working in an area of the code that you understand thoroughly. If you've been neck-deep in data access code, start looking for responsibilities there. If you're the user interface go-to person in your organization, the `Initech.UserInterface` namespace might be your best bet. It's a great idea to begin under familiar circumstances.

If you're somewhat confident in your ability to remove and/or invert dependen-cies, the best place to start is a location in the code that has historically been a sore spot for maintenance. If your application hasn't yet been released to production, don't think that you're clear of problem maintenance areas. Where are you getting the most defects reported from your QA team? What area of the application receives the most requests for functionality changes? What part of the code sends developers into a fetal position at its mere mention? These are all areas of maintenance friction that you can help to address by removing coupling and inverting dependencies.

Regardless of where you start, you'll have to work in small, controllable chunks. The crux of this approach is to work on changes incrementally.

### 9.5.3  *Work incrementally*

Unlike the incremental refactoring to logical layers outlined in chapter 8, the incre-mental nature of this refactoring is multidimensional. The first dimension is the incre-mental units within the codebase. This part *is* similar to the steps outlined in chapter 8, except that this time, you're refactoring dependencies into interfaces in baby steps, running your tests after each change.

The second dimension is the incremental use of the decoupling techniques out-lined previously in this chapter. In our experience, trying to implement a container-based IoC implementation as the first refactoring of a tightly coupled piece of code is a large and overwhelming undertaking—especially when you're first starting to refactor the codebase. Instead, our suggestion is to incrementally apply each technique within each unit of code you're working on. As you move forward in the process, the impact of the changes required will become less and you'll be able to apply multiple techniques simultaneously.

---

### Tales from the trenches: Choosing the end goal

When initially analyzing one project that we joined, it was obvious that some of the main problems were due to not using dependency injection. The project was already quite large and had a fairly mature codebase (a typical brownfield application). We had to determine how we were going to loosen the coupling by implementing dependency injection while still allowing the project to continue to move forward.

The first step in this process was to start with using poor man's dependency injection. It allowed us to easily convert one class at a time with minimal impact to the remainder of the codebase and the overall project. Using poor man's dependency injection allowed the team to address decoupling in an extremely incremental fashion. We could pause and resume the refactoring work almost at will depending on whether more pressing tasks came up. The result was that we rarely felt as if we were hemmed in by doing this work.

Our initial goal when we started the dependency injection refactoring was to make use of an IoC container to resolve all our dependencies. As we moved further along in the initial refactoring to poor man's injection, we realized that the task we'd taken on was much larger than we'd initially thought. That, in combination with the learning curve that the team would endure when implementing an IoC container, pushed the effort-to-benefit ratio too high. Rather than risking a large impact on the project, we decided that we wouldn't take the final step to an IoC container at that time.

Because we chose to implement our dependency injection refactoring one step at a time, we were able to switch gears partway through and reassess what was best for the project. In the end, our initial goal was never met, but we did improve the code and address some of the major issues that we'd seen in our initial analysis.

---

Detaching the code that you're working on from the remainder of the application is one of the keys to being able to work incrementally. The first step to doing this, and one that's quite effective, is to begin working with interfaces instead of concrete classes.

#### 9.5.4 *Start by introducing interfaces*

So which decoupling technique should you start with? Well, the easiest and the one with the smallest amount of impact to the codebase is using interfaces. Change the code to use interfaces for its internal variables. Don't worry about inverting dependencies just yet. Converting dependencies to interfaces will be trying enough. You'll have to create new interfaces for objects, modify existing code to make use of those interfaces, and finally, retest the code to ensure that everything still works.

As we mentioned earlier, this process will become easier as you get further into the codebase. More and more of the classes will already implement interfaces, and making use of the interfaces will be a simple change task.

Once the code you're working on is using interfaces in as many places as possible, you can now work at the next step: inverting the dependencies.

### 9.5.5   *Apply the dependency inversion principle*

Our second recommended refactoring step is to take code that has been decoupled through the use of interfaces and begin to invert the dependencies within it. There are two options available to you here. Both require that you start to move your dependencies to field variables and to have them provided through constructor injection. You've seen how this can be achieved in earlier examples, but listings 9.15 and 9.16 show a piece of code before and after the dependency inversion principle is applied.

**Listing 9.15   Before applying dependency inversion**

```
public class DocumentFinder( )
{
    public IEnumerable<DocumentDto> FindByTitle( string titleFragment )
    {
        DocumentRepository repository = new DocumentRepository( );       ◁─┐
        IEnumerable<Document> documents =                                  Creates
repository.Find( x => x.Title.Contains( titleFragment ) );             dependencies
                                                                           inline
        DocumentToDtoTranslator translator =
new DocumentToDtoTranslator( );
        IEnumerable<DocumentDto> documentDtos =                          ◁─┘
translator.Translate( documents );

        return documentDtos;
    }
}
```

Next (listing 9.16) is the same code after applying dependency inversion.

**Listing 9.16   After applying dependency inversion**

```
public class DocumentFinder( )
{
    IDocumentRepository _documentRepository;
    IDocumentToDtoTranslator _translator;

    public DocumentFinder( ) : this( new DocumentRepository( ),
        new DocumentToDtoTranslator( ) { }

    public DocumentFinder( IDocumentRepository documentRepository,
        IDocumentToDtoTranslator translator )                          ◁─┐ Uses
    {                                                                      constructor
        _documentRepository = documentRepository;                         injection
```

```
        _translator = translator;
    }

    public IEnumerable<DocumentDto> FindByTitle( string titleFragment )
    {
        IEnumerable<Document> documents =
_repository.Find( x => x.Title.Contains( titleFragment ) );

        IEnumerable<DocumentDto> documentDtos =
_translator.Translate( documents );

        return documentDtos;
    }
}
```

Hopefully by this point, you'll see why the listing 9.16 is more desirable from testability and maintainability perspectives.

Once the dependencies have been inverted, the two available choices are between implementing poor man's dependency injection (constructor chaining), as you did in listing 9.16, or to go straight to an IoC container implementation. Both options require about the same amount of effort, although there will be some initial setup, coding, and configuration when implementing the IoC container. Unless you're being prevented from using an IoC container, we suggest that you make the immediate leap to this technique.

Again, implementing the IoC container should be done incrementally. Do not, we repeat, do not try to configure your container with all dependencies all at once. Doing so can be confusing and can lead to missed configurations. Furthermore, this type of oversight can be a difficult one to track down. Worse, it's also a problem that can go unnoticed for long periods of time. Configuring your IoC container is one task that we keep in the smallest possible pieces of work that we can, even when we're doing new development.

If you decide to go the route of poor man's dependency injection, don't fear. That approach will put your code in a wonderful position to implement an IoC container when you decide to use one. The changes to code will be minimal and the effects immediate. Although poor man's dependency injection isn't necessarily the absolutely ideal step to take, it will still make your code testable and will reduce the barriers to progressing to an IoC container in the future.

All through the process of refactoring your code using these techniques, you've quite possibly broken existing automated tests. Additionally, you've introduced a number of new points of testability. Now is the time to look at what has been going on with respect to those tests.

### 9.5.6  *Review (and add) unit tests*

The process of changing the code to require the injection of the dependency will offer you a new testing point within the application. With dependencies removed from a class, it's in a much better state to be unit tested. This is because you can now create it without having to worry about the requirements of its dependencies. If unit tests exist for the class, now is a perfect time to review them. If they don't, it's an even more perfect time to add them.

Begin making use of mock objects to better test your classes in isolation. They're ideal for mocking your dependencies and for testing the behavioral interaction between a class and its dependencies (see chapter 4). This strategy will allow you to increase the quality of your codebase and ensure that quality is maintained by running these new tests as regressions on future code changes or enhancements.

Our final suggestion, and one we're going to keep repeating, is that you refactor to single responsibility where required. Decoupling your code gives you the perfect platform to make use of the open/closed principle to enable your attempts to refactor to single responsibilities. The single responsibility principle: we've talked about it before, we're talking about it now, and we'll continue to mention it in the future.

On a brownfield project, these are the approaches that we suggest should be taken. None are magical potions that make effort required when decoupling your code disappear. Instead they're meant to help manage the work in units that a person can easily keep track of and ensure a quality outcome to the effort.

> ### Don't forget to test the IoC container
>
> If you decide to go with a third-party IoC container, don't forget to test that it's configured. Take the time to write a test that will quickly verify that the configuration of the container is without error.
>
> We mentioned earlier that mass configuration can lead to missed values and, ultimately, hard-to-trace errors. By writing a test to verify configuration, you're adhering to the idea of failing fast. This quick feedback on failure of the container configuration will save you grief in the long run.

Although the fast feedback provided by your test writing efforts is great, there are other, less immediate, benefits that your codebase will see.

### 9.5.7   *See the benefits*

The benefits of decoupling your code tend to be intangible at first. Decoupling won't increase the speed of your code's execution, it won't eliminate defects from the application, and it won't make your code more robust. All these things still depend on the code within each of the dependencies.

Instead, what you'll notice over time is that you can fix defects more quickly. Code that isn't tightly coupled to its dependencies can be tested more easily in isolation. This fact effectively makes the code under a particular test smaller, and the less code you're executing per test, the easier it is to thoroughly verify it. As a result, developers will be able to isolate, verify, and fix defects quickly and with limited impact on the overall codebase.

Another benefit that will occur is the ability for developers to quickly and easily switch out application functionality when required. No longer will the team cringe at the prospect of a client's desired changes. Instead they'll know that the impact will be limited and isolated. On top of that, they'll see that the application of the open/ closed principle will make new or changed functionality easy to develop in isolation and with confidence.

From these benefits, you'll notice an overall decrease in development costs. True, there will be a large effort (and associated cost) outlay initially as you decouple your brownfield application, but in the long term costs for maintenance will be far lower than other projects. The reduced effort and increased confidence outlined in the two previous benefits are the direct cause of the decreased expense of development and maintenance. Because applications usually have a longer life in maintenance mode than they do in development, this is a powerful benefit and not one to be ignored.

## 9.6  *Summary*

We dove fairly deep into a few related topics in this chapter. Starting with problems stemming from coupling, we walked through an example where we decoupled a class from its dependencies. We also showed how this can vastly improve the testability (and thus, the maintainability) of your brownfield application.

Along the way, we covered some important principles, starting with the dependency inversion principle. Related to that is the concept of inversion of control and dependency injection.

Decoupling a brownfield application can occur in many different ways. The techniques used may be as simple as the use of interfaces instead of concrete classes, and as complex as dependency inversion and injection. Although all can be used on a brownfield application, implementing them requires much effort and an incremental approach.

By slowly decoupling an application class by class, you introduce a great many benefits into your codebase. Testability increases through the use of mocks and behavior-based testing. Replaceability increases through the use of interfaces and dependency inversion. Practices such as the open/closed principle become much easier to adhere to.

As with any refactoring effort, there's a cost. On a tightly coupled brownfield application, the cost may be very high and the initial outlay of that effort may be hard to sell. In the long term, costs will diminish. Maintenance costs will decline. Enhancements and changes to the system will seem effortless, and their cost will coincide with that effort.

Don't read into this that decoupling your code is a silver bullet for all things software development. It's just one of many pieces, such as single responsibility, open/ closed, Liskov substitution, and DRY, that make up a greater whole.

We've been slowly narrowing our focus over the last three chapters. In the next chapter, we'll narrow it further by looking specifically at your user interface.

# Cleaning up
# the user interface

## 10

**This chapter covers**

- Pain caused by highly coupled UIs
- Importance of separating concerns in UIs
- Useful UI patterns to work toward
- Refactoring to those patterns

The user interface (UI) has traditionally been a bone of contention for developers on many brownfield applications. As often as we're told to keep the UI simple, it takes only the slightest lapse before some business logic starts mixing with our layout code.

It doesn't help that historically Microsoft has provided little guidance. Since the days of classic ASP, we've been encouraged to put complex logic into our page code. The page-behind method of .NET did little to alleviate this except to move the logic to an equally untestable area: the code-behind.

WinForms applications haven't fared much better. From the beginning, we've been inundated with demos that showed us how to drag and drop database connections onto a page, wire them up to controls, and call it a day. Although these work well for...uh...well, actually, we can't finish that sentence. Drag-and-drop software doesn't work well, even in demos.

Adding to the issue was the framework that *did* originally come out of Microsoft for WinForms applications: the Composite Application Block. Although this framework did provide a way to divorce the UI from the business logic through a publish/subscribe model, the Composite Application Block proved complex and cumbersome for many people. It required an understanding of some advanced concepts to utilize the model to its full potential. As of this writing, its successors, Prism and the Managed Extensibility Framework, appear to be a step in the right direction, but the single responsibility principle has eluded Microsoft in the UI.

That's enough nay-saying (for now). As usual, let's start with the pain!

## 10.1 Pain points

This chapter's pain points start with a real-life (and abridged) code sample in listing 10.1.

**Listing 10.1 Sample code-behind for a web page**

```
public partial class MySubscriptions : System.Web.UI.Page
{
  // ... Local field declarations ...

  protected void Page_Load(object sender, EventArgs e)
  {
    try
    {
      m_domain = ConfigurationManager.AppSettings["My.Domain"];
      m_username = ConfigurationManager.AppSettings["My.UserName"];
      m_pwd = ConfigurationManager.AppSettings["My.Password"];

      subscriptionservice.ClientCredentials
.Windows.ClientCredential.Domain = m_domain;
      subscriptionservice.ClientCredentials
.Windows.ClientCredential.UserName = m_username;
      subscriptionservice.ClientCredentials
.Windows.ClientCredential.Password = m_pwd;
      subscriberservice.ClientCredentials
.Windows.ClientCredential.Domain = m_domain;
      subscriberservice.ClientCredentials
.Windows.ClientCredential.UserName = m_username;
      subscriberservice.ClientCredentials
.Windows.ClientCredential.Password = m_pwd;

      messagingservice.ClientCredentials
.Windows.ClientCredential.Domain = m_domain;
      messagingservice.ClientCredentials
.Windows.ClientCredential.UserName = m_username;
      messagingservice.ClientCredentials
.Windows.ClientCredential.Password = m_pwd;

      if (Common.VerifySecureConnection()) {
```

```
        if (Common.EnsureUserIsLoggedIn()) {
            if (subscriberservice
.HasSubscriberSelfServeBeenRegisteredFor(
                Members.Web.Current.MemberId.ToString()))
            {
                try {
                    m_localization = new Localization();
                    m_localization.ApplicationKey = "Subscriber Self Serve";
                    m_localization.CategoryKey = "MySubscription";
                    m_localization.Culture = new System.Globalization
.CultureInfo("en");

                    lit_Subscription_Title.Text = m_localization
.GetResource("lit_Subscription_Title");
                    lit_Subscription_SubTitle.Text = m_localization
.GetResource("lit_Subscription_SubTitle");
                    lit_Subscription_Intro_Copy.Text = m_localization
.GetResource("lit_Subscription_Intro_Copy");
                    lit_Subscription_Customer_Name.Text = m_localization
.GetResource("lit_Subscription_Customer_Name");
                    lit_Subscription_Customer_Email.Text = m_localization
.GetResource("lit_Subscription_Customer_Email");

                    //get error/confirmation messaging if passed in
                    if (Request.QueryString["message"] != null
&& Request.QueryString["message"].Length > 0)
                        lit_Subscription_Error.Text = m_localization
.GetResourceWithCategory(
Request.QueryString["message"], "Errors");

                    Member member = new Member(CMembers.Web.Current.MemberId);
                    Members.Profile profile = member.GetProfile();
                    lbl_Subscription_Customer_Name.Text = string
.Format("{0} {1}", profile.Firstname, profile.Lastname);
                    lbl_Subscription_Customer_Email.Text = member
.GetPrimaryEmailAddress().Email;
                }
                catch { }

            }
            else
                Response.Redirect("registration.aspx", true);
        }
      }
    }
    catch (System.Threading.ThreadAbortException) { }
    catch (Exception)
    {
        m_error = true;
    }
  }
}
```

Note that listing 10.1 shows only the Page_Load event—and even that has been short-ened. The original class, which includes custom Render and PreRender code, is a much stronger example of UI code run amok. But including that would look too much like an excerpt from a Douglas Coupland book. We're not famous enough to be afforded such latitude.

To get more specific, here are some ways a tightly coupled UI can cause problems:

- Screens (web pages and forms) are hard to fit into a unit-testing harness.
- It's difficult to focus on the specific code when changes are required to the UI and it's intermingled with other logic.
- You duplicate code when you port over to a different interface (such as for mobile devices).
- You duplicate code between similar screens.
- A tightly coupled UI leads to large, hard-to-read classes in a screen's code-behind.
- It's hard to determine what's screen logic and what's business logic.
- Screens become fragile. Adding new functionality is difficult.

This list isn't exhaustive, and we're sure you've experienced your own brand of pain from a monolithic UI. Few people can withstand the psychological kick to the stomach that occurs when you first open a six-thousand-line code-behind file.

That said, techniques, tools, and patterns are available that can help you overcome these past indiscretions. Let's start our look into those with a discussion of separation of concerns.

## 10.2 Separating the UI layer's concerns

A disconnect usually exists between the goals of a user and those of a developer. The user wants to open an application and interact with widgets on the screen to do some meaningful task. The developer, on the other hand, wants to write the code to perform the meaningful tasks and simply needs a way to test it with a GUI. Any GUI.

A (too) common way to test that code is to build a "quick" UI around it and start clicking things. In fact, often the tendency is to start from the UI and work your way to the database. This tendency can lead to too much code in the UI. After all, it's easy to drag a button onto a form, double-click it in the designer, and then start typing away in the `click` event for your shiny new button.

It's easy to see why this approach is the natural tendency. Many developers think in terms of UI. When there's a requirement to add a new consultant to a timesheet system, immediately a picture of a data entry screen with labels and text boxes is conjured.

Indeed, clients very often word their requirements in terms of screens. "We need a screen to search for jobs by date. We also need a screen to search for jobs by customer." As a dutiful developer, you go about building a prototype to show the client, who promptly says, "I love it. Deliver it by the end of the week. Actually, I'm feeling generous. Make it next week."

The result is as brownfield an application as you've ever laid eyes on.

Listing 10.1 highlights some rather nasty properties. First is that this code is hard to test. It's launched from the UI, which means that in order to test it, you'd need to launch the application and wait for the page to load.

> **Testing UIs**
>
> Okay, we lied a little. There are other ways to test code embedded in a UI without launching it manually. GUI test runners, such as NUnitForms for WinForms and WatiN and Selenium for web applications, will automate these UI interactions for you. But UI testing should test only the UI, not the underlying business logic.
>
> Additionally, some mocking frameworks (notably TypeMock) do allow you the flexibility to test the seemingly untestable.

Furthermore, consider all the responsibilities of this page. You can count service configuration (much of it duplicated), authentication, localization string management, and profile retrieval among them. This code is hardly a shining example of single responsibility principle.

In short, if an application is going to violate SRP, it will very likely happen in the UI. In fact, Visual Studio makes it easy to do so. For the rest of this chapter, we'll help you fight the natural instinct to "whip something together for a demo" that has been instilled through years of Rapid Application Development (RAD) demos.

Let's start by exploring the components of a user interface.

## 10.3    *Components of a user interface code*

We've spent so much time trashing monolithic user interface code that you're probably wondering "Enough already! What's the alternative?"

There are several. All of them have the same goal: to compartmentalize the code into specific roles. The typical roles are as follows:

- Code that represents the object(s) being manipulated on the screen
- Code used to display information on the screen
- Code that manages the interaction between the two

The first two items have well-established names. The first is called the model and the second, the view. The third depends on how you manage the interaction between model and view.

We'll talk about each component in detail now.

### 10.3.1    *The model*

The model is fairly intuitive. The model is whatever object you're displaying, editing, deleting, or otherwise managing on the page. It could be something simple, like a username and password for a login screen, or it could be complex, such as a collection of calendar months, each of which contains a number of tasks associated with the day of the month. Whatever data is being rendered or manipulated is the model.

Note that the model doesn't need to correspond to a specific domain object in your domain model. In chapter 8 we discussed refactoring the application to a domain-centric approach in which the domain model was the most important aspect of the architecture. Here the model is specific to the screen. It contains (or should contain) only the information needed for the screen it's created for.

This *may* correspond to a domain object but it doesn't have to. Say you need to display a portal screen that shows a username along with a collection of current projects for the company. In addition, the screen shows the outstanding invoices and any employees currently unassigned.

Chances are you don't have a specific domain object that has all this information. Instead, you can create a screen-specific class (that lives outside your domain) that has all the information you need and populate it from your domain model.

> **Working with screen-specific classes**
>
> Screen-specific classes are a type of data transfer object (DTO). They're simple, lightweight objects responsible only for shuttling data from one place to another—in this case, from the domain model to the screen. Screen-specific classes are sometimes referred to as view models.
>
> There are benefits to using DTOs instead of full-fledged domain objects. First, it helps divorce your UI from changes to the domain. Of course, rarely does the domain change without a corresponding change in the UI, but with DTOs, you can break up the work so that you don't need to do it all at once.
>
> Another advantage, as we've already discussed, is that you can combine domain objects into screen-specific objects that may not make sense as full-fledged domain objects. An example is a portal page that collects information from a variety of sources like the one described earlier.
>
> If you go this route (and we highly recommend you do for all but the simplest applications), you'll need a separate layer whose responsibility is to translate between domain objects and DTOs. Don't worry. It's not as arduous as it may sound. Furthermore, there are tools that can handle much of the plumbing for you. One we like is AutoMapper.[1]

By creating this layer of screen-specific classes, you allow the domain model and the UI concerns to exist without any knowledge of each other. If you're diligent at keeping the screen-specific classes absent of any logic or business knowledge, you'll also be one step closer to eliminating that logic from the uppermost levels of the UI concerns, such as the view.

Speaking of the view, that's our next topic of discussion.

### 10.3.2 *The view*

However you define your model, whether as a screen-specific DTO or an actual domain object, you need some way to represent the data on the screen. This is where the view comes in.

---

[1] http://www.codeplex.com/AutoMapper

At its core, the view is responsible for display only, though some UI validation can be thrown in as well. It decides where the text boxes and labels and drop-down lists are positioned, and it may be the first point of contact for the events that are fired from it.

Generally speaking, the view should be, to put it bluntly, dumb as a sack of door-knobs. Again, just how dumb depends on the presentation pattern, but even in one that allows it more latitude, the view doesn't do much more than forward calls on to another class.

Web applications provide a natural separation point for views: HTML. Anytime you're writing HTML, you're working with the view. JavaScript kind of muddies the waters a bit because with it, you can do some powerful things, especially with Ajax calls. We'll get into this a bit more when we talk about implementing Model-View-Controller.

In brownfield applications, both WinForms and web, the view is a good place to start major refactorings. In the absence of any directed effort, the view is often an obvious sign of bloat. Most developers can easily recognize when it's doing too much, even if they have only a vague idea of what to do about it.

The big question still is how you're going to make the view and the model work together without introducing any business logic. That's where the interaction class comes in.

### 10.3.3  *The interaction*

How the model and view interact is part of the difference between the various patterns to be discussed shortly. In most cases, the view has some knowledge of the model. The Passive View (see section 10.4.1) is the lone exception where the view has no knowledge of the model whatsoever. Before diving into the details of the various interactions that can be used in the next section, let's talk about why you care about these separations.

### 10.3.4  *Why the separation?*

Now that we've discussed the various components of a user interface pattern, it's time to address the burning question: why do you need this separation?

The answer should be obvious by this point in the book. We're strong proponents of testable code as one of your goals toward maintainable code. User interfaces are inherently tough to test in an automated fashion. Yes, there are GUI testing products such as NUnitForms and WatiN, but by and large, you'd like to test your underlying code in as friction-free a manner as possible.

So to achieve this goal, we repeat a common theme from part 2 of this book: apply the single responsibility principle and separate the UI into its individual concerns. And for the most part, this means having a view to render and interact with your data, a model to represent what you're interacting with, and the goo that holds it all together. Separate concerns means each component can be tested in isolation.

With that said, the view is still a bit of a sticking point. No amount of refactoring is going to change the fact that, at some point, you need to render a "screen" (a form or a web page). This screen still requires a certain amount of baked-in infrastructure in order to test adequately.

Because of this infrastructure, and the fact that the real business logic is contained outside the view, many teams will often forego testing the view altogether. After all, you'd assume that if a `click` event is wired up to a button, you wouldn't need to test to make sure the `click` event was actually fired. The .NET Framework wouldn't last too long if the event mechanism weren't reliable.

The danger with this line of thinking is that you have this entire layer of code that's not being tested. And it's easy to fall back into the practice of putting large blocks of "testable" code into the view.

"What's the harm in adding a check to ensure the phone number is the right length into the view?" you ask yourself one day while you're working on your air-conditioning management software. All goes well until the day you sell your product to a company in Greenland that has six-digit phone numbers. As you test your system to see if it can handle the new phone number format, it would be nice if those tests included the validation in the UI.

So we tend to favor views that don't have a lot of logic to them, if any. As we talk about the various UI patterns, you'll notice that this is sometimes a balancing act between views that provide a good experience for the user and views that don't contain a lot of untestable code. With that in mind, it's time to expand on our sparse discussion on the interaction and look at some specific patterns that you can refactor your brownfield application to use.

## 10.4 User interface patterns

Now that you understand the components of a good UI layer, we can talk about popular patterns used to implement them:

- Passive View
- Supervising Controller
- Presentation Model
- Model-View-Controller

**NOTE** You may have heard the term Model-View-Presenter as a UI pattern as well. The person who originally documented the pattern, Martin Fowler, split it into the Supervising Controller and the Passive View in 2006.[2] They are variations on the same idea but differ in the level of control provided to the presenter.

We'll take a look at the first three in this section as they have the most direct bearing on brownfield applications. Later, in section 10.6, we'll examine Model-View-Controller in more detail.

---

[2]  http://martinfowler.com/eaaDev/ModelViewPresenter.html

### 10.4.1 *Passive View*

Figure 10.1 shows a representation of the Passive View.

In the Passive View, you have a model and view as described in section 10.3. You also have a presenter, which handles the interaction between the two.

The defining characteristic of the Passive View is that the view has no knowledge of the model whatsoever. All interactions are handled entirely by the presenter.

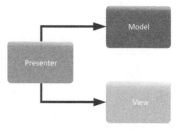

**Figure 10.1  The Passive View. The presenter mediates between the model and the view, which have no knowledge of each other.**

Let's consider an example. Say you have a music catalog application and a form that displays the details for a given song in appropriate controls (such as a textbox for the title and artist, and a drop-down list for the genre). Let's ignore events like Save for now and deal only with one-way communication. That is, you'll display a selected song.

Because we have no knowledge of the model, you can't create a Song object and send it to the view. Instead, you need to set the value for each UI element explicitly. Listing 10.2 shows the view code and listing 10.3 shows the presenter.

**Listing 10.2  View code for a Passive View**

```
public class SongDetailView : Form, ISongDetailView          ◁─┐  View
    {                                                         ❶  interface
    public string Title                                  ◁─
    {
        get { return textBoxTitle.Text; }
        set { textBoxTitle.Text = value; }
    }

    public string Artist                                 ◁─❷  Setting UI
    {                                                         values
        get { return textBoxArtist.Text; }
        set { textBoxArtist.Text = value; }
    }

    public string Genre                                  ◁─
    {
        get { return listBoxGenre.SelectedItem.ToString( ); }
        set
        {
            int index = listBoxGenre.FindString( value );
            listBoxGenre.SelectedIndex = index;
        }
    }

    public string AddGenre( string genre )
    {
        listBoxGenre.Items.Add( genre );
    }

    // ...and so on and so forth
}
```

As a bit of a teaser, notice the implementation of an interface on the page class ❶. We'll come back to this after the listing for the presenter. Also, you need to set the value of each UI component explicitly ❷ as the view has no knowledge of the model.

**Listing 10.3  Presenter for Passive View**

```
public class SongDetailViewPresenter
{
    private readonly ISongDetailView _view;
    private readonly ISongRetriever _songRetriever;
    private readonly IGenreRetriever _genreRetriever;

    public SongDetailViewPresenter( ISongDetailView view        ◁──┐   ❶ Dependency
      ISongRetriever songRetriever,                                      injection
      IGenreRetriever genreRetriever )
    {
        _view = view;
        _songRetriever = songRetriever;
        _genreRetriever = genreRetriever;
        loadGenres( );
    }

    private void loadGenres( )                                   ◁───┐
    {
        var genres = _genreRetriever.GetAll( );
        foreach ( var genre in genres )
        {
        _view.AddGenre( genre.Name );
        }
    }                                                                       ❷ Passive view
                                                                               methods
    public void ShowSong( int songId )
    {
        var song = _songRetriever.GetById( songId );
        _view.Title = song.Title;
        _view.Artist = song.Artist;
        _view.Genre = song.Genre;
        // set other properties
    }
}
```

Notice the use of dependency injection ❶—described in chapter 9—to provide the dependencies to your presenter. Elsewhere, some other piece of code is responsible for creating the view and the other two components used by the presenter. That's not the presenter's job.

Now let's talk about the heart of the Passive View ❷. Because the view has no knowledge of what it's displaying (it doesn't know what a song actually is), you need to tell it explicitly what to display for each field. You set the view's `Title`, `Artist`, `Genre`, and other properties explicitly. You even need to manually add each genre to the `ListBox`.

If this pattern seems unduly chatty, well, you're right. One of the characteristics of the Passive View is that the view usually requires a large number of methods and/or properties. That's because you need to interact with each UI element individually.

> ### `ISongRetriever` or `ISongRepository`
>
> In the sample code, we inject an `ISongRetriever` into the class. From the code, it's clear this is used to retrieve an object (presumably, some sort of `Song`) from a datastore. So why not call it an `ISongRepository`, as we'll discuss in chapter 11?
>
> Depending on the architecture, you may not allow your UI to talk directly to your domain objects, including repositories. Earlier in the chapter, as well as in chapter 8, we talked about a translation layer that converts domain objects into screen-specific DTOs for manipulation in order to divorce the UI from changes to the domain. This is where the `ISongRetriever` comes in.
>
> Whether or not you wish to directly inject a repository or some other intermediary class depends on the complexity of the screen and a certain degree of personal preference. The primary goal is that we've separated the concern and injected the dependency.

As a result, the view is, in a word, stupid. It knows very little about what it's doing. In the example, if you told the view to display the song's artist in the `Title` textbox, it would do so happily.

But that blissful ignorance is also part of its power. As we mentioned in section 10.3.4, one of the major reasons you're applying a UI pattern in the first place is to enhance testability. With the Passive View, your view has little to no logic of any sort in it. So you don't care too much that it can't be tested. You can test everything up until the point where a field is shown on the screen. A developer looking at the view, which is essentially a shell for data, can figure out what it does quickly. Indeed, you'd be hard-pressed to find a bug in listing 10.2.

> ### Why no interface for the presenter?
>
> You may have noticed that we implemented an interface for the view (`ISongDetail-View`) but not the presenter (`SongDetailViewPresenter`). This strategy is borne out of experience.
>
> Typically, we introduce interfaces to handle dependencies between objects. That is, if we want to test the presenter, we need to handle its dependency on the view and the "song retriever" (see the previous sidebar).
>
> But usually nothing depends on the presenter. Most of the time, it's our point of entry into a screen. Yes, other classes will be responsible for creating them (usually the view itself) but those classes don't interact with the presenters they create. The presenter is created and it's let loose.
>
> Put another way, we don't generally have any classes that require a presenter to be injected into it, nor do we swap out one implementation of a presenter for another. Hence, there's no need for an interface on presenters.

There's one glaring omission from our view that we've been ignoring. What happens when the user clicks a button or raises some other event in the view? How does the view know what to do with it? We'll table that question until section 10.4.3 when we discuss events in your UI.

---

**Careful with your controls**

We've been in projects where the implementation of a Passive View involved exposing the underlying UI controls in the view to outside callers. For example, rather than exposing a `Title` string property, we'd expose a `TextBox` control called `Title`.

Don't do this. Ever. That is *not* the way to a Passive View. It's an antipattern that combines the chattiness of a Passive View with the untestability of having everything in one monolithic class. You get the worst of both worlds.

Controls should never be exposed outside the view, if you can help it. If you need to add a reference to `System.Windows.Forms` or `System.Web.UI.Controls` (or even to the namespace directly above each of those) to your presenter, you're courting disaster. The whole reason for separating concerns is to decouple your application and make it testable. Tying your presenters to a UI framework isn't the way to go about this.

---

In summary, use the Passive View when you want the ultimate in testability. It will allow you to test absolutely everything except the .NET Framework itself. By its nature, the Passive View requires a lot of interaction with the presenter. For simple views, such as a login screen, it is quite well suited. If your screen requires a lot of interaction between the UI elements (for example, in complex validation scenarios), you may want to consider one of the other patterns that we're going to cover now.

### 10.4.2 *Supervising Controller*

Next on our list is the Supervising Controller, depicted in figure 10.2.

We'll save you flipping back to the Passive View for comparison. The only difference between figure 10.2 and figure 10.1 is the arrow from the view to the model. The Supervising Controller is similar to the Passive View except that the view knows about the model and can take advantage of it.

Just how *much* advantage the view takes is where many applications can fall back into brownfield territory. Your goal is to keep things testable so only simple data binding logic should take place in the view. The .NET Framework includes powerful tools in both WinForms and web applications for binding controls to objects. The Supervising Controller uses its knowledge of the model to make use of these data binding capabilities.

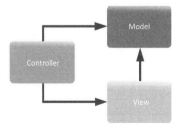

**Figure 10.2 The Supervising Controller. Unlike the Passive View, the view has direct access to the model.**

**Presenter or controller? Make up your mind**

Yes, figure 10.2 refers to a controller although figure 10.1 calls it a presenter. That's an unfortunate circumstance of naming and how the patterns evolved. The Supervising Controller derived from the now-retired Model-View-Presenter pattern. In his discussion on it, Martin Fowler even includes a note asking whether it should be called a controller or presenter. We used controller in the diagram to match the name of the pattern but will refer to it as a presenter throughout the chapter, again to avoid confusion with Model-View-Controller but also so we can use the term *presenter* collectively when we refer to both Supervising Controller and Passive View.

On behalf of the industry and the English language, we apologize.

Let's revisit the example from listings 10.2 and 10.3 but this time using a Supervising Controller. Listings 10.4 and 10.5 are the corresponding view and presenter.

**Listing 10.4   View code for a Supervising Controller**

```
public class SongDetailView : Form, ISongDetailView
{
    public Song Song
    {
        set
        {
            textBoxTitle.Text = value.Title;
            textBoxArtist.Text = value.Artist;
            listBoxGenre.SelectedText = value.Genre.Name;
            // ...and so on and so forth
        }
    }
    public IEnumerable<Genre> Genres                    ①  Data
    {                                                       binding
        set
        {
            dropDownListGenre.DataSource = value;
            dropDownListGenre.Bind();
        }
    }
}
```

Note that in listing 10.4's version of the view, you can take advantage of the .NET Framework's data binding mechanism to bind to a list of Genre objects ①. Now let's look at listing 10.5.

**Listing 10.5   Presenter for a Supervising Controller**

```
public class SongDetailViewPresenter
{
    private readonly ISongDetailView _view;
    private readonly ISongRetriever _songRetriever;
    private readonly IGenreRetriever _genreRetriever;
```

```
    public SongDetailViewPresenter( ISongDetailView view
      ISongRetriever songRetriever,
      IGenreRetriever genreRetriever )
    {
        _view = view;
        _songRetriever = songRetriever;
        _genreRetriever = genreRetriever;
        loadGenres( );
    }

    private void loadGenres( )
    {
        _view.Genres = _genreRetriever.GetAll( );
    }

    public void ShowSong( int songId )
    {
        _view.Song = _songRetriever.GetById( songId );
    }
}
```

No change here...

...but this code is much simpler

The code for the Supervising Controller is considerably more concise than for the Passive View. It's so much more concise that you may be wondering why you'd bother with the Passive View.

Consider what you're giving up with the Supervising Controller. It's not obvious from this simple example but that's because the scenario is very contrived. In the real world, this form probably resides in a much more complex application. For example, the user may select a song from a tree view and the form needs to keep track of a history of all songs displayed in it for Previous/Next support (because users have gotten used to the metaphor in browsers). Plus, perhaps it has the ability to add Genres to the master list on the fly—not to mention the ability to listen for changes to the data made by other users accessing the same list of genres in their own instances of the application.

These are a lot of scenarios to keep track of. Any one of them could be the source of an obscure bug. In these cases, you'll be glad you went to the extra trouble of removing the logic required to keep everything in sync out of the view and in the presenter where it can be tested.

On the other hand, if your data synchronization is straightforward and you've got the stomach for having untestable code, a Supervising Controller does lend itself to code that's easier to understand at first glance. It's a case of ensuring the application is more readable or more testable. As with most trade-offs, the deciding factor will ultimately depend on your project dynamics.

Another area of difference between the two types of MVP pattern is in the handling of events. Let's take a look at that in detail right now.

### 10.4.3 *Event handling in the Passive View and the Supervising Controller*

We've ignored events long enough. It's all well and good that you show a bunch of data on screen, but what happens when you click the Save button? How does information get from the view back to the presenter?

There are two ways a view can communicate to the presenter:

- By holding a direct reference to the presenter/controller and calling methods on it
- By publishing events that the presenter subscribes to

**DIRECT REFERENCE**

In this scenario, the view contains a reference to the presenter by way of a private variable. As the view raises events (as users click buttons, select list items, and otherwise interact with the form), the view calls appropriate methods on the presenter. The presenter will then perform whatever logic needs to be done and may optionally update the view.

**EVENT PUBLICATION/SUBSCRIPTION**

A publish/subscribe mechanism is another alternative. Here, the presenter subscribes to appropriate events that are raised by either the view or the model itself. In the Passive View, the view must raise the events as it does not contain any reference to the model. In the Supervising Controller, the events can be on the view or the model.

In most cases, it makes sense to apply the events to the model. For example, if you have a list of cascading drop-down lists (for example, Country, State/Province, City), you'd likely put a `PropertyChanged` event on the corresponding properties of the model class.

Note that this approach is easier to justify when you have a screen-specific model. If you're using your domain model object, adding events to handle screen interaction is a bad idea and you'd be better off adding events to the view instead. Better yet, switch to a screen-specific model.

There are advantages to each approach. A direct reference is often easier for developers to navigate. User events follow a direct path of method calls from view to presenter to model back to presenter and back to view. With the publish/subscribe scenario, you can't use the built-in IDE navigation tools to trace through a request. When you see an event being raised, you need to use other ways to determine which objects are listening to that event.

Also, direct references tend to make for easier unit tests. Most mocking frameworks allow you to raise mock events, but this isn't always for the faint-hearted. The goal of each of these patterns is to make the UI more maintainable. Complicated unit tests that no one wants to touch are only a half-step above complicated UI classes that no one wants to touch.

However, the event mechanism does allow a cleaner separation of concerns. The view has no knowledge of how it was created or how it's being controlled. Presumably, this would make it easier to swap one view implementation for another.

The publish/subscribe model is also well suited for complex asynchronous scenarios. Let's take a timesheet submission application as an example. At the end of the month, you'd like to be able to submit your timesheet to various people from a certain screen. Perhaps the system has to go through a complicated automated approval process that could take several minutes. Eventually, you'd like an email confirming whether it was successfully submitted to each person, but there's no point waiting around for that. (Okay, you may not trust such a system when it deals with your paycheck but let's assume you have faith in the submission mechanism.)

In this case, perhaps you'd like the view to raise an event to the presenter, which in turn raises an event of its own to a message queue that's processed on a first-come, first-served basis.

However you choose to handle user clicks on a screen, remember the underlying goal is maintainability. If you find that raising events causes a lot of friction because the view is so chatty, try a direct reference approach. By the same token, if having a direct reference to the presenter is causing too tight a coupling with the view, consider switching to event publication/subscription to reduce the dependencies.

Our favored approach is with a direct reference, but it's not a position we'll defend to the death, or even to the slightly injured. It has worked for us in the past as long as we had the discipline not to overload either the presenter or the view. That said, Microsoft tends to favor the event publish/subscribe model with its Prism framework for Windows Presentation Foundation (WPF) applications.

This section was noticeably short on code samples. We'll address those later in section 10.5. First, let's finish this section with one final alternative for your UI.

### 10.4.4 *Presentation Model*

A slightly different approach to screen synchronization is the Presentation Model, as shown in figure 10.3.

This model is a little different from the other patterns. You have a whole new class to deal with. Instead of a presenter, there is a Presentation Model. This differs from the regular model in a couple of ways. It's created specifically for the screen in which it's used. Although that's similar to the idea of screen-specific DTOs mentioned in section 10.3.1, it has more responsibility. The Presentation Model controls both the state and the behavior of the screen.

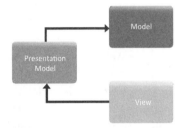

**Figure 10.3   In the Presentation Model, the view keeps itself synchronized with a screen-specific Presentation Model object.**

In effect, the class acting as the Presentation Model performs all the actions that a view might perform. It determines when to enable and disable elements, gets and sets values for fields, populates lists, and so forth. But it does so without referencing any specific user interface components. Text boxes, drop-down lists, radio buttons, and the like are still held within the view. But the view monitors the Presentation Model and updates itself whenever the Presentation Model changes. Because of this, the view requires extra code to synchronize itself with the Presentation Model and the Presentation Model requires code to synchronize itself with the domain model.

Think of the Presentation Model class as an abstraction on top of the view. It does everything you'd expect a view to do, such as store and maintain the state of the screen and control the interaction between the various elements on the screen. But it uses internal variables to store the state, not UI elements. So it doesn't require a reference to either `System.Windows.Forms` or `System.Web.UI.WebControls`.

Where does the actual domain model fit in? It's still used, though typically it's wrapped within the Presentation Model class. The Presentation Model class will use the domain model to control its own state and behavior, and the view will react accordingly. In effect, the Presentation Model class acts as both model and presenter.

---

**The Presentation Model and WPF**

Despite our relative dismissal of the Presentation Model pattern, it's the pattern of choice for WPF applications. Though the documentation calls it Model-View-ViewModel, it's essentially the same pattern.

WPF makes it much easier to create the Presentation Model (or ViewModel) classes that abstract the view. It provides an infrastructure that makes it easy to synchronize with your view, even providing two-way binding support. The result is that you can exercise your view in tests simply by exercising your Presentation Model. The only code remaining untested is the statements that bind the view to the Presentation Model.

Comparatively speaking, you won't see too many brownfield WPF applications, at least not at the time of this writing. Be aware that they do exist. Although we may consider rewriting a GUI in WPF to take advantage of its testability, in this book we focus on the more traditional UI patterns that we understand and feel are more prevalent in brownfield applications at the moment.

---

We'll forego the code sample of the Presentation Model because it's not nearly as common as the other three (although that's changing as WPF becomes more prevalent; see the sidebar "The Presentation Model and WPF") and we're not, to be completely honest, nearly as knowledgeable about it. The goal of the Presentation Model is to pull all reasonable behavior out of the view so that it can be tested in isolation. It's useful if you have a screen with a lot of complex state-based behavior because it provides an abstraction between the actual domain model and how the screen/view works. If that's important to your application, it may be a good alternative to the Passive View or the Supervising Controller. However, in our experience, the annoyance of having to synchronize the Presentation Model with both the view and the model is usually enough to push us to one of the alternatives.

Now that we've covered some of the most common UI patterns, let's talk about how you can refactor your existing brownfield code to make better use of these patterns.

## 10.5  *Refactoring to MVP*

We've now covered three ways to structure your UI. If your brownfield application is typical, it probably uses none of them. Indeed, if it's like the ones we've seen, it very likely uses much less famous patterns, such as House of Cards and Sheer Force of Will.

In this section, we'll look at tips on refactoring your UI to one of the patterns discussed here. We'll focus on the Passive View and the Supervising Controller, the most common ones, but you can apply the same tips if you decide to move toward a Presentation Model. With that, let's dive in head first. The underlying steps are shown in figure 10.4.

### 10.5.1 *Write your test first...if you can*

There's an inherent danger involved with refactoring your UI. Typically, we recommend writing a test before refactoring in order to make sure you don't break anything during your travels. With the user

interface, accomplishing this isn't as easy. Automated user interface testing tools still have a somewhat spotty track record when it comes to return on investment, especially for complex screens.

A relatively safe way of working is to avoid changing code as you refactor if possible. In chapter 8, we talked about defining seams while you draw your layers. You're doing the same thing here—you're defining the seam between your model, your view, and your presenter. As you work, you'll move code out of the view into its own testable class. As soon as you do so, get a test in place.

Resist the urge to optimize the code until the test has been written. Ideally, you'll be able to cut and paste the relevant code from the view into some other piece of code, which can be instantiated directly and is easier to test. This strategy minimizes the risk of breaking something during your refactoring and sets the stage for optimization when you're finished. Regardless, you need to look at the existing code and determine what pieces of it belong in which of the appropriate UI layers (or other layers that you've created in your codebase). This task is going to be at the front of your mind, so let's take a look at it next.

### 10.5.2 *Identify the components*

In each of the patterns we've discussed, we've mentioned three components: the model, the view, and the presenter. (The Presentation Model is slightly different but the underlying idea is the same.) In order to refactor, you first need to identify these components.

#### THE MODEL

The model is often the easiest thing to pick out for a screen. The model is the actual business object being acted on in the screen. If your web page displays a list of administrators for your discussion board, the model will be a list of administrators. If you're displaying a screen that allows users to dynamically manipulate an organization chart, the model is the list of employees displayed on the screen and the relationships between them.

Be careful not to limit your scope too much when determining your model. Often the screen displays more than you think. For example, say you've got a page that displays the details of one of your branch offices. On it, you can change details such as the name of the office, the contact person, and the address.

On first glance, the model for this page appears to be the details of the office. That is, you would have an `Office` class with properties like `Name`, `ContactPerson`, and `Address`.

But how are you selecting the contact person? Are you displaying a list of employees assigned to that office and allowing the user to choose one? If so, that list of employees is also part of the model. The same holds for the address if you're showing a list of states or provinces on the page. So in fact, the model is several pieces of data: the `Office` object, a list of `Employee` objects, and a list of `State` or `Province` objects.

There are a couple of ways we could potentially collect this information into a single model. Our personal preference is to use a DTO as mentioned in the sidebar in section 10.3.1. With this approach, you can create a specialized object whose sole purpose is to hold information for the specific screen you're working on. This technique gives us ultimate flexibility when it comes to refactoring the screen later to change or add to its functionality.

---

**Don't shy away from objects**

Another option we've seen used for a model is `DataSets`.

`DataSets` make for a nice demo, usually one that contains the phrase "...and I did it all without writing a single line of code" at least twice. But they come with quite a bit of baggage. Untyped, they're prone to errors because you need to reference things using strings. Often, these strings map directly to database columns, and it's never a good idea to marry your UI logic to a specific data implementation.

These days, custom objects are easy to build and still allow you to take advantage of built-in data binding capabilities. Most controls bind equally well to objects as they do to `DataSets`.

Objects give you the advantage of discoverability: it's easy to see what your domain model looks like. Compare that to `DataSets`, where the schema is buried in syntax such as `ds.Tables[1].Rows[3]["ArtistName"]`.

We've come down on `DataSets` already and will do so a little more harshly in the next chapter. `DataSets` have their place (though it's a place we've never visited in several years), but once you start rigorously testing your code, you'll find their usefulness wears thin quickly.

---

Another alternative is simply not to collect the various pieces of data at all. Because of the tight integration between the view and the presenter, you could request each piece of data individually whenever you need it.

Once you've determined the information that's going to be acted on for display, you need to figure out how you're going to go about doing that display. Let's move our focus to the view components.

## THE VIEW

Once you've identified the object you plan to act on, the next step is to determine what the view should do. Identify the tasks that the view must perform in order to display its data and then list the physical actions that can be taken on the view.

In general, the view consists of the user interface widgets (the text boxes, dropdown lists, grids, and so on) that display the data and that the user interacts with. The view should be the only layer of your application that contains a reference to `System.Windows.Forms` or `System.Web.UI`.

Your goal is to keep your view as stupid as reasonably possible. You may say to yourself, "When the Update button is clicked, the view needs to calculate the shipping cost and taxes so that it can display a subtotal to the user." If you do, give yourself an electric shock (it worked for Pavlov[3]).

The view does *not* need to calculate the shipping cost and taxes. Instead, it needs to record the fact that the Update button was clicked and pass that information on to the presenter. That's all it's capable of doing: showing the data it's told to display and letting someone else know that a widget was interacted with.

The "someone" that the view interacts with could be the model or it could be the domain model (if you're using the DTO pattern to fill the Model portion of the MVP/MVC implementation you've chosen). Bear in mind that, as much as possible, you'd like to keep any business logic outside of the view. Tax and shipping calculations sure sound like business logic to us.

Instead, you should let the presenter determine what to do with those raw values (in this case, perform tax and shipping calculations) and then take the required actions. This leads us to the last component to identify.

## THE PRESENTER/PRESENTATION MODEL

We've left the presenter for last because it falls under the category of "everything else." Whatever isn't view or model is handled by the presenter.

This separation isn't as easy as it may sound. For example, how much do you want the view to do? We talked about having a view that had no knowledge of the model (the Passive View). We also discussed giving the view more responsibility in the Supervising Controller. Your choice of pattern will determine how the presenter looks and behaves.

To define your presenter, you must define how the view will interact with it. Because we're working with a brownfield application, you have the advantage of knowing how the screen is already behaving. So you have an idea of how much power you want to give to the view.

Ultimately, the deciding factor should be testability. How testable would you like the screen to be? For extreme testability, the Passive View is the way to go. With this pattern, the view can't even blow its nose without first being told to do so. Almost anything you do on the screen can be tested.

---

[3] http://wikipedia.org/wiki/Ivan_Pavlov

Passive View may be a good option if the screen has historically had a lot of bugs. In this case, it helps to be able to test the interactions between the view and presenter so that you can expose existing bugs and new ones through tests.

But you also must balance this option with the chatty interface (between the presenter and the view) that will arise due to this increased testability. Because the view can't do anything on its own, there will be a large number of simple methods like `Get-Province` and `SetShippingCostLabel`. They're all testable, mind you, but be prepared for an explosion of small methods.

Another factor in your decision is whether the current screen makes use of built-in data binding capabilities. For example, do you have a list box or repeater control that's bound directly to a `DataSet` or a list of objects? If so, it makes sense to move toward a Supervising Controller that allows for this scenario. If not, be prepared to populate these controls manually through the use of custom `AddListItem` methods on your view.

In general, we like the testability of a Passive View but will often use a Supervising Controller to make our lives easier. If possible, you may find it useful to start with a Passive View simply to get into the habit of testing everything. There's little question of how much power to give to the view because the answer is always none. It's harder to accidentally sneak logic into a view that has no place for it.

Once your team is in the habit of writing tests against the presenter and is comfortable handing a model into the view, you can move toward a Supervising Controller. By this time, you should be more familiar with how to separate concerns and have probably felt some pain in writing seemingly meaningless tests to ensure a text box is set properly. A Supervising Controller pattern still isolates the various concerns nicely but allows the view to deal with the model directly.

You still need to take care that you don't do too much work in the view. If your view is performing any action that you feel should be tested (like calculating shipping costs), this should raise a flag that the view is overstepping its bounds.

That said, if your screen already uses a lot of built-in data binding functionality, a Supervising Controller is the obvious choice. Figure 10.5 shows the major selling

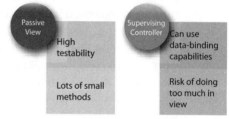

**Figure 10.5   A Passive View is more testable than the Supervising Controller but at the risk of being more chatty.**

point and downside to each implementation. Once you've identified the model, view, and interaction, you can start doing the code manipulation.

### 10.5.3 *Isolate the code*

With your boundaries defined (if only on paper), now you can start moving code around. By now, you should have an idea about how your presenter will behave. If you are using test-driven development (and we recommend that you do), you are now in a position to write a test against the presenter.

If you aren't ready to try TDD, that's fine as well. In the end, your goal is the same: testable code. As long as you move toward a state where there are tests in place, you're in a good place. We'll continue the discussion using TDD but it's easy enough to follow along assuming you write the tests afterward.

Your first test should be one that ensures the presenter and view can communicate with each other. It can (and should) be as simple as asserting that you can create a presenter and that it has a reference to the view. Then, you create the presenter and provide it with a view so that the test can pass. (Don't worry—we'll show an example of this in the next section.)

From there, you can flesh out the presenter's behavior. Doing so will involve moving logic out of the view into the presenter. What should happen when the Calculate Subtotal button is clicked? Well, we should probably have a method called `Calculate-Subtotal` on the presenter. So you create a test for the presenter for such a method to ensure it works as expected. Then you create the `CalculateSubtotal` method and make sure it passes your test.

## Writing tests for existing code

You have an advantage at this stage in that the code is already written. This fact makes the tests easier to write because you can write knowing how the implementation will look.

But this knowledge can be a double-edged sword. Tests that are tailored too much to a specific implementation may be useful in the short term. In the longer term, it could mean that when you refactor your code, you need to also change your tests due to the internal implementation change. Frequent refactoring of your tests should be a clear sign that your tests are overspecified and may be testing things at too granular a level.

For a more detailed discussion on this, see Roy Osherove's *The Art of Unit Testing* (Manning, 2006).

Working back and forth between the presenter and the view, you can slowly get the UI into a more testable (and tested) state.

For the most part, you should strive toward *moving* code rather than rewriting it. Your single purpose is to move the screen to a state where it's tested. Once you've achieved that goal, *then* you can optimize the code within the presenter, view, or model. But until you've got your safety net in place, resist the urge to make things better within the code you're moving.

The application may work against you. Your application may not yet be properly layered, and even if you move all the relevant code to the presenter, it may be doing too much. A good example we've encountered often is a common data access class with static methods on it to retrieve various bits of data.

We've already talked a little about how to manage this in chapters 8 and 9: by slowly teasing apart the layers and introducing dependencies into the presenter as appropriate.

Say you have a button click event that extracts data from several controls, performs a database lookup, and then updates several text boxes. Let's start with the click event itself. What does it do? It retrieves data from the form, performs some action, and then updates the form again. Breaking this down, you could have appropriate methods on the view to retrieve the data and other methods to set the values of controls. Once you have those in place, the presenter can then do everything the click event on the view did: retrieve data (this time from the view rather than directly from the controls), perform a database lookup (via an injected dependency as in chapter 9), and update the display with new values (again, by calling appropriate methods on the view). All concerns are nicely segregated and testable.

It's getting painfully obvious that we need to show an example. Let's do that now.

### 10.5.4  *A sample refactoring*

Let's make this theory a little more practical and work through a simple example.

For that, you'll need a piece of suitably brownfield code to start with. Let's tackle a nice, controversial control from ASP.NET: the GridView.

The page we'll refactor is in the administration section of an application that manages bookings for bands. It lists the bands whose tours are currently being managed by the application.

The screen is a simple application of the GridView. It lists the names of some artists and allows the user to edit the name of the artist or delete them. At the top, there's a way to add new artists to the list.

Listing 10.6 shows the code that's executed when the page is first loaded.

**Listing 10.6   Code-behind for a page showing a list of bands**

```
public partial class BandList : Page
{
    protected void Page_Load(object sender, EventArgs e)
    {
        if ( !IsPostBack )
        {
            bindPage( );
        }
    }

    private void bindPage( )                                   Static data ❶
    {                                                          access class
        DataSet data = TwilightDB.GetData( "twi_getArtists", "Artists" );
        gridViewBands.DataSource = data.Tables[0];
        gridViewBands.DataBind(
        );
    }
}
```

Right off the bat, we can see a few problems with listing 10.6. It's using a static class ❶ to retrieve the data required to display. Furthermore, it's passing in the name of the stored procedure that needs to be called. This code doesn't lend itself to a decoupled application.

But remember, your goal is not to change any of the existing code, but only to implement a pattern that allows you to test this code so that you can change it later. So you'll need to swallow your pride and let the static class be for now.

From this code, you can easily deduce your model. It's a list of artists. You may argue that the name of the new artist is also part of the model, but it's better off on its own. It's a single piece of data that can be requested when needed. For the most part, you'll be dealing with a list of artists.

So the view consists of a GridView, a TextBox, and a Button. The model is a Data-Set containing information about the artists. That leaves you with the presenter. Since you're binding the GridView directly to the list of artists, a Supervising Controller pattern makes sense in this case.

Let's write a test to get ourselves started. We'll start simple and write one that proves we can create a presenter and provide it with a view. See listing 10.7.

**Listing 10.7    Test to prove we can create a presenter**

```
[Test]
public void Should_create_presenter_with_view( )
{
    var view = MockRepository.GenerateStub<IBandListView>( );
    var presenter = new BandListPresenter( view );
    Assert.That( presenter, Is.Not.Null );
}
```

There isn't much going on in listing 10.7. All we've proven is that we can create a presenter and that it isn't null. But it's an important first step because we've made the decision that the presenter requires an IBandListView in its constructor. That is, we're claiming that we'll need a reference to an IBandListView object at some point.

We're kind of getting ahead of ourselves with that assumption. After all, how do we know that we'll need a reference to the view from the presenter at this point? Also, if we aren't actually doing anything with the view in this test, why bother mocking it at all? Why not pass in null to the presenter?

All valid questions—but we're going to sidestep them and move on. Maybe the next test will make things a little clearer, but for the time being let's implement the code that makes this test pass. See listing 10.8.

**Listing 10.8    Presenter class for our band list page**

```
public class BandListPresenter( )
{
    private readonly IBandListView _bandListView;

    public BandListPresenter( IBandListView bandListView )
```

```
    {
        _bandListView = bandListView;
    }
}
```

Again, we've cheated pretty heavily here by assigning the `bandListView` parameter to a class field. If you were doing true TDD, the code would pass just as easily if you'd left out that line in the constructor. We do encourage you to start with baby steps and implement only what you need, but that's not the focus of this chapter so we must take some shortcuts.

At this point, you have a presenter that can accept a view interface. You haven't defined what that interface looks like yet, and at this point, you don't need to. But let's take a look at the code-behind for the view and see what you need to do to get things started. Listing 10.9 shows the changes you need to make.

**Listing 10.9   Code-behind converted to a view**

```
public partial class BandList : Page, IBandListView
{
    private readonly BandList _presenter;

    public BandList( )
    {
        _presenter = new BandListPresenter( this );    ◁──❶ Presenter
    }                                                         initialization

    protected void Page_Load(object sender, EventArgs e)
    {
        if ( !IsPostBack )
        {
            bindPage( );
        }
    }

    private void bindPage( )
    {
        DataSet data = TwilightDB.GetData( "twi_get_artists", "Artists");
        gridViewBands.DataSource = data.Tables[0];
        gridViewBands.DataBind( );
    }
}
```

Listing 10.9 isn't too different from listing 10.6. You've made the class implement the as-yet-undefined `IBandListView` interface and added a reference to the new `Band-ListPresenter` class. Notice that you create the `BandListPresenter` ❶ in the constructor and pass the view (`IBandListView`) into it.

This approach seems a little odd. In the view, you maintain a reference to a presenter. And in the presenter, you maintain a reference to the view. Doing so is necessary for the MVP patterns to work because of all the communication that needs to occur between them.

It's time to speed things up a bit. We'll forgo the unit tests here (they're included in the sample code accompanying this chapter) and skip to the implementation.

> ## Lies! Untruths! Falsehoods!
>
> Okay, okay, you don't *really* need to maintain references between the classes to make the view and presenter work together. We've talked already about using events. In this scenario, the view still creates the presenter and passes itself to it, but after that, the view can forget about the presenter. It will raise events whenever it does something meaningful and rely on the presenter to listen to those events.
>
> You can decouple the view and presenter even further and have what's called an event aggregator manage the events. Here, a separate centralized class keeps track of event publishers and subscribers. The view will register itself as an event publisher with the aggregator and the presenter will subscribe to those events. Neither class needs to know of the other's existence.
>
> This pattern is powerful and flexible and is becoming increasingly popular. A full discussion is beyond the scope of this chapter, but we encourage you to investigate the topic further.

Listings 10.10 and 10.11 show the view and the presenter, respectively, after refactoring out the non-UI logic to the presenter.

### Listing 10.10  Final view implementation

```
public partial class BandList : Page, IBandListView
{
    private readonly BandList _presenter;

    public BandList( )
    {
        _presenter = new BandListPresenter( this );
    }

    protected void Page_Load(object sender, EventArgs e)
    {
        if ( !IsPostBack )
        {
            _presenter.ShowArtistList( );          ◁──  ❶ Presenter
        }                                                  performing task
    }

    public void BindTo( DataSet artistList )       ◁──  ❷ View displaying
    {                                                     data
        gridViewBands.DataSource = artistList;
        gridViewBands.DataBind( );
    }
}
```

And now take a look at the presenter in listing 10.11.

### Listing 10.11  Final presenter implementation

```
public class BandListPresenter( )
{
    private readonly IBandListView _bandListView;
```

```
public BandListPresenter( IBandListView bandListView )
{
    _bandListView = bandListView;
}
public void ShowArtistList( )              ◄──┘  ❸ Presenter
{                                                  retrieving data
    var artistList = TwilightDB.GetData( "twi_get_artists", "Artists");
    _bandListView.BindTo( artistList );
}
}
```

The changes in listing 10.11 are minor, and it may be difficult to see the impact they have. All you've done is move code around into different classes.

But notice that the BandListPresenter doesn't have any references to user controls—which means it can be tested without requiring any user interaction. Yes, you still have that nasty static method call in there ❸ but at the very least, you can implement an integration test around this class so that you can refactor it further.

In addition, because you've injected the view into the presenter, you write a test with a fake or mock IBandListView class that behaves in a controlled manner (and again, that doesn't require references to a user control library).

The view's responsibilities have been crystallized as well. You've absolved the view of its responsibility to display a list of artists ❶. Instead, it now says, "Once I'm done loading, tell the presenter to do all the work and show the artist list."

Once the presenter has its data, it turns around and passes the buck back to the view by calling the BindTo method ❷. But that's also a good thing. The presenter is responsible for collecting the required data. Once it has what it needs to display, it says, "Okay, view, here's what you need. Show it on the screen somehow." The BindTo method takes a DataSet as a parameter, which means it isn't capable of retrieving the data it needs to display. It needs to be told what to display—which is in keeping with the goal to make the view as stupid as possible while the presenter does all the heavy lifting.

NOTE    The MVP patterns aren't limited to the page level. Your user controls can be converted to the pattern as well. The same principles apply, though take extra care when defining the interface in which you interact with the control. If you aren't careful, the main page view that contains the user controls can end up even messier than before.

You've only scratched the surface of all the refactoring that needs to be done in this page. The sample code that accompanies this chapter separates responsibilities even further by moving the data access to a separate class and even providing an intermediate class to convert the data into a DTO for use in the view. Unit tests are provided for all except for the data access class, which we'll cover in the next chapter.

Before we close this chapter, we're going to talk about one final presentation pattern: Model-View-Controller.

## 10.6  *Model-View-Controller*

The final user interface pattern we mentioned in section 10.4 was Model-View-Controller (MVC). MVC predates MVP by many years, at least as an officially recognized pattern. In fact, the MVP patterns are derivatives of it and are sometimes considered to be an evolution of MVC to accommodate some of the features of modern IDEs. Figure 10.6 shows how the pieces interact.

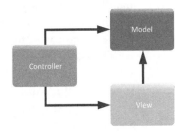

**Figure 10.6  Model-View-Controller. Like the Supervising Controller, the view has access to the model.**

Comparing this to figure 10.2, you might think that MVC isn't so far removed from the Supervising Controller. The controller retrieves a model, then sends it down to the view. The view can interact with the model as it does with the Supervising Controller.

In fact, the Supervising Controller, the Passive View, and Model-View-Controller are all variations on the same theme. Their overall differences can be hard to discern when looking at them for the first time.

Where MVC differs is that the view and the controller are more clearly separated. There isn't much, if any, communication between the two. In most cases, the controller launches the view, and then goes away. When the view wants to do something, a new controller is created and an appropriate action is taken.

By contrast, in the patterns discussed in section 10.4, the view has a constant connection to the controller, either through direct reference or by events raised from the view and/or model. The presenter has to do quite a bit of synchronization with the view to maintain state. The presenter needs to stick around to keep things in order.

In MVC applications, events raised by the view are typically routed to a centralized location in the application, a front controller. Based on the action raised, the front controller then decides what to do.

Typically, this process means instantiating another controller and performing an action on it (calling a method on the instantiated controller class). That method does whatever processing is necessary, and then retrieves the model appropriate for the action, selects a view to display, and sends the model down to the view, which renders itself. The process then repeats.

As you can imagine, there are differences in how a UI using MVC would be implemented. Let's take some time to compare MVC and MVP.

### 10.6.1  *Comparing MVC and MVP*

MVC and the various flavors of MVP may appear similar on paper. But if you've never seen an MVC implementation, it can seem quite foreign to developers who haven't worked outside of .NET.

In general, MVC is well suited to web applications because of their stateless nature. The pattern lends itself to having a controller launch a view and then disappear until an action is performed on the view. Controller actions are often designed so that they handle state management intrinsically: everything the action needs is provided to it. It doesn't need to request anything from the view and usually doesn't even have access to the specific view that launched it.

That said, it isn't trivial to implement MVC in an ASP.NET Web Forms environment without outside help. Microsoft has gone to great lengths to make Web Forms seem stateful, and it's difficult to circumvent this out of the box. Server-side web controls were designed specifically to maintain state on the web, and MVC is better suited for scenarios where state isn't mandatory from one call to the next.

To use MVC in ASP.NET, you'll probably find it necessary to use a framework designed specifically for this purpose. As of this writing, there are two popular ones: Castle MonoRail from Castle Stronghold and ASP.NET MVC from Microsoft. MonoRail has the advantage of maturity—it has several years on Microsoft's offering. MonoRail is an open source project, and although ASP.NET MVC is not open source, as of this writing, its source is available for download. Both products are free.

By contrast, the Passive View, Supervising Controller, and Presentation Model work better in stateful environments, such as Windows Forms applications and out-of-the-box Web Forms applications. The MVP patterns require much more interaction between the view and the presenter, so they don't have the luxury of being disconnected in the same way they are in an MVC implementation. Events that are raised by the view are handled by the same presenter instance that launched the view. Often, a view will have a reference to its presenter, and vice versa.

When discussing the difference between MVC and the MVP patterns, a good rule of thumb is to examine the entry point of a screen. If the view is the first class instantiated, chances are it's one of the MVP patterns. If the controller is the initial point of contact, it's probably an MVC pattern.

Think of a typical Web Forms application. A user navigates to an .aspx page. This page is the view. In the code-behind, you create your presenter and pass the view class to it. This configuration is an MVP pattern. By the time the presenter is created, you've already determined which view will be shown.

In an MVC world, the controller class is the first piece of code that runs. It executes any code that needs to be done, and based on the action that was requested (and in some cases, on the results of the code that was executed), it will determine which view to display and pass control over to it. The order of instantiation is the opposite of how it's done in an MVP scenario.

The starting point isn't the only difference between the two patterns, but it's a good guideline for understanding the differences between the two styles, as illustrated in figure 10.7.

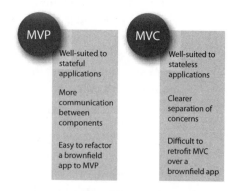

**Figure 10.7   Some differences between MVP and MVC. MVP is usually better suited to brownfield applications.**

You may be wondering why we haven't spent as much time on MVC as with MVP. Good question. Let's answer it.

### 10.6.2  Refactoring to MVC?

There's a reason we've isolated the MVC pattern on its own: MVC isn't conducive to brownfield applications.

As we've mentioned, MVC is useful for web applications. But Web Forms wasn't designed to have a controller as its entry point. Microsoft wants you to start from the view. Plus, they *really* want to help manage the state of your web page for you. This desire permeates every aspect of Web Forms, from the ViewState, to the ASP.NET page life cycle, to the server-side controls.

To circumvent this, you must intercept requests before they get to the .aspx page and handle them differently from how they're handled in a traditional Web Form. You can achieve this goal through the use of HTTP handlers, which is how frameworks such as Castle MonoRail and ASP.NET MVC are able to do it.

However, once you introduce such a framework, you're no longer able to use your existing web pages in the same way. The purpose of the MVC framework is to circumvent the issues arising from the built-in ASP.NET state management mechanism.

Also, the entire notion of an .aspx page is turned on its head. You don't navigate to a specific page anymore. Instead, you navigate to a route and the framework translates that route into a controller action, which in turn renders an appropriate page.

We aren't suggesting that you discount MVC by any stretch of the imagination. We're huge fans of the pattern because of the increased control it provides and, more importantly, because of the clearer separation of concerns (read: testability). It's our pattern of choice for the UI...for greenfield web applications.

For brownfield applications, we feel the costs of refactoring to it outweigh the benefits. As it is, you wouldn't so much refactor your UI as you would rewrite it. Each page would have to be rewritten in the new "controller-first" style, and the URL for that page would be different than the original—which means breaking existing links to that page.

In addition, because MVC applications are more suited to stateless environments (like the web), ASP.NET server-side controls are harder to manage. One of the key features (notice we didn't say "advantages") of server-side controls is their ability to manage view state. When a form is submitted, the control is able to retain its state even though the page was reloaded.

Many server-side controls rely on the Web Forms view state management pipeline in order to function properly. With the pipeline being subverted in an MVC environment, you'd need to find a workaround.

Finding a workaround isn't such a big deal for simple controls like a text box. But for complex ones, like a third-party grid, it can be a big challenge to replace the control with something else that's more conducive to a stateless web (such as a control that uses only HTML and JavaScript).

The same holds true for WinForms application though it's not quite as drastic a change. With WinForms, you don't need to worry about breaking s, but there's considerable work involved to migrate to MVC.

In both cases, one of the main reasons for our position is that there's already an alternative—three of them in fact: the Passive View, Supervising Controller, and Presentation Model. Any of these is more than adequate to work toward.

For WinForms in particular, they're a natural fit because of the stateful nature of WinForms. With MVP, you can take advantage of both separation of concerns and the event model provided by form controls.

The same goes for Web Forms. Although we may not agree that making web applications behave like WinForms applications is a wise model, the practice does lend itself to using one of the MVP patterns.

And so concludes our whirlwind tour of MVC. As we mentioned, it's our preferred pattern for brand-spankin'-new web applications. MVC is garnering a lot of interest in recent months due to the release of Microsoft's ASP.NET MVC implementation, and we encourage you to investigate it. We recommend *ASP.NET MVC in Action* (Manning Press, 2009) as a good way to learn about it. But for the focus of this book, it pays to be familiar with the various flavors of MVP.

## 10.7   *Summary*

We covered a lot of ground in this chapter and still there's much we've left out. The user interface is an important facet of a brownfield application because many such applications begin their journey to brownfield in the UI. All it takes is one demo application released to production.

In this chapter, we outlined some of the common pain points you may experience from such a user interface. We reiterated the importance of separation of concerns, particularly in the UI.

We also dove pretty deeply into the components of a UI and discussed ways you can configure these components, via the Passive View, the Supervising Controller, and the Presentation Model. Each of these patterns provides a certain trade-off between flexibility and readability, and each has its place in various scenarios.

From there we talked about how to refactor to a less coupled user interface and how you can approach the refactoring. We provided a somewhat detailed example of one such refactoring, though the supplemental code sample goes more in depth.

We closed the chapter with a discussion about Model-View-Controller. Although it's an important pattern and well worth the effort to learn, MVC is more suited to greenfield web applications. In general, you don't refactor to MVC so much as you rewrite the UI in it. But MVC is a well-known pattern, and we provided a comparison between it and the other patterns in this chapter.

From the user interface all the way to the database, chapter 11 awaits! Let's see what's in store in the data access layer.

# *Refactoring data access*

**This chapter covers**

- Isolating data access components
- Understanding data access layers
- Using options for data access

In chapter 8, we talked about the logical layers that are found in most applications. In chapter 10, we discussed one of them: the user interface. In this chapter, we'll move to the other end of the application: the data access layer (DAL).

The majority of applications need to persist data to a storage medium of some type. As a result, developers continue to spend a large portion of their project budgets writing code to store, retrieve, and manipulate data. The results are the many and varied implementations affectionately known as data access layers.

Most developers have seen almost as many ways to implement a DAL as they've seen projects. It seems that everyone has his or her own idea of how to best handle the problem of data persistence. We've seen implementations from the simple and naive to the robust and complex. Although each has its own benefits for a project, they all seem to have pitfalls that must be dealt with.

This chapter will explore the data access layer patterns and antipatterns that we (and very likely you) have seen implemented on real-world projects. We'll stop short of claiming to have a silver bullet solution that you'll be able to take to work tomorrow and implement with ease and success. Instead, we'll identify problem areas with data access that you should be aware of and explore techniques that can help you avoid those pitfalls.

## 11.1  Pain points

Huey stared at the method in a sort of trance. He'd received word from his DBAs that a column name from one of the database tables had to be renamed due to an integration issue with another application. He'd just spent the entire morning looking through various web pages in the application, all of which contained a method similar to listing 11.1.

---

**Listing 11.1   Brownfield sample (read at your own risk)**

```
protected void Page_Load(object sender, EventArgs e)
{
    if ( !IsPostBack )
    {
        string artistSql = "SELECT ArtistID, ArtistName FROM Artists";
        DataSet artists = SqlHelper.ExecuteDataset( connectionString,
CommandType.Text, artistSql );
        artistName.DataSource = artists.Tables[0];                Data access in  ❶
        artistName.DataBind( );                                    codebehind

        string tourSql = "SELECT TourID, TourName FROM Tours";
        DataSet tours = SqlHelper.ExecuteDataset(connectionString,
CommandType.Text, tourSql);
        tourName.DataSource = tours.Tables[0];
        tourName.DataBind();
    }
}
```

For a few more minutes, Huey looked at this method, almost willing it to fix itself. He was getting weary making the same change over and over again. "Whose bright idea was it to embed hardcoded SQL directly in an ASPX page's code-behind?" ❶ he thought. As it was, he'd already caught himself making a typo in the new column name on one page, a problem he discovered only by accident after running the application for a spot-check. ("I wish I had time to read chapter 4 in this brownfield book," he muttered to himself.)

Meanwhile, Lewis was having issues of his own. He'd spent the better part of yesterday afternoon chasing down a bug—the user profile page would no longer update the user's email address.

Lewis had looked for the logic for several hours in the code before finally going off on a rant to his co-worker, Jackson. After Lewis raged on for about 30 seconds, Jackson interrupted him: "Why are you looking in the code for this? All that's handled in a stored procedure."

Lewis calmly returned to his desk and opened the database. After looking through the stored procedures, he finally found the one he needed (listing 11.2).

**Listing 11.2  Sample stored procedure**

```
CREATE PROCEDURE change_user_info (
     @userName            nvarchar(50),
     @requestType         int,
     @newValue            nvarchar(1000)
) AS BEGIN
     DECLARE @field          nvarchar(100)
     DECLARE @sql            nvarchar(2000)

     IF @requestType = 1 SELECT @field = 'password'
     --IF @requestType = 2 SELECT @field = 'email'
     IF @requestType = 3 SELECT @field = 'passwordQuestion'

     SELECT @sql = 'UPDATE Users SET ' + @field + ' = '''
         + newValue + ''' WHERE UserName = ''' + @userName + ''''
     EXEC ( @sql )
END
```

❶ Commented out logic

Lewis scanned the stored procedure until he found a commented line ❶ that effectively ignored any updates to the email address. After removing his fist from the monitor, he started asking around to see who had made the change (because sadly, the stored procedures weren't included in source control). Apparently, another team member, Michael, had commented it out temporarily due to another issue (users were providing incorrectly formatted email addresses).

These are two of the most infuriating pain points you'll see in your data access code. In the first case, a seemingly simple change in the backend has had far-reaching effects throughout the UI.

In the second case, the physical and logical separation of business logic adds an enormous amount of friction to the ongoing development and maintenance efforts. Although the argument has been made that more business logic in a stored procedure allows for easier patching of the application, in our experience brownfield applications will regularly feel pain from this approach.

One of the reasons for this pain is the prevalent attitude that changing code in stored procedures won't break anything. The problem with this sentiment is that very often, you *do* break something. You just don't know it until someone runs the application and exercises the stored procedure.

Even more dangerous is the situation where a stored procedure has branching or conditional logic in it that executes different SQL depending on parameters provided to it. The impact of a change—in either the conditional logic or the execution path within one condition—is much harder to determine.

Having confidence in both of these types of changes is difficult at best; yet developers firmly assert that the application will be just fine after making such changes. All it takes is one updated stored procedure without comprehensive prerelease testing, and a system of any size will come crashing to the ground in a fiery heap of finger pointing, accusations, and lost confidence.

**NOTE**   A situation like this is not hyperbole. We've seen it. If you're lucky, you won't. But forgive us for not putting any money on it.

Through the remainder of the chapter, we'll work to provide you with tools and techniques that can be used to help bring these pains under control. The first step is to make sure your data access is all in one place.

## 11.2  *Isolating your data access*

Chapter 8 discussed the concept of logical layers within an application. One of the layers that almost every developer can relate to is the data access layer. The rationale behind creating any logical layer is to separate it so that changes to it will have the smallest impact on other parts of the application. Unfortunately, data access is one area where the impact of change can quickly ripple through an entire application.

**NOTE**   By *impact of change*, we mean the extent to which changes in one area of the application require changes in other areas. If a fundamental change to a feature is required, there's not much you can do to minimize this risk. But as you gain experience, you'll learn to recognize when the changes you're making are because of fundamental feature changes versus badly layered code. To reiterate one of our overarching mantras from part 2 of this book: get rid of any code that causes ripple effects.

If you've jumped straight to this chapter, shame on you! Go back to chapter 8 and read about refactoring to logical layers. Before you do anything with your DAL, you must ensure that it's encapsulated into its own isolated area of the application. The primary reason for encapsulation of the DAL is that you want to effect change without worrying about ripple effects.

For some brownfield applications, getting to a point where there's an isolated data access layer is going to take some time and effort. But as described in chapter 8, it can be done incrementally one function at a time. Figure 11.1 is adapted from figure 8.9 in that chapter.

If you have a highly coupled data access scheme in your brownfield application, the key is to relayer incrementally in small chunks. If you try to isolate and encapsulate the entire DAL at once, you'll run out of time before your client or manager asks you to deliver another piece of functionality. In a worst-case scenario, refactoring to a cleaner DAL could mean pulling code from places as far off as the user interface and everything in between.

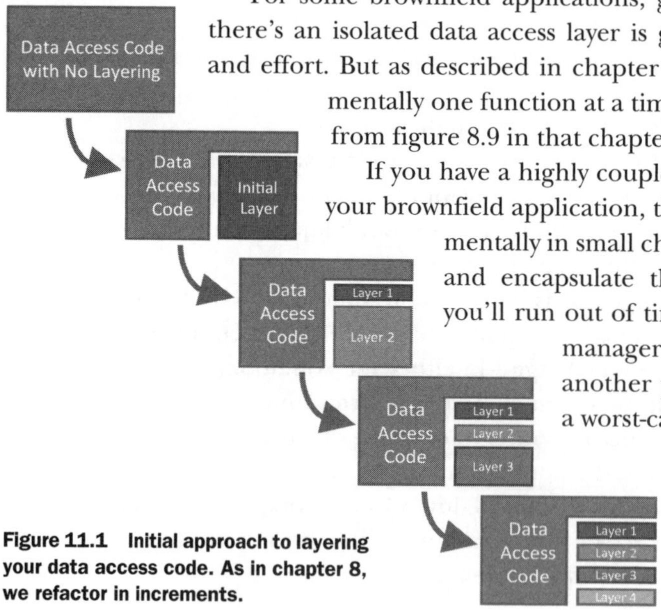

**Figure 11.1   Initial approach to layering your data access code. As in chapter 8, we refactor in increments.**

Another scenario is multiple occurrences of what should be the same code. Brownfield applications can be rife with duplicate code. If data access logic and components are spread from top to bottom in the application, we guarantee you'll find duplicate code. It might be code that manages the life cycle of a database connection, or it could be similar SQL statements that were unknowingly written in two or more places. Infrastructure and CRUD functionality (create, read, update, and delete; the four operations performed on data) will be the two areas where you spend most of your time refactoring.

Although not directly related to infrastructure, there's one other area of a data access refactoring that you'll most likely encounter: DataSets. DataSets have served a purpose in the .NET Framework, but they're one of the leakiest abstractions that you'll find in a brownfield codebase. DataSets that are used from the DAL all the way up to the UI are automatically imposing a tight coupling between your user interface and the datastore's structure. Controls that are bound to a DataSet must work directly with table and column names as they exist in a datastore.

---

**DataSets**

We've emphasized this point in chapters 8 and 10, but just to make our opinion clear, DataSets are evil. Their data-centric view of an application runs contrary to the complexity of the business logic, the diversity of the user interface, and the ability for a developer to reuse code. DataSets are, essentially, a method to expose the tables in a database to the user for them to be able to add, modify, and remove individual records.

Our recommendation is that you avoid using DataSets. Period. We understand that it's likely you'll be inheriting brownfield applications that are deeply rooted in DataSet–driven design. With the proliferation of code-generation tools and object-relational mappers (discussed later in this chapter), it's easier than ever to use a rich domain model rather than default to DataSets.

---

With many applications containing DataSets throughout the entirety of the codebase, it's not going to be an easy task to refactor them out of the way. Later in this section we'll talk about refactoring CRUD. At that point, we'll begin to discuss how to realistically and reliably remove DataSets from your codebase.

Before getting to that, let's take a look at the infrastructure.

### 11.2.1 Refactoring infrastructure

From the perspective of data access, infrastructure consists of any code that's required for the application to work with the external datastore. Examples include creating and managing connections and commands, handling return values and types, and handling database errors. Essentially, infrastructure will be anything except the actual

SQL used to interact with the datastore and the entry points for the application to access the data.

Initially, when refactoring a vertical slice of the application to nicely encapsulate its data access components, you'll spend a lot of time on infrastructure. That very first piece of infrastructure you attack could encompass many facets: connection/session management, command management, transaction management, integrating with an object-relational mapper, and possibly others.

Once you've created the first portion of your layer, you'll find it's much easier the next time around. You recognize areas of duplication easier and see areas of isolation much more clearly. That's because when you refactor the first piece of functionality, it's not as easy to see which pieces will need to be reused. Beginning with the second piece of functionality, it becomes clearer where you can make your code more efficient and reduce duplication.

Related to noticing duplication is the mentality trap that you must build out all the connection management functionality in the first pass regardless of whether it's needed. It's easy to say to yourself, "Well, we'll need support for relationships between multiple tables eventually so I'll just add in the code for it now." Attempting to build in all possible future required functionality is inefficient. Instead, only do the refactorings that are needed for the piece of code you're working on at that time.

### Challenge your assumptions: Premature optimization

Chapter 7 introduced the concept of premature optimization. To recap: deciding, in advance of ever executing the application in its whole, that the code needs to be optimized is referred to as *premature optimization*. The desire to optimize is premature since the system's bottlenecks have yet to be identified.

There's nothing wrong with "fast enough" when discussing performance of your application. If you attempt to optimize your code before checking to see if a performance problem exists, you'll almost certainly spend time increasing the efficiency of the wrong piece of code. Until you can run the application and accurately profile its execution, you won't fully understand the areas that require attention.

In one project we were on, well-formed arguments were made for the addition of a complex caching system to ensure processing performance. Luckily the team chose not to do the work in advance of the profiling effort. Once profiled, the results clearly pointed us to a different portion of the application as the largest bottleneck that we had. The change required to alleviate the bottleneck was an easy fix, quick to deploy, and very effective. Waiting for the profiling to occur before making the decision on where to invest resources and effort in performance saved our client money and maintained the simplest codebase possible.

Performance shouldn't be ignored. Nor should it be addressed haphazardly. Your primary goal should be a working application. Once that's been achieved, it can be tuned based on actual performance testing. And remember, *perceived* performance is more important than *actual* performance.

If you create only the minimum functionality required at any given time, it's entirely possible that you won't create support for something like transaction management in your first pass at refactoring. And that's fine. If it's not needed, there's no sense in guessing at how it should work for code you've not looked at yet. (Recall "You ain't gonna need it" from chapter 7.)

Putting off writing this code doesn't mean that you won't ever implement transaction management. Rather, it means that you'll do it when the need arises. There's a good chance the application will have the need for transaction management. But when you're doing these refactorings, the need may not arise right away. Avoid the temptation to implement for future use; it's a pitfall that will create rework or, worse yet, code that's never used and thus hasn't been verified.

Taking an incremental approach will allow your infrastructure code to grow organically. The nature of anything organic is that it will morph and adapt to its environment. Expect these changes to happen with your data access infrastructure code. Not only will you add new functionality, like transaction management, but you'll also be refactoring code that you've already modified during previous work on the DAL. Don't worry about this. In fact, embrace it. A codebase that has evolved naturally will be much easier to maintain and work with in the future.

In the end, what you're looking to achieve is data access infrastructure that adheres to the DRY principle ("Don't repeat yourself"; see chapter 7), functions as desired, and lives in isolation from the rest of the logical layers and concerns within the codebase. None of these are insurmountable goals. It can take time to achieve them, though.

The other area of your data access that will require attention is the part that does the actual work: the CRUD operations.

### 11.2.2 *Refactoring CRUD*

Between refactoring infrastructure and refactoring CRUD, the former can be considered the easier of the two. Creating a connection to a database usually happens only one way for an application. CRUD code, however, has subtle nuances in what it's attempting to achieve. Two queries to retrieve data may look very different on the surface. If you take the time to look at the goals of both, you may find that they're working toward similar end points. Listing 11.3 shows an example of two different SQL statements doing the same thing.

**Listing 11.3  Similar SQL code**

```
// Retrieve customer data, version 1
SELECT NAME, ADDLINE1, ADDLINE2, ADDLINE3, CITY, PROVINCE, POSTAL
          FROM TBL_CUSTOMER WHERE CUSTOMERID = @CUSTOMERID      Returns
SELECT NAME, DISCOUNTPLANID, STATUSID, ACTIVE            multiple result sets ❶
          FROM TBL_CUSTOMER WHERE CUSTOMERID = @CUSTOMERID

// Retrieve customer data, version 2
SELECT NAME, ADDLINE1, ADDLINE2, ADDLINE3, CITY, PROVINCE, POSTAL,
     DISCOUNTPLANID, STATUSID, ACTIVE
   FROM TBL_CUSTOMER WHERE CUSTOMERID = @CUSTOMERID    Return single result set ❷
```

As you can see, the two statements in listing 11.3 are essentially identical in intent. Both retrieve the same data for a customer. But the first returns two result sets ❶ and the second only one ❷. So they don't *quite* do the same thing. If you wanted to refactor your application from one approach to the other, you'd have some work to do.

Because of issues like this one, as well as the fact that refactoring tools for SQL are relatively sparse and underutilized, refactoring CRUD code so that it follows the DRY principle can be an arduous and time-consuming task. Much time can be spent consolidating queries so that there are fewer of them to manage. Consolidation isn't a bad goal, but your initial refactoring of CRUD code should be done without this goal in mind.

Rather than trying to minimize the number of queries, focus more on encapsulation and coupling. If you're able to encapsulate CRUD code into the DAL in such a way that it's loosely coupled, you're in a better position to make further changes later: you've reduced the impact of changes to this code.

Consolidating CRUD code will almost certainly require the use of automated integration tests (see chapter 4). These tests are the insurance that you need when changing column names, rolling two SQL statements into one, or performing other changes to the CRUD code. They'll be the only way that you can confidently, and efficiently, ensure that nothing has been broken with the changes you've made.

Too often developers implement what they believe to be innocent changes to a SQL statement only to have unforeseen impacts on other parts of the application. If you're not using automated integration tests when making these types of changes, you'll run a high risk of releasing an application that's broken. Without tests, the only way to ensure that no regression errors are introduced is to manually test all the functionality in the application. If your projects are anything like ours, your project manager will, to put it mildly, not be impressed with this prospect. Having automated integration tests in place will mitigate a lot, but not all, of those risks.

### Tales from the trenches: Working with a net

On a recent project, we were required to implement lazy loading (more on this later in the chapter) capabilities to the application. We were lucky that the application had a nice suite of automated integration tests that could be run against the entire data access layer.

When implementing the lazy loading, a small bug was introduced where one field wasn't being properly loaded with data. One of our integration tests caught the error and reported the failure prior to the developer even checking in the code, long before it was ever released to a testing environment. That single failing test saved our team from the embarrassment of breaking already working code as well as many hours of searching through the code to find the problem.

Although that wasn't a refactoring of CRUD, the practice and benefits are the same. Automated tests when changing code functionality are insurance for developers. You don't want to have to ever use it, but you're happy you have it when the need arises.

Another technique that we've used with success is to refactor code into a single data access entry point. For example, instead of having one call to retrieve a customer address, another to retrieve phone/fax information, and another for office location, consider having one entry point to retrieve *customer information*: a call to retrieve all the data that was previously accessed through three separate calls. Listing 11.3 can be considered an example of this, as the second example was essentially a consolidation of the first.

---

**More on premature optimization**

When consolidating CRUD calls, you may worry about possible performance issues. After all, why retrieve all the customer information if all you need is the phone number?

Worrying about performance optimizations before implementing the code is judging a book by its cover. The first goal in your codebase is to make it maintainable. Build it so that it's easy to understand (and performance optimization code usually doesn't qualify). If you do this and performance does become an issue, *then* you deal with it. Again, this all falls back to the idea of letting your codebase naturally evolve.

Premature optimization plagues our industry. As developers, we look at code and immediately see some little thing that we think can help to optimize the performance of the code. We rarely take into account that the microsecond that we're optimizing may go unnoticed by business users. Instead, developers spend time working out the nuances of increased performance at the cost of our project's budget and often the readability and future maintainability of the code.

Instead of prematurely optimizing, write the code so that it works and then profile the application against the requirements set out by the business. As developers, we find that the optimizations we often see when reviewing code aren't the real problems that the business encounters when using the application under load.

Remember, there are very few things (in code and in life) that you'll want to do prematurely.

---

Regardless of the approach you take to refactoring the data access portion of your application, strive toward working in isolation. As we've explained, your data access code should evolve naturally like any layer in your application. Make sure changes made to the DAL have the least possible impact on the rest of the application. So before moving on, let's do a quick review of the concept of an anticorruption layer from chapter 8 as it relates to data access.

### 11.2.3 *Anticorruption layer*

Recall from section 8.4 that an anticorruption layer is a means of implementing a contract over your layer to isolate the calling code from changes to it. In the case of data access layers, the anticorruption layer provides you with the ability to refactor the data access components at will while limiting the effects on the application.

One technique for creating an anticorruption layer is to have the layer implement interfaces, and then have the calling code work with those interfaces. Let's take a look at an example that demonstrates an anticorruption layer over your data access.

The data access layer must implement an interface that sets the contract with the rest of the application. Listing 11.4 shows such an interface for a generic data access class.

**Listing 11.4  Sample generic data access interface**

```
public interface IRepository<T>              ◁─┐   Generic
{                                            ❶   interface use
    IEnumerable<T> FetchAll();
    void Add( T itemToAdd );
    void Update( T itemToUpdate );
    void Delete( T itemToDelete );
    T FetchById( long itemId );
}
```

The technique in listing 11.4 seems like a good way to promote code reuse in the application (remember DRY?). By making the interface generic ❶, it should work in many situations with any class you throw at it. This interface will do a good many of your basic CRUD operations.

A notable exception is searching based on some criteria. For example, finding a customer based on their city isn't something that the interface in listing 11.4 should support, because the functionality is specific to a particular class. For such cases, you can add a new, more specific interface:

```
public interface ICustomerRepository : IRepository<Customer>
{
    IEnumerable<Customer> FetchByCityMatching( string cityToMatch );
}
```

Notice the reuse of the generic interface, IRepository<T>, and that we've added a new method to it. The DAL class that implements this interface will be capable of all the CRUD operations as well as finding customers in a given city. In the meantime, you have two usable interfaces that you can start using in your code.

The creation of this anticorruption layer provides a couple of benefits. First, you can mock out the data access layer (see chapter 4), isolating its behavior and dependencies from the tests being written. This increase in testability is a kind of proof that you've implemented the anticorruption layer correctly.

Although testability is a huge benefit for the developers (both current and future) working on the application, it isn't the primary reason to implement the anticorruption layer. Rather, it allows you to later refactor the code at will without fear of having to change code outside of the anticorruption layer. As long as the contract's interface is adhered to, any changes in the data access layer are effectively being done in isolation. And it's this isolation that allows you to continue down the refactoring path.

For completeness, figure 11.2 shows a class diagram for the interfaces described in listing 11.4 and the previous snippet, as well as the classes that implement them.

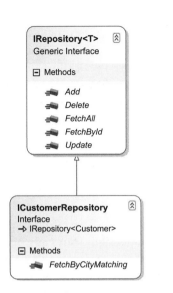
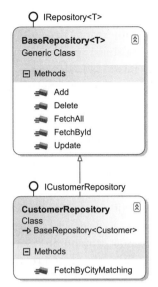

**Figure 11.2  Interfaces and implementations for a generic data access scheme. The `IRepository` interface and `BaseRepository` implementation provide most of the basic operations.**

Related to the idea of isolating the data layer is that of centralizing your business logic. We'll tackle that topic next.

## 11.3  *Centralizing business logic*

In the "Pain points" section of this chapter, we mentioned applications that have business logic strewn throughout the codebase. In the previous chapter, we also discussed how to isolate the concerns of the user interface and to remove business logic-and data access-related code from it. The data access layer of the application requires the same attention to isolate it from business logic.

A data access layer that contains business logic has at least two concerns: managing persistence and performing business logic. Separation of concerns, as you learned in chapter 7, is a vital practice in making your code more understandable, changeable, reversible, and ultimately more maintainable. The pain point that we outlined earlier, where a developer spends time trying to find a piece of logic only to be told that it exists in a place more suited for data storage, is poor maintainability. Pushing business logic into irregular locations is poor asset management.

There's a reason you want to isolate your business logic, as you would your other components. Simply put, it changes. Business logic in particular is far from static. It changes as the business changes, as management changes, and as the customers change. It even "changes" in an application as the development team learns more about it. It behooves you to ensure that it's centrally located so that you can easily respond when the inevitable change happens.

When refactoring business logic out of a DAL, you'll usually find it in one of two places (and often both): in stored procedures, and nestled in the existing data access code. Both situations will provide challenges when refactoring, but they can be solved.

### 11.3.1  *Refactoring away from stored procedures*

Let's assume you have some stored procedures with logic in them that's clearly business logic. Refactoring business logic out of them can be a touchy situation. In the simplest scenarios, the business logic stands out: the stored procedures have clearly defined controlling logic in them. They contain if...else statements or logic that throws business-specific errors. And you'll find other nuggets of information that are obviously business related, such as statements to calculate the shipping costs of an order. These are the easy items to refactor.

Where you'll run into difficulty is when you encounter stored procedures that contain complex joins, aggregation, groupings, or WHERE clauses. In these cases, it's often hard to determine how to break out the logic into manageable chunks or even to determine what's business logic and what's CRUD.

Our path of choice is to leave these procedures alone. The effort required to untangle and replicate SQL statements that are making significant use of vendor-specific language capabilities is not well rewarded. Besides, many complex SQL statements will be related to the retrieval of data, often for reporting. Rarely do people go to such lengths when performing updates, inserts, or deletes. As a result, leaving complex and convoluted SQL SELECT statements in stored procedures is a valid choice when refactoring a data access layer.

---

### Command/query separation

A not-so-new but increasingly popular idea to consider is command/query separation. The basic idea is that each method can be either a command or a query, but never both. A command performs some action, like updating a row in a database, whereas a query returns data to the caller.

The concept is becoming more and more important as a means to build scalable applications using a publish/subscribe model. For example, we could have some data in a cache for a quick response time. When the data changes in the database, it publishes a message to indicate so. The cache subscribes to that message and updates itself accordingly. In this case, the publisher publishes messages about changes (commands) and the subscriber queries for those changes.

Another way of thinking about the two is that commands are for creating, updating, and deleting data, and queries are for reading data.

We won't claim any sort of expertise on the subject, but it's an idea worth considering for a great many scenarios.

---

Although it's acceptable that some stored procedures are too difficult to refactor business logic out of, it's important to try to remove all logic from stored procedures that are altering data. Inserts, updates, and deletes should be free from logic if you expect maintenance developers to be able to easily work within your application.

**The challenges aren't all technical**

Unfortunately, not all refactoring problems can be solved through code. In many cases, you'll encounter resistance to the idea of moving logic out of stored procedures in the form of overprotective DBAs. Typically in these situations, developers aren't allowed direct access to the database and changes to existing stored procedures must be approved through a process we call "Death by 1,000 Quick Questions."

Joking aside, this reluctance to "give up" business logic is often a reaction to a bad experience in the past. Regardless, you'll have a challenge ahead of you wrestling it back into your code. How you approach that is more an exercise in team dynamics than in code refactoring—which is our way of saying we don't have any hard-and-fast answers.

Most of the arguments in favor of logic in stored procedures are based on good intentions but are impractical. In our experience, a well-designed business layer in code is far clearer and less fragile than having it in the database. It's easier to verify and, in the end, more maintainable. In our humble opinion, your mileage may vary, opinions expressed are solely those of the authors and not their employers, and so on and so forth.

You must tread a fine line when refactoring business logic out of procedures, and it's centered on the WHERE clause. Specifically, what's business logic and what's simply a data filter? In some cases, we obviously need to do the bare minimum, like so:

```
UPDATE TBL_CUSTOMER SET STATUS = @STATUS WHERE ID = @ID
```

In other cases the WHERE clause is less clear. Take this example:

```
UPDATE TBL_CUSTOMER SET STATUS = @STATUS WHERE CITY = @CITY
        AND (PROVINCE = 'BC' OR PROVINCE = ' ' OR PROVINCE IS NULL)
```

The existence of the AND and OR clauses could be construed as business logic or could be the bare minimum required to do the job. In other words, it could be a filter or it could be a business rule.

You'll see this dilemma often if you're working to refactor business logic out of the stored procedures in your brownfield application. The only way to clarify this situation is to dig deeper into the intended use of the stored procedure. In the end, it will be a judgment call.

The next area where you'll see business logic is in the data access code itself. Let's see how you can get it out of there.

### 11.3.2 *Refactoring out of the data access layer*

Once you have refactored business logic out of stored procedures (or if you've been so lucky as to avoid this problem), there's still the chance that you'll find business logic buried in your DAL. Indeed, we've been guilty of creating code in this manner ourselves.

Although having business logic in your DAL may not seem as big a problem as having it in stored procedures, it still should cause concern. As with business logic in stored procedures, locating it in the DAL makes it more difficult for developers to find it when they're working with the code. As we've mentioned a number of times, your application will spend more time in maintenance than any other part of the application's life cycle. If a practice such as locating business logic in the DAL increases the difficulty of working with the application during that long portion of its life, you're increasing the overall cost of the application.

Business logic should be kept where it makes the most sense: in the business layer. But, as with stored procedures, maintaining this separation can be fraught with difficulty at times.

Your primary concern when starting these refactorings should be to relocate any obvious business logic. In some cases you'll perform a simple refactoring that only requires you to move code from one part of the application to another. Other times you'll be facing a daunting task that requires the skills of a surgeon to slowly whittle out pieces of offending code and patch it back together in a better location.

**WARNING**    At the risk of sounding like a broken record, before making such changes, you need to have confidence that the changes you're making don't break the application. Create unit and integration tests *before* you start.

On top of having the confidence provided by automated tests, consider working in isolation during this time. Two ways to achieve isolation are by branching the version code repository or, if you've created an anticorruption layer, creating new concrete classes based on the contract/interface you've defined. Both options allow you to reverse your changes easily if your refactoring goes awry.

As with stored procedures, removing business logic entirely from a DAL can be a lofty goal in some brownfield codebases. Be aware of the cost-benefit ratio involved while you work. Watch for situations where your efforts to refactor would be too great because you could sink into a pit of refactoring quicksand (the more you refactor, the more you *need* to refactor). As always, external factors play a role in your refactorings and you should ensure that you're not biting off too much at one time.

In the next section, we'll spend some time talking about features of a DAL you should consider during your refactoring.

## 11.4   *Features of a DAL*

Moving business logic to a centralized location is an important separation of concerns that makes a good starting point in refactoring your data access. But you should take into account other issues as you define your DAL. This section will talk about concepts that will improve your data access code for future work.

If you're working with a hand-rolled data access layer (which isn't unusual in brownfield applications), some of these will seem like a lot of work to implement. We won't disagree with you. Luckily, there are alternatives in the form of third-party tools

for object-relational mapping or code generation. Both will be discussed later in the
chapter, but first, figure 11.3 outlines the features we think are important in a good DAL.

There are many places to start this discussion, but the one that makes the most sense
is encapsulation.

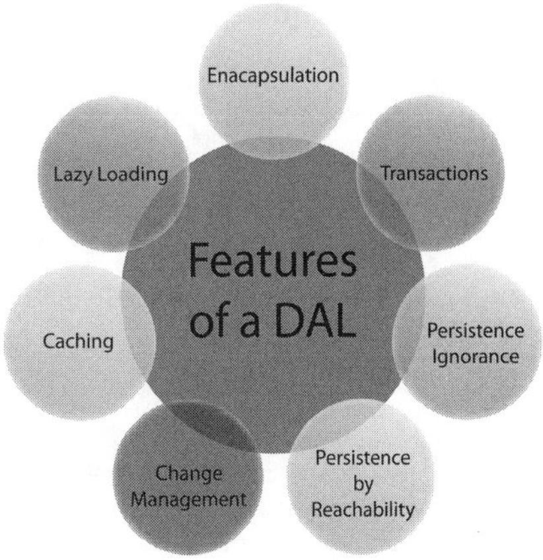

### 11.4.1 Encapsulation

To begin our discussion on encapsulation in
a data access layer, let's look at an example of
bad encapsulation. Here's a common brownfield scenario:

**Figure 11.3  Features of an effective data
access layer. Some are easier to implement
than others.**

```
// ...
var customerRepository = new
    CustomerRepository( );
customerRepository.OpenConnection( );
var customerList = customerRepository.GetCustomers( );
customerRepository.LoadOrdersFor( customerList );
customerRepository.CloseConnection( );
// ...
```

Notice how the service layer has intimate knowledge about how to open and close the
connection used by the data access component. We have bad encapsulation at the
DAL. There's no reason for the service layer to know why or how this is occurring. Yes,
we've encapsulated how the connection is opened and closed, but a good DAL
shouldn't require knowledge of connections.

Other common "mis-encapsulations" include passing around a connection string
or connection object, the handling of data access return values as checks for errors,
and checking for specific database types throughout your code (and this includes
System.DBNull). Although the existence of these issues is by no means a sign that the
application won't work (we've seen dozens of applications with these encapsulation
flaws that are fully functional in production), they *are* signs of problems to come.

Poor encapsulation will lead to code changes requiring what's known as the *shotgun effect*. Instead of being able to make one change, the code will require you to make
changes in a number of scattered places, similar to how the pellets of a shotgun hit a
target. The cost of performing this type of change quickly becomes prohibitive, and
you'll see developers resisting having to make changes where this will occur.

Good encapsulation and good separation of concerns are closely related. Working
to get your brownfield DAL to have both of these will put you in a better position to
work with the remaining items that we'll explore in this section.

### 11.4.2 Transactions/Unit of Work

You've likely dealt with database transactions at some point. They're one of the cornerstones of data integrity and reliability.

The question with transactioning is how it's implemented. If you're working with a raw data access tool, such as ADO.NET, transactions are probably maintained at the database connection level (though the `System.Transaction` namespace, introduced in .NET 2.0, has helped alleviate this need). This means your DAL must reuse the same connection on any call, leading to the code snippet shown earlier in section 11.4.1, where calling code is responsible for managing the connection. Another scenario is when connection objects are passed into the DAL between calls, as in listing 11.5.

**Listing 11.5   Managing connections through business code**

```
// ...
var connection = DataAccessHelper.GetConnection( );
var transaction = connection.BeginTransaction();
var customerRepository = new CustomerRepository( );
var orderRepository = new OrderRepository( );
customerRepository.SaveCustomer( connection, transaction, customer );
foreach ( var order in customer.Orders )
{
    orderRepository.SaveOrder( connection, transaction, order );
}
transaction.commit();
```

Instead of a leaky abstraction that forces the connection object management out to another layer, you should be striving for data access layers that intrinsically know how to use a transactional approach. You can achieve this with a standard ADO.NET connection object in a number of ways, but you can make it easier.

Enter the Unit of Work pattern. In this pattern, instead of making numerous separate calls to the database you'll bundle a number of calls together and push them through at the same time. The pattern allows the code to open a transaction immediately before the first call is executed, keep it open (and thus the transaction alive) during the remaining calls, and commit or roll back the transaction when the final transaction has been completed. Figure 11.4 depicts one way it could work.

Implementing the Unit of Work pattern stops you from having to move a connection object through your code but still gives you the power of a transactional system. Unit of Work can be implemented in various degrees of complexity. At its simplest, it will manage transactions and mass execution of data calls. In more complex implementations, the calls to the database will be reconciled in the correct order so that no relational constraint errors occur.

As you can imagine, Unit of Work isn't a commonly implemented pattern in hand-rolled data access layers. It's not widely known and can be difficult to implement fully. But if your application is suffering from poor encapsulation due to failed attempts at transactional support, implementing a simple Unit of

**Figure 11.4   Database calls are queued in the Unit of Work and executed in a single transaction.**

Work pattern is a good option. Note that we said *simple*—again, invoke YAGNI and implement only the functionality required to support your code's current needs. Any more is wasteful.

### 11.4.3  *Persistence ignorance*

As with many concepts in this chapter, we're going to reach back to the concept of separation of concerns when we discuss persistence ignorance. Persistence ignorance is the concept whereby your business entity objects (`Customer`, `Order`, `Invoice`, etc.) have no knowledge about the infrastructure required to perform data access (CRUD) operations against them.

So how does persistence ignorance tie back to separation of concerns?

Without persistence ignorance, entity classes will start to see other concerns creep into them. Take the class definition in listing 11.6, which shows a simple `Customer` entity.

**Listing 11.6  Class with no persistence ignorance**

```
[TableMap("tbl_customers")]
public class Customer {

    [PropertyMap("customer_id")]
    public property long Id { get; set; }

    [PropertyMap("name")]
    public property string Name { get; set; }

    [PropertyMap("mailing_address")]
    public property string Address { get; set; }

    [PropertyMap("is_active")]
    public property bool Active { get; set; }
}
```

Immediately you'll notice extra information along with the properties: the `TableMap` and `PropertyMap` attributes. Without knowing anything about their implementation, you can guess from their names and values that they're probably used to map the `Customer` class to a database table named tbl_customers and the properties to columns, like customer_id or name.

Having the mapping information directly in the class constitutes a poor separation of concerns. The DAL has crept into the domain model via the attributes. If, for whatever reason, changes were required to data access (such as renaming a column), the separated DAL wouldn't stop changes from rippling to code in other layers.

As with many things that don't have a good separation of concerns, the `Customer` class in listing 11.6 also violates the single responsibility principle. There are two scenarios that would require changing it:

- When you change the way that a customer is modeled within the application
- When the datastore storing a customer changes

As mentioned in chapter 7, poor adherence to the single responsibility principle makes code more difficult to change, verify, and maintain—hardly traits you want to incorporate into your application.

Instead, you'd rather see something like this:

```
public class Customer {
    public property long Id { get; set; }
    public property string Name { get; set; }
    public property string Address { get; set; }
    public property bool Active { get; set; }
}
```

The entity itself is devoid of any knowledge of the datastore or the methods used to perform data access. All of that knowledge is contained elsewhere, presumably within the data access layer.

Persistence ignorance doesn't obviate the need to map your business classes to database tables. But you want to do it in a place where you can maintain good separation of concerns and single responsibility. You could use something as simple as a `CustomerMapper` class that takes a `DataReader` and converts it into a `Customer` object.

Or you could achieve your goal using an object-relational mapper. Listing 11.7 shows an example of how this mapping could be achieved.

**Listing 11.7 Sample mapping file using an object-relational mapper**

```
public class CustomerMap : ClassMap<Customer>
{
    public void CustomerMap() {
        WithTable("Customer");                      ❶ Table mapped to

        Id(x => x.Id, "CustomerId)                  ❷ Property mapping
            .GeneratedBy.Identity();
        Map(x => x.Name, "CustomerName");           ❸ General property mapping
        Map(x => x.Email, "EmailAddress");
        Map(x => x.Phone, "PhoneNumber");
    }
}
```

There's no need to get into the details of the syntax, but the intent should be intuitive. The database table that the `Customer` class maps to ❶ is described. Next ❷, the `Id` property is mapped to an appropriate column and a description of how it's generated is provided. Finally ❸, individual properties are mapped to corresponding columns.

Note that you have *not* eliminated the need to change your code if the name of a column changes. But you've separated it from the `Customer` class itself so that if this situation arises, you know exactly where the change should be made because that's this class's single responsibility.

**NOTE** Listing 11.7 isn't theoretical. It uses an open source library called Fluent NHibernate that builds on yet another open source library, NHibernate. For more information on Fluent NHibernate, visit http://fluentnhibernate.org.

When you're rolling your own DAL, or if you've inherited one in a brownfield project, you rarely find that it has this level of separation. The result is that changes to the data structure, or to the entity model, will ripple through the codebase. As soon as that happens, there's a significant increase in the risk that you've made changes that have unknown or unintended consequences. Usually that results in errors that aren't caught until the application is in front of testers or, worse, the end users.

Although persistence ignorance has huge benefits when it comes to code maintenance and development, it isn't something that's supported in its purest form in many DALs, be they hand-rolled or otherwise. When you're refactoring your brownfield DAL, take stock of the situation you're in. If your domain model and database are stable, perhaps the need for persistence ignorance isn't a priority.

But if your datastore and/or domain model are changing often, or if you have no control over the datastore, take a hard look at incorporating persistence ignorance during your refactoring. Having to review the ripple effects of datastore changes will only slow down your efforts if you have poor separation of concerns.

### 11.4.4 *Persistence by reachability*

Persistence by reachability builds on persistence ignorance. Consider the code in listing 11.8.

**Listing 11.8  Walking an object graph to persist all the data**

```
public void Save(Invoice invoiceToSave) {

    _invoiceRepository.Save(invoiceToSave);
    _customerRepository.Save(invoiceToSave.Customer);

    foreach(var lineItem in invoiceToSave.Items)
    {
        _invoiceRepository.SaveItem(lineItem);
    }
}
```

Most of us have written code along these lines in our career. To update a group of related entities, you walk along the object graph in the appropriate order, saving each as you go.

Of course, this example is trivial. In real life, walking the depths of an object graph, especially one with multiple nesting levels, quickly creates a call stack that can go several levels deep.

Instead, wouldn't it be nice if you were able to run the following code and have it take care of that complexity for you?

```
public void Save (Invoice invoiceToSave) {
    _invoiceRepository.Save(invoiceToSave);
}
```

You may say, "Well, that's all well and good, but you just moved the saving of the Customer and the LineItems into the _invoiceRepository.Save(...) call." And indeed, if you were rolling your own DAL, that may be exactly how to achieve persistence by reachability. But the end result is the same: saving an invoice should, by nature of the business rules, also entail saving the customer and line items implicitly.

In the end, regardless of how you get there, you've achieved a state of persistence by reachability. You've created a data access layer entry point (in this case the `_invoiceRepository.Save(…)` method) that will navigate the object graph without the calling code having to coordinate the effort.

**NOTE**    Those of you familiar with domain-driven design will recognize this concept as one of the properties of an *aggregate root* in a repository.

The definition of persistence by reachability is that the DAL will traverse and save any entity and entity data that it can find by navigating the properties on the entities. If the data is publicly available on an entity, the DAL will persist it. Not only that, but it will do it to the full depth of the object graph.

Implementing persistence by reachability in a hand-rolled DAL isn't easy. Usually, half-hearted attempts contain a lot of duplicate code and a less-than-palatable level of brittleness. Because this tends to happen, many people will forego taking a DAL to this level and instead will use a variation on listing 11.8.

With some care and attention, it's possible to make code that has pieces of persistence by reachability in it. However, the time and effort required to do so usually isn't trivial, and with typical time pressures, incorporating it into a DAL is often not a realistic option.

Having said that, most third-party object-relational mapper (ORM) implementations do implement persistence by reachability to some degree. If you have extremely complex object graphs that you're constantly traversing to save or update data in the datastore, consider refactoring your DAL to use an ORM. Although doing so does introduce other potential issues (which will be addressed later in this chapter), the benefits typically outweigh the costs.

### 11.4.5  Dirty tracking

Imagine a scenario where you have 1,000 line items in an `Invoice` object and you save the `Invoice`. The code could make up to 1,001 database calls, saving each line item as well as the invoice itself.

For brand-new invoices, you'd expect this to happen. But what if it was an existing invoice? Say you had loaded an invoice with 990 line items from the datastore, modified 2 of them, and appended 10 more line items? When you save that invoice, should the code save all 1,000 line items again? Or just the 10 new and 2 updated ones?

Hopefully you chose the latter. And accomplishing parsimonious updates isn't all that complicated. The DAL needs to be smart enough to identify objects and data that have been modified, added, or deleted. Once these items can be identified, you're able to perform data persistence much more parsimoniously.

One of the most common, and primitive, ways to implement this is the most intuitive: an `IsDirty` flag. Listing 11.9 shows this on the `Customer` entity.

**Listing 11.9   Primitive `IsDirty` implementation**

```
public class Customer {
    public property long Id { get; set; }
    public property string Name { get; set; }
    public property string Address { get; set; }
    public property bool Active { get; set; }
    public property bool IsDirty { get; set; }
}
```

The key to listing 11.9 is that each of the first four property setters would change the state of the `IsDirty` flag. Although listing 11.9 is a viable solution, there are some issues with it. First, this example is capable of monitoring only a Boolean state, which can make it difficult for you to distinguish between an entity that has been added versus one that has been altered. Second, you need quite a bit of code to ensure that the `IsDirty` property is set when any value is changed. Single responsibility starts to break down when you have code internal to the entity performing these tasks. At the very least, it usually means you can no longer use automatic setters for the other properties because you'll need to pepper the code with calls to `IsDirty = false`.

**NOTE**   Setting an `IsDirty` flag is a good candidate for aspect-oriented programming, as described in chapter 8. We don't explicitly need to mark the entity as dirty; instead, we add a dirty-tracking aspect that would weave this into the code itself.

Moving these responsibilities out into their own cohesive areas of the codebase isn't overly difficult to do, but it can be time consuming. As a result—and as with so many of these important data access features—you're not likely to see anything more complicated than the naive `IsDirty` implementation in brownfield codebases, if they have any dirty tracking at all.

As with any of these features, dirty tracking may or may not be important in your application. Indeed, there's an element of premature optimization to implementing it. If your application relies heavily on a robust and well-defined domain model (such as one developed with domain-driven design), you'll likely benefit from having dirty tracking as a core component in your DAL. Otherwise, it may well be within your performance guidelines not to deal with it at all.

Another feature shown in figure 11.3 is lazy loading, which is discussed next.

### 11.4.6   *Lazy loading*

Consider again the `Invoice` with 1,000 line items. What if you wanted to display only the customer information of the invoice? It wouldn't be efficient to load its data as well as the information for each of the 1,000 line items, each of which could require a lookup from the Product table as well as possibly the Category table.

One naive way around the abundance of data retrieval is to have one data access call that retrieves only the invoice data and another that retrieves the full object graph. A cleaner solution is to use a single call that retrieves only the basic invoice details initially and that loads the line items only when they're requested. This is where lazy loading comes in.

When implemented properly, lazy loading will defer the execution of reads from the datastore until the last possible moment prior to the information being required for processing by the application. Take, for instance, listing 11.10.

**Listing 11.10    Manual version of lazy loading**

```
public void DoSomeStuff(Customer customer) {

    var invoiceRepository = new InvoiceRepository();
    var invoice = invoiceRepository.FindByCustomer(customer);

    // Do some stuff with the invoice

    invoiceToProcess.Items.Load();

    foreach(var item in invoiceToProcess.Items) {
        // do work with the items
    }
}
```

Here, you're using one form of lazy loading called *lazy initialization*. When you retrieve the invoice, the `Items` collection hasn't been populated. Later, when you want to work with the `Items`, you make an explicit call to load them into the `Invoice`. In this way, you reduce the burden of making database calls when they're not needed.

Although the code in listing 11.10 is more efficient, it's a bit of a leaky abstraction. It requires the calling code to know that the `Items` aren't loaded when the invoice is retrieved. You've allowed some of our DAL to creep into the business layer where it doesn't belong.

A better implementation is one where the calling code has absolutely no knowledge of the state of the data access call. Instead, it assumes the object graph is always preloaded. Listing 11.11 shows how that code would look.

**Listing 11.11    Virtual proxy version of lazy loading**

```
public void DoSomeStuff(Customer customer) {

    var invoiceRepository = new InvoiceRepository();
    var invoice = invoiceRepository.FindByCustomer(customer);    ❶ Initial
                                                                    loading
    // Do some work with the invoice

    foreach(var item in invoiceToProcess.Items) {
        // do work with the items
    }
}
```

The first thing that you'll notice is…well…nothing. There's no way to look at the code in listing 11.11 and tell whether the `Items` collection is preloaded or if it's being lazy loaded. As in listing 11.10, the basic invoice information ❶ is loaded, but there's no explicit call to load the `Items` collection. For all you know, the `Items` are all there. But behind the scenes, they don't exist until the first call to the Items collection. At that point, the lazy loading mechanism kicks in and a call is made to the database to retrieve the items.

Here we have an example of the *virtual proxy* version of lazy loading. You always assume the Items collection is loaded. But in fact, the Invoice will contain a proxy object, which is an object that only *appears* to be an object of the same type as Items. When the first request is made to the Items collection, it's loaded from the database.

**NOTE**   For completeness, we'll mention that lazy loading can also be implemented using either a *ghost* or a *value holder*. A ghost is similar to a virtual proxy except that it's an actual instance of the object being loaded. But it's only partially loaded, likely with just the ID. Likewise, a value holder is also a substitute like the virtual proxy, except that it's a generic object that must be cast to its actual type after retrieving it from the database.

Using virtual proxies may seem like voodoo, but it's very much possible. And because of it, you can achieve what you want: code that's clear and decoupled from infrastructure concerns in the business logic. You can now work with your Invoice object without worrying about whether you're affecting performance with extraneous database calls.

Of the different implementations of lazy loading, lazy initialization is the easiest to implement. It's intuitive to grasp and straightforward to implement. But it places a burden on the caller to ensure it makes the appropriate call to load the properties.

The remaining implementations also vary in complexity. Each has its strengths and weaknesses, but none of them is trivial. Again, the traits of your particular application will best guide you. For a brownfield application, lazy loading could be a case of premature optimization. There's no reason to implement it if users aren't experiencing performance problems. Perhaps none of your objects have very deep graphs. If you're lucky enough that that applies to you, you've dodged a lazily loaded bullet.

### 11.4.7  Caching

No discussion of data access is complete without considering caching. Yet retrieving data from a datastore can be a costly operation. If you're retrieving the same data over and over again and it's not changing, why not keep a copy locally and use that instead of constantly going back to the datastore?

If the DAL is hand-rolled, many teams will neglect to add any caching to their systems. Sometimes a lack of caching is just an oversight, but in other cases, it's because caching isn't always as simple as it seems on the surface. For example, how long do you keep data in the cache? If it's a list of U.S. states, it could be indefinitely. But what about a shopping cart for an online purchase? Ten minutes? An hour? A day? Or maybe based on an event, like the user logging out or the session ending? The correct answer, of course, is "It depends," which is what makes the question of invalidating the cache so complex.

Another reason that caching is often absent from a brownfield application is that infrastructure concerns can start to enter the design conversation. For instance, how should you implement efficient caching for an application that will be residing in a web farm? What about caching data so that it's available across sessions? Both of these are problems that commonly need to be solved when dealing with caching. There may not be simple solutions for them, though.

---

**Tales from the trenches: Caching woes**

On one project we had the chance to see a hand-rolled implementation of caching go horribly awry. The idea was simple: implement a caching scheme so that we wouldn't have to make large numbers of calls, through a horrifically slow connection, to the datastore.

It all seemed so idyllic at the start. The code was written and it existed for quite some time while the team continued to develop around it. When the time came to do performance testing on the application server components, a disaster occurred. Making only two data requests to the middle tier from the client caused the application to stop responding. After some panicked performance profiling, we found that the caching scheme was bringing a high-powered middle-tier server to a grinding halt, so much so that it required a hard reboot of the machine.

The culprit was the mechanism by which we determined when data should have been cleared from the cache. Fortunately, we were able to change the caching to perform better in relatively short order, and the application's performance was greatly improved and deemed adequate when compared against our goal metrics.

The lesson for our team was twofold. First, caching, when implemented incorrectly, can be as much of a problem as it can be a solution. Second, profiling and performance metrics should be incorporated into any test plan. With them in place, we can make informed decisions on where to get the largest gains for the smallest effort.

---

Caching is a valuable component to a fully featured data access layer. But like the other topics described here, it's a performance optimization technique. As mentioned before, prematurely optimizing your code isn't a practice you should have. With caching, you must understand where you're seeing bottlenecks caused by repetitive data access. You must also have a strong understanding of the volatility of the data that's being accessed. The combination of those two things will help you determine where caching can be of benefit to your brownfield application.

### 11.4.8  *Tips on updating your DAL*

Now that all the features from figure 11.3 have been covered and you have a sense of which ones you'd like to implement, how can you upgrade your existing DAL?

There are two issues with your current brownfield DAL (if we may be so bold). First, it's probably functionally incomplete: it does some, or even most, of what you want, but not everything. Second, your DAL might be unmanageable. Any time a bug arises in the DAL, it requires a search party complete with Sherpa to determine where the issue is and, more importantly, how to fix it.

**Beware the hidden gem**

The unmanageable code problem isn't native to the DAL by any stretch. But it's usually a nice example of one of the major pitfalls of brownfield development: the hidden "gem" (other words come to mind, but let's use this one for now).

A hidden gem is a piece of code that does a specific, focused task, but when you review it, you think it's useless and your first instinct is to delete it. But removing it will introduce defects that are hard to trace and even harder to understand.

In our experience, if you encounter code like this, your best bet is to leave it alone and find a way to do what you want some other way if possible.

These scenarios aren't mutually exclusive. It's possible that your existing DAL is an incomplete mess. Regardless, once you've decided you want to add new data access functionality, you have two choices:

- Add the new functionality to the existing code.
- Create a new DAL side by side with the existing one and add new functionality to it. Over time, you can (and should) migrate the existing functionality to it.

The first option will depend on how extensible your existing DAL is. If you can easily add new functionality without duplicating a lot of code (or by refactoring the duplication into a separate location), then by all means that should be your choice. But brownfield applications aren't generally known for being extensible, and you'll often find that a task that at first seems easy will turn into a multiday ordeal.

That said, you should consider carefully before creating a new DAL alongside the existing one. It's easy to make plans to migrate the existing DAL into the new one over time, but that task is often given a priority only slightly above "review TODO comments." The reality is that you'll likely have two DALs to maintain for some time, so be sure to balance that against the heinousness/incapability of your existing one.

**Final warning**

We've beaten both points to death, so this will be the last reminder. Before you start messing with your DAL, you should have two things in place:

- Integration tests to ensure your code still works after you've changed it
- An anticorruption layer to make it easier to back out your changes should things go horribly awry.

That's it for the discussion on features of a DAL. If you do decide you want to build a DAL, you're in luck. You have a number of options available other than building it yourself. In the next section, we'll review them.

## 11.5   *Options for creating a DAL*

You have three main options when creating a new DAL. Although we're only covering three, and doing so at a very high level, you'll find that other options are available. On top of that, each of these options has different flavors, each with its own benefits and pitfalls. Remember that the solution you choose has to work for your project, its developers, and the maintenance team, and it must also support the end goal of the business. Your current DAL will play a role in your decision as well.

### 11.5.1   *Hand-rolled*

Hand-rolled DALs have been the cornerstone of .NET applications since the framework was introduced. As the name implies, this style of DAL requires that developers create all the required functionality from scratch, using only classes from the .NET base class library (such as ADO.NET).

The capabilities of hand-rolled DALs are usually basic. For example, there may be no implementation of the Unit of Work pattern in the DAL, or the caching will be a simple hash table with no concept of expiration. As a result, the DAL might either have no support for transactioning or support with poor separation of concerns.

Although support for edge case scenarios can be added to a hand-rolled DAL, the biggest concern is the amount of effort that can be required to build it. Not only that, but you have to be concerned with the correctness of each feature added. Some of these problems can be alleviated through good unit and integration testing (see chapter 4), but there will still need to be a concerted manual testing effort to ensure that the features are working correctly.

Another concern is that a hand-rolled DAL will probably be application specific. Consequently, the support and maintenance developers will need to learn, and understand, the intricacies of a particular DAL on an application-by-application basis. In many environments, these developers are responsible for more than one application, and if each has a different DAL implementation, they'll potentially need a deep understanding of more than one data access codebase.

**NOTE**   Application-specific DALs aren't always a bad thing. Theoretically, an application-specific DAL contains only those features needed for the current application and nothing more. An application-specific DAL is a testament to YAGNI...assuming it's feature complete and implemented properly.

This effort can be alleviated in two ways. The first is to have common patterns used on several applications' DALs across the organization. However, because each application may have different technical needs in its DAL, this plan can quickly break down as features are added in one application but not in others. Once that starts to happen, it's as if each DAL was designed and written independently of the other. At this point you have all the pitfalls of a fully hand-rolled DAL with the added consequence that it now contains features you don't need.

The second option is to completely separate the data access layer and reuse it through many applications, the so-called *corporate DAL.*

Designing a cross-application, corporate DAL introduces a number of issues that won't have entered your application development practices before. Here's a list of some of those issues:

- Functionality support
- DAL defect and resolution management
- Release and version management
- Integration with other applications

Each of these items introduces tasks, processes, and techniques that will drive your teams toward managing a fully fledged project that's internally specific to the institution. Although this result isn't necessarily a bad thing, there has to be a solid understanding of the task that's being taken on as well as the overhead that it will create. Considering the number of good alternatives, tread carefully before taking on your own internal company DAL. Some of the high-level considerations you must take into account when deciding between these two DAL strategies are shown in figure 11.5.

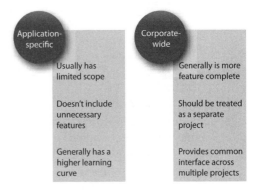

Figure 11.5  Hand-rolled DALs can be application specific or corporate wide. Each has advantages and disadvantages.

The second option when building a DAL is to generate it automatically.

## 11.5.2  Code generation

In an effort to reduce the tedious, and error-prone, nature of writing DALs by hand, people sometimes turn to code generation. A code generator is able to look at your database and generate an object model based on it. Typically, the developer uses templates to further refine how the classes are generated.

Like hand-rolled DALs, the results of code generation are completely dependent on the skills of the developers who design the templates. We've seen instances of generated code that range from horrific to elegant.

Although generating code is perceived as a technique that greatly reduces the effort required to create a DAL, don't underestimate the amount of effort required for the initial design and creation of the templates. It's certainly easier to design and write a generation template than it is to hand-roll an entire DAL, but you need to factor in overhead.

Tooling for template creation, maintenance, and execution is available in a number of products. Some code-generation systems come with prebundled templates that create code in commonly known patterns. If your project environment allows for it and you've chosen to use code generation, we suggest you look into using one of these tools. Third-party tooling will preclude your team, and the future support and maintenance teams, from having to maintain an in-house, custom generation engine.

---

### Creating your own code-generation engine

Creating your own generation engine is a great academic exercise in software development. But when you look at the larger picture, the generation engine is another project and codebase that needs to be maintained and supported through the life of the application that's consuming the code it generates.

As we're trying to simplify the brownfield application we're working on, introducing another project is often counterproductive to that goal. If you're considering creating your own generation engine, it's best to treat it like a separate project, using the existing brownfield application as the testing ground.

---

Another maintainability concern is the learning curve for the tooling and templates. As with any tools, developers must learn to work efficiently and effectively with the code-generation engine and templating language. Granted, some tools are better than others, but you still have to consider the impact of this learning curve.

The nature of code generation is that it creates code that you include in your application. Code that exists in the application is code that your team must understand and maintain. It may be generated automatically, but that doesn't mean that the development or maintenance team doesn't have to be able to navigate and understand it. Like any other code in your application, generated code is a maintenance burden that you must be willing to take on.

Like with hand-rolled DALs, you should be concerned about edge cases and one-off needs when implementing code generation. You can handle these scenarios in a number of ways, but the one constraint that you have to constantly work around is the fact that a certain portion of your codebase is completely volatile. If you manually modify generated code, be fully aware that those changes will be eliminated the next time the generation engine is run. Partial classes and inheritance are two of the most common techniques used to overcome this issue, but both introduce complexity and readability concerns into the codebase.

When contemplating the use of code generation in your brownfield application, be aware of the maintenance, extensibility, and quality issues they can introduce to the codebase. In an ideal world all of these concerns can be mitigated, but we have yet to see an ideal world. In reality we find that code generation is used for an initial period on a project (usually greenfield), and then as the project matures it's abandoned in favor of maintaining and extending the previously generated code by hand.

Some popular code generators include SubSonic, MyGeneration, and CodeSmith.

The final option for creating a DAL, and our personal favorite, is to use an object-relational mapper.

### 11.5.3 Object-relational mappers

The final option to discuss in this section is object-relational mappers (ORMs). Like generated solutions, ORMs are an implementation of a DAL that helps minimize effort in the development phase of the project. With an ORM, the developer typically defines the object model independent of the database and provides a way of mapping the object model to the database. The ORM then takes care of generating the SQL statements required to perform CRUD operations on the object model. In most cases, the SQL generation happens within the ORM itself; all your application needs to do is reference the appropriate assembly.

**NOTE** Although some ORMs generate code as well as use precompiled assemblies to provide functionality, we'll limit our discussion to those that don't generate code. The previous section covers many of the pertinent details for ORMs that generate code.

The major benefits and drawbacks of ORMS are shown in figure 11.6.

The first advantage is that third-party ORMs are usually very feature complete. Many incorporate most, if not all, of the features discussed in section 11.4.

A good example of feature completeness is lazy loading. In brownfield applications, hand-rolled and generated implementations often don't have lazy loading implemented at all. In many third-party ORMs, lazy

**Figure 11.6   ORMs can provide a lot of benefit, but be prepared for possible resistance and a learning curve.**

loading is just a matter of configuration. When talking about performance-related DAL techniques, such as lazy loading and caching, the ability to turn the features on and off is beneficial when avoiding the pitfalls of premature optimization.

Another benefit of using an ORM is that there will be much less code to maintain in your application's codebase. You won't have to write any code to map your object to a database table, and in many cases, you won't even need to write SQL statements. All of that's provided by the ORM.

It's not all sunshine and daisies, of course. We've glossed over the major feature of ORMs: the mapping. At some point, you need to tell the ORM how to map your objects to one or more tables. In the worst-case scenario, the mapping process will require you to create a class or file that says something like "Map the `Customer` class to the Customers table, the `ID` property to the CustomerID column, the `FirstName` property to the FirstName column, etc., etc." And that's not to mention the intricacies of one-to-many and many-to-many collections. Although there have been inroads in making mappings easier to manage, the fact is that with an ORM, you'll spend a lot of time dealing with configuration on some level.

Furthermore, an ORM, like any third-party library, requires ramp-up time. To be sure, any DAL will require developers to spend time learning about it, but one of the drawbacks of ORMs is that when you run into problems, most of the time you can't solve the problem by throwing more code at it like you can with hand-rolled or generated solutions.

That said, a few ORMs are popular enough that you could *reduce* ramp-up time by finding a developer who is already well versed in the one you've chosen.

A final note on ORMs in general. Because the SQL is "magically" generated outside your control, you'll often hit resistance to the ORMs from overprotective DBAs who believe autogenerated code (or indeed, any SQL outside a stored procedure) is inefficient or, worse, a security risk.

With most database engines, you won't run into the same resistance. Nearly all the time, the SQL generated by ORMs is either just as efficient as you'd generate yourself, or efficient enough to the point where the difference is negligible. Furthermore, all SQL generated by ORMs is parameterized and thus isn't susceptible to SQL injection attacks. Given that, we have yet to convince any sufficiently paranoid DBA of these facts.

Three popular object-relational mappers for .NET are NHibernate, iBATIS, and LLBLGen Pro.

## An emphasis on ORMs

Although we've tried to remain objective throughout the book, we're going to take a departure here and express our strong opinion in favor of ORMs.

Quite simply, we feel the benefits of an ORM far outweigh the costs and that once you're familiar with them, they'll save you a tremendous amount of time and money over the life of your projects. The time savings come from development time; developers won't need to create as much code. The other savings is because there isn't as much code to maintain.

There are plenty of arguments against ORMs. The learning curve can be higher, particularly because when you run into issues, it will usually be with the configuration of the mapping, which isn't always intuitive. The mappings can be fragile; they may not be strongly tied to your database or your object model. So if you change the name of a column in your database, the application will still compile. The SQL is dynamically generated and thus is not as fast as it could be if you take advantage of database-specific features or stored procedures.

By the same token, there are counterarguments to each of these. "Learning curve" is one of the prerequisites to surviving in our industry. Integration tests will catch any mismatches between your mapping and your database or object model. And with the performance of today's databases, dynamic SQL is on a par with stored procedures. In any case, we have yet to work on a project where the ORM was the source of performance problems.

If all of this sounds like a long-standing and well-rehearsed argument, you're right. You'll see these points/counterpoints along with many others when you start diving into the concept.

*(continued)*

We revert back to our experience: ORMs have saved our clients money, plain and simple. And lots of it. Not just in development time but in maintenance, which we've said many times is much more important. Although we've encountered brownfield projects where implementing an ORM wasn't the right solution, it wasn't because of the limitations of the ORM tool or lack of experience of the team. Rather, it was due to project constraints such as time to delivery or scope of the rework.

Thus ends our discussion on creating (or configuring) a data access layer. Each of these three options—hand-rolled, code-generated, or object-relational mapper—has its place. Often the options are limited (at least at first) by corporate policy and your team's ability and schedule. Rolling your own DAL is a good trial-by-fire exercise because most people have done it themselves at some point, and if you're like us, you've likely done it without giving it much thought early in your career.

Before wrapping up our journey into data access, we'd be remiss to neglect the deployment aspect of the subject.

## 11.6 *Improving the deployment story*

Regardless of the solution that you choose, or are moving to, for your data access layer, one of the primary friction points on brownfield projects is the consistent and correct deployment of data access components. We've regularly worked on projects where releases to testing, and even production, have sent incorrect versions of vital assemblies or stored procedures, or sometimes were never even sent at all. These release failures are unacceptable. Nothing sours relationships between clients and testers and the development team faster than poor releases or regression errors (errors that were fixed in a previous release but that have recurred).

The first topic is a comparison of stored procedures versus inline SQL statements with respect to application deployment.

### 11.6.1 *Stored procedures versus inline SQL statements*

Each data access technique from section 11.5 offers costs and benefits to the deployment story. Some say that stored procedures are easier to manage because they can be deployed separately from the main application. This deployment benefit is achieved only if joint deployments (both the application and the stored procedures) are well managed and performed correctly all the time. Independent deployments are only as good as your ability to test the production configuration with the stored procedure to be released. If you can't perform that integration testing with confidence, you can't be sure that the deployment will be effective and trouble free. Brownfield applications in particular are susceptible to deployments without the means to properly test.

At the other end of the spectrum, inline SQL statements in your application eliminate the need for the integration concerns that were pointed out for stored procedures. They also provide an easier application deployment because all the data access artifacts are contained within the assemblies to be deployed. Deployment of hot fixes will, however, require you to deploy application components instead of just a database-level component.

A system that uses an ORM is similar to one that uses inline SQL statements. Deployment is simpler because you need only release the required third-party assemblies correctly. But by the same token, changes to the database typically require a redeployment of the application as you need to update the mapping between the database and the object model.

Another aspect of deployment is how you manage different versions of your database.

### 11.6.2 *Versioning the database*

Changes to your database (such as new tables or modified columns) are common during the life of an application. When they occur, they're often a source of frustration during deployment. You must remember to execute update scripts in a certain order, and if anything goes wrong, the database can be left in an unknown state. Having a deployment process in place that will support schema changes with minimal effort is essential for the long-term maintenance and multirelease requirements of many applications.

Luckily, there are tools out there, both open source and commercial, that will help solve this deployment problem. Some will automate a good portion of the database versioning by comparing an existing production database with the development database and generating the change scripts. Others require you to create the scripts but will automate their execution and may offer the ability to roll back if any one of them fails. Almost all of these tools are useful in some way, and we encourage you to investigate them. Some examples include Red Gate's SQL Compare, Ruby on Rails Migrations, the Tarantino project, and Migrator.NET.

The best way we've found to use these tools is to integrate them into the release portion of your automated build script (see section 3.7 in chapter 3 for more on using automated builds for releases). If your release process automatically creates all the required scripts for the next release and you're continually applying these scripts through the automated build process, the pain of datastore changes will be greatly mitigated on your project.

Finally, let's talk about a common issue with brownfield application deployments: connection strings.

### 11.6.3 *Managing connection strings*

One of the most common data-related failures is an incorrect connection string. For example, you deploy the application to the test environment with a connection string that points to the development database.

No matter how much you abstract away your connection string management, somehow your application needs to know which database to communicate with. Short of hard-coding a map of deployment servers to database names, addressing this problem involves updating a configuration file or two. And we're willing to bet that you have, at some point in your career, deployed an application without remembering to update a configuration file.

The deployment of connection information isn't necessarily a data access concern; it's related to release management. Any time a configuration differs from one environment to another, it's ripe for automation during the deployment process.

For example, say you store your connection string in the `<connectionstrings>` section of your app.config. A basic way to handle connection strings in a multi-environment scenario is to create three app.config files (one for dev, one for test, and one for prod) somewhere in your folder structure. Each one would contain the appropriate connection string in the `<connectionstrings>` section. Then you could create a "deploy to test" task in your automated build that would copy the appropriate app.config file to the appropriate folder *before* compiling the application for deployment to test.

Although somewhat of a brute-force method, this technique is still an effective way of ensuring the application is properly configured for the target environment. At the very least, it removes "update the app.config file" from the list of deployment steps.

When looking at data access techniques for your brownfield application, don't forget to evaluate the current deployment story as well as how that story will change if you decide to use a different DAL technique. Deployments are often the forgotten part of the application development process. Data access deployment seems to be the most forgotten and, as a result, the most problematic. Paying close attention to this area on your project will pay dividends in developer and client happiness.

## 11.7  Summary

This chapter explored one of the most commonly written components of projects. Data access is also one of the most complex components that you write for your applications. As a result, it's the bane of many a brownfield project's existence.

This chapter pulled together quite a few techniques from previous chapters. Using these methods, along with performing a thorough examination of the needs of the application, will go a long way to reworking flawed or failed code. In this chapter we talked extensively about the fundamentals of a good data access layer. These fundamentals will guide you toward the best possible solution for your project. Applying those fundamental concepts to the three main types of data access techniques (hand-rolled, code-generated, and ORM) is a major step in determining both if your current solution is sound and if another solution is viable.

With all the data access-specific content you learned in this chapter, don't forget about the fundamental practices that we outlined in the rest of the book. Understand that you'll have to release the data access components to one or more environments and what that will entail. Remember that working in isolation, both behind an interface and in an isolated area of your version control system, will allow you to work through issues without severely impacting the current development effort.

Finally, don't forget that doing anything with confidence is of the utmost importance. The developers working on any new data access code must be confident that what they're building is working. Your project team, and the client as well, need to be confident that the changes you make won't result in regression issues. The best way to build this confidence is through the use of well-written automated tests, which is another one of the fundamental techniques we covered at the start of the book.

Reworking, rewriting, or replacing a data access layer can be an intimidating task. The ideas and information we presented in this chapter will reduce any apprehension that you may have when working in this area of your brownfield project.

In the next chapter, we'll move to an area that often causes problems in brownfield applications: how to handle external dependencies.

# 12

# *Managing external system dependencies*

**This chapter covers**

- Interacting with external systems effectively
- Testing the interaction with an external system
- Reviewing useful patterns for dealing with external systems

No application is an island. That's true now more than ever. Today's applications are expected to not only provide their own functionality but also pull data from a supplier's website, transform it using a third-party library, and republish the results to both your own database as well as that of, say, the HR department.

Indeed, there are entire products, services, frameworks, and companies dedicated solely to the purpose of integrating disparate systems. As companies have grown, shrunk, and merged, their systems often struggle to keep up. Many an "interim" solution has been in production for many years, forming a tenuous bond between two completely separated applications.

In this chapter, we'll examine common problems that come with managing external dependencies. Then we'll look at the types of dependencies you'll encounter and discuss techniques for managing them effectively. We'll also provide examples of ways to implement these techniques.

As usual, let's first review the pain points.

## 12.1  Pain points

These days, working with an external system is almost a given in an application, like having a UI or a database. But like those other aspects, if it's not done properly, your application can turn brown in a hurry.

Consider an application that uses a document repository to store documents about the oil and gas industry. An administrator adds documents on a regular basis, providing metadata about each one that's stored in a database.

The documents are indexed using Microsoft Indexing Service. As users search for them, the application converts their queries into a format that the Indexing Service understands. The results are combined with the results for any metadata criteria that are provided and displayed on the screen.

Things are moving along nicely until the company decides to upgrade to Windows Server 2008. The server is configured using the new Windows Search capabilities built into Windows Server 2008. While the Indexing Service is still available, Windows Server 2008 doesn't allow it and the search functionality to run at the same time. One must be turned off before the other is turned on.

Now arises the dilemma of depending on an external solution. Faced with this problem, you can either: (a) update the code to use the new Windows Search interface, or (b) leave the application running on its own server (the old server) that uses the Indexing Service. Depending on the size of the company, option b isn't always feasible.

Unfortunately, the code to search the Indexing Service is hard-wired into the screen. To change it, you need to open the code for the page itself. When updating the mechanism you use to index documents, you now have to touch the code that also searches metadata and displays the results to the user. By this point in the book, you should recognize the inherent risks in such an operation.

Let's look at another example.

Your search page uses a third-party grid control to display the results. Eventually, a user discovers a bug that occurs when using Google Chrome to view the results. A quick search of the vendor's website reveals that the latest version of the grid is compatible with all the latest browsers, and you happily go about upgrading.

During the upgrade, you quickly discover that there was a breaking change in the new version that affects your application. An interface changed on one of the methods you use and you can no longer call it in the same way. And as luck would have it, you call it everywhere in your UI, as you can see in figure 12.1.

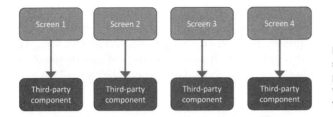

Figure 12.1   Example of four screens calling the same third-party component. What happens when something changes in the third-party component?

Now you have a no-win decision to make. Here are your choices:

- Stick with the old grid and postpone support for the new browser.
- Stick with the old grid and implement HTML and JavaScript hacks to accommodate the inconsistencies in it.
- Upgrade to the new version and fix every instance of the breaking change.

None of these choices are palatable. The first is more of a marketing faux pas than anything else. The second and third both involve a considerable amount of development and, worse, it will be error-prone development.

These are but two examples of the ways external systems can have an effect on your code. It's not hard to come up with others:

- A web service changes the format of the data it returns or changes the signature of a method you call.
- A web service becomes unstable.
- A legacy component will no longer be supported and you need to move to a different component.
- The interface for an external system is cumbersome to use.
- You wish to expand the functionality of your application but the external system doesn't support some of the features you need.

We've painted a pretty bleak picture. Let's see what you can do to make it a little brighter. First, we'll describe the different ways you can integrate with a system.

## 12.2  *Types of external system dependencies*

Before looking at how to mitigate your risk, let's differentiate between two types of external dependencies:

- Compile-time dependencies
- Runtime dependencies

### 12.2.1  *Compile-time dependencies*

A *compile-time dependency* is one in which the dependency on the external system is resolved when the application is compiled or built. Essentially, these are the third-party libraries and controls you use to build and run your application.

These systems are usually less risky than runtime dependencies because you need to make a conscious decision to change the dependency; unless you decide to physically remove one version of a library and insert a newer one, your code will not break.

NOTE   Way back in chapter 2, we recommended that you include all third-party libraries and tools used by the application in your version control system. In addition to reducing the friction of having to track down all the pieces of your application, this approach cuts down on the risk of one developer inadvertently installing the wrong version of a library or control on his or her machine.

Sooner or later, you may need to actually do an upgrade to a newer version of a library or component. This upgrade can often be a small nightmare if there are calls made to it all over the code. Later, in section 12.3, we'll look at ways to minimize the risk of such an upgrade.

### 12.2.2  *Runtime dependencies*

By contrast, a *runtime dependency* is one where the dependency isn't resolved until the application is running. Furthermore, it's often not under your direct control.

A web service is a good example, whether it's internal or external. If you're using a supplier's web service to retrieve purchase order data and the service goes offline, your application may fail (if you haven't allowed for this contingency; more on this later). Unless it's a planned outage, you probably won't even have any warning about your application failure.

Runtime dependencies represent a more volatile risk because you don't have the same control over them as you do with compile-time dependencies. If something changes in a compile-time system, you have the option of simply ignoring it and sticking with the version currently being used. Not so with runtime dependencies. If they change, you may have to change along with them.

### Dynamically loaded libraries

You may be wondering about libraries that are dynamically loaded at runtime. Say you have a process that, when the application is built, retrieves the latest version of certain assemblies and puts them into a plug-in directory.

We consider these compile-time dependencies because you still have control over them at the time the application is built. Although they may not be compiled in with the application, if they're part of your build process, that means you can write tests around them to ensure they act as expected.

The good news is, regardless of the type of integration you have, compile-time or runtime, the methods are the same for dealing with them effectively. But it's good to identify what type of integration you have for each external system as the type of integration will have a bearing on decisions you make concerning your system.

Next, we'll talk about what you can do to manage your external systems.

## 12.3 Handling external systems

The insurance industry is predicated on a single concept: managing risk. You pay an insurance company a certain amount of money so that they can assume the risk of some catastrophic event that you don't have control over, such as a fire in your house.

In your software, external systems are a risk. You don't have the same control over them that you do over your own code. You need to "buy insurance" to reduce the risk of a loss if something should happen to those systems that are beyond your control.

By this point in the book, you may have figured out what that insurance is, so we'll give away the ending: apply OO principles (chapter 7), layer your application appropriately (chapter 8), and isolate the dependencies you have on the system (chapter 9).

Indeed, you've already seen examples of external systems. In chapter 9, we explored third-party inversion of control containers and, in chapter 11, object-relational mappers. These are two examples of external systems over which you have limited control. You're at the mercy of the interfaces these libraries provide. Although it's true that a number of frameworks are available for each and you have a choice of which one you choose, you must almost always make compromises.

Chapter 8 introduced the concept of an anticorruption layer. To review, an anticorruption layer is one that you add between two other layers to protect the top layer from changes to the bottom one.

Let's take another look at one of our pain points from section 12.1. Recall the third-party component used throughout the UI as depicted in figure 12.1 earlier.

As we mentioned in that section, this arrangement can lead to problems when you want to upgrade. Here's where an anticorruption layer can be used for protection, as shown in figure 12.2.

Here, we've added a layer of code between the screens and the third-party component. The screens no longer interact with the component directly; the component deals with a class of your own design. Behind the scenes, this class will still work with the third-party component, but from the screens' perspective, a screen no longer has any knowledge of that third-party component.

**NOTE** This discussion on anticorruption layers is a long-winded way of saying "abstraction" from chapter 7.

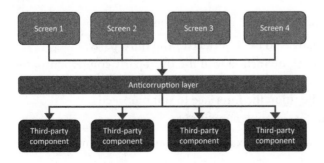

**Figure 12.2 The same drawing with an anticorruption layer added. Now the screens call out to your own service, which passes the calls on to the third-party component. If the component changes, only the anticorruption layer needs to be changed.**

**Tales from the trenches: The "internal" external dependency**

When looking at integrating with other systems during one project, we encountered a dependency that was, shall we say, less than wonderful to integrate with. The person who created the public-facing API for the dependency had done a poor job. It wasn't even a truly external dependency. It had been created, and was being maintained, by our client's internal programming department.

During discussions on how to deal with the difficulties that the API presented, we decided to draw a clear line in the sand. If the code wasn't under our full control, we'd treat it as if it had been purchased. This was an important distinction for us to make: if we weren't involved in the development or the release planning for the dependency's codebase, then that codebase presented a potential point of change and thus risk.

Once we made this decision, we wrote an anticorruption layer that wrapped the "external" dependency. Instead of our application's code directly interacting with the public, and potentially changing, API of the dependency, it now worked directly with a single piece of code that was completely in our control. No longer did changes to the "external" dependency's API affect the code deep in our application. Those changes needed to be dealt with only in one location.

On top of that, the application's code was able to call this dependency in a way that appeared to seamlessly integrate into the fluency and standards that had been set for our codebase. There was still one location where we had code that did make that direct call to the "external" dependency. The nice thing was that all that nasty code was centralized.

Sure enough, a few months after developing this portion of the application, we were advised that changes to the "external" dependency were coming. When that happened, the impact to our codebase was minimal, the stress of retesting was focused, and the changes were quickly implemented.

Determining whether a component is external isn't always easy to do, especially if the codebase is controlled by the same department, or even part of the development team you're working with. In the end, treating an internal library as an external one may be more work, but it can save you from some large refactorings if changes do occur.

An anticorruption layer provides some important benefits:

- Protection from changes to the interface of the third party
- Testing of the screens' interaction with the third-party component without having to explicitly create that component
- Simplification or alteration the interface to suit our needs
- Swapping out of different implementations

At this point, it'd be useful to see an example of an anticorruption layer at work.

## 12.4 Example 1: A sample refactoring

Let's say you have a Windows Forms application that reads a web service. The service is provided by Twilight Stars from previous chapters, and it provides information on upcoming tours and locations for various artists. Our application (see figure 12.3) is a ticket-purchasing app that reads this data so the business can sell tickets to appropriate shows.

The tabs list the data in different ways depending on how the user wishes to search for the data. Each tab makes use of a custom control that manipulates the data in various ways. Listing 12.1 shows the `OnLoad` event for one such control.

**Figure 12.3  Ticket Chooser, a sample application that reads a web service**

---

**Listing 12.1   `OnLoad` event for control that calls a web service**

```
protected override void OnLoad( EventArgs e )
{
    base.OnLoad( e );
    TwilightStarsSoapClient client = new TwilightStarsSoapClient( );
    DataSet tours = client.GetTours( );
    DataTable artistTable = tours.Tables[0];

    foreach ( DataRow artistRow in artistTable.Rows )
    {
        // Add artist row to control
        // Then add nested tour and locations
    }
}
```

As you can see in listing 12.1, we're expecting to get a `DataSet` back from `Twilight-StarsSoapClient`, which is the web service.

Now let's see the code for another control in listing 12.2.

---

**Listing 12.2   `OnLoad` event for a different control**

```
protected override void OnLoad( EventArgs e )
{
    base.OnLoad( e );
    TwilightStarsSoapClient client = new TwilightStarsSoapClient( );
    DataSet ds = client.GetTours( );
    DataTable artistTable = ds.Tables[0];

    // Iterate through the dataset and add a row for each tour, then
    // nested rows for each date and location
    // ...
}
```

There isn't much difference between these methods except omission of the nitty-gritty details where most of the work is done. We won't show the corresponding code from the last tab, but suffice it to say, it calls the same web service.

So there are three controls. All use the same web service and retrieve the same data from it.

Let's assume that Twilight Stars updates the web service. They have some new developers on board that recognize the blatant evil of `DataSets` (see the sidebar "Don't shy away from objects" in chapter 10) and have decided carte blanche to change the web service to return serializable objects instead.

As a consumer of the web service, this decision is a problem for you. Now you need to open each of these controls and modify them. If you're lucky, Twilight Stars notified you of the impending change before it happened to give you some lead time to make changes. Even then, you need to make the change at the same time Twilight Stars does to minimize downtime, assuming they don't provide an overlap period where both interfaces are maintained.

---

**What are they thinking?**

An argument could be made that Twilight Stars shouldn't change the public interface to their web service. Regardless of the new developers' desire to use objects instead of `DataSets`, there are clients' needs to consider. Changing a public interface is not to be taken lightly.

That's an excellent—and moot—argument. The fact is, it's Twilight Stars' web service and they can do whatever they want to it. You can work with them to try to convince them otherwise, or you can look for another vendor. Maybe you'll be successful; maybe you won't.

The reality is that when you rely on another company's web service, you're ultimately at their mercy. It's the nature of third-party dependencies: you don't have control over them.

---

What could you have done to minimize the impact of such a change? That's easy. The answer is to go back and reread chapter 8.

We'll save you some time flipping back. To isolate your exposure to a third-party dependency, you need to isolate it behind an anticorruption layer. In this case, that means creating a layer above it that *you* control.

Let's start with the quick and dirty solution to this problem. In it, you simply wrap the web service in another class. Let's call that class `TwilightStarsProxy` for reasons we'll explain later. Its implementation is simple, as you can see in listing 12.3.

**Listing 12.3   Implementation of `TwilightStarsProxy`**

```
public class TwilightStarsProxy
{
    public DataSet GetTours( )
```

```
    {
        var client = new TwilightStarsSoapClient( );
        return client.GetTours( );
    }
    public DataSet GetTourDates( int tourId )
    {
        var client = new TwilightStarsSoapClient( );
        return client.GetTourDates( tourId );
    }
}
```

Pretty simple. Your `TwilightStarsProxy` class exposes the same methods that the web service does. Each method creates a reference to the web service and returns the contents of the corresponding method.

The changes to the corresponding code in the controls is equally trivial. We'll show the same excerpt from listing 12.1, except using our new proxy class (listing 12.4).

**Listing 12.4    Updated `OnLoad` event for our control**

```
protected override void OnLoad( EventArgs e )
{
    base.OnLoad( e );
    TwilightStarsProxy client = new TwilightStarsProxy( );   ←—  ❶ Using a
    DataSet tours = client.GetTours( );                              proxy
    DataTable artistTable = tours.Tables[0];                         class

    foreach ( DataRow artistRow in artistTable.Rows )
    {
        // Add artist row to control
        // Then add nested tour and locations
    }
}
```

The difference between listings 12.4 and listing 12.1 is that you don't create a web service reference ❶. Instead, you create an instance of your proxy class.

Note that we're being a little naive in our approach. It may not be a good idea to create a reference to the web service in the proxy in every method. By the look of our `OnLoad` method, it's possible that it's being called more than once. So it might be useful to create a reference to the web service in the proxy's constructor. Then again, that decision may have ramifications as well. Just bear in mind that there are various options available and the one you choose should match your particular scenario.

**NOTE**    In listing 12.3 we've implemented an example of the Proxy pattern. Its goal is to provide an interface for some other object so that you can control how it's used. This pattern is ideally suited for creating an anticorruption layer over third-party dependencies in the way described here.

With the proxy class in place, you can guard against the changes proposed by Twilight Stars. If they change their web service to return objects rather than `DataSets`, you're no longer forced to update all your controls to use their object structure. You can update the proxy class so that it retrieves the new objects from the web service and converts them back into the DataSet structure your controls are expecting.

Adding a layer that ties us to DataSets may seem like a dubious benefit given the swipes we've taken at DataSets. But because we're working with a brownfield application, there could be dozens of places where you make a call to this web service. It may not be practical to change each and every one of them, even assuming you're able to write tests to verify that it's done correctly. By isolating the calls to the web service, you minimize the impact of future changes to the external web service. Although we're very much in favor of eventually moving away from DataSets to an object graph that's easier to maintain, the nature of brownfield applications is such that you may need to deal with them in the short term.

Your anticorruption layer can also play a role in the conversion from DataSets to objects when you do move in that direction. Because you control access to the web service through a proxy class, you can return whatever you want from that proxy. For now, you're returning DataSets because that's what was originally returned from the service and the original development team decided not to change it. But if you hide the web service behind a proxy, you could (and in many cases, should) convert what's returned from the web service into something you're more familiar with.

Let's assume you've created the TwilightStarsProxy class as outlined in listing 12.3 earlier. You're returning DataSets from it because that's what was originally returned from the service. Later, you decide you don't want to deal with DataSets in your controls. You'd rather work with, say, a Tour object that references an Artist and a list of Tour-Dates, as shown in figure 12.4.

With a proxy class in place, you can take the DataSet returned from the web service and convert it into such a structure. You also still have the benefit of minimizing the risk of changes to the web service. If Twilight Stars decides they want to return objects instead of a DataSet, you can update your proxy class to convert their objects into yours, just like you would if you wanted to continue using DataSets.

Furthermore, let's revisit the assumption that dozens of controls are accessing the web service. Say you have a proxy class that returns the data from the web service as a

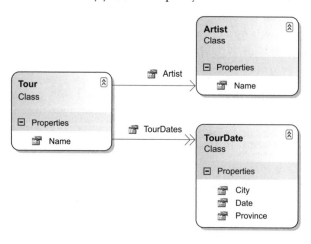

Figure 12.4  A class diagram of a possible structure you'd like to use instead of DataSets

> **The dangers in class naming**
>
> The change we describe here, converting a `DataSet` into an object, is a good example of why it's a bad practice to name classes based on the pattern used. The goal of the Proxy pattern is to control how an object is accessed. But now we're also altering the interface for this web service, which is an example of the Adapter pattern. As we mentioned in chapter 7, though it's useful to recognize patterns and talk about them, it's usually best to avoid hard-wiring your classes to them if you can help it.
>
> As it is, it's best not to get too hung up on names. Although you get bragging rights for recognizing when a proxy turns into an adapter, in reality it's not going to help you finish your work any faster.

`DataSet` and that each control is referencing the web service through the proxy. Later, you decide you'd like to use objects instead.

You can make this change incrementally: you can introduce a new method on the proxy class that returns a list of `Tour` objects rather than a `DataSet`. In this manner, you don't need to update the controls all at once. You can visit each one at your leisure and have them call the new object-returning method. Once they've all been upgraded, you can remove the method that returns the data as a `DataSet`.

If you decide to go this route, try to avoid an inevitable trap that occurs: you start out with good intentions of migrating from one style to another but along the way you get sidetracked. As the months go by, you don't get around to converting all the controls and you're left with a hybrid class where developers aren't sure which method to call (though you can mitigate this confusion through the use of the [Obsolete] attribute).

Let's take a bit of a diversion from external dependencies and see what else you can do to improve this sample application. In the next section, you'll apply some other techniques from previous chapters to the code. While it doesn't have to do explicitly with external dependencies, think of it as an extended sidebar.

### 12.4.1 *Extending the refactoring—a recap*

We're going to step out of the chapter for a little while. So far in the book, we've talked in fragments about how to incrementally alter bits and pieces of code to make it better. We've run through the UI and the data access layer, discussed layering and dependency injection, and explored some OO principles. Let's revisit our example briefly and see what else can be done to make it better, not just from a third-party dependency perspective but as a whole.

This section isn't meant to be a full-fledged practical application of the book's principles but we feel it's worth at least talking about how you might go about applying some of them in practice. The sample code provided with this chapter shows some of the fruits of our labors.

Recall earlier that we referred to our initial change to a proxy class as a *quick and dirty* solution. We were able to quickly isolate the call to the web service with minimal effort, partially because of the simplistic example. So let's go a bit further into it based on what little we know about the code so far.

In our previous examples, you could safely assume that the code in the controls wasn't being tested. In listing 12.1, the web service is directly referenced in the OnLoad event of the control itself. This code doesn't lend itself to a decoupled and testable design. There's a good chance this code isn't even being tested in an integration test, unless the framework is loading up the controls.

Your first step is to create a safety net. Doing so means getting the code in a state where it can be tested. This task will be difficult without changing the code, but if you apply techniques we discussed in previous chapters, you can try to layer the application gently and move code with relative confidence.

First, you need to get as much code as you can out of each control. As you'll recall from chapter 10, you can refactor this screen to a Model-View-Presenter implementation. Because you're working with DataSets, a Supervising Controller makes sense. That way, you don't need to change as much code because you can make use of most of the existing data-binding code.

You can see that the data is retrieved from the Twilight Stars web service. When you migrate your code to a presenter, you should also inject a proxy class into it using the techniques of chapter 9 as well as the anticorruption layer discussed here and in chapter 8.

When you've finished, each control should have a presenter that looks something like listing 12.5.

### Listing 12.5   Skeleton presenter for our controls

```
public class ListByArtistPresenter
{
    private readonly ITwilightStarsProxy _proxy;
    private readonly IListByArtistView _listByArtistView;

    public ListByArtistPresenter( IListByArtistView listByArtistView )
        : this(listByArtistView, new TwilightStarsProxy( ) )
    {
    }

    public ListByArtistPresenter( IListByArtistView listByArtistView,
    ITwilightStarsProxy proxy )
    {
        _proxy = proxy;
        _listByArtistView = listByArtistView;
    }

    public void Initialize( )
    {
        var tours = _proxy.GetTours( );
        _listByArtistView.LoadTours( tours );
    }
}
```

Poor Man's dependency injection ❶

Notice the use of poor man's dependency injection ❶ to allow the creation of a presenter with only a view. The view can then create this presenter and pass itself to it without needing to know where the presenter gets its data. See listing 12.6 for that implementation.

**Listing 12.6   Skeleton view for control**

```
public partial class ListByArtist : UserControl, IListByArtistView
{
    private readonly ListByArtistPresenter _presenter;

    public ListByArtist( )
    {
        InitializeComponent( );
        _presenter = new ListByArtistPresenter( this );
    }

    protected override void OnLoad( EventArgs e )
    {
        base.OnLoad( e );
        _presenter.Initialize( );
    }

    public void LoadTours( DataSet tours )
    {
        // Code to populate ourself from the DataSet
    }
}
```

❶ Presenter getting knowledge of the view

Using dependency injection means that the view doesn't need to know all the dependencies the presenter has when it creates the presenter ❶.

The sample code for this chapter shows this change as well as other refactorings and corresponding tests. We've also gone a little further and applied techniques from part 1 of the book by using a more efficient folder structure and adding an automated build.

This brief section was a bit of a sidebar. Although we didn't go too in-depth, it does show some of the thought process involved when you tackle a brownfield application. Real-life examples will be much less cut-and-dried but the same basic principles apply: break it down into manageable chunks and work iteratively and steadily toward your end goal.

Let's get back to the topic at hand. We have a couple more examples to work through, but first let's talk about some limitations of anticorruption layers and discuss how far you should take the practice.

### 12.4.2  *Limits of isolation*

Throughout the chapter, we've claimed that you can *minimize* the risk of changes to external systems through the use of an anticorruption layer. The use of the word *minimize* instead of *eliminate* is intentional.

You can't foresee all changes a third-party component could make. It's possible that the component changes in such a fundamental way that you can't alter its interface to match what your code is expecting. Perhaps the company that made the component has gone out of business and a suitable replacement doesn't exist. Or may the web service no longer returns all the data you were previously expecting.

These examples are usually exceptional circumstances. They're by no means an argument against anticorruption layers. If someone is trying to make the argument that adding a layer over a WCF service is a waste of time because the company could go bankrupt anyway, they are being shortsighted.

An anticorruption layer can save a tremendous amount of work if it's well designed. If you find you need to update the public interface of your anticorruption layer every time the object it's hiding changes, that could be a sign that you aren't hiding the dependency but merely sugarcoating it.

That said, the question will inevitably come up: how far do you take your anticorruption layer? We'll tackle that question next.

### 12.4.3   *How far do you go in minimizing your risk?*

Ah, the age-old question when abstracting a third-party interface: which components do you abstract? How far do you take the abstraction? When do you apply abstraction and when do you leave the code as is?

These aren't easy questions; the answers will vary from application to application. You need to be able to recognize when you're coupling yourself to a third-party implementation and to assess when it's appropriate to create an anticorruption layer around it.

Furthermore, even after you've decided to create the layer, you must decide how it should look. If you aren't careful, you could end up with an interface that's no better than the third-party component at protecting you from changes.

Obviously, it doesn't make sense to abstract every aspect of your application. Taking this idea to the extreme, you'd create an interface for even the built-in form controls, like `TextBox` and `Label`.

The reason you don't, of course, is because these controls are stable. They don't change often, and even when they do, the effort involved to update your application would likely not be as much as it would be to maintain a separate layer over top of the controls.

When considering factors in the decision to abstract, you'll return to the concept of risk. For a given external system, what's the risk involved if you decide *not* to create an anticorruption layer over it?

---

**Assessing the risk**

When deciding whether or not to abstract a system, consider the risk involved. Here are some questions that can help guide you:

- How stable is the system? Does it change often? Is it reliable?
- What would be the effort involved if it did change? Would you need to examine several dozen classes or is the integration isolated to only a small area?
- Is it a runtime system or a compile-time system? If it changes, will you be forced to update the application?

More often than not, a gut feeling can be accurate, provided you consider all the risks and discuss them with your team. But if there's any dissension, it's best to err on the side of caution and create the anticorruption layer (or, depending on the dissenter, "reorganize" your team).

Consider one example we've already discussed: object-relational mappers (ORMs). As a rule of thumb, these are systems that you *wouldn't* create anticorruption layers around. Here are some reasons why:

- The ORM is a compile-time dependency. If a newer version of the library comes out, you can safely ignore it.
- Most existing ORMs, both open source and commercial, are very stable.
- The ORM should already be isolated in the data access layer. Any changes made to accommodate a newer version don't need to be made application wide.

Deciding whether to add an anticorruption layer to a component isn't always easy. In general, there are no major downsides to adding one except for the extra work involved in both creating and testing it. Adding an anticorruption layer reduces the coupling of the application, and in most cases, makes the application more maintainable.

---

### Anticorruption layer for inversion of control containers

We've also mentioned IoC containers as another example of third-party containers. As of this writing, a new project has been created to act as an anticorruption layer over IoC containers. It's called the Common Service Locator library and can be found at www.codeplex.com/CommonServiceLocator. The idea is that you can code to its interface rather than having a hard dependency on a particular product, which has traditionally been an argument against wider adoption of IoC containers in general.

It's too early to say whether or not the library has long-term prospects. But in our opinion, if it encourages decoupled code and the use of IoC containers, whether commercial, open source, or hand-rolled, it gets our stamp of approval.

---

For brownfield applications, it usually doesn't make sense to add another layer just for the sake of it. As we've mentioned throughout the book, refactoring should be done on an as-needed basis. If you're using a third-party component successfully and don't have an anticorruption layer around it, there probably isn't any point adding one as soon as you finish reading this chapter.

Instead, wait until the component needs to be upgraded before adding a layer over it. That's an ideal time because you're already making changes to the code, especially if the new version has an updated interface. As we recommended in chapter 4, you should be writing tests for any code you add or modify. So if you're updating code to work with a new version of the component, you can modify your code to work with an interface of your own design, thus making it more testable and reducing your exposure for future upgrades.

On the other hand, if you *are* experiencing pain with the current version of the component, there's no need to wait for an upgrade to add an anticorruption layer. Working from the same chapter 4 recommendation, as you address bugs or add features that relate to the component, you can add the layer incrementally. Using techniques from chapter 9, you can inject the anticorruption layer into your code to reduce the coupling now. But again, only do this if you're feeling pain.

This example is just one way you can add an anticorruption layer to your application to minimize the risk of an external dependency. There are a couple more scenarios we'd like to walk through for third-party dependencies. We'll start with the same example as before but this time from the perspective of the web service.

## 12.5  *Example 2: Refactoring a web service*

In this example, we return to the web service of the previous section. This example will be much simpler, but it's still important.

During this refactoring, we'll pretend we're Twilight Stars, the company that runs the web service. We'll assume that the service has already been modified to return objects rather than a `DataSet`, as shown in listing 12.7.

**Listing 12.7   Initial web service returning an array of objects**

```
[WebMethod]
public Artist[] GetArtists()
{
    var ds = TwilightDB.GetData("twi_get_artists_and_tours", "Artists");
    var artists = new List<Artist>();
    foreach (DataRow row in ds.Tables[0].Rows)
    {
        var artist = new Artist();
        artist.Id = (int)row["ArtistId"];
        artist.Name = row["ArtistName"].ToString();
        artists.Add(artist);
    }
    return artists.ToArray();
}

[WebMethod]
public Tour[] GetTours()
{
    // Code to create a list of Tour objects
}
```

We've omitted the code for the `GetTours` method, but it's the same idea as `GetArtist`. Its full implementation is included with the sample code accompanying this chapter.

Twilight Stars has some clients that would like to use a WCF service rather than an Active Server Methods (ASMX) web service. Perhaps they're merging with another company and wish to offer a unified service model. Or maybe they want the option of supporting the queuing capabilities of Microsoft Message Queuing (MSMQ). We could make up any reason you like, but the end goal is that Twilight Stars wants to introduce a WCF service to replace the ASMX.

They can't outright replace the ASMX; for a time, they'll need a phased approach to give clients time to migrate over to the new service. So for a little while, Twilight Stars will need both an ASMX service and a WCF service offering the same functionality.

The WCF should look like the ASMX service, as shown in listing 12.8.

**Listing 12.8   Signatures for WCF service**

```
[ServiceContract]
public interface ITwilightStarsService
{
    [OperationContract]
    Artist[] GetArtists( );

    [OperationContract]
    Tour[] GetTours( );
}
```

For the implementation of this interface, you won't want to duplicate the existing code. And as you've probably guessed, the way to do this is to encapsulate the common functionality into a separate class (see listing 12.9).

**Listing 12.9   Encapsulated functionality**

```
public class WebServiceTranslator
{
    public Artist[] GetArtists( )
    {
        var ds = TwilightDB.GetData("twi_get_artists_and_tours",
            "Artists");
        var artists = new List<Artist>();
        foreach (DataRow row in ds.Tables[0].Rows)
        {
            var artist = new Artist();
            artist.Id = (int)row["ArtistId"];
            artist.Name = row["ArtistName"].ToString();
            artists.Add(artist);
        }
        return artists.ToArray();
    }

    public Tour[] GetTours( )
    {
        // GetTours implementation
    }
}
```

The changes to the ASMX and WCF services are shown in listing 12.10.

**Listing 12.10   WCF implementation and updated ASMX**

```
[WebService(Namespace = "http://tempuri.org/")]
public class TwilightStars : WebService
{

    [WebMethod]
```

```
        public Artist[] GetArtists()
        {
            return new WebServiceTranslator( ).GetArtists( );
        }

        [WebMethod]
        public Tour[] GetTours( )
        {
            return new WebServiceTranslator( ).GetTours( );
        }
    }

    public class TwilightStarsService : ITwilightStarsService
    {
        public Artist[] GetArtists()
        {
            return new WebServiceTranslator().GetArtists();
        }

        public Tour[] GetTours()
        {
            return new WebServiceTranslator().GetTours();
        }

    }
```

In listing 12.10, the third-party component you want to abstract is the transport mechanism. You have a dependency on how the objects are being publicly exposed. Previously, it was through ASMX web services; in the new example, it is through ASMX web services and WCF.

This example is almost right out of the Object Oriented 101 Handbook under encapsulation. But it's important to always be on the lookout for opportunities to avoid duplication. As it is, web services are almost as notorious as web pages for having far too many responsibilities. Even without the requirement to support a WCF service, the original implementation of our ASMX service in listing 12.7 wasn't very maintainable. Web services, in general, should be kept lean, with most of the work being done in other, more testable classes.

This example may seem straightforward but it demonstrates an important concept. When you're dealing with a hard boundary, such as with a web service, it helps to keep the code in that boundary at a minimum while most of the work is delegated elsewhere.

Our last example is another common scenario: managing a third-party component.

## 12.6   *Example 3: Wrapping a component*

Let's do a slightly different but still musically themed example. Say you have a simple search application (figure 12.5) that people use to enter a search term and the application tries to find corresponding music files in a specified folder.

The user selects a folder and loads their metadata (Title, Artist, Album, etc.) into the grid. As the user types in the Search Term text box, the window filters the results in the grid.

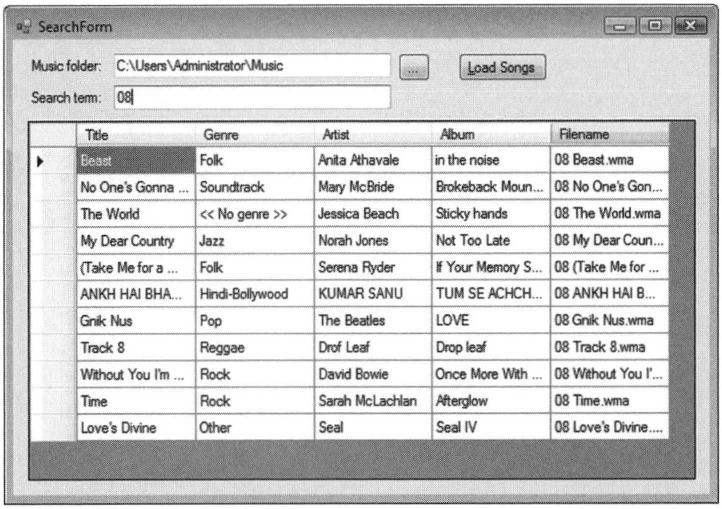

**Figure 12.5** This sample application provides a simple search function against a music library. It uses two different third-party libraries to extract the metadata from each file.

Fortunately, there are third-party libraries that handle reading metadata from music files. Unfortunately, the previous team chose two different ones: one to search MP3 files and another to search WMA files. Of course, they don't do it in the same way.

Listing 12.11 shows how the MP3 files are loaded; listing 12.12 shows the code for loading the WMA files.

**Listing 12.11  Loading MP3s using a third-party library**

```
private List<Song> GetMp3s( )
{
    var filePath = textBoxFolder.Text;
    var files = Directory.GetFiles( filePath, "*.mp3",
            SearchOption.AllDirectories );
    var songs = new List<Song>( );

    foreach ( var file in files )
    {
        var id3 = new UltraID3( );
        id3.Read( file );
        var song = new Song
                    {
                        Title = id3.Title,
                        Artist = id3.Artist,
                        Album = id3.Album,
                        Genre = id3.Genre,
                        Filename = Path.GetFileName( file )
                    };
        songs.Add( song );
    }
    return songs;
}
```

**Listing 12.12  Loading WMAs using a third-party library**

```
private List<Song> GetWmasFromFolder( )
{
    var musicFolder = textBoxFolder.Text;
    var dataManager = new MediaDataManager( );
    var mediaData =
        dataManager.RetrieveSingleDirectoryInfo( musicFolder );
    var track = mediaData.Track;
    var songs = new List<Song>();
    foreach (MediaData.TrackRow row in track)
    {
        var song = new Song
        {
            Title = row.Title,
            Artist = row.Author,
            Album = row.AlbumTitle,
            Genre = row.Genre,
            Filename = Path.GetFileName( row.FileName )
        };
        songs.Add(song);
    }

    return songs;
}
```

❶ Listing retrieval

Notice in listing 12.12 that the library allows us to retrieve the files only from the root directory ❶. That's not entirely true. There's another method, RetrieveRecursive-DirectoryInfo, that retrieves the WMA files from subfolders. The problem is that there's no single method that retrieves all WMA files from both the root folder *and* its subfolders. So you need to abstract some of this code into a separate method and call it twice, once for the root and once for the subfolders (this has been done in the sample code accompanying this chapter).

The net result is that the buttonLoad_Click method looks like listing 12.13.

**Listing 12.13  Click event for the Load button**

```
private void buttonLoad_Click( object sender, EventArgs e )
{
    var songs = GetWmasFromFolder( );
    songs.AddRange( GetWmasFromSubfolders( ) );
    songs.AddRange( GetMp3s( ) );
    dataGridViewSearchResults.DataSource = songs;
}
```

Listing 12.13 may not be the most coupled code we've seen, but it's certainly a lot more knowledgeable than it needs to be. You can see how we've implemented two separate methods to load WMAs, one from the root folder and another from its subfolders.

There's the usual laundry list of problems with this code; here are two issues:

- It's highly coupled to the specific third-party libraries that load the songs.
- It contains business logic directly in the form, a clear violation of the single responsibility principle.

Fortunately, cleaning this code up is straightforward. You've already taken a decent first step by encapsulating the third-party libraries in separate methods. That step will make it easier to move the necessary code out of the form.

One of the major problems with this code, other than coupling to the components within the form, is that the logic to load the songs is more complex than it needs to be. Because of the limitations of each library, the form has to first load the WMAs from the root folder, then load them from the subfolders, and finally load the MP3s.

We need to hide this complexity. Ideally, we'd like the buttonLoad_Click method to say, "Load all the songs from this folder" without having to differentiate the type of file or having to deal with subfolders. In this way, the buttonLoad_Click method's code has less knowledge about the process required to get the files and thus is less brittle and more resilient to change. Listing 12.14 shows our ideal buttonLoad_Click method.

**Listing 12.14 Click event we want to have**

```
private void buttonLoad_Click( object sender, EventArgs e )
{
    var folder = textBoxFolder.Text;
    var songs = _songRepository.GetAllFrom( folder );
    dataGridViewSearchResults.DataSource = songs;
}
```

The code in listing 12.14 is much cleaner. The form makes use of a new object, _songRepository, to get the list of songs to display. All the complexity is hidden behind a façade for us. Listing 12.15 shows the new interface for this object. We think you'll agree that this interface, from the perspective of the form, is much nicer to deal with.

**Listing 12.15 Interface for the SongRepository object**

```
public interface ISongRepository
{
    List<Song> GetAllFrom( string folder );
}
```

The implementation of the SongRepository object will be familiar to you: it's the same code cut and pasted from the original form. You can take a look at the sample application to see it in its entirety, but we'll show the code for the GetAllFrom method in listing 12.16.

**Listing 12.16 GetAllFrom method on the SongRepository implementation**

```
public List<Song> GetAllFrom( string folder )
{
    var songs = GetWmasFromFolder( folder );
    songs.AddRange( GetWmasFromSubfolders( folder ) );
    songs.AddRange( GetMp3s( folder ) );
    return songs;
}
```

The code in listing 12.16 is similar to that shown in listing 12.13. But the difference is that it's encapsulated in a separate class. We can now safely upgrade either third-party component, swap in a different one, or even add one that reads a different type of music file (for example, CDA or AAC files).

You may have noticed a common theme in all three examples. In each of them, we solved our problem by adding another layer between our code and the third-party component. This strategy was deliberate; it's almost always a surefire way to make your brownfield application more maintainable. Layering your application is an excellent way to reduce your exposure to "risky" components and keeping it decoupled and testable.

Let's expand on this idea with another "extended sidebar" on adding a layer around the Microsoft Office API.

### 12.6.1  Made for wrapping: Microsoft Office integration

Although our previous sample focused on a third-party .NET library, where the wrapping technique particularly shines is in wrapping Component Object Model (COM) or COM+ objects. A fantastic example of its power is in managing Microsoft Office integration.

The history of Office development is steeped in Visual Basic for Applications (VBA) and COM. VBA is notorious for being rather loose with its programming conventions. A good many of the methods on Office objects have optional parameters, something VBA can handle with ease. C#, on the other hand, is not so lucky. All parameters must be provided to methods in C# (at least as of this writing with .NET 3.5).

Add to this the long and checkered history of Office development and we are left with methods that can take over a dozen optional parameters.

Consider the `Open` method on the `Excel.Workbooks` object shown in listing 12.17.

**Listing 12.17  Open method on the `Excel.Workbooks` object**

```
Function Open( _
    Filename As String, _
    UpdateLinks As Object, _
    ReadOnly As Object, _
    Format As Object, _
    Password As Object, _
    WriteResPassword As Object, _
    IgnoreReadOnlyRecommended As Object, _
    Origin As Object, _
    Delimiter As Object, _
    Editable As Object, _
    Notify As Object, _
    Converter As Object, _
    AddToMru As Object, _
    Local As Object, _
    CorruptLoad As Object _
) As Workbook
```

Although this code is easy enough to handle in VBA, calling it in C# requires something like this:

```
object f = false;
object t = true;
object o = System.Reflection.Missing.Value;
Excel.Workbook book = m_application.Workbooks
    .Open( spreadsheet, f, f, o, o, o, t, o, o, t, f, o, f, o, o );
```

In short, listing 12.17 is just screaming out to be wrapped, even after including variables for `false`, `true`, and `System.Reflection.Missing.Value` to make the calling code more readable. And we haven't even mentioned the joys of dealing with earlier versions of Office, where the signatures are slightly different.

This scenario is where a layer between your code and a third-party component becomes less an academic exercise and more of a way to maintain your sanity. You can add a class, say `ExcelFacade`, that can expose only the methods you want and with the parameters you need.

For example, if you always open Word documents the same way, you could define a method, `OpenDocument`, that takes a single parameter, `DocumentPath`. All the other parameters are hidden behind the class.

### Intent-revealing naming

We can't understate the usefulness of what may seem at first glance to be a simple concept. As you can see in listing 12.17, the `Open` method is nearly indecipherable. Why are we passing `false` in the second, third, eleventh, and thirteenth parameters? Someone who isn't familiar with the `Open` method (and that includes us even a week after we've written this code) will be hard pressed to determine the best way to call it. Some parameters seem to contradict others and require detailed analysis of the documentation. For example, three of the parameters are `ReadOnly`, `IgnoreReadOnlyRecommended`, and `Editable`.

*Intent-revealing naming* is a concept whereby you name your methods based on the goals of the caller. Our `Open` method violates this practice because of all the optional parameters and the need to provide `Missing.Value` for the majority of them. Yes, it's used to open a document with all the permutations of parameters. It would be more useful to have separate methods for more common scenarios. By creating wrappers around the call, you can provide a more meaningful method name more aligned with your purpose.

Office products are also quintessential examples of how to deal with upgrades. The ubiquitous nature of Microsoft Office can be useful when you're developing applications that integrate with them. But that ubiquitous quality comes with a price: what version of Office is installed? And just as important, what version of Office could they possibly install in the future?

Word 97 doesn't have exactly the same methods in its object model as Word 2007. If the `Open` method takes a new parameter in a newer version of Office, it's much better for your mental state if you've wrapped the Word COM object in its own layer so that you need to change it just in the one place.

That's the last of our examples. Between the three of them, you should sense a common theme when dealing with third-party dependencies: to create a buffer between you and them. We'll close this section with a brief discussion of internal dependencies that you have no control over.

### 12.6.2  *The dependencies don't have to be third-party*

Although we've focused only on third-party dependencies, everything we've talked about applies equally well to internal dependencies.

Brownfield applications are often laced with some complicated dependency graphs. In one project we encountered, a data access assembly contained references to a service assembly. Then, through the magic of reflection, that service dependency loaded a separate instance of the data access assembly to access a different object. In short, it went to a lot of trouble to create a circular dependency.

Think of any class as a third-party component. Examine how you're using that class and consider how you would *like* to use it. Is the interface complex and/or fragile? Does it require a lot of setup? Is it an internal web service? A common company web service? If so, you have the option to change it—it *is* your code, after all.

But you have another option. You could apply one of the patterns and techniques we demonstrated here to simplify things. It may not be the ideal solution, but the reality of brownfield applications is that you have to pick your battles. Sometimes it can be useful to wrap a complicated class in another layer of abstraction with the intent to clean up the underlying class at a later date.

NOTE   If wrapping ugly code rather than fixing it sounds like a cop-out, it is. The phrase "lipstick on a pig" comes to mind. When you're faced with the decision to clean up a class or hide it behind an adapter, you should make a concerted effort to refactor it. Are you sure you don't have time at least to add tests around it before popping it behind an interface? No, seriously. Are you *very* sure?

Before we close out this chapter, we thought it'd be useful to provide the names of some of the patterns we've discussed here and throughout the book.

### 12.7  *Design patterns for dealing with third-party dependencies*

We'll finish up with a quick discussion of some patterns that can be useful when abstracting third-party dependencies. Some of them we've talked about already even if we haven't assigned a name to them. We'll explore them here so that you can match the concepts to names if they come up in conversation. The patterns are listed in figure 12.6.

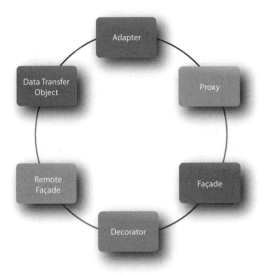

**Figure 12.6  Useful patterns for dealing with external dependencies. All deal with the same theme of hiding parts or all of the access to the dependency.**

Each of these patterns is a variation on the same theme: they represent a layer of abstraction over another component or system of components. Where they differ is in their intent.

---

**Patterns in brownfield applications**

Although we try not to focus on the jargon, the underlying concepts behind each pattern name are useful for brownfield applications. It's often easier to refactor to a pattern than to design one from scratch. Sometimes, you can't see where another layer could be beneficial until you see the code in place and the way classes interact.

Also, many times an additional layer doesn't become obvious until the need arises. You may not consider wrapping a `TextBox`, for example. But the first time the client asks for autocompletion behavior, or some other feature that isn't included in a basic `TextBox`, it answers the question "What are the odds of this ever changing?" rather definitively. If it's changing once, chances are it will change again. (Incidentally, to refer to our earlier comparison at the beginning of the chapter, insurance companies tend to follow the same principle when they hike your rates after a car accident.)

---

Our first pattern is the Adapter.

### 12.7.1  Adapter

The Adapter pattern should be familiar to you. We've talked about the Adapter previously, including in the first example in this chapter.

An adapter comes in handy if you're using a component and want to use a different interface to access it. Perhaps the existing one doesn't meet your needs. Maybe you need it to implement a specific interface to make it work with yet another third-party component. With an adapter, you create a layer above the component you wish to modify and expose the methods and properties that you actually need to use.

Let's review the first example of this chapter. The original web service returned a `DataSet`, which we were using happily. Then the company decided it wanted to return a list of domain objects.

Rather than rewrite all our code, we could add an adapter to the mix. We'd already created a proxy class to control how we access the web service, but we could also add in an adapter. This adapter would take the list of objects retrieved from the web service and convert it back into a `DataSet` until we're ready to make the switch over to the list of domain objects.

Another pattern we've discussed is the Proxy.

### 12.7.2  Proxy

A proxy is simply a class that controls access to some resource. They're commonly used for wrapping web services. In fact, when you connect to a web service, Visual Studio creates a proxy class for you, as shown in figure 12.7. This figure shows an example of a remote proxy, which is a variation on the Proxy. With a remote proxy, you interact with a local object, which handles the nitty-gritty of connecting to the remote resource (in this case, a web service).

Proxies are valuable for hiding the manner in which you connect to a resource. By adding a proxy, you decouple a client from knowing exactly how it connects to a service. This approach allows you to test the calling code without having to configure an actual connection to the service.

Next up: the Façade.

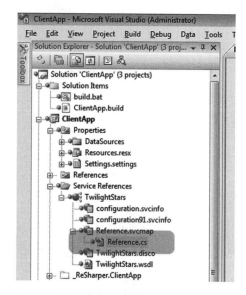

Figure 12.7  When connecting to a web service, Visual Studio generates a proxy class to control access to it.

### 12.7.3  Façade

The keyword for the Façade pattern is simplicity. You take a complex system, often involving several objects, and simplify it behind a single interface that's easier to use in your client code. It allows you to stay focused on a class's core functionality without getting mired in the complexity of a third-party interface.

The third example in this chapter, from section 12.6, used a façade to simplify the complexity of loading the music metadata. Before we added the interface from listing 12.15, our form had to perform some acrobatics to retrieve this information.

Once we moved that behind a façade, it became much easier for the form to manage. Even though the underlying code barely changed, we effected a useful change for our maintainability.

A façade is helpful when dealing with third-party components that have been in use for a long time. Typically, the companies behind them add more and more functionality until even the simplest task becomes an exercise in self-restraint. We mentioned Microsoft Office as one example. Third-party grid controls are another.

Adapter, Proxy, and Façade are the three patterns we've used directly in this chapter. In the next section, we'll zip through a few others we've found useful in both brownfield and greenfield applications.

### 12.7.4  Other patterns

The previous three patterns are ones we've used or talked about explicitly. But there are others that are equally useful in managing third-party dependencies. This isn't a patterns book—for that, we recommend Martin Fowler's *Patterns of Enterprise Application Architecture* (Addison-Wesley Professional, 2002), Eric and Elisabeth Freeman's *Head First Design Patterns* (O'Reilly Media, 2004), and, of course, the original Gang of Four's *Design Patterns* (Addison-Wesley Professional, 1994). Here we'll provide a brief description of other patterns you may find useful.

#### DECORATOR

A decorator is useful when you have a class that doesn't quite do everything you need. With a decorator, you wrap the class and provide additional functionality on top of it. In a typical implementation, the client code must create the object being decorated. Thus, it doesn't totally hide the object being decorated, so exercise caution when using it as a means to reduce exposure to third-party components.

#### REMOTE FAÇADE

The Remote Façade, like its namesake, is used to simplify an interface. It differs in its focus. Whereas a façade is a general way of simplifying a complex process, a remote façade's specific purpose is to provide a coarse-grained way of accessing a fine-grained object.

Think of a remote façade as a bulk accessor. On a `Customer` object, instead of calling `GetPhoneNumber`, `GetEmailAddress`, `GetFaxNumber`, and `GetMobileNumber`, a remote façade would provide a method, `GetContactInfo`, that does all that for you. It collects other accessors into a single one to minimize the number of calls you need to make, which can be an issue if you're making the calls over a network connection.

#### DATA TRANSFER OBJECT

We've mentioned data transfer objects (DTOs) before, in the context of binding screens to objects. They're representations of one or more objects designed (often for a single purpose or screen) to reduce the number of calls to the underlying object(s) they represent. Additionally, DTOs are often used to transport data in over-the-wire scenarios (web services, for example) in place of more complex, harder-to-transport objects.

DTOs are similar to a façade in that they simplify one or more objects. But they're often implemented as a "dumb" class, usually just with getter properties (setters are usually unnecessary as the values are set in the constructor arguments), for the purpose of binding a screen or some other object. A façade, on the other hand, is all about simplifying a complex process that often involves more than one class.

That should do it for design patterns. You may not have thought that so many could apply to such a simple concept, but each has its place. Hopefully, they got you thinking about how to handle some of the issues you've had with external dependencies on your brownfield project.

## 12.8   *Summary*

There's a quote often attributed to either David Wheeler or Butler Lampson that says "Any problem in computer science can be solved with another layer of indirection." This chapter is a testament to that quote. Third-party dependencies can expose you to considerable risk, and in this chapter we demonstrated what those risks are and how you can minimize them.

We started with our usual pain points, though you don't have to get too far in your career to experience them firsthand. We followed with a distinction between compile-time and runtime dependencies before launching into the crux of the discussion: how can you reduce your exposure to third-party dependencies?

To demonstrate, we provided three examples, taking a bit of a departure with the first to discuss larger issues and tie things back to other topics in the book. In the examples, we worked with a web service on both sides as well as with two third-party compile-time dependencies.

Finally, we closed by applying some names to the patterns we used in the examples and with a reminder that these techniques apply equally well within your own codebase, even without third-party dependencies.

It's been quite a journey and we're just about to wrap it up. In our final chapter, we'll take a step back from the code and the environment. We'll return to the social and political concerns of chapter 1 and see what we can do to keep the momentum going.

# *Keeping the momentum* 13

**This chapter covers**

- Balancing refactoring and new features
- Knowing (and pushing) your team's limitations
- Fitting refactoring into the schedule
- Moving to a culture of quality

It's been quite a journey. You've worked your way through source control, automated tests, object-oriented concepts, user interfaces, and data access. For the final chapter, we're going to set aside the code and circle back to some of the softer aspects of brownfield applications that we mentioned in chapter 1 and make sure you can keep the enthusiasm of your team high.

So, for the last time, let's talk about pain.

## 13.1 Pain points

It may seem odd to talk about pain points when the chapter won't be discussing utilities or concepts. But waning enthusiasm is probably the most important pain point you'll experience if you don't work actively to avoid it.

It's common to start a brownfield project with a lot of enthusiasm. The existing team is heartened by the fact that the code they've been mired in during the last 6

**Figure 13.1**
**Without a consistent and conscientious effort to improve, a brownfield application reverts back to its old self very quickly.**

to 18 months will finally be fixed. New team members bring a renewed energy. Perhaps even the client is onboard with the promise of an app that will be "even better."

Six months into the project, things look a little differently (see figure 13.1). Yes, the application might be in a slightly better state. The code is probably a little cleaner in the version control system (VCS), and maybe there are unit tests and even a continuous integration server. Perhaps some of the forms have been refactored to an MVP pattern.

But watching the team's day-to-day efforts, it becomes clear that they're no better off than before the brownfield project started. A looming deadline early on forced them to cut corners. The client changed requirements at the last minute. One of the team members didn't see any benefits from the early work and went back to his old cut-and-paste habits. Another latched on to the latest framework without considering whether the team had the cycles or the core knowledge to maintain it, so certain sections of the app look vastly different than others.

In short, although there may be minor improvements to either the ecosystem or pockets of the code, the project has reverted back to its previous path. So it's critical that the team maintain the early momentum it builds up. Maintaining any momentum gained can involve drastically changing your course.

## 13.2  Changing your course

Consider a young boy running down a hillside. At the top of the hill, he points himself in a vague direction, but after that, his course is pretty much set by gravity and physics until he hits the bottom. He barrels down the slope barely able to get his legs under him as he runs, let alone consider what direction he's going.

A brownfield project is a lot like that—but instead of a cute, uncoordinated little boy, it's a large, lumbering, three-ton beast barreling down the side of a mountain at the speed of a freight train.

And it's your job to change its course.

You have two options. The first is to throw up a roadblock in an attempt to stop the beast so you can start fresh on a new course. If the roadblock is high and strong enough, the beast will stop with a thud and knock himself silly. If he manages to get up, maybe he wanders around in a daze for a little while before tearing down the mountain again on a different path—the correct path, we hope, but there are a lot of ways down a mountain and only one is the correct way.

If the roadblock isn't strong enough, the beast will crash right through it because of the momentum he's built up. He may stumble or flinch a bit, perhaps veering off in the right direction for a few steps, but eventually he reverts back to his original path of destruction (see figure 13.2).

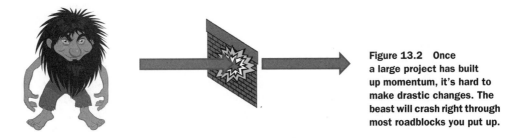

**Figure 13.2** Once a large project has built up momentum, it's hard to make drastic changes. The beast will crash right through most roadblocks you put up.

The second way to change the beast's course is through small nudges at regular intervals. You look at the end goal: where you want him to end up. Every so often, you give the beast a little push in that direction and he changes his course slightly each time. By the time he reaches the bottom, you've provided enough tiny course corrections that he ends up exactly where you wanted (see figure 13.3).

With this method, there's no expectation that the beast (your project) will quickly go the direction you want. Instead, you need a clear goal in mind and a plan for how to reach it—not just "We need to make things better so let's add unit tests." Our suggestion is to continually nudge the project so that you end up as close to your desired endpoint as possible. Throughout the book, we've repeatedly suggested the use of incremental change techniques. Incremental changes are the implementation of those nudges that your project needs.

One of the most important things you can do is manage your team's expectations. Good intentions alone won't sustain a brownfield project. What you need is a dedicated, directed, and, just as important, long-term effort by everyone involved. There must be more than a vague "We're going to do things differently from now on" resolution made in a fit of year-end budget planning and justification.

All too often, development teams dive into a brownfield application expecting to see instant results. When those results don't come as quickly as expected, a team can get frustrated and revert back to what they feel are tried-and-true methods.

Despite your head brimming with all the possibilities we've spent 12 chapters outlining, proceed with caution. In our opinion, each of the topics that we've covered has an excellent improvement-to-effort ratio. Each will take time both to implement and to realize the benefits. It's imperative that the team realizes this going in.

Now that you've held your horses, let's talk about how to walk before you run.

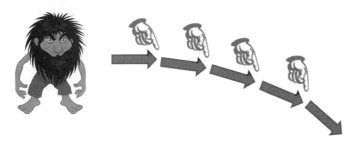

**Figure 13.3** Nudging a project to change its course slowly and steadily over time provides a smoother transition than an all-at-once, or "big bang," approach.

## The importance of setting expectations

We can't stress this point enough. If you're creating a specific goal to make your codebase more maintainable, it's vital that everyone be in for the long haul.

The reason is that a failed brownfield project can be dangerous. As discussed in chapter 1, morale is a factor in brownfield applications. If you think the morale of your team/project manager/client is low at the beginning of a brownfield project, consider what it'll be like if you lift their hopes, then fail yet again due to unrealistic expectations.

It's difficult to recover from a failed brownfield project. In many cases, your project manager or client may be leery about spending time to clean up what, to them, could be a working application. If you spend good money with long-term promises of maintainability and you don't follow through on those promises, you've doomed not only your project but all future brownfield projects.

Clients expect results for their money (they're funny that way). If you don't deliver, they have a good case to be cautious the next time some young upstart asks for leeway so they can "make things better."

## 13.3  *Setting the pace*

When planning your path, the dynamics of the development team is crucial. Not everyone works at the same pace or has the same experience (and the two aren't necessarily, or often, correlated). Perhaps the eager developer can race through code but often forgets edge cases. The senior consultant spends a lot of time at a whiteboard before putting finger to keyboard. Two others are productive when they pair together but aren't nearly so effective on their own.

The point is, you must evaluate your team's current velocity before you can commit to making the changes outlined in this book. How much solid work can the team do under normal conditions? Does the team work at a steady pace? Does the code often have bugs? Are existing bugs being squashed regularly or do they give rise to more bugs? If your company is located near Banff, does productivity drop off drastically in the first two weeks of snowboarding season?

Furthermore, the team's underlying capabilities must also be taken into account. Take on only what you're capable of. Although your collective heads may be brimming with possibilities, it's vital that you curb your enthusiasm until you've spent enough time researching each new concept.

The good news is that each chapter in this book talks about a stand-alone concept that can be implemented when the team is ready. For example, you can start by researching VCSs and how to use them effectively. When you feel you have a good grasp on the concept, try implementing (or moving toward) a more efficient folder structure in your existing VCS. If you aren't happy with your current system, consider moving to a new one.

Once you have a handle on your version control, start looking into continuous integration (CI). Then move on to the rest of your ecosystem. After that, you can

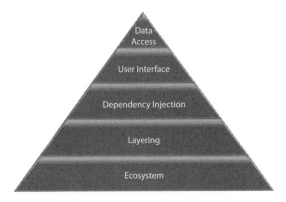

**Figure 13.4** Each topic lays a foundation for the one above it. Make sure you have a good grasp of each one before moving on.

investigate ways to layer your application and try refactoring the UI and the data access layer. Many of these topics build on earlier ones (see figure 13.4), but none of them needs to be done in tandem with another.

The important thing is to work at a pace you can handle. Yes, the code will still be in a bit of a tizzy in the early stages, and you may feel physical pain looking at it. But consider the alternative. If the team tries to do too much, too quickly, you'll be worse off than you were before. You'll have an application with incorrect versions of third-party libraries in version control, a CI process that does only half of what you need it to do, tests that are ignored, dependency injection used in some places and not others, and some parts of applications in appropriate layers and others in their original state. In short, it'll still be a mess, but this time it'll be an inconsistent mess.

### The dangers of "too much, too fast"

It's possible to cripple a project if you take on too much at once. Sometimes this happens when one small refactoring leads to another slightly larger one, then to a larger one, until you are re-architecting the application just so you can populate a list box in a maintainable way.

These cumulative refactoring binges often leave the project in a dysfunctional state. We've been on both ends of the conversation that ends "I just need to finish up one small refactoring, then we'll be good to go" while the rest of the team waits patiently for an application that works.

So to borrow from Aesop, slow and steady will win this race, especially at the beginning. Make sure the entire team is comfortable with the state of affairs before introducing a new change into the mix.

Another important aspect is a regular review of the work you've done. Whether or not you're doing this now, it's a good idea to get together as a team periodically to make sure everyone is still comfortable working with the code (or, at least, no less comfortable than before).

The purpose of the periodical review isn't necessarily a code review (although code reviews can be beneficial in certain scenarios). Rather, it should be a discussion of overall changes to the codebase since the last meeting and what's planned before the next one. Team members can also voice their successes, failures, and concerns.

Here's a list of sample questions that could be addressed:

- What major shifts in architecture have been introduced?
- Is everyone familiar with (and happy with) the check-in process?
- Does anyone have questions about the ORM you're in the process of adding to the project?
- Are you at a stage where you can introduce an MVP pattern to the UI?
- Does anyone feel they need some mentoring on the recent changes made to the code?
- Is everyone convinced that real value has been added with the new concepts?

This meeting is also an excellent opportunity to review any code metrics you're tracking. Chapter 5 talked about how to use code metrics to get an overall sense of your project and what areas could be improved with a minimal effort. Your brownfield progress review meetings are an opportune time to review those metrics to learn how to address the problem areas and see whether the practices you've implemented have made a difference.

These meetings aren't meant to be formal. They're round-table discussions to make sure you're on track and still delivering value. It's okay—and even encouraged—to rely on gut feeling.

By the same token, don't leave anything unsaid if you're uneasy about something. As the adage goes, there are no stupid questions. For example, perhaps you don't feel comfortable implementing an IoC container this early in the project. Maybe you aren't clear on the concept yet and need more time to try it out in a controlled environment. You might feel a lunch 'n' learn session would help get the team on the same page. It is incumbent on you to mention this at the progress review meeting.

### Time box the meeting

Brownfield review meetings can get out of hand for many reasons. Team members could disagree on an implementation of a design principle, there may be different ideas on what areas of the application to clean up next—heck, your team may just plain not get along.

It's important to recognize when a discussion isn't furthering the goal and needs to be set aside. (It's also important that you follow up on the issue, something that's often forgotten in the heat of a discussion.) Be sure you leave enough time to address the major points of whatever agenda you have set.

In the next section, we'll take a common mind-set to task: the "spring cleaning" phase.

## 13.4  *The "spring cleaning" iteration*

When a brownfield application gets to the point where the team decides direct action is needed to get it back on track, there's often a tendency to initiate a "refactoring iteration": for the next iteration, no new features will be added and no bugs directly addressed. Instead, the team will spend all day, every day, simply refactoring the application to clean up this mess. The intent is that future iterations will be that much easier because of the work you put in up front.

This approach is the "too much, too fast" issue taken to the project level and isn't what we generally refer to as a good idea.

There are several problems with this approach. First, it's naive to assume you can fix all, or even some, of your brownfield issues in a single iteration. If you can accomplish this, we'd question if what you're working on is a brownfield application at all. You'd be hard pressed to implement even half the topics in this book in a reasonable amount of time, especially if the team is not well versed in them. Like the basket of cleaning products in figure 13.5, the number of options you have can be overwhelming.

Second, we feel that a spring cleaning iteration is a little insulting to your client. You're essentially admitting to them that the application is in such a sorry state that no further work can be done on it until the code is cleaned up. Whether or not that's actually true, you shouldn't hold the client accountable for it.

Finally, very often areas needing refactoring are found in the normal course of work. If you take out the day-to-day interaction with the code, you'll lose sight of what made the application hard to work with on a regular basis.

**Figure 13.5  No one likes spring cleaning. So don't do it.**

Instead, you should fall back on an idea we've mentioned before: changing the team's culture. A better approach than initiating a refactoring iteration is to look at your development process as a continuous process. Indeed, this is why the process is often called continuous integration. From this day forward, your team is making a collective effort to do three things:

- Add new code that's maintainable
- Make any old code you touch maintainable
- Eliminate pain and friction in your processes

Essentially, you're making a pact with your team. This pact states that you'll continue to work on new features and bug fixes but that you won't stand for any process or code that causes you pain or friction. Any time you can't do what you want to do easily, you promise to take a long hard look at why that is and make every effort to fix it.

Chapter 6 talked about introducing a culture of quality in your team to fight your defect backlog. In that process you instill the ideal that you won't tolerate defective code. This objective is worth reiterating here because much can be gained by achieving this goal. A developer who will make a genuine effort to remove duplication, reduce friction, and eliminate pain points has skills that extend far beyond the current brownfield application.

---

### Tales from the trenches: "We can't do it"

A common defense against changing your culture to use many of the techniques we've discussed in this book is "Our team won't be able to absorb that much information." In our experience this claim is usually false. Sure, we've seen situations where some people on the team are either so resistant to change or so uninterested in augmenting their skills that they can't make the transition. But more often we've discovered that the team as a whole can make the leap to a new culture.

On one project, none of the developers had experience with any of the practices outlined in this book. Some had heard talk of things like unit testing and test-driven development, but none had ever attempted these practices. That was about to change.

Initially the learning curve was steep, painful even, and littered with lessons that needed to be learned, repeated, and instilled until they were as natural as riding a bike. In the span of 6 to 8 months, the development team had converted its practices to be in line with what you've read so far in the book. That team is proof that it can be done and that no past experience is needed to make this transition.

Furthermore, by the time they wound down and left the project, the developers on the team were strong advocates of the practices presented here. They may not have had all the knowledge and experience necessary to head off and teach others, but they did have the passion. As one put it shortly after he'd moved on to another project: "It's made development fun again."

Remember that. Developing software doesn't have to be filled with pain and angst on a daily basis. Make it fun by killing as many pain points as you can.

---

Changing your team's culture isn't easy to achieve. It's frighteningly easy to become complacent and fall back on old habits in a brownfield application. Phrases like "I know exactly where to fix this. I don't need to write tests for it first," or "Ugh, I don't want to deal with this mess right now, I'll just add a TODO comment and get my work done" often run through our heads. You might feel like the extra bit of knowledge you've gained on object-oriented practices gives you license to forget the basics. After all, it may not be perfect but at least it's better than the way it was, right?

This thinking highlights a common attitude when you get a few months into a brownfield application. You'll start to recognize problem areas and even potential solutions, but you don't feel comfortable enough making the required changes just yet, out of fear either that you'll do it the wrong way or that you'll take too long and launch a refactoring binge. Instead you stick to the tried-and-true method in the hope that the code will blend in with its surroundings until someone else deals with it.

**What if not everybody is on board?**

We've made a large leap of faith assuming everyone will accept the extra time and effort required to bring both the team and the application up to a more maintainable state. Anyone from a team member to a project manager to a client could poison that effort with a simple "I don't buy it."

There's no way to sugarcoat it. This attitude is a problem—potentially a big one. You can't ignore it, and if after all your efforts you can't convert the naysayer(s), you have some tough decisions to make.

The easiest case is when the dissenter is another developer. It may seem harsh, but if the entire team is in agreement except for one person, you simply have to make that person go away. Whether that's by moving him or her to another team or something more drastic, someone who's working daily with the code and isn't totally committed to improving it has no business being on the team. This is just an extension of the pain point aspect of your pact: if something (or someone) is causing pain, find the cause and remove it.

If the party pooper is a project manager or your client, you'll have to be more discreet or diplomatic in your efforts. It's possible to make progress on a brownfield project without support from above, but you'll be seriously limited in the scope of the changes you can make. If the objections are coming from the client, it may be a reaction rooted in their lack of confidence in the project team due to past failures. Although it can take longer, starting by setting a track record for consistent, high-quality, and timely deliveries sets a strong stage for clients accepting your suggestions.

Or, and we're only partially kidding, find another job. As one highly skilled developer we know says, "Change your environment, or change your environment."

A common counterargument to all this evangelism is our old nemesis, the clock. We'll tackle that now.

## 13.5 *Making the time*

We can hear the counterargument now: "This talk of culture and continuous improvement is all well and good, but I have to get back to the real world." Given that you're still expected to deliver value in the form of new features and fixed bugs, it can seem futile to fit time in to fix vast, embedded architectural problems when all you need to do is modify the validation rule for a text box.

One seemingly counterintuitive way to make time is to pull in another team member and collaborate. Almost everyone has encountered the phenomenon of "talking it out," whereby a solution to a problem presents itself simply by explaining it to another person. And if it doesn't, now there are two people who are aware of the problem and you can work through it together (see figure 13.6).

Furthermore, developers working in a group are far less likely to knowingly introduce bad code. Admit it, when no one was looking, you've checked in code you weren't proud of. Would you've done it if a peer had been looking over your shoulder while you wrote it?

When talking a problem out with someone, you'll often discover a simple solution. The act of learning together will help you both further your understanding of design principles, unit-testing techniques, object-relational mappers, or what have you.

It could very well be that you decide the code isn't in a good state, or the team isn't quite ready, to refactor it completely. This is perfectly acceptable. In the early stages of

**Figure 13.6   Pair programming is an excellent way to introduce new concepts to a team.**

your efforts, you'll need some trial and error to balance refactoring and new features.

But it's rare that nothing can be done *now*. For example, maybe you aren't at the stage where you can implement an IoC container, but that shouldn't stop you from refactoring some responsibilities out of a monster method into their own classes.

Both Martin Fowler's *Refactoring: Improving the Design of Existing Code* (Addison-Wesley Professional, 1999) and Michael Feathers' *Working Effectively with Legacy Code* (Prentice Hall PTR, 2004) provide excellent techniques for quick refactorings that can provide a lot of improvement for little effort. More importantly, these refactorings can set the stage for later when you can finish the work you start today.

The important thing is not to forge ahead the way you did before. Instead, make the time to analyze and evaluate the code you're working on instead of dumping in code by rote.

In the early stages, frequent collaboration with the team will be useful. Formal meetings aren't needed, but quick discussions, maybe around a whiteboard, about what's working and what's not are. Harness the power of the hallway conversation. If you find a good blog post about how to refactor dependencies, share it. If you find a new way to structure your build file and want to try it out, get together with a co-worker and start playing.

Communication between the team members, whether at an individual or a group level, will greatly improve the team's ability to implement change and improve a floundering project. Don't stop with sharing ideas via email or Instant Messenger. Get together on a daily basis and have every developer on the team briefly state what they're doing and submit any potential questions or problems they may have. Keep it quick and stick with it for the duration of the project. Soon developers and other team members will see that this face-to-face method of communication really works and can keep the team's momentum flowing.

It may seem as if bringing other people in will reduce your efficacy, but you'll often find that the opposite is true. If two people work on a problem, many times they'll accomplish more than if they both worked on two problems separately. And in almost every case, the resulting code will be cleaner.

Earlier in the chapter we mentioned that change will involve a serious shift in expectations all the way up the chain of command. Quick fixes may not be quite so quick at first, but you must persevere. Like learning any new skill, learning to do things the right way takes time and practice, but over time it becomes easier. And you'll eventually become aware that bug fixes and features don't take as long as they once did.

Before we close the book, we thought it would be fun to revisit our hapless developer from the preface of the book who had just started with Twilight Stars and was facing some dire prospects.

## 13.6   *A milestone retrospective*

A blank email form stares back at you from your computer screen. The project manager, Jackson, has asked for everyone's input on what worked and what didn't work for the most recent version release of the Twilight Stars flagship product. As you reflect on the experience, you can't help but smile. The team has come a long way in a short time.

After the debacle that was phase 1, you had a serious discussion with Jackson, as well as Martin, the client. This was one of your early successes; Martin had long since stopped talking directly with the development team by that point. During that conversation, you asserted yourself more than you had in the past. Without getting emotional, you laid out the issues with phase 1, including, but not limited to the following:

- The length of time it takes to get up and running for a new developer
- The lack of a coherent defect tracking system
- Recurring bugs due to fragile layering
- Inconsistent application of unit and integration tests

The underlying theme, you said, was a lack of confidence in the application from all members of the team. Over the course of 2 hours, you made a passionate plea to Jackson and Martin to allow you 6 months to try to repair this lost confidence, not with silver bullet solutions, but with a directed effort to change the mentality of the entire team. They agreed, thanks in no small part to your claim that deliverables would continue, though with more direct involvement from Martin on prioritization.

### 13.6.1   *Early success*

You knew the road to success would require long-term gains to make the process maintainable, as well as quick wins to show progress. To handle the latter, you focused on the ecosystem to help close the feedback loop for potential problems.

To prepare for the new developers brought in to replace the recently departed ones, you reorganized the source code tree in your VCS so that they wouldn't have to go through the same pain you did to get up and running. By the time the first developer arrived, she was able to retrieve the latest version of the code from the VCS and compile the application with no further steps.

Once that was in place, it was almost trivial to add the project to a continuous integration server. Initially, all it did was retrieve the latest version of the code and compile it, but that was enough to start the shift in mind-set for the team. Once email notifications started appearing whenever the application wouldn't compile, developers quickly learned the value of following the check-in dance before each check-in.

To counter any possible trepidation in the process, you added a bit of levity to the CI process. Whenever a build failed, you configured the CI server to play the chorus from "Broken" by Evanescence over a loudspeaker in the team room.

> **Don't go overboard**
>
> Despite your good intentions, we don't suggest playing a song over the loudspeaker for very long. It will quickly become a huge distraction to anyone who is heads-down in coding mode. There are other, less intrusive, ways to keep the team informed of the build status. For example, some teams use a large screen in the team room that displays the build status at all times.
>
> An application such as Big Visible Cruise (http://code.google.com/p/bigvisiblecruise), which provides an easy visualization for projects that use the CruiseControl CI product, would also help.

After adding CI, you introduced a test project into the mix so that any failing tests would also produce a failing build. Coupled with the CI environment, this was an important step in the project; it meant that the team would put a much greater effort into not only testing their code but automating those tests.

### 13.6.2   *Introducing and maintaining a culture of quality*

The ensuing weeks were a tough ride. The existing code was highly coupled and nearly impossible to test. The team's frustration was palpable as they constantly peppered you with questions about how to add tests for new features in code, a step that was traditionally done in a web page's code-behind file against a static data access class. It required a few lunch 'n' learns, several one-on-one/pairing sessions, and regular code reviews just to get many of them to the point where they were confident enough to check in code more regularly than once a week. A careful review of the current application's architecture and a discussion of how the various layers should look was necessary in order to move things forward.

And although one or two of them took to it very quickly, a couple resisted the move to automated tests and continued the way they normally had, writing untested code. It wasn't until you incorporated code coverage into the automated build to report any major drops in the percentage of untested code that they began to take the idea seriously.

When the team members started to get the hang of automated testing and were familiar with some of the common object-oriented principles (especially single responsibility), you instituted weekly meetings to review the defects and code statistics. It was another uphill battle convincing team members to take defects seriously, and you had to lead by example. You chuckle when you recall the look on Jackson's face when you outright refused to take on a new feature because three new bugs were logged against the most recent milestone.

After that, it was much easier to get the team on board with the same line of thinking. When, after 4 weeks, the defect list shrank slightly, you'd have thought your team had won the Super Bowl.

### 13.6.3 *Every rose has some thorns*

Despite your successes, there were some bumps in the road. Productivity in the early stages dropped significantly, causing the team to miss deliverables for the first two milestones. The client, Martin, was initially critical of your performance because of this. Yes, you were able to demonstrate that the deliverables you *did* achieve had fewer defects reported, but given the project's history, he wasn't sympathetic to your plight. Now, with the release behind you, relations are still tense but Martin has admitted, tentatively and grudgingly, that he is on board with the new focus on quality. Your team's near-feverish disdain for defects has helped in this regard.

Then there was the now-infamous ORM debacle. Having enjoyed much early success setting up the ecosystem and teaching the team about layering, you got cocky. One afternoon, you introduced an ORM into your codebase in an attempt to rid yourself of the bug-ridden data access strategy that currently poisoned the application.

The move was met with an almost instant and universal pushback. The development team, still reeling from many other new concepts, had no idea how to debug issues that arose in classes that used the mapper. And the DBA steadfastly refused to grant appropriate table-level permissions you requested to implement your data access strategy.

Although you still believe that moving to an ORM is the correct path for the project, you now realize what social and political barriers you'll face when you next try to make this transition. The end result of this effort was only an afternoon of lost code, but a valuable lesson was learned.

### 13.6.4 *Increasing confidence*

Still, you had to admit the progress was tremendous. One needed only to look at the deployment to production. For the previous release, the team needed a weekend-long outage with several infrastructure people on call. For this one, it was almost a nonevent. You created a build script to deploy the relevant components to the appropriate servers. Included in the release were database update scripts and configuration files.

Before the release, you began practicing the deployment on a test environment. When the kinks were worked out, all that needed to be done was to create a build configuration for the production environment. Once that was done, deployment was, literally, a single command in the console. The ease with which you deployed the application went a long way to improving relations with both the project manager and the client.

Now you're facing a blank email message on your screen, thinking how you can summarize the previous release succinctly. In the end, you focus on the confidence gained: confidence the team has in its direction and confidence that the client has gained in the product. There's a greater sense of code ownership from the developers and an improvement in everyone's standards. Successes have been steady, and failures have been reversible. Much remains to be done, but you feel confident that this brownfield application is on the right path.

## 13.7   Summary

This chapter has been a departure from the code-centric ones of late but necessarily so. A successful project is more than the sum of the ecosystem, architecture, and design of the application. As developers who are more comfortable with code than in meeting rooms, it's all too easy to ignore the fact that real people have a stake in the application and have different goals than you do.

In this chapter, we returned to the softer side of brownfield projects to explore ways to keep the team motivated over the long haul. Remember that during an extended development process, which most are, falling back into the old practices that originally tainted the codebase can happen. Fight that possibility by setting expectations at all levels of the project stakeholders group.

When setting expectations, try to enable working in small, indiscernible ways that all contribute to the larger goals. Although the temptation will be to make sweeping changes to achieve the stated goals, remember that you still have to deliver software to your clients. Don't let the desired work effort interfere with that delivery, but also don't allow the delivery to interfere with the goals of the work effort. It's a fine line that requires you to ensure that you have clear and frequent communication occurring between the development team and the rest of the project stakeholders.

Our journey is over. We've taken the walrus's advice from *Alice in Wonderland* and talked of many things. It's our sincere hope that you'll be able to take at least some of the techniques in this book and apply them to your brownfield project successfully. (We won't begrudge your applying them to your greenfield projects either.)

Better yet, we hope we have piqued your curiosity enough to look into the topics in more detail. Although we've tried to focus on fundamentals, which are less affected by the technology changes that define our industry, new ways of approaching old problems constantly arise. We wish you luck and success in your application and feel certain that you are now able to approach obstacles with confidence.

# APPENDIX
# *Our .NET toolbox*

Over the course of our careers, we've used many different tools to be as effective as possible at our jobs. As we've moved through technologies, from language to language and from platform to platform, many tools have fallen by the wayside— which isn't a bad thing. It's the natural evolution of our careers and the technologies that exist within them.

Equally important is that the tooling we use within one technology and platform continually evolves. We watch for pain points in our development process and we also watch the ongoing creation of tools that are available for our current platform. It's this constant change of tooling that allows us to get as close as possible to optimal development performance.

With that constant change in mind, we've compiled a list of some of the current tools we can't do without on projects. Some, like CruiseControl.NET and TeamCity, are duplicate solutions to the same problems. In those cases we don't differentiate. Instead, read it like this: we'll work with either, but never neither.

As we've tried to emphasize, this list is constantly changing. Make no mistake: keeping up with the steady stream of new technologies, tools, and practices is a daunting task. But the time invested in becoming skilled with these tools is valuable. There's no way that you'll be able to take this list; spend a weekend with it, the internet, and your development environment; and expect to be able to work proficiently with these tools. Be willing to invest the time, and the returns will pay dividends.

## *Productivity tools*
- ReSharper—www.jetbrains.com/resharper
- CodeRush—www.devexpress.com/coderush
- TestDriven.Net—www.testdriven.net

### Automated testing tools

- NUnit—www.nunit.org
- MbUnit—www.mbunit.com
- RhinoMocks—www.ayende.com/projects/rhino-mocks.aspx
- Moq—http://code.google.com/p/moq/
- SQLite—www.sqlite.org

### Continuous integration and automated builds

- CruiseControl.NET—http://ccnet.thoughtworks.com
- TeamCity—www.jetbrains.com/teamcity
- NAnt—http://nant.sourceforge.net
- NAntContrib—http://nantcontrib.sourceforge.net

### Metric generation

- NCover—www.ncover.com
- NDepend—www.ndepend.com
- Simian—www.redhillconsulting.com.au/products/simian

### Data access

- NHibernate—www.nhforge.org
- Fluent NHibernate—www.fluentnhibernate.org
- IglooCoder Commons WcfNHibernate—www.igloocoder.net/wiki/wcfnhibernate.ashx
- NHibernate Profiler—www.nhprof.com
- AutoMapper—http://automapper.codeplex.com

### Inversion of control and dependency injection

- Castle Windsor—www.castleproject.org/container
- StructureMap—http://structuremap.sourceforge.net
- Autofac—http://code.google.com/p/autofac/

### Aspect-oriented programming

- Castle Windsor—www.castleproject.org/container
- PostSharp—www.postsharp.org

### User interface

- Castle MonoRail MVC—www.castleproject.org/monorail
- ASP.NET MVC—www.asp.net/mvc

### Logging

- log4net—http://logging.apache.org/log4net

## *Source control*

- VisualSVN Server—www.visualsvn.com/server
- TortoiseSVN—http://tortoisesvn.tigris.org
- AnkhSVN—http://ankhsvn.open.collab.net
- VisualSVN—www.visualsvn.com/visualsvn
- KDiff3—http://kdiff3.sourceforge.net
- Git—http://git-scm.com
- Mercurial—http://mercurial.selenic.com/

## *Code profiling and diagnosis*

- dotTrace—www.jetbrains.com/profiler
- ANTS Performance Profiler—www.red-gate.com/products/ants_performance_ profiler
- Fiddler2—www.fiddler2.com

---

### Challenge your assumptions: Someone else might be doing it better

One of the key ideas we discussed time and again in this book is that you should constantly *challenge your assumptions* when working in this industry. When looking for ideas and guidance, remember that this is an industry. It's not just the .NET developer community.

Don't be afraid to look past your community (no matter if it's .NET, Java, Ruby, or even COBOL) for good ideas. Many ideas in this book trace their roots to the Smalltalk community. Others point back to Java. Look into these communities, and others, and be open and willing to learn from them.

Also, don't isolate yourself in an object-oriented world when looking for ideas. Look beyond to procedural (yes, we said what you think we said) and functional programming paradigms. We can guarantee you one thing: our industry, and especially the .NET platform, are too young for any of us to know how to do everything right all the time.

Be humble, far reaching, and adventurous when you challenge your assumptions.

# *index*